Of Things of the Indies

Of Things of the Indies

Essays Old and New
in Early Latin American History

James Lockhart

Stanford University Press
Stanford, California

Chapters 1 through 8 are based in varying degrees on earlier publications. The copyrights for the original versions are held by Duke University Press (Chapter 1); the *Latin American Research Review* (Chapter 2); the University of California Press (Chapters 3 and 5); Elsevier Science Publications Ltd. (Chapter 4); the Ibero-Amerikanisches Institut Preußischer Kulturbesitz (Chapter 6); the University of Toronto Press (Chapter 7); Dumbarton Oaks (Chapter 8). Where relevant, permission has been given by the copyright holders for the publication of the present versions.

Stanford University Press
Stanford, California
© 1999 by the Board of Trustees of the Leland Stanford Junior University
Printed in the United States of America

CIP data appear at the end of the book

To Betsy and John

Contents

Preface

E SSAY COLLECTIONS tend to be much alike, bringing scattered pieces by an author together in one place, perhaps rescuing some items from venues where the readers most likely to understand them would never see them. This book is the same. Perhaps it is a little unusual in that four of the twelve chapters are published here for the first time, another (Chapter 4) represents a basic reorientation of the original version, and yet another (Chapter 2) has been extensively revised and expanded. Indeed, at least slight changes have been made in all the items previously published.[1]

I would not claim that the volume has a single theme, but it has something of a predominant tone, rather colloquial, for nine of the twelve items originated as talks. Though some primary research is to be found here and there, the general thrust of the pieces is explanation of the implications of my larger research campaigns and monographic books for another audience, usually simply a wider one, but in certain cases some special group I do not normally reach, such as the editors of historical narratives or linguists. I have always had a strong interest, of an epistemological nature, in historiography, and I believe it shows here. Perhaps the reader will also see in the totality of these pieces that although I have had a Peruvian and a Mexican phase, have studied first Hispanic and then indigenous society, and my research interests have seemed to evolve from more social to more cultural and linguistic, it is all from a certain point of view very much the same kind of thing, interrelated when not interdependent.

The individual chapters of the volume have their own separate histories, which are of considerable interest to me and conceivably to some others. I have not wanted, however, to burden the preface with a detailed listing and discussion,

---

[1] The title of the book first came to me as *De rebus Indiarum*, but I quickly decided that it would be wrong for someone who has as little Latin as I do to use it in that form. Also, it might be construed as meaning "Of *The* Things of the Indies," a mighty systematic survey rather than a modest miscellany with some common threads running through it.

which appears instead in the Appendix. I do say that although I have made it easy for the reader to avoid this rehearsal of origins, as a person with a historiographical bent I recommend that you give it a look.

The first item in the collection was originally published in 1969, and the last was written in 1998, with other pieces falling at various points along the intervening time. Readers may notice that the 1980's are very lightly represented in this volume. The culprit is my book *Nahuas and Spaniards* (1991, the companion volume to *The Nahuas After the Conquest*, 1992), which absorbed most of my smaller productions of around that time. That collection and this one do not quite make a pair or a larger unit; *Nahuas and Spaniards* contains far more in the way of primary research and is aimed much more tightly at a specific monographic target.[2]

It was the retrospective aspect of writing Chapter 12 a few months ago that moved me to prepare the present volume at just this time (for I had long meant to do something similar),[3] and perhaps the mood accompanying that piece even gave a certain coloration to the whole volume.

------

[2] I had, it is true, much the same hope as I do for this volume, that it could help demonstrate the unity of the things I do and accustom people to a somewhat different normal range of activity for practitioners of early Latin American history than has been the case.

[3] I honestly had; in the preface to the second edition of my *Spanish Peru* (1994), p. xi, I speak in particular of my plan to put what is Chapter 2 here in a volume of essays. I first began mentally organizing pieces for this volume in the late 1970's, when most of the things in it were yet to be written. Some of my notions about what it would contain have been realized; others were quite far off the mark.

Almost the main item was going to be a piece on Africans and slavery, not to say anything strikingly new, but to try to get something clear once and for all. Already twenty-five years ago works had appeared that showed (1) that hardly anything about Spanish American African slavery was new, but had been fully anticipated in Spain (the same would be true for the Portuguese sphere); (2) that where there was a significant local indigenous population, Africans including as slaves were intermediary between the Spaniards and the Indians in every conceivable sense; and (3) that however important the economic aspect of slavery was, the cultural aspect was at least as much so, for the practice was viable only with people transported a long distance, divorced from their original social context, and

I wish to thank those who issued the invitations leading to so many of the articles in this book.[4] Without the nudging, which at the time I often rather resented, not wanting to get derailed from my larger projects, several of the chapters would probably never have been written. I also thank the students at different levels who have served as audiences for

---

culturally distinct from all local populations, hence dependent on the owning group and equipped to learn necessary skills quicker than those still inside their original social and cultural milieu. Yet scholars not only outside the field of Latin American history, but even some within it, have repeatedly shown a lack of comprehension of these basic matters. I have been kept from my plan not only by other activities and the great and healthy growth of the historical literature on Africans in Latin America, but by a sense of not knowing how to make things clearer than they already are.

Other pieces earmarked for inclusion in the volume, once they had been written, were an article on the evolution of the word *criollo* and a look at the body of writing often called "chronicles." "Criollo" or "creole" has long been one of our field's most misleading anachronistic stereotypes. For most of the first three postconquest centuries, in most contexts, it referred to people of African, indigenous, or mixed descent who were in some sense displaced from their origins. The word's history is a topic of vast importance still little understood.

With the chronicles, I meant to attempt to define the social profile of the authors in a more sophisticated way than is usually done, and to assess the works not merely as self-expression but as historical sources, as which they have been and continue to be greatly abused. It finally came to me that both these enterprises are large-scale research projects, not something to which an article could do justice, and the first of them especially implies perhaps a lifetime of work in the records of many countries.

[4]I must admit that I forget just who it was (perhaps Herbert Klein) that invited me to take part in a Conference on Latin American History session on social historiography with Karen Spalding and Fred Bowser; my commentary there was the first germ of Chapter 2. Jack Greene later organized an American Historical Association session for the full version, and he was also primarily responsible for the invitation leading to Chapter 11. Several people at the UCLA Center for Medieval and Renaissance Studies, with John Elliott behind them, invited me to do what became Chapter 3. I believe it was Rolena Adorno who was responsible for the publication of the first version of Chapter 4, and it was surely she and Kenneth Andrien who asked me to do what became Chapter 5. Günter Vollmer asked me for a contribution to Enrique Otte's Festschrift, which resulted in Chapter 6. Germaine Warkentin invited me to do what became

much of the material at various stages, and especially my graduate students over the years, often the only ones who seemed to understand what I was up to, and whose work has by now gone far toward giving my own a context.[5]

J. L.
Frazier Park, California
July, 1998

Chapter 7; Geoffrey Symcox was ultimately responsible. Elizabeth Hill Boone asked me to give the presentation at Dumbarton Oaks which became Chapter 8. Peter Bakewell and Susan Socolow had me come to Emory to give the talk which led to Chapter 12.

[5]I mention first their published books: Kicza 1983; Super 1983; Cline 1986; Haskett 1991; Himmerich 1991; Schroeder 1991; Offutt 1993; Horn 1997; Restall 1997; and Terraciano forthcoming. Nearly all of these have reflected back very meaningfully on my own doings, and most of them will be found mentioned in this volume. Other members of the group have produced articles and dissertations (some of the latter now on the way to ultimate publication) that have been no less helpful to me than the books. I will point specifically to Ganster 1974, Hunt 1974, Smith 1974, Tutino 1976, Flory 1978, and Wood 1984 as dissertations that have had as great an impact on myself and the field as many a book; they in every respect deserved a publication which for various reasons never occurred. It is fortunate that under modern conditions allegedly unpublished dissertations circulate among scholars almost as well as formally published books.

My thanks to Rebecca Horn, Mary Ann Lockhart, Richard Yatzeck, and Anne Sheldon for their proofreading, to Kevin Terraciano (and Doris Namala too) for help with the bibliography, and to John Hébert and Susan Danforth for help with the map. Leslie Walton and Kate Washington saw the book through the press. I appreciate the friendly attitude of Norris Pope and Susan Socolow toward the present enterprise.

Of Things of the Indies

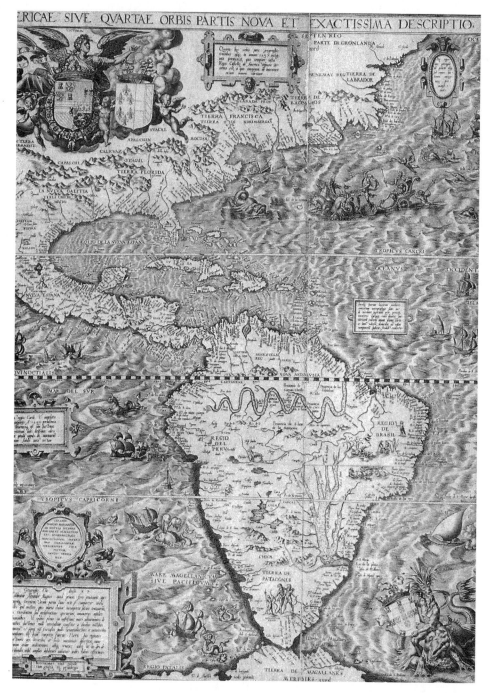

Detail of the 1562 Diego Gutiérrez map of the Western Hemisphere
(by permission of the Library of Congress, Washington, D. C.).

1. Encomienda and Hacienda: The Evolution of the Great Estate in the Spanish Indies
(1969)

W HAT THE SPANISH colonial period added to pre-Columbian America can be described briefly as the contents of two complementary master institutions, the Spanish city and the great estate. Historians have now begun to penetrate deeply into these subjects, and soon it will be possible to deal with Spanish American colonial history from its vital center rather than from its surface or periphery. While the colonial city is the less well explored of the two themes, its study can proceed on a firm footing, since the continuity of location, function, and even formal organization must be evident to all. Understanding the great estate has proved more difficult, for the estate had a greater diversity of forms and changed more than the city, both in law and in substance. The most serious problem, not always recognized as such, has been the apparent lack of connection between the encomienda of the conquest period and the hacienda of the mature colony.

Early in this century some scholars assumed, quite logically, that the encomienda must have evolved directly into the hacienda. The restricted rights of the encomendero were thought to have become gradually confused with land possession through some process never revealed in detail. Then in a series of publications written mainly during the 1930's, Silvio Zavala and Lesley B. Simpson proved to general satisfaction that this identification was false.[1] The encomienda had no juridical connection with land, and as time passed, it grew weaker rather than stronger, until, in Mexico at least, it was little more than an annuity.

Most historians today would no doubt agree that there is some sort of equivalence between encomienda and hacienda, as well as a certain temporal correlation in that one declined as the other emerged. But after the massive and successful

---

[1] Zavala 1935 and 1940; Simpson 1966 and 1934–40.

drive to establish the encomienda's juridical history, scholarly opinion has tended to insist more on the separation than on the connection. Charles Gibson made a fair assessment in saying that "the two histories are now regarded as distinct."[2]

Before going on, it may be of interest to consider why scholars have so readily tolerated a gap breaking one of the major continuities of Spanish American development. A large part of the reason is that, until all too recently, the top item on the research agenda was to define the legal framework of the Spanish empire. Historians concerned with the subtleties of legal concepts and procedures felt little inclination to pursue any continuity between a governmental, tribute-collecting institution, the encomienda, and a private, land-owning institution like the hacienda.[3]

In the period since World War II historians of Spanish America have gone beyond legalism, but rather than stepping directly onto the firm ground of social and economic reality, they have often leaped past it to statistical research and highly categorical or topical analysis. For the great estate the favorite categories have been land and labor. Unfortunately it is not much easier to see the continuity between encomienda and hacienda from the viewpoint of land and labor studies than from that of pure legalism. What could be the connection between a landless institution and one based squarely on the legal ownership of large tracts? Where was the continuity

---

[2]Gibson 1966, p. 118, n. 12.

[3]It is no accident that the now discredited thesis of the essential identity between the two institutions was upheld most strongly by scholars in less legally oriented disciplines, like the geographer George M. McBride (1923, pp. 43–45), or by such Latin American historians (principally Bailey W. Diffie) as were interested mainly in social and economic matters. Some geographers remain unimpressed by the notion of the landless encomienda to this day. In his article of 1967, Ralph A. Gakenheimer fully equates the encomienda with landholding, apparently unaware of the tempests which the issue has stirred up among historians. Diffie (1945, pp. 62–67) was the last major North American historian to support the McBride position of a gradual merging of encomienda into hacienda. In the introduction to a reprint of the same work (1967, p. xxvi) he abandons this view while still maintaining that the encomienda at least facilitated control over land by Spaniards.

between an institution which procured shifting labor by virtue of a governmental grant and one which depended very largely, it has been thought, on a permanent force of debt peons?[4]

A final basic factor inhibiting work on the continuous history of the great estate has been lack of knowledge about the encomienda as a functioning institution, for scholarship was long forced to rely almost exclusively on legislative and other indirect sources. The veterans of encomienda studies were themselves perfectly aware of the problem. Simpson specified that the lack of records concerning the actual operation of an encomienda in the early period was a source of uncertainty.[5] Lewis Hanke once devoted two whole pages of eloquent prose to the absence of "the intimate and varied source materials needed for a real history of the encomienda system," and urged caution on those who would draw firm conclusions about the institution.[6]

In recent years better sources have indeed come to light, and scholars have begun to interpret the new information. Notarial records are proving to be an excellent if incomplete

---

[4] As an aside it will bear mention that the doctrine of the separate encomienda and hacienda has never achieved quite the orthodoxy among scholars in Spanish America that it now enjoys here. There are at least two good reasons. First, the Spanish Americans have a broader conception of the agrarian problem, including in it social, cultural, and other elements. Second, the detailed demonstration of the sad juridical destiny of the encomienda applies in all its rigor only to central Mexico (an area, as it now seems, where the weakening of the encomienda occurred sooner and more evenly than in any other major region). As recently as 1965 Juan Friede (1965, p. 82), certainly no stranger to the work of Zavala and Simpson, published an article defending in its pure form the older notion that the encomienda gradually became confused with property rights. He even mentions (without specific sources) late sixteenth-century encomienda titles that included lands, waters, and forests. His article's main frame of reference is New Granada. For Chile Mario Góngora accepts the landless nature of the encomienda in the strictest juridical sense, but indicates a link with landowning at the level of local legal practice. (Borde and Góngora 1956, p. 29. The sections on the colonial period are by Góngora.)

[5] Simpson 1966, p. xiii.

[6] Hanke 1949, pp. 84–85.

means of exploring the manifold economic activities of encomenderos and their subordinates in the crucial central areas of Mexico and Peru.[7] Much can be learned about land-holding aspects of the encomienda through painstaking research with land titles in a restricted locality.[8]

The postwar years have also brought a more complete, realistic, and articulated picture of the hacienda, yielding new points of comparability with the encomienda. François Chevalier's now classic description of the Mexican hacienda provided the first adequate social view of the institution; more recently Charles Gibson in *The Aztecs Under Spanish Rule* modified the stereotype of debt peonage and showed that in the Valley of Mexico haciendas operated even during the late colonial period with a relatively limited skeleton crew outnumbered by temporary or seasonal help coming from the Indian towns.[9]

The main purpose of the present paper is to bring the separate histories of encomienda and hacienda into some connection with each other. Such an undertaking means advancing a bit beyond previous interpretations. It does not require rejection of the juridical history established by Zavala and others, however, since the continuities to be observed here are mainly social and economic in nature. Only one aspect of the legal history of the encomienda seems to call for comment. Both Zavala and Simpson recognized that in practice encomenderos could own land, but they tended to give the impression that there was literally *no* juridical link between the encomienda and landholding.

Nevertheless, aside from de facto patterns, there was a certain indirect legal connection which can be demonstrated from the encomienda titles themselves. North American scholars have generally accepted Simpson's interpretation that from the inception of the encomienda in the Antilles it was first of all a grant of the right to collect tributes, however

---

[7]Miranda 1965; Lockhart 1968, pp. 11–33, 206, and passim.

[8]Borde and Góngora 1956; partial use of this technique is to be found also in Fals Borda 1961.

[9]Chevalier 1963; Gibson 1964. Borde and Góngora 1956 deserves mention for its portrait of the hacienda as well as for its land-title research. Góngora 1960 is also invaluable.

prominent a feature labor use may have been.[10] Yet Zavala's more detailed treatment of the institution's development shows that the original encomienda or repartimiento of the Antilles was a grant of the right to use labor, with no initial link to royal tribute in fact or theory.[11] It was only in the course of a long legislative and administrative campaign that the crown and its officials succeeded first in adding the tribute idea to labor use, and later in restricting the encomendero's rights to the enjoyment of tributes alone.

Actually there were two strands of institutional development, perceptibly distinct even though always intertwined. On the one hand, there was the "encomienda," created by high officials. This was a governmental office similar to the encomienda of the Spanish military orders, strictly limited in tenure, and essentially conceived as a concession of the right to collect and enjoy the king's tribute. On the other hand, there was the locally inspired "repartimiento," stemming from the original ad hoc division made in Hispaniola by Columbus, and spreading to other areas through a process of diffusion at the local level. This was a much more amorphous institution, without much framework of legal theory, but basically concerned with labor use.

Even in legal format, the arrangements existing in Mexico and Peru during the conquest period owed more to the repartimiento of the Antilles than to the official conception of the encomienda. The word "repartimiento" triumphed in both popular and official usage to designate the actual geographical area of the grant.[12] The titles of encomiendas in

---

[10]See for example Simpson 1966, pp. xiii and 8.

[11]Zavala 1935, p. 2.

[12]F. A. Kirkpatrick (1939, pp. 372–79) maintained that aside from its other recognized senses, the word "repartimiento" should be acknowledged as a synonym of "encomienda," not only for the Antillean period, but on up to the time of Solórzano and the *Recopilación*. The point is a valuable one, if only to make scholars aware to what extent our notion of "encomienda" is an ideal construct. The two words were not strictly synonomous, however, and to delve a bit deeper into contemporary usage may be revealing. The term "encomienda" was very little used in the Spanish Indies in the sixteenth century; it referred to the institution in the general sense, "the encomienda," and it occurred in set legal phrases, such as to have or receive

the period before the New Laws do not emphasize tribute; in
fact, they hardly ever mention that word. (The title forming
the frontispiece of Simpson's *Encomienda in New Spain*,
granted in Yucatan in 1544, is no exception.) What was
assigned, to take the documents literally, was not tribute but
Indians, who were to work on the encomendero's properties,
his *haciendas* and *granjerías*; in Peru as in the Antilles,
mines were often mentioned as well.[13] If the titles are accepted at face value, then, the standard encomienda of the
conquest period was not in itself a grant of property, nor did it
provide a specific legal vehicle for property acquisition. But it
was addressed to a man presumed to be a property owner, who
could otherwise take little advantage of the grant in its own
terms. Góngora shows that in Chile encomenderos cited their
official position as justification for receiving grants of land
(*mercedes*) within the limits of their encomiendas, and even
for preventing such concessions to others in the area.[14]

Still, legal connections between landowning and the encomienda remain tenuous. A far more significant link is to be
found in the realm of actual practice, though the present state
of research prevents its thorough analysis. One can say with
some assurance that during the conquest period encomenderos in all the major regions of the Spanish Indies regularly

---

Indians "in encomienda." But when we speak today of "an encomienda," we are using the word as contemporaries rarely did. This
sense was rendered almost always by "repartimiento," even in such
legalistic writings as Juan de Matienzo's *Gobierno del Perú* (1967).
The popularity of the term "repartimiento" among the Spaniards of
the Indies certainly must have been related to the word's connotations of labor use and territoriality. It is similarly significant
that the crown preferred "encomienda," and that this term became
more prevalent in the seventeenth and eighteenth centuries as the
legal institution lost its "repartimiento" attributes. The term "encomendero," unlike "encomienda," came into instant and univeral use
upon its introduction in the Antilles. To the status-obsessed Spaniards the word smacked of a noble title, very reminiscent of the title
of "comendador" in the military orders, with which indeed it was
sometimes confused.

[13]Representative titles are quoted in Zavala 1935, pp. 294–309,
and in *The Harkness Collection* 1936, pp. 168–70. Here "haciendas"
means just properties; "granjerías" is "(agrarian) enterprises."

[14]Borde and Góngora 1956, p. 29.

owned land as private individuals and that many of their holdings were inside the limits of their own encomiendas.[15] When the nature and extent of these holdings are understood in detail and in time depth, someone can begin to write the systematic institutional history of the Spanish American great estate. For the present, only provisional conclusions can be drawn about any actual derivation of individual haciendas from individual encomiendas.

The state of knowledge concerning landholding as a de facto aspect of the encomienda has already been very well outlined by Silvio Zavala. In his *De encomiendas y propiedad territorial* . . . he demonstrated a drastic legal separation of encomienda and landowning. Nevertheless, the course of his argument required him to adduce several cases of land use and ownership by encomenderos. Shortly thereafter, in carrying out a study of the institutional history of Guatemala, he unearthed documents proving that the heirs of Bernal Díaz del Castillo, while encomenderos of San Juan Chaloma, had gradually built up an hacienda there through land grants and purchases from Indians. This was evidence, Zavala said, of the "sustained tendency of the encomendero's family to convert itself—by specific entitlement distinct from the encomienda proper, that is, by land grant (merced) or purchase—into the proprietor of lands contained within the jurisdiction of the encomienda towns. Thus an hacienda would be born under the cloak of the encomienda, though independent as to juridical title." The encomendero could "create an hacienda within the encomienda."

One type of information is lacking now as in 1945, when Zavala wrote, and that is the relative frequency with which this phenomenon occurred. Zavala pointed to the only conceivable way of finding out. It could be done, he said, at least for certain regions of the Indies, "on the basis of a scrupulous comparison of encomienda titles with titles supporting territorial property in the same region, inquiring at the same time into kinship between the families of the encomenderos

---

[15]This is the common conclusion of Miranda 1965, Borde and Góngora 1956, and Lockhart 1968. See also Zavala 1940, pp. 22–23 and 85, and 1945, p. 56.

and those of the hacendados."[16]

In its inherent significance Zavala's analysis of this subject is at least as weighty as his voluminous work on the legal history of the encomienda. Buried as it is in a minor publication on a different subject, however, it has been little noted, and historians have not followed his prescription for further research. Only one work of high scholarly standards attempts to trace a detailed account of landowning in a restricted area from the conquest period to independence and beyond—Jean Borde and Mario Góngora's *Evolución de la propiedad rural en el Valle del Puangue*. While estimable and indeed epochmaking, this book does not represent quite the type of research that Zavala envisioned. First, though there are precious bits of information and analysis, systematic investigation of the encomienda is lacking. Moreover, the authors make no attempt to go deep into family histories and interrelationships. Such research will demand a concentrated, special effort to master an enormous amount of detail. Góngora finds that some encomiendas in the valley studied gave rise to haciendas in Zavala's sense, and others did not. Of exceeding interest for the present paper, however, is the fact that the family of the valley's greatest encomendero, starting in the first generation, built up a large hacienda in the valley center, the only one in the whole region to maintain the same ownership through the entire colonial period.[17]

Aside from this, relevant information must be sought mainly in works basically concerned with other themes. Chevalier's study is not systematic at the local level, and he is much more interested in haciendas and sugar plantations than in the encomienda. He gives some examples of encomendero families who came to own great properties near their encomiendas in central Mexico, but retreats from any pronouncement on trends, since there were many other haciendas not traceable to that origin.[18] Gibson in his *Aztecs* demonstrates that some used the encomienda as an opportunity to acquire land, and he gives the names of several

---

[16]Zavala 1945, pp. 58–61.
[17]Borde and Góngora, 1956, pp. 43, 60, 224.
[18]Chevalier 1963, pp. 93, 97, 119–22.

encomenderos who became property owners. But he also believes that there were many other modes of land acquisition.[19]

Elsewhere the findings are also suggestive but fragmentary. Orlando Fals Borda's local study of a highland community in Colombia, while oriented toward Indians, does show that the original encomendero of the region not only acquired a large property that became one of the area's most "aristocratic" haciendas, but even gave it the name (Aposentos) under which it continued to be known until today.[20] For Yucatan, Arnold Strickon asserts that when encomiendas were finally abolished in the eighteenth century, the encomenderos tended to buy up the core area of their former grants, the *planta*, where the headquarters of the developing hacienda was located.[21]

From these examples a pattern seems to emerge. In most regions there eventually came to be a considerably larger number of haciendas than there had been of encomiendas.[22] As the Spanish sector expanded and more families grew rich and powerful, non-encomenderos managed to acquire large tracts of land in areas originally dominated by encomenderos. But in a typical case, if there be such a thing, the oldest, stablest, most prestigious, and best-located hacienda would have stemmed from the landholdings of the original encomendero and his family. Research that could establish the general validity of such a pattern, however, would require years and the effort of many people. And even when accomplished it would probably not reveal the heart of the matter. Unless it went far beyond land titles, it could only demonstrate a certain genealogical relationship, and we can be almost certain that even this relationship did not exist in many regions, especially in the thinly settled cattle areas

---

[19]Gibson 1964, p. 275.

[20]Fals Borda 1961, pp. 14, 111–12, 130, 132. The founder of Aposentos was the original encomendero in effect, since his single predecessor left the Bogotá region immediately after the first conquest, without ever taking possession of the encomienda.

[21]Strickon 1965, p. 44.

[22]Gibson estimates some 160 haciendas for the Valley of Mexico in the late colonial period, as opposed to about 30 encomiendas in the years after the conquest (1964, pp. 61, 289).

where the encomienda tended to be weak or absent.

Legal history yields few links between these two institutions which in turn dominated the Spanish American countryside, while any actual line of descent cannot yet be traced in detail. Accordingly, the only means available to establish the connection is a phenomenological comparison of the two. This in itself could never prove—nor is it meant to prove—that the hacienda arose out of the encomienda, but it can show that the change was far less than a transformation. The comparison, to be just and fruitful, must range broadly over associated practices and structures which, one could maintain, were not a part of the institutions proper. This procedure is necessary because the true comparability exists at the level of de facto practice, social organization, and broader functions. Neither encomienda nor hacienda ever found adequate legal expression of its full impact on society.

First of all, we may compare the two institutions as to proprietorship.[23] It will be immediately apparent that the encomendero and the later hacendado were cut from the same cloth; they were patriarchs of a special kind who ruled both the countryside and the city. Following both custom and law, the encomendero lived and maintained a house in the city to whose jurisdiction his encomienda belonged. Similarly the hacendado, while not a full-time urban resident in most cases, kept a large town house and held citizenship in the nearest city. The urban role played by both types expressed itself in the domination of the municipal council. In the

---

[23]The treatment that follows is so generalized that specific footnoting seems inappropriate. The terms of the comparison are drawn from the descriptions of the encomienda and hacienda referred to in footnotes 7 to 9. Particularly important for the hacienda is the material in Chevalier 1963, pp. 230–31, 268–307. The whole comparison applies primarily to regions of sedentary Indian settlement. It holds above all for the former centers of Indian civilization, Peru and Mexico, and with slightly diminished force for adjacent regions such as Colombia, Chile, or Guatemala. In fringe areas like Paraguay or Venezuela, the encomienda assumed a great variety of forms, though it appears to me that these various arrangements were in each case as close an approach to the classic estate form as conditions permitted, with some residual influence of the tradition of *rescate*, a mixture of trade and booty.

conquest period, the councils of most cities consisted exclusively of encomenderos. The later hacendados never
achieved such a complete monopoly of urban office, since
miners in some places and merchants in others were also
council members, but nevertheless the dominance of the
hacendado over municipal councils was the norm.

Each institution in its time was a family possession, the
main resource of a numerous clan. Each gave rise to entails;
but, with or without legal devices of perpetuation, each had a
strong tendency to remain in the family. As the effective
heads of society, both encomenderos and hacendados felt
themselves to be an aristocracy whatever their origins and
negotiated for honors and titles from the king, particularly
coats of arms and membership in Spain's military orders.

The balance between country and city shifted considerably
from encomendero to hacendado. The encomendero stayed
ordinarily in his city residence, as luxurious as he could
afford to make it, and went to his encomienda as rarely as
once a year on a trip which combined a pleasant country
excursion and a tour of inspection at tribute-collecting time.
He did not have a house for himself on the encomienda,
though he would often build or preempt structures there to
house his subordinates and to store products. In contrast, the
typical hacienda had an impressive country house as one of
its outstanding features. Yet though some hacienda houses
were like palaces, at least as many were fortress-warehouses,
massive and utilitarian compared to the hacendado's town
house with its carved balconies and fountains.

The hacendado and his family could be counted on to live
in town as much as possible. On occasion, if times were bad,
an hacendado might not be able to afford the heavy expenses
of ostentatious town living, and would sit out months of
involuntary exile in the country, or at least send the lesser
members of his family there. But when times were good, he
and the family would live mainly in the city and travel out to
the hacienda for one good long vacation and inspection tour,
much like the encomendero. Both types were rural-urban,
with their economic base in the country and their social ties
in the city. Only the balance between the two poles changed,
corresponding to the slow and uneven movement of Span-

iards and Spanish life out into the countryside through the course of the colonial period.

What one might call the staff of the two institutions was nearly identical. Both encomendero and hacendado had large collections of relatives, friends, and guests who partly lived on the bounty of the patron, partly worked for him. More specifically, both encomendero and hacendado had in their hire a steward called a majordomo, who took over nearly all the practical management of the estate. The man in this post would be well educated and would enjoy reasonably high standing in the Spanish world; yet he remained socially subordinate to the employer. Like his master the steward was urban-oriented; he was at home in the city markets, where he borrowed money, bought supplies, and sold the estate's produce.

On the encomienda, or at least on large encomiendas, there were beneath the majordomo a number of combined tribute collectors, labor foremen, and stockwatchers, often called *estancieros*.[24] Though their function was of considerable

---

[24]"Estanciero" clearly derives from *estancia*. On the face of it, this would seem to constitute a linguistic proof of the intertwining of tribute collection, labor use, and land exploitation in the encomienda, since "estancia" was the most commonly used word all over the Indies in the conquest period for private holdings whether devoted to livestock or to crops. If the encomienda's tribute collectors were named after their agricultural functions, that would be a very strong indication that such functions were seen as an important regular feature of the encomienda in practice. I believe that such an interpretation is essentially justified, but there are two factors tending to obscure it. First, "estancia" had another meaning, particularly well established for Mexico by Gibson (1964, pp. 33 and 475, n. 13). In this sense it designated an area where a small group of Indians lived remote from the main group. Estancieros would often be found in such places, so that this sense of "estancia" could have influenced, or conceivably have been the real origin of their name. Both meanings of "estancia" go back to the Antillean period, and examples can be found in the Laws of Burgos (see Simpson, 1936–40, 1: 4, 23). Second, "estanciero" was not the only word applied to the lowest employees of encomenderos. They could be called simply majordomos like the head stewards, and in Mexico they often went by the name of *calpisque*, after the indigenous tribute collectors. A third alternative name, *capataz*, had the strongest agricultural connotations of all, but was quite rare during the conquest period.

importance, their status was the lowest possible within the Spanish sphere. Typically they originated in the humblest strata of Spanish peninsular society or came out of marginal groups such as sailors, foreigners, or blacks. The later hacienda had exactly the same kind of low-level supervisory personnel, sometimes still called estancieros—which significantly was the first word for cowboys on cattle haciendas. They still came from the same social strata, belonging to the Spanish world, but at the very fringes of it. By this time, mestizos were commonly found in such work, along with blacks, mulattoes, and poor Spaniards, but their relationship to Spanish society as a whole was precisely that of the earlier estancieros. These people lived more in the country than in the city, though often against their preference. In any case, they spoke Spanish, rode horses, used Spanish weapons, implements, and techniques, and thus constituted a Spanish-urban extension into the countryside, taking their norms from the cities.

At the lowest level, in both cases labor was performed by Indians or near-Indians, divided into two distinct worker types, as will be seen shortly. We must also take into account the ecclesiastical personnel of the great estate. Each encomienda was supposed to have its *doctrinero* to minister to the native population, and this person might also serve as the encomendero's private chaplain. The priest present on the larger haciendas duplicated these functions.

In one aspect it would be natural to expect a thorough transformation—in the evolution from public to private, from a semi-governmental office to an agricultural enterprise. Here too, however, a great deal of continuity can be observed. On the governmental side, encomenderos had the nominal paternalistic duties of protecting and instructing their Indians. Although their post was not supposed to entail true jurisdiction, it is clear that they did in fact rule over their Indians during the early period, openly calling themselves their *señores* or lords. Hacendados, as mere property owners, lacked any legal justification whatever for such a role; yet they too often achieved it in practice. As recognition of their power, the authorities would often give them positions such as captain of the militia or alcalde mayor, and they would end by exercising formal jurisdiction as well.

Even on the economic side, in the evolution toward a private agricultural enterprise, there was no lack of common elements in encomienda and hacienda practice. On the encomienda traditional, unsupervised Indian production ordinarily had primacy, but the encomendero would regularly go on to take possession of land, often on or near his encomienda. (Usually, but by no means always, he received a formal land grant from the town council or the governor.) On these holdings, most commonly called estancias,[25] he would raise crops and livestock for his own establishment and for sale in town markets or mining camps.

Of great importance in the agricultural labor force of the estancias were Indians falling outside the legal framework of the encomienda. Almost everywhere certain Indians soon came to be attached personally to individual Spaniards, who might or might not be encomenderos; in the circum-Caribbean region these people were called *naborías*, and in Peru *yanaconas*. Indians of this type, plus some black and Indian slaves, formed a permanent skeleton crew for the estancias, under the supervision of the estancieros. They were aided by a much more numerous force of encomienda Indians performing "tribute labor," particularly at times of maximum work load.[26] In the case of Peru we know that the yanaconas of the conquest period had the use of plots which they cultivated for their own sustenance.[27] From a very early time there were also non-encomenderos with much the same kind of estancias, though their position was rather precarious, and their possibilities were limited at first because of uncertain access to seasonal labor by encomienda Indians.

All of the above characteristics persisted into the hacienda

---

[25]In Peru and adjacent areas, often *chácaras*.

[26]For the sake of clarity, the above presentation makes a clean distinction between estancia activity and unsupervised tribute producing. Actually a common practice was for the encomienda Indians to grow tribute products on certain land set aside for the purpose, under as much or as little supervision as the majordomo saw fit to apply. There was no basic difference between this arrangement and an estancia.

[27]Matienzo 1966, pp. 26–27.

period. We should not forget that our term "hacienda" is a scholarly convention; seventeenth-century Spanish Americans used "estancia" at least as often to designate a large landed property, retaining the earlier meaning of this word.[28] Ownership of land by Spaniards expanded greatly as the hacienda began to emerge, but the Indian towns still held much land themselves. Even more important, the hacienda did not exploit all of its sometimes vast holdings intensively; instead, certain restricted areas were cultivated under the direction of majordomos. To do this work the hacienda possessed a more substantial crew of permanent workers than the estancias of the conquest period. (The workers' names at this time were *gañán* in Mexico and still "yanacona" in Peru.) But they were still aided by a large seasonal influx of laborers from the independent Indian towns, impelled now by direct economic considerations rather than by encomienda obligation. Sometimes the villagers floated in and out according to their own and the hacienda's temporary needs, but in some places, as in Yucatan, they had a regularized obligation very reminiscent of earlier labor arrangements.

Both resident labor and nonresident labor, under both encomienda and hacienda, were still very close to pre-Columbian systems of periodic obligatory work. All types of workers performed something less than full-time duties, and obligations were usually reckoned by the household rather than by the individual. Also rooted in the pre-Columbian period were the so-called personal services which were so prominent a feature of the early encomienda. Many of these were inherited by the hacienda. This is especially clear for Peru, where in the twentieth century hacienda workers still delivered produce to town and provided rotating servants in the town house of the hacendado, as was once done for the encomendero.[29]

---

[28]Both Chevalier and Gibson give evidence for this, but see above all Borde and Góngora 1956, p. 58.

[29]Mario C. Vázquez 1961, pp. 26–31. Beyond the bare statement that the main elements of the Spanish American estate were brought from Spain, the present article hardly touches on the question of antecedents, because both the Spanish estate and possible Indian forerunners are very incompletely studied. It appears, here as in

The renowned self-sufficiency of the hacienda (actually better considered as vertical integration or diversification, as we will see) was also anticipated in the conquest period. Using their rights to Indian labor and produce as a base, encomenderos created networks of enterprises in almost all branches of economic activity that were locally profitable, though livestock and agriculture always occupied a prominent place. They did their best to make coherent economic units of these varied holdings, each supplementing and balancing the others. The whole estate was under unified management, since the majordomos were responsible both for official encomienda activities and for enterprises of a more private nature, as were the estancieros at a lower level.

The tendency to build complete, diversified estates, then, was already observable at a time when the Spanish sector of the economy was generally booming under the influence of newly opened mines and the demand of the nascent Spanish towns for all kinds of supplies. This fact throws a different light on the "self-sufficiency" thought to be so characteristic of the later hacienda, which has often been explained very largely as a response to depressed conditions. Much the same type of structure appeared earlier in response to social and economic forces of quite a different kind. The vision of society which the Spaniards brought with them to America included a clear picture of the attributes of a great estate and its lord. Aside from his mansion and numerous servants, guests, and vassals, he must have land, cattle, and horses, and various agricultural enterprises from wheat farms to vegetable gardens. From the early conquest period, this ideal constituted a fixed pattern of ambition for successful Spaniards. First the encomenderos and then the hacendados exerted themselves to carry it out to the last detail, even where

---

other facets of Spanish American life, that Spanish influence was concentrated in the upper and middle levels, Indian influence at the lower, and that the indigenous element was recessive. Often it is hard, when analyzing any one trait, to make a clear decision on whether it is Spanish, indigenous, or a coincidence of both. The ambiguity holds even for something as distinctively native as the special services of the Incas, some of which were very close to practices on European estates.

local conditions rendered it economically irrational.

But by and large the great estate scheme was economically rational as well as socially desirable. Everything the estates produced was wanted in the cities; taken together these products helped create a Spanish as opposed to an Indian economy. The desire to assemble a complete set of varied holdings was not inconsistent with a thoroughly commercial orientation. Self-sufficiency is very hard to distinguish from the diversification or integration of a commercial enterprise, and the complete refusal to specialize, which may strike us today as amateurish, characterized not only the lords of estates, but the merchants of the time as well. In an age of commercial rather than industrial capitalism, characterized by slow transportation and small markets, there was little thought of expansion and usually little justification for it. The constant effort of the most acute commercial minds was to monopolize, drive out competition, and sell at high prices to the severely limited market. The hacienda would carry the tendencies toward self-sufficiency and monopoly to their logical conclusion, without ever sacrificing market orientation.

In fact, though inspired perhaps in part by social ambition, the hacendados' desire for lands which they would not exploit fully made very good economic sense. Monopolizing the land discouraged the rise of competitors in the immediate neighborhood. If the hacendado had actually developed production on the whole vast expanse, however, he would have flooded the city market, as sometimes happened in any case. It seems probable that the size of urban markets and the amount of silver available were the real factors limiting hacienda production at any given time. The most obviously market-oriented establishments in the Spanish Indies, the sugar plantations, still did not typically become specialized, but raised much of their own maize, wheat, and cattle. A drive toward self-sufficiency, diversification, or completeness—for the three cannot be separated—was a constant in Spanish American estates from the early sixteenth century onward.

All in all, the replacement of the encomienda by the hacienda involved only a shift in emphasis, whatever the factual details of institutional development. A semigovernmental domain, serving as the basis of a private economic unit, gave way to a private estate with many governmental characteristics. There was also a significant movement into the countryside, but both institutions stretched from the city into the country, and indeed their main function was to connect the two worlds. The estate ruled the countryside in the city's name; it brought country products to the city and the elements of Spanish culture and society to the country. After the city itself, the estate was the most powerful instrument of Hispanization in Spanish American culture. During the early period, when Indian structures were relatively intact and Spanish cities relatively small, the estate could emphasize government and tribute collection over active supervision. As Indian structures deteriorated and the cities grew, supervision increased; the city came into the country.

The perspective here suggested makes it possible to treat the evolution of the great estate as one single line of development underneath the changing forms on the institutional surface. To judge from certain portions of their works, scholars like Zavala, Miranda, and Gibson have long had a good subjective understanding of this deep continuity, but they have never chosen to give it methodical expression. The standard works still tend to speak in terms of three successive systems: encomienda, repartimiento, and hacienda. The internal history of each system is worked out separate from the others; each new stage is seen as requiring a much greater transformation than was in fact the case.[30]

But looking beneath the level of formal institutions and administrative policy, the evolution could be expressed in simplest terms as follows. At all times there were private Spanish holdings in the countryside with workers attached to them, and these holdings always drew temporary labor from surrounding Indian settlements. From the conquest period until the present century, the constant trend was for the Spanish properties and their permanent crews to grow, while the Indian settlements and their lands and production

---

[30]A notable exception is Gibson's treatment of the transition from repartimiento to informal hacienda labor in Mexico (1964, pp. 235–36).

shrank. It now begins to appear that Spanish agricultural enterprises, generally speaking, never achieved complete reliance on a resident working force during the colonial period. (Scholars familiar with conditions in the late nineteenth and twentieth centuries have projected into the early period the solid, sedentary force of debt peons thought to characterize more recent times.) The people from surrounding settlements came to work on the estancias and later haciendas, first through encomienda obligations, then through the mechanism of the repartimiento,[31] and finally through individual arrangements, but they were always the same people doing the same things. In the conquest period the greatest landowners were the encomenderos, whose estancias formed an integral if informal part of their estates. Yet from the very beginning there were other Spaniards with similar holdings, both small and large. Encomendero families or their legal successors seem often to have retained, consolidated, and even expanded their properties, which may have had a special aura of permanence and nobility. But the lands of the non-encomenderos increased even more, until the countryside contained several times the number of great estates present in the conquest period. This development paralleled the large expansion of the Spanish or (broadly speaking) urban sector. The organization and social composition of those who owned and managed the estate hardly changed from the age of the encomienda to the hacienda of the eighteenth century.

Giving importance to these basic social and economic continuities does not require one to believe that the encomienda as an institution involved landholding, or that it evolved directly into the hacienda. As far as agriculture and landownership are concerned, the technical antecedent of the hacienda was the estancia rather than the encomienda. One may retain a narrowly legal definition of the encomienda as the right to enjoy labor and tribute and of the hacienda as pure landownership (though the latter interpretation is more

[31]The central Andean region, which had an exceptionally strong pre-Columbian tradition of obligatory rotary labor, and apparently suffered less population loss in the highland regions, remained at this stage longer than Mexico. See Phelan 1967, pp. 60–65.

rarely made). At the same time, it is quite possible to appreciate that the Spaniards tried to use each legal framework in turn as the basis of the same kind of great estate. Ideally this would have combined jurisdiction with vast possessions of land and stock. In the encomienda only the governmental aspect was formally expressed, and the rest was left to the spontaneous action of socioeconomic ambitions and opportunities. The hacienda was just the opposite, giving legal status only to landownership and leaving the jurisdictional aspects to de facto patterns. This basic, essentially unitary social institution, the great estate, was quite fixed as to ideal attributes and social organization, and it maintained constant its function as intermediary between the growing Spanish cities and the receding Indian towns. It evolved along two simple lines—constant rise in the legal ownership of land and change in the balance of the labor force, as permanent workers increased and temporary workers decreased.

Let us view the great estate, therefore, as a basic social pattern with certain permanent attributes and a few recognized principles of evolution. By so doing, we can hope to understand the increasingly complex picture that is emerging as research proceeds to areas other than Mexico. Each region in the Spanish Indies seems to have produced a different form of the encomienda and a different timetable for its downfall. The same is true for the repartimiento or *mita*. Some areas suffered greater population loss than others, and at varying rates; others had little or no population to start with. Some estates arose from holdings associated with encomiendas, others from lands accumulated by administrative and judicial officials, others from humble wheat farms. From region to region the hacienda veered toward pastoralism, cereal production, sugar growing, and other activities. But we can cope with all these variations if we understand them as retarding, hastening, or modifying an institution that was ultimately embedded in Spanish social practice and had its own coherence, its own dynamics of development.

One may conclude that the rise of the hacienda was essentially a development rather than a struggle. The evolution of the great estate responded to such realities as the size of cities and Spanish populations, the degree of acculturation among the Indians, and the nature of Spanish society in early modern times. The royal policy of discouraging an independent aristocracy and the humanitarian campaigns to protect the Indians deserve intensive study in themselves, but the struggles over these matters cannot be said to have greatly affected the evolution of the great estate. Wherever it might appear that the crown or the church became a prime mover in its development, one will find on close examination that deeper forces were at work. Crown policy has been credited with the destruction of the encomienda, but natural developments in the Indies had doomed the institution in the central areas (as opposed to the periphery, where it flourished for centuries). On the one hand, the fortunes arising from commerce and mining were not directly dependent upon the encomienda; on the other hand, the sheer growth of Spanish society produced newly powerful families who began to carve out estates of their own, undermining the inflexible encomienda system.

Historians have commonly observed the general tendency of the conquest period to set basic patterns for later times. The hacienda, taking shape in the late sixteenth and seventeenth centuries, has appeared to be a major exception. But the interpretation of the great estate set forth here reintegrates the hacienda into the general picture. From the broader perspective one may argue that the conquest period created the function and the basic social and economic modes of organization, while following years brought mainly growth or shrinkage—in other words, quantitative change. Such a view implies that perhaps scholars investigating the history of the hacienda should begin at the beginning. One of the complaints that one might bring against the renowned work of Chevalier is that, faced with a vast body of material on the hacienda, he accepted a conventional view of the conquest period and the encomienda, without submitting them to the same kind of analysis which he applied to his more immediate subject.

In general, those who engage in future research on forms of the great estate should take into account the institution's multiple dimensions and not limit themselves to "hacienda studies," or to the study of "land and labor systems," or most especially to "rural history." In all known embodiments the Spanish American great estate was closely related to the city, indeed almost inseparable from it. Early Spanish American history has three principal elements: the city, the great estate, and the world of indigenous settlements. Of these only the latter were truly and thoroughly rural. The function of the great estate was to mediate between city and country, to carry back and forth supplies, people, and ideas that were vital to the growth of Spanish American civilization.

Epilogue
(1995)

IF I ASK myself why this piece has been anthologized several times over the years, I come to the conclusion that, the perennial interest in the hacienda aside, one of the main reasons is that it attempts to do something not often done. Tying the conquest period to following times in terms of large trends may seem a necessary, basic enterprise, but it has not in fact been much undertaken in recent decades, largely because of lack of the requisite primary research to compare.

When I came on the scene, I found a well developed juridical literature on the encomienda of the conquest period and a newer literature on the hacienda of the mature period, dominated by Chevalier, Góngora, and Gibson, still in gestation and expanding quickly, more social and economic in orientation. My work on the initial period in *Spanish Peru*, being likewise socially oriented, presented many points of departure for comparison with the corpus on the hacienda and made possible a mediation between the two existing bodies of research.

In the 1970's interest in the hacienda grew, grew, and grew, at the expense of many other kinds of study. One major historian after another devoted a book to the topic. As the rational economic nature of the hacienda became ever more obvious, the parallel with the encomienda along the lines I had drawn was strengthened, and as its market orientation, its consolidation in response to markets, became clearer, it was even more apparent that the two types of estates fit along a single line of evolution. But the great majority of the new studies concentrated on times later than the conquest period, often much later, for whereas Chevalier's research began in the late sixteenth century[32] and centered on the seventeenth, many of the successor studies concentrated on the eighteenth.

For Chile and Peru some work did come along that began at the beginning and carried the story forward into the seventeenth century. Góngora's *Encomenderos y estancieros* (1971) and Davies' *Landowners in Colonial Peru* (1984) showed encomienda families across the generations using the estancias associated with their grants as the beginning for agrarian enterprises of various kinds, which turned out not to be Chevalier-style haciendas but businesses adapted in size and nature to their respective settings.[33] The point has been made, but we could still use more studies of the operation of encomienda and other estates before 1570 to balance the work on the time thereafter, especially for Mexico.

My plea that historians not study estates as purely rural and agrarian entities fell largely on deaf ears. Finally, though, Van Young's *Hacienda and Market* (1981) appeared, making clear once and for all that city and estates were inseparably connected, that the size and nature of the city determines the market and hence the size and nature of the estates, and that the whole complex functions as a single entity. With that, the picture was quite complete, and Van Young's book could be said to have brought to an end the period of the field's great preoccupation with the hacienda.

The version of the encomienda-hacienda article appearing here is hardly changed from the one originally published in 1969; I have done little more than alter a few individual words that because of developments of the intervening time strike my sensibilities in a somewhat different way. I have left the word "hacendado" as it was, though I have become ever more aware that the owners of haciendas were rarely if ever called that in the time to which I refer; they almost always had

---

[32]As is apparent in Chevalier's belief that the term "estancia" begins to turn up in documents at that point, when in fact it had been there from the Caribbean phase and all through the Mexican conquest period up to that time without interruption.

[33]See also Ramírez 1986, a study of estates in the Lambayeque region of northern Peru from conquest to independence.

broader interests and did not define themselves by hacienda owning alone.[34] In general, by the time I wrote the article I had reacted against the crucial aspects of the French feudal view of the hacienda, but along the edges I see that I was still enough affected to think it more monolithic and seigneurial than I do now.

Looking at the article today, the main thing I miss is a sense of the presence and importance of smaller estates. I gave to the great estate a role which in fact was played by an estate system including some mix of smaller and larger estates at any given time and place depending on the conditions, a mix varying to the point that some situations would support no larger estates at all—and yet the principles of operation and development were constant. It was in the fall of 1969, a few months after the article had appeared, while I was doing research on the Mexican Valley of Toluca in the late sixteenth century, that I first became aware of the coexistence and cooperation of larger and smaller estates.[35] Other scholars began to fill in the picture, and Brading's *Haciendas and Ranchos* (1978) made it as clear as one could wish. Adding this dimension would not alter the general direction of the development over the centuries or affect its continuity. The encomenderos' estancieros, former estancieros who had gone independent, and truck gardeners around cities in the early times relate to later *labradores* and *rancheros* in the same ways as the encomienda relates to the hacienda. Estates large and small participated in the general labor procurement systems of their times.

As these things sank into my mind, I began to take a broader and more abstract view of Spanish American estate

---

[34]Another matter in which the terminology could be refined has to do with the term "repartimiento." I may have been affected here by the fact that at the time of writing the article I had done much more research in Peru than in Mexico. In my subsequent years of work in and on Mexico I never studied encomienda terminology directly, but my present impression is that although indeed the word "encomienda" is not used in Mexican records as generously as it is in modern scholarship, "repartimiento" in its Peruvian sense, referring to the grant and the jurisdiction of the encomienda, is not common either.

[35]See Lockhart 1976a and Lockhart 1991, pp. 202–42.

organization. If one adds a few more components and variables to the elements provided for encomienda and hacienda structure here, the framework becomes applicable to things as different as textile shops, silver mines, and sugar mills. The ownership, staff, and labor force vary with the nature of the enterprise, responding especially to how profitable and how technical it is. Small agrarian estates are truncated versions of the larger ones. All the enterprises can be seen as much the same thing, being quite predictable adaptations to particular conditions, sharing the same temporal and regional arena of variation as encomienda and hacienda. In due course I expounded this view of things somewhat systematically, if briefly.[36]

My original notion in writing the encomienda-hacienda article was to begin a large process of spelling out the significance of work such as my *Spanish Peru* for later times, for I was then as I am now of the opinion that Latin American history is all of a piece, that the only two periods based on a sharp break are precontact and postcontact (and even there I find a host of basic continuities). It is not that subsequent phenomena were determined for all time in the conquest period, but they have their beginning there and a continuous development thereafter, and the true trajectories of evolution, the spectra of variation, and even their rationale can hardly be grasped without seeing the entire chronological sweep from its start.

But having with this article accounted for the first substantive chapter of *Spanish Peru*, I met with frustration in thinking of doing the same for other chapters. Studies like those on the hacienda were simply not to be found for the other topics, and in many cases they still are not. With the appearance in 1971 of Brading's *Miners and Merchants*, one began to see the possibility of something comparable for mercantile organization, but it would have skipped from the 1550's to the 1770's. Succeeding studies pushed the time back earlier into the eighteenth century, and finally Hoberman's *Mexico's Merchant Elite* (1991) filled the chronological gap to

---

[36]Lockhart 1976, pp. 21–26, and Lockhart 1984, pp. 274–75 and passim. See also Chapter 5 in this volume, especially pp. 128–31.

the extent that one could attempt something on the order of my "The Merchants of Early Spanish America."[37] Similar surveys could now probably be done with Audiencias and their judges, and possibly also with some portions of the ecclesiastical world, as well as in the very rapidly expanding subfield of the study of women and gender. Perhaps with Africans as well. With the crafts and maritime life, not yet.[38] I do hope, though, that as primary research on given topics across the centuries from first contact forward mounts (and it by no means needs to reach comprehensive coverage, but merely be enough to allow some triangulation), people in our field will take the opportunity to work out the longer trends it implies.

---

[37]Now in this volume as Chapter 6.

[38]Mining is unusual. The barrier in this case is not a lack of studies for the seventeenth and eighteenth centuries, but the paucity of knowledge about how the industry really functioned and was organized in the beginning.

2. The Social History of Early Latin America: Evolution and Potential

(1972, revised and expanded 1989)

"SOCIAL HISTORY" should be readily definable as the study of historical phenomena which transcend the individual and manifest themselves in human groups. But such a definition includes almost all meaningful history; it seems to fit precisely those political and institutional studies with which social history is ordinarily contrasted. Since our main concern here is with practical historiography rather than with precise definitions of broad genres, I will simply indicate through description and elimination the kind of history I mean.

Social history deals with the informal, the unarticulated, the daily and ordinary manifestations of human existence, as a vital plasma in which all more formal and visible expressions are generated. Political, institutional, and intellectual history, as usually practiced, concern themselves with the formal and the fully articulated. Social history bears the same relation to these branches as depth psychology does to standard biography. While it often discusses humble or obscure individuals, the correlation is not perfect, since study of the daily life and family connections of the famous is certainly social history, of a very valuable sort. Indeed, any branch of history can be converted into social investigation by turning attention from its usual main object of study, whether laws, ideas, or events, toward patterns in the lives and actions of the people who produce them.

Often it is impossible or undesirable to make a distinction between social and economic history. One can, however, discern a fairly distinct type of economically-oriented research which is concerned more with amounts and techniques of production than with the organization, conduct, and wider connections of the people involved. It tends strongly toward statistics and macrophenomena, and has a great deal in common with institutional history. In our field of early Latin America, it has often been practiced by French scholars and French-influenced Latin Americans. This useful branch of historical writing is also not our present concern.

The potential significance of social history for the so-called colonial period is easy to see. Formal institutions in early Iberoamerica, however important in adjudication and legitimation, were weak and spotty, lacking the manpower, the mechanisms, and even generally the will to carry out the activist policies of their counterparts in the twentieth century. Even when apparently locally influential, they were so only by virtue of grafting official attributes onto concentrations of social-economic resources, forming conglomerate structures of which the official aspect was more the symbol than the active principle. The main cohesive and dynamic forces of life were the needs, customs, techniques, and ideals of individuals acting in informal groupings; taken together these of course constitute society, so that early Latin American history is or should be to a large extent social.

Though E. G. Bourne sensed all this over eighty years ago, socially oriented studies have only recently come into their own. They were long nearly absent from the field (the national period lagging even farther behind), until finally the harbinger, demography, appeared after World War II, followed by full-fledged social history in the late 1960's. The years up to about 1975 saw the appearance of a series of major publications. With related kinds of ethnohistory and detailed demography, social history continued for some time to be the dominant strain among English-speaking historians of early Latin America and in some sense perhaps still is, though it has become broader and more eclectic. Latin Americans have largely continued to equate progressivism with the French school, though they read the English-language literature, and one or two major figures, above all Mario Góngora, have moved in that direction.

Why should such a movement emerge just when it did? One might imagine some connection with the persistent present-mindedness of the 1960's, strong echoes of which have stayed with us to this day. Social history touches a substream of continuity existing under more quickly alternating intellectual currents, governments, and even formal institutions. It therefore deals with matters that are of immediate relevance to the present. Scholars of our time in the social sciences have maintained a preoccupation with twentieth-century "development." Social history certainly bears on development. It can show, for example, that the role of foreign entrepreneurs in Latin America was not only prefigured but fully anticipated by first-generation Spaniards and Portuguese in the colonial period. It can show that Spanish American cities in the sixteenth century had the same structure and function as today. A double process of migration to the cities and expansion of urban-European life outward, beginning in the conquest period, is what brought the Latin American countries as we know them into being; the continuation of the process is what their further "development" must inevitably consist of. The study of society in the early period quickly reveals the bankruptcy of the traditional-vs.-modern dichotomy in interpreting development.

Despite all this, it is not clear that development studies had much influence on early Latin American historians. To take the only example about which I have intimate knowledge, they surely had no influence on me. Rather, I always had a negative reaction to the condescension and restricted perspective that are involved in viewing another society and culture primarily as a problem. On the conscious level, my motivations in the early 1960's were: a deep sympathy for that combination of restraint and energy so characteristic of sixteenth-century Spaniards, not unrelated to my love of Renaissance music; and on the other hand a dissatisfaction with then current knowledge of Latin American history, which seemed to me to be miscellaneous, to lack a core. My intuition was that a close study of society would reveal that core and make sense of the whole. My colleague David Brading also wrote me once of his love for Guanajuato and everything concerned with it. Generally it appears to me that social historians are more likely to be motivated by a positive fascination with their subject and an intellectual curiosity about it than by the moral outrage of the developmentalists.

Probably neither outside pressures nor conscious inner motivations are crucial to the rise of the social history movement. The time of social history came largely because the field had worked its way through the sources down to those which have obvious social content. According to a principle which may be called the law of the preservation of energy of historians, scholars in a given field usually take the easiest (most synthetic) sources first. When the easiest source is exhausted, or at least when it ceases to produce striking new results, a new generation of historians takes the next easiest, and so on.

There is a cycle of sources, from more to less synthetic, with corresponding kinds of history. For early Latin American history, the main elements of the series are (1) contemporary books and other formal accounts, which we call "chronicles"; (2) official correspondence; (3) the internal records of institutions; (4) litigation; (5) notarial records. With the chronicles, a sort of narrative history is practically ready made; the scope of reference is then gradually reduced as one proceeds through the series until in the notarial records the historian is confronted with an individual item about one ordinary person on one day of his or her life. The sources also get less and less accessible as one proceeds down the list, both in the physical sense and in the sense of requiring more special skills for use. They become more primary, minute, local, fresh, and of more direct interest to social history.

The early Latin American field has now completed its first full cycle of surveying the (written) sources, and it is in this light that we can view the question of the relation of the newer, close social investigation to older types of work. Mainly we will find the succeeding stages complementary rather than directly contradictory; there is merely the difference between a less and a more complete view. One type of correction is usually necessary. At every step historians have assumed that the portion of reality they were working with was the whole reality, and have made generalizations accordingly. The non-existence of Spanish artisans, merchants, and women in the new areas was presumed from their near absence in the bare military narratives of the conquest. Scholars working in vast collections of metropolitan legal records came to imagine that the "state" was all-powerful, or at least all-important, while those working with ecclesiastical reports made the "church" the sole transmitter of Iberian civilization.

Epic and institutional history

The historians who used the chronicles to write the epic of the conquest and interpret the lives of the great conquerors did work of lasting validity, in the sense that their narrative facts are mainly correct, that they saw something of the sweep of the process and recognized many of the critical junctures. It goes without saying that commercial, technical, social, and ethnohistorical dimensions must be added to their picture. But aside from other dimensions, there is a strong element of social convention or tradition, unrecognized by the older writers, in the very ostensible acts of military conquest. The psychological portraits by Prescott or Ramón Iglesia, acute analysts of character though they were, often rested on a false supposition of the uniqueness of acts which were actually within a well defined tradition. Prescott thought only a spirit as daring as Cortés could conceive of Moctezuma's capture, not realizing that to seize the cacique was standard procedure. The social background juts into surface events in ways the older writers could not know. No one can fully understand Columbus's troubles as a governor of Spaniards without taking into account the abysmally low status and prestige of sailors in Spanish society, or the extreme Spanish contempt for foreigners.

The literary sensitivity of an Iglesia or a Marcel Bataillon is by no means outmoded; rather it requires extension. The art of subtle reading of documents represents one of the most real technical contributions we historians can make to colleagues in other disciplines, as the Swede Åke Wedin has shown, and it needs to be extended to all kinds of sources, not merely chronicles. But we have also seen by now that it is only too easy for textual criticism, in a vacuum, to outsmart itself. Sometimes the slightest glimmer of a contact with social reality, a triangulation through other kinds of documents, will answer a question more certainly than the most stunning textual pyrotechnics. For example, Bataillon used great virtuosity to impale the chronicler Pedro Gutiérrez de Santa Clara on his many plagiarisms, mistakes, and absurdities, and would surely convince a neutral, uninformed person that the writer had never left his native Mexico for Peru. Yet Juan

Pérez de Tudela (1963) points out many examples of the chronicler's sure touch on matters of social detail not to be found in his sources, proving his presence in Peru beyond reasonable doubt. From my own Peruvian research I could multiply the instances of Gutiérrez de Santa Clara's originality and authenticity.

The successors to the epic writers and commentators were the institutional historians who dominated Latin American historical scholarship during the time between world wars and somewhat beyond. With them too we find that the descriptive-analytical core of the work retains much validity, while the general perspective and conclusions need modification. The repeated occurrence of this phenomenon at every stage of the field's evolution is a negative commentary on the naive common belief that a work's ostensible "conclusions" are the most important part of it. Actually they are almost always the most ephemeral part. The classics of the field have had importance for their creative reconstruction and skillful presentation of important subject matter, including the identification of key concepts and patterns, and second for the method they used, as a model for other studies.

As one example, there is little wrong with Roberto Levillier's biography (1935–42) of late sixteenth-century Peruvian viceroy don Francisco de Toledo. The vicissitudes of the viceroy's official career and the extent of his legislation are there delineated in a way that for the most part we have no particular reason to change. But social history has made us aware that Viceroy Toledo did not single-handedly create the Spanish colony of Peru; in most cases he was merely codifying a state of affairs that had come about spontaneously in previous decades. The same holds true for such viceroys as Mendoza, Enríquez, and Velasco in Mexico. A process of rationalization and stock-taking occurred regularly about a generation after Spanish arrival in any given area, when the first great movement of creation and destruction had run its course. Robert Ricard's classic *Spiritual Conquest of Mexico* (1933) remains as a faithful reproduction of the mendicant orders' own view of themselves; it gives an admirably rationalized portrait of their internal history, aims, and methods—but not of their achievements. Basing himself only on friars' reports, Ricard thought the countryside was empty except for the friars and some very dimly seen Indians. We know now that the rural *doctrina* or parish was usually tied to an encomienda, and the encomienda in turn to an already existing Indian entity and jurisdiction; that the friars were outnumbered in the very areas where they were working by Spanish stewards and retainers of the encomenderos, by miners, small traders, and Hispanized black slaves. Rural church activity in the more settled areas, indeed, was often largely a function of the encomienda and of Spanish secular society. The widespread assumption, stemming from Ricard and other similar work, that the church was the primary conveyor of Spanish social-cultural influence is not tenable. In my opinion the great mechanism of Europeanization was not formal instruction but ordinary contact between Europeans and Indians, measured in manhours, and the primary Europeanizing agent was the local Iberian and already Iberianized population going about its daily business—not the church, except insofar as it was a part of that population.

Thus the institutionalists, until after World War II at least, mainly took their institutions at face value. They therefore produced an ideal picture, with emphasis on formal structure. The actual operation of the institutions at a local level, or indeed at any level, received little attention. It was inevitable that there would be a movement, dictated by both the sources and the logic of the subject, from this generalized and formalistic institutional history toward more individual or regional studies, and this movement, when the time came, had in it the germs of social history.

It is worthy of note that that massive monument of institutionalism, Clarence Haring's *Spanish Empire in America* (1947, actually conceived in the 1930's), though it has done perhaps more than any other work to reinforce the notion of a rigid and powerful Spanish state, was written with some realization of limitations and exceptions, as well as a strong sense for such tidbits of social history as appeared in the administrative sources Haring used.

The intellectual history written from closely related sources—official correspondence and pamphleteering—stands in much the same relation to social history as does formal institutionalism. Mainly concerning the controversies over Indians and the encomienda, it is unassailable as the history of a polemic, but tells little about the social reality beneath it (even though that dimension was often crucial in determining the positions of the participants in the debates). A certain sophistication is required to keep the two aspects apart; many readers of the intellectual historians have failed to maintain the distinction. In the case of the most famous exponent of this branch, Lewis Hanke, there was little enough excuse for readers' confusion. Hanke said repeatedly that he was study-ing attitudes and ideas.[1] In one memorable passage of *The Spanish Struggle for Justice* (1949, pp. 84–85), which struck me forcibly when I first read it as a graduate student, he not only disavowed any firm conclusions on the encomienda as a functioning organ, but put his finger on the lack of sources which would elucidate its ordinary operation and the neces-sity of locating such sources, if any should exist.

---

[1]This I always took to be Hanke's main emphasis, but at times (1971) he has implied belief in a stronger impact of laws on behavior than he had expressed earlier.

The social historians are not absolute skeptics about the power of law and formal ideas, nor are they in the main guilty of a simplistic distinction between law and reality. If there is such a thing as reality, then law is clearly a part of it. The frequently used term "social reality," as contrasted with law, is merely a convenient expression meaning the potentially observable, verifiable behavior and behavior patterns of an existing population. No one imagines that law is without relation even to this more narrowly defined social reality. But social history teaches us three basic lessons about the relationship: (1) Most Iberian legislation was reactive. If there was an ongoing dialectic of law and social reality, law's role was usually that of the antithesis. (2) Iberian law tended to be descriptive rather than actively formative. Charles Gibson has called it "an approximation of historical happening, or a commentary upon it" (1964, p. 235). (3) Legislation was written in a highly formulized style that almost amounted to a code, and even when directly influential could not and cannot be taken literally. For these reasons as well as for more obvious ones, it is generally hard to deduce much about social reality from a given law or debate prior to knowledge of the whole context. Most of the general principles of interpretation one can draw up are negative, such as the principle that legislative reiteration indicates noncompliance.

Social history in search of sources

Institutionalism held the stage for so long that an intellectual dissatisfaction with it became manifest rather far in advance of that true exhaustion of its characteristic sources that had helped bring the epic stage to a conclusion. Though there were still viceroys' biographies unwritten and Audiencia correspondence unread, important scholars in the field began to strain in the direction of social or economic history, usually staying as close to traditional sources as possible.

The simplest way was to work with legislation on social matters. This was the method of Richard Konetzke, who compiled relevant royal cedulas (1953–63), and also wrote some articles about social trends, based on these and similar materials. While valuable as one kind of formal institutional history, such work is no closer to social reality than any other legislative study. In fact it is more distant, for in the whole panoply of idealistic and quixotic royal ordinances, social legislation has a peculiar unreality. Not only were Spanish social concepts more archaic and artificial than concepts of administration and commerce, but the crown knew and cared far less about the amorphous society of the Indies than about the administrators it appointed or the export economy that produced its revenues.[2]

Actually, royal ordinances can be a very valuable source for social history. The cedularies of the Spanish crown contained decrees of two different kinds, *de oficio* and *de parte*. The former, ordinances of a general nature addressed to governors, were the main concern of investigators like Konetzke. But the more voluminous de parte decrees, concern-

_____

[2]Guillermo Céspedes del Castillo (1957) used mainly metropolitan administrative sources to produce an exceptional synthesis of Spanish American social history for the sixteenth and seventeenth centuries. It is interesting to observe on the one hand how much Céspedes was able to achieve through intuition and sophistication, and on the other hand how the nature of the sources often forced even an acute, socially oriented scholar into a legalistic and metropolitan stance, with consequent retention of several received ideas that would be hard to defend today.

ing individuals, do not suffer from the typical shortcomings of the general legislation. Usually they are in response to petitions, and whether they concern the recovery of property, the grant of a coat of arms, or a recommendation, they give authentic information about a dimension of the individual in the Indies that is often not otherwise documented.

Frank Tannenbaum's *Slave and Citizen* (1946) was also an attempt to do social history with legal-institutional ma- terials. It took for granted the strong, active state and church of the institutionalists; as these phantoms then dissolved under the light of closer study of society, the "Tannenbaum thesis" of mild treatment of slaves in Latin America was left with little to stand on. Yet Tannenbaum did have enough knowledge of Iberian society to see and emphasize that the Iberians possessed a living tradition or social convention of slave holding, and that having such a tradition was very different from having none. While research was pulling one leg from under Tannenbaum's thesis, it was adding support to the other. Though "mild" and "harsh" are probably the worst imaginable categories to measure it, there was a difference between Latin American slave-holding practice even in structurally similar situations, at least as to rate and manner of the absorption of the slave group into European society. Herbert Klein in *Slavery in the Americas* (1967) started with much the same sources and perspective as Tannenbaum, but, by virtue of some quite solid statistical information about employment patterns and relative positions of blacks and mulattoes in the later period, plus a more specific geographical focus and the sheer force of intuition, he put much more emphasis on social-economic practice than had Tannenbaum.

One of the most outstanding feats of legerdemain per- formed in the field at this stage was that of C. R. Boxer, who without going in any way beyond the traditional sources of "empire history" as practiced by the British—travelers' accounts and correspondence from both local and metro- politan officials—produced preliminary social-economic surveys (1952–65) of much of colonial Brazil that have long retained their usefulness and still cannot be considered entirely superseded. Boxer's relative lack of preconceptions, his faithful reporting of detail, his attention to reports of people on the spot, and his English traveler's eye for social and commercial significance, whatever the main thrust of the documentation, were all great strengths. Nevertheless, it is likely and indeed in some cases apparent that Boxer could not utterly transcend the limitations of the sources and the genre. Significant elements of the population remained untreated or unsuspected; the picture of others, such as the paulistas, is a typically one-dimensional "governor's portrait"; categories of analysis imposed by Boxer from the outside are now yielding to ones growing out of closer examination of the material (thus "plantation," or the anachronistic, Anglo-Saxon notion of "prejudice").

Another striking phenomenon of the period when the field was groping for social history sources was the work of Gilberto Freyre. With Freyre it becomes obvious, as was already implied to a certain extent with Tannenbaum and Boxer, that the sources are not necessarily and absolutely the only factor dictating what kinds of history are done. Some fields develop more clearly in this fashion than others; when there is a high degree of political or ideological interest in a subject, its study may veer far indeed from that steady march through the sources which, though perhaps blind, is natural, organic, and in a sense logical. Such deflection has been minimal in the early Latin American field. Some may think this is for the better, some for the worse. I do not deplore it. National image building is doubtless a valid and creative human endeavor; at the same time, it is often antithetical to the search for truth and the investigation of historical reality. Freyre's work is a major example of the intrusion of twentieth-century political-intellectual movements on pre-independence historiography. For historians, his writing was valuable above all as a stimulus toward social investigation, directing attention as it did away from formal structures while emphasizing the centrality of informal institutions, social conventions, and the ethnic-cultural make-up of the population.

Freyre's sources appear quite varied (with travelers' accounts after all at the core), but they do not merit prolonged discussion because he used them with impressionistic levity, as a guide to a private vision, in the manner of a novelist. One feels that in a sense his childhood was his most basic source, and that the rest was used to illustrate and bring alive a world already imagined. That world is childlike in its lack of any time dimension. The task of deciding what the primary chronological reference is in *The Masters and the Slaves* (1933) is exceedingly difficult; apparently the time is more than anything else the early nineteenth century, whether Freyre realized it or not. At any rate, one can deduce from subsequent writings by Boxer, Stuart Schwartz, and others, that Freyre projected a late and idealized version of the "plantation" back onto the whole colonial period, totally ignoring and implicitly denying the long and dynamic evolution of the sugar-producing complex and accompanying population.

It is unlikely that any basic advance could have been made toward an understanding of Iberoamerican society as long as the main sources used were legislation, chronicles, and official correspondence. Not only was little social infor- mation to be found there; until other sources gave a context, what social data did exist were unintelligible. It is difficult to convey to a layperson the utter uselessness of broad, syn- thesizing generalizations on social matters presented by contemporaries. "The sons of the conquerors are impov- erished." "All Spaniards in the Indies are considered hidalgos." "Creoles are deprived of high office." Not one of these statements, found repeatedly in correspondence, is anywhere near the truth. Critical reflection might have convinced scholars that such dicta were not literally true. But even after we have concluded that a general statement is affected by formula or bias, what meaning can we attach to it? None, until we have either direct and reliable information on the careers of large numbers of individuals of the type referred to, or a relatively exhaustive statistical survey (the latter being in most cases impossible). Once a notion of the real state of things has been in some manner obtained, it is instructive to return to the original statement, which one now for the first time fully comprehends. Comparing the reality with the statement reveals the political position or other interest of the person who made it. In this way one can also acquire a sense of the vocabulary being used; contemporary recipients of governors' reports understood them far better than we usually do today.

One redeeming feature of these sources was their inconsistency. While in general they built up a version of society approximately as distorted as the picture of the twentieth-century United States purveyed in political campaigns for the presidency, at times there was occasion for concrete references greatly at variance with their general tenor. Particularly in the chronicles one is forever meeting with suggestive examples: the black slaves escape from camp, and one becomes aware that there are black slaves; some Spanish women get killed, and their existence too is authenticated; guns are manufactured for approaching hostilities, and one becomes aware of the extent of local Spanish technical know-how and self-sufficiency. The most striking such anomaly in the chronicles, the building of brigantines for the siege of Tenochtitlan by Cortés's forces, led C. Harvey Gardiner to write a forward-looking biography (1950) of the man most responsible, ship's carpenter Martín López.

On the edges of institutionalism

At length, the field moved on to sources containing fuller, more direct, and more systematic information about various aspects of life—not necessarily leading to "social history" in our more specific sense; more often indeed, to economic or macrodemographic research. Such sources were of many kinds. Most typically they were the internal records of a well defined organization or institution, consisting of day-to-day entries which might have become the basis of reports, but themselves did not have that character. These sources include such documents as registers of emigrants or departing ships, parish records, tribute and tax rolls, and the like; census records, where they exist in any detail, are a somewhat similar source. Most materials of this nature lend themselves readily to a statistical approach, though there are some that do not, such as the minutes and other records of corporations—municipal councils, cathedral chapters, or charitable organizations.

Ever since the end of World War II there has been a strong

interest in documents like these, and it will indubitably
continue. The quest for organized and centralized sources is
legitimate. Concentrated materials are not merely more
convenient for the scholar; they make it possible to attain a
higher degree of completeness, or to deal with longer time periods and broader areas, without exceeding human limitations. But inevitably the more centralized source is more
manufactured, tampered with; it tends to force one into
certain avenues of research regardless of one's real main
interest. We get primarily what the persons writing the
records were interested in communicating, rather than the
facts and patterns they took for granted, which are usually
precisely the matters of greatest interest to social history. In a
statistically-oriented source, what is left out is often forever
beyond reach. The more unorganized, haphazard, and miscellaneous the source, the more likely that one can discover
new basic patterns, suspected or unsuspected—not as the
principal subject matter of the document, but as a byproduct,
something to be picked out by a perceptive reader. Of course
the limitations of any one source need not be a serious matter
if historians will stop the practice, too prevalent in our field,
of basing a whole approach on one kind of source alone.

For economic history, the documents in organized series
represented an obvious and important opportunity to determine amounts and trends for shipping, production, and
prices. Such work as that of Pierre Chaunu on Atlantic
shipping (1955–56) represents a very adequate response to
this challenge (see also the work of Alvaro Jara on silver
mining production). The pitfalls—lacunae and unofficial
activity—are clear, and therefore relatively easy to compensate for. Both ships and silver mines were finite in number,
highly concentrated geographically, and under quite close
surveillance. We have every reason to accept the results of
such research, particularly as to trends. It is always of interest to show their correlation, or lack of correlation, with
trends in other aspects of society. For the rest, one can only
say that work of this kind is not the answer to a social historian's prayer. By its nature it turns toward the most
centralized, formally structured aspects of the imperial establishments; its sources are characterized by a paucity or total

lack of information about people and informal practices. Chaunu's work was actually in a way a step backwards for social history, since it redirected attention to metropolitan agencies and the sealanes, subjects which the field was tending to abandon as relatively peripheral to the story of the formation of Latin American society. As for silver mining, one can easily maintain that it was more than peripheral. Yet though it provided the economic base of European-style society in large parts of Spanish America, it also stood somewhat apart from the mainstream of social evolution in city and countryside. We know even in the twentieth century how easy it is for the mining sector to become an enclave. There is much greater direct significance for social history in such work as Enrique Florescano's study (1969) of the price of maize in eighteenth-century New Spain. Even here, because of the depersonalized nature of the source, almost no advance is made toward directly understanding the functioning of the haciendas that produced the maize.

Drawing social significance from serialized documents proved to be the special domain of the demographers, above all of Woodrow Borah and associates at Berkeley (1948 to present). Some may find it surprising that this branch of investigation appears here, only part way through our survey of sources and methods, when demography and the quantitative approaches connected with it have been held by many to be the field's most modern, advanced development. Certainly demography's potential is far from exhausted even today; but there is something beyond it, and no one type of endeavor can or should hold our exclusive attention forever. Macrodemography is very closely related, in both source material and method, to the kinds of economic research mentioned just above. Borah indeed has a distinguished record as an economic historian; he has worked, among other things, on price trends in colonial Mexico (1958).

It will emerge in the remainder of this paper that large-scale demography has been succeeded in part by an attempt to look more closely at various sides of social reality, as reflected in more local or less organized sources. This movement is parallel to and contemporary with a similar trend among European historians, though there the subsequent work has often itself remained primarily quantitative (see Franklin Mendels 1970). European historical demographers turned from the study of total population trends to more intensive investigations of smaller groups, going as far as the (rather skeletal) reconstitution of individual parishes and families, and in recent years demographers of Latin America have increasingly done the same sort of thing. The motivation is partly lack of confidence in the results obtained by macroinvestigation, partly the fact that knowledge about gross trends often reveals little about the structures and patterns of most interest to social historians.

Given Borah's own writings on method, this is not the place to treat demographic sources and methods per se. But surely there should be a dialogue between two approaches as closely related in subject matter and underlying theme as statistical demography and the close study of the lives of people. As to method, social history can make a contribution through helping to clarify and refine the categories. For the later period of census-taking, the place to start is no doubt an intense study of the use of increasingly elaborate terminology in the censuses themselves. Changes and ambiguities in the census-takers' use of categories can tell us as much, about both social concepts and social realities, as the raw figures. In work on the earlier period, the categories remain broad and relatively undefined, in striking contrast to precisely articulated procedures of source analysis and extrapolation. To get at the content of these categories, one must go beyond the "demographic" sources proper. Advances in broad-based, close study of people's lives have gradually done much to fill in what it meant to be "Spanish," "Indian," and "mestizo" at given times and places, so that we can better interpret the statistical results, but much still remains to be done in this respect.[3]

Nor are the actual census categories the only ones important for interpretation. Other tools of analysis, such as the category "labor," need refining. For example, demography

---

[3]Borah himself gave a good beginning to the enterprise of category analysis in his penetrating, almost unknown essay, "Race and Class in Mexico" (1954).

tells us that the Indian population of Mexico declined while the black population rose. Nothing is more natural than to suppose (with David Davidson, 1966) that the blacks were brought in to replace Indians, labor to replace labor. In lowland areas where the Indian population almost disappeared, this interpretation seems to hold true. But for an area such as central Mexico, investigation of what blacks were doing shows them mainly in various intensive, skilled, or responsible activities, and certainly not replacing Indians in the maize fields. Once the role of the blacks is understood, we can interpret the increase in their numbers as related to (1) the growth of the Spanish world with its infinite need for auxiliaries; (2) the continuing lack of enough fully acculturated Indians for such posts; (3) the growth of wealth and capacity to buy slaves. There seems hardly any relation to raw Indian numbers.

The demographers have not made their own special sources and subject matter into a total explanation of Latin American history to quite the same extent as did many of their predecessors, although the tendency can be detected. If a generation of undergraduates was taught that Indian population decline was the reason for falling silver production and the rise of the hacienda, the fault was only partly that of Woodrow Borah, who in *New Spain's Century of Depression* (1951) was careful to weigh other factors as well. But until various close studies of a more local nature could be made, it was really impossible to weigh other factors. As to mining, Peter Bakewell's work on Zacatecas in the sixteenth and seventeenth centuries (1971) and David Brading's on Guanajuato in the eighteenth (also 1971) prove definitively that the size of the overall Indian population of the country was a negligible factor. Silver deposits, mercury supplies, technology, finance, and organization seem to be the totality of relevant variables. Insofar as labor availability was important at all as a determining factor, it can only have been skilled, experienced labor; even at the bottom of the curve, there were enough Indians, many times over, to work the mines, if simple numbers would have availed. The case of the great center of Zacatecas is striking. The town grew, mines extended, and production went up, while the Mexican Indian population went down. Zacatecas hit a peak in the first three decades of the seventeenth century when Indian population was reaching a low point, then declined through the later part of the century as Indian population began to recover.

For the hacienda, such clarity cannot be attained. Indian population decline was certainly important in affecting the chronology of the hacienda's development in some areas; that it hastened its rise was all Borah ever said. But the first systematic work on the evolution of the hacienda in a single area, Mario Góngora's study of the history of landholding in Chile's Valley del Puangue (1956), not only presents resources, markets, and the growth of the Spanish world as the essential motor of development, but specifically denies any straightforward connection between the granting of land and Indian population loss. Later William Taylor (1972) and Robert Keith (1976) were to publish regional studies from which one can deduce, in the first case, that the lack of a strong local Hispanic market severely retarded the development of the mature hacienda system, and in the second case, that the presence of such a market soon brought it into existence. François Chevalier, too, though he like his contemporary Borah tended to explain the hacienda largely as a response to depression and population loss, gave a relatively full-bodied portrait of the institution, which, by showing its social coherence and interconnection with every stratum and aspect of Spanish American society, implied that it might in some form be almost coterminous with that society. My own work on Peru in the conquest period (1968) showed that social and economic goals, patterns of behavior, and types of organization usually associated with the hacienda were then already dominant, in loose association with the encomienda, so that with the predictable growth of Spanish society the predominance of something like the hacienda seems inevitable.

The general perspective rising from closer studies is considerably different from that which arises from macrodemography. It would appear from the former that trends in pure numbers of people rarely if ever actually originate social patterns; such trends work mainly to accelerate or decelerate developments rooted in society, culture, and technology. Even in the matter of the timing of important trends, close substantive studies usually give at least as much importance to the growth of the Spanish world (only partly a demographic phenomenon) as to decline in Indian population, despite the great disparity in sheer numbers in the early and middle colonial periods. We become aware that with the broad, unarticulated demographic categories necessary for the earlier period, a correlation cannot be presumed to be an explanation. It does, however, represent a hypothesis and direction for research.

Smaller-scale, more intense statistical studies can reconstitute more refined information from sources not organized to deliver it in any straightforward way, and by the 1970's such studies were ceasing to become a rarity. Edgar F. Love (1971), for example, studied exhaustively the ethnic status of the marriage partners of blacks and mulattoes in a Mexico City parish for a hundred-year period in the seventeenth and eighteenth centuries. While the results were not unexpected, Love established the nature and extent of mixture among lower urban groups beyond all reasonable dispute. For eighteenth-century Chile, Jacques Barbier (1970) used the extensive genealogical literature on the Chilean upper class to carry out a study which measures statistically the degree of endogamy of holders of titles, offices, and property entails, making quite fine distinctions of category and chronology. Love's study sticks close to the parish register, while Barbier ranges more widely and makes illuminating use of more substantive accounts of the careers of certain individuals, which is of course easier to do with a group much written about.[4] Barbier's article was one of several indications around this time that by the mid-eighteenth century an upper group of creoles was in a position of considerable wealth and great official influence almost everywhere in the Indies. Research of these types could readily and usefully be combined with the career pattern approach of social history proper, but such has rarely if ever happened. In the era of late Bourbon census-taking, there are many possibilities. The censuses themselves are so much more methodical and articulated that statistical-

---

[4]This work and more has since been incorporated into Barbier's book *Reform and Politics* (1980).

demographic work with them could serve as a time-saver and a sensitive guide for more direct studies of social configurations.

Some of the sources of the serial type seem to lend themselves not only to statistical compilations, but to a more immediate study of social patterns. Outstanding among these are the registers of permits issued to New World emigrants, such as the Archive of the Indies began to publish in its *Pasajeros a Indias* (Bermúdez Plata, 1940–46). The entries give not only the emigrant's name but usually the names of his parents, his birthplace, and his destination. Sometimes occupation and other particulars are added. Seeing the apparent potential of such a source, Peter Boyd-Bowman (1964–68) made an ambitious attempt to go over from the purely statistical approach of compiling discrete bits of data which lack intelligibility except in the aggregate, to the large-scale accumulation of actual case histories, each of which would have its own directly perceptible pattern.[5] It would thus be possible to manipulate large amounts of data while retaining direct comprehensibility at every step, with a consequent gain in reliability of conclusions and interpretations; above all, patterns would emerge that could never come out of more atomistic data. But the documentary base proved unable to sustain this pretty dream. The entries of the Seville registers do not tell enough about the emigrants; so few occupations are listed as to give a false impression. Above all, the broad Atlantic stretches as an unbridgeable gap. Though Boyd-Bowman has utilized various supplementary sources, there is no equally methodical and centralized listing in the Indies; as a result of the limited repertory of names and deliberate repetition of the same name in families, it is usually impossible to identify a given person in the New World with his homonym in the Pasajeros, even if you can find him, without other kinds of evidence. Failure to recognize this caused social history pioneer Tomás Thayer Ojeda recklessly to identify the conquerors of Chile with Pasajero entries,

---

[5]A brief statistical summary of this and later compilation subsequently appeared in Boyd-Bowman's "Patterns of Spanish Emigration to the Indies until 1600" (1976).

bringing about an extraordinary longevity among that group.

For macroresearch, then, the Pasajeros have turned out to be useful mainly in the same way as other sources of this type: as the basis of statistics on gross trends for the kinds of data they provide systematically, above all information about regional origin. In many other respects, Boyd-Bowman's *Indice* is an excellent research tool. The absolute volume of migration will probably long remain uncertain, but the work of Boyd-Bowman and others has established that the general order of magnitude was greater, at an earlier time, than once thought. From the beginnings, there were enough Iberians in the New World to form complex, largely self-contained societies. Also the quick transition from an initial, geographically determined, overwhelming Andalusian predominance to a broad cross-section of Castilians is a very clear trend. The significance of it is not so clear; we are as far as ever from knowing whether Spanish American civilization can be said to have Andalusian origins.

At one time I had a rather strong distrust of the Pasajeros as a source for investigating trends of immigration, particularly for working out short-term shifts and trends for individual areas. The reasons were several. Those who have watched the process closely know that many people who received permits to go to the Indies actually never left Spain; others, a very large proportion, went to areas different from their declared destination. On the other hand, many or most emigrants for one reason or another went unregistered; at least this is a natural conclusion to draw from the fact that only a small fraction of the names of Spaniards in Peru in the conquest period can be located in the Pasajeros. All this induced me to carry out a separate investigation of the origins of Peruvian Spaniards (1968, pp. 237–39), counting all I could find in all types of sources, with the single criterion that they must have been physically in Peru. The resulting list turned out to have a regional distribution very close indeed to that seen in the entries in the Pasajeros giving declared emigrants to Peru for the same years. Apparently the biases balance out or are irrelevant, and the emigrant registers are a trustworthy and sensitive indicator of trends in overall volume and regional composition.

Whenever and wherever similar registers can be found on this side of the Atlantic, they can easily become the basis for both statistical surveys and systematic observation of careers, informal structures, and behavior patterns. An outstanding example of such a document is the complete or nearly complete listing of the European-born Spaniards in Mexico City in 1689, published by J. Ignacio Rubio Mañé (1966). The original document gives each individual's name, Spanish origin, and present occupation, and often the approximate wealth and time of arrival as well; Rubio Mañé also located over half of the Spaniards in local parish records of marriages and burials. Even a quick statistical overview of the data shows much of interest: for example, how very few European Spaniards were in government, and how many were in humble positions. A year of research, tracing these same individuals in all kinds of other Mexican documentation, would enable one to write an illuminating book. On the basis of multiple career patterns, it would show the nature of the first-generation Spaniards' ties to and role in the local society and economy, and it would help in the process of refining what have been two of the field's most corrupt categories, "creole" and "peninsular."

Another source which might have the potential for a macrostatistical approach on the basis of perceived patterns rather than discrete phenomena is the famous set of regional surveys we call the *Relaciones geográficas*. However, they tend more to economic than to social detail, and an attempt by Alejandra Moreno Toscano (1968) to use French quasi-statistical methods on them led neither to new conclusions nor to appreciable refinement of old ones. Like the emigrant registers, the Relaciones geográficas seem primarily helpful as research tools, as one resource we can use in reconstructing individual careers and local communities, but insufficient in themselves.

Institutional sources of various kinds also offer opportunities for close studies of administrative entities and personnel, with inevitable social implications. The social aspect first became an important and integral part of institutional studies with John Phelan's *Kingdom of Quito in the Seventeenth Century* (1967). At root a study of Quito's Audiencia, and by no means mainly intended as social history, the work nevertheless gives a full-length portrait of the president, Antonio de Morga, with attention to the shape of his career as typical of advancement patterns, and with much evidence of the intertwining of his official and social life. Aside from the usual materials, Phelan made an intensive study of *visita* proceedings, which with the related *residencias* loom ever larger as an important source for the crucial informal activities of officials.

The next step was to deal systematically with the careers of larger numbers of officials. David Brading did this, among other things, in his *Miners and Merchants in Bourbon Mexico* (1971), for the Audiencia of New Spain, and Leon Campbell shortly thereafter published an article (1972) with similar research on the Audiencia of Lima. Both reached revolutionary conclusions on the old question of whether creoles were deprived of high office in the Spanish Indies. Their sources were standard, except for close attention to visitas and other litigation; anyone who had had the perspicacity to distrust creole correspondence could have discovered these facts long ago, by merely asking the question: *who* were the members of the Audiencias?

For his *Sovereignty and Society* (1973), dealing with the *Relação* or high court of colonial Brazil, Stuart Schwartz discovered and exploited an even more centralized and informative source, the metropolitan files of appointment dossiers, which give the judges' social and regional origins, education, and previous careers. These data, together with study of their activities, marriages, and investments in Brazil, made it possible to assemble capsule biographies of large numbers of officials over a long period of time. As a result, one can establish the important interrelation between social status or regional origin on the one hand and official activity on the other. An ongoing process of absorption of some of the judges into the upper levels of local Brazilian society emerges as a clear trend. Others, however, eventually went on to different assignments in the transatlantic Portuguese world. This is social history pure and simple; at the same time, it gives the main elements for explaining the nature of the court and its official activity. A mere study of the court's formal organization and of the legal philosophy and intellectual caliber of its members could never give as good a basis for understanding the general role and profile of the tribunal.[6]

On the face of it, the minutes of local corporations appear promising for social history, since they deal with relatively large numbers of people in a rather normal daily situation, nearly outside the great hierarchies. But municipal council records, the most common such source, have led to little beyond conventional formalistic treatment. Social historians who have wandered among these materials have usually become disillusioned with them, largely because of their aridity in personal detail; even so, establishing council membership is always a good tool in identifying and tracing the trajectory of important local families and interests, when done in conjunction with other types of research on the region (as seen for example in Bakewell's 1971 study). The debate between Boxer (1965) and Dauril Alden (1968) over whether or not Brazilian councils were aristocratic and self-perpetuating could never be resolved out of those records alone. The question must be settled by establishing family connections and status through study of other local documents. Once a deep study of a local society has been made, the dry council records come to life. Where before one saw only the admission of so-and-so to the council, one may now recognize that a body of estate owners is admitting its first merchant to membership, with all that action implies.

A source of this type that is much more amenable to social history are the records of lay brotherhoods, at least those of the Portuguese *Casa da Misericórdia*, as proved by A. J. R. Russell-Wood in his *Fidalgos and Philanthropists* (1968). These documents include a much larger slice of life than those of the municipal councils; the Misericórdia was a prestigious organization which was led by the rich, but also admitted

---

[6]Carrying the evolution a step further, Mark Burkholder and D. S. Chandler later published a book (1977) based on a survey of dossiers for all the Spanish American Audiencias from the late seventeenth century to the end of the colonial period; in a study of this scope, of course, they were not able to look closely into local ties and activities of the judges in the many different areas.

plebeian members and was in contact with the poor. Because of legacies left by members, the Misericórdia transcribed many testaments and property inventories, and admission procedures often necessitated a rather realistic and explicit evaluation of social status. Thus one gets at least a glimpse of family fortunes over some generations, of changing investment patterns, of the degree of social mobility, and of some important social types or categories.

On the basis of the brotherhood records, Russell-Wood clearly demonstrated the existence of a complex urban society in Brazil from an early time, a society amazingly like its Spanish American equivalent in organization, function, and tendency. Whatever its economic base, colonial Brazil was no mere rural plantation society; the master-slave dichotomy is not an adequate analytical tool to comprehend it. What we see is a complete European-type urban-oriented society in operation, with a strong tendency to grow because of entry of European immigrants into its middle levels and Africans into its lower levels.

The Misericórdia records have the great advantage of containing social data in a highly concentrated, centralized, and usable form, so that one can quickly get a long time perspective; Russell-Wood ranges over some two hundred years. On the other hand, Misericórdia documentation is not sufficient in itself; no type of document really is, but there *are* collections which concern the main activities of the people who figure in them and thus catch them head-on—administrative sources for administrators, estate records for estate employees. The Misericórdia was not anyone's main activity, and it is not possible with its records alone to construct good career samples, so that very basic aspects remain untouched. For example, though one thrust of the new material was to show the extent of urban-centeredness of the whole society, arousing the suspicion that Brazilian estate owners might have been as urban-oriented as their Spanish American counterparts, Russell-Wood retained the concept of a rural aristocracy as worked out in the previous generation by Boxer and Freyre. The Misericórdia records contribute literally nothing to this subject, except that the putative rural aristocrats belonged to at least one urban organization, the

Misericórdia. It was left to later scholars using wider sources to approach closer to the matter.[7]

Apparently the records of other brotherhoods will be even less able than those of the Misericórdia to serve as the sole basis of social investigations. The Misericórdia had a dominant, nearly monopolistic position among the Portuguese organizations; no single Spanish brotherhood could compare with it, and some of its functions were carried on in Spanish America by various branches of the church proper. There the brotherhood records are often consolidated today in archives of the *Beneficencia*. Taken together, these materials seem to have much the same characteristics as Misericórdia records. They can serve as an initial guide, and they permit surveying rather long periods of time; but though a fresh and intimate source, they are too peripheral to large areas of social life to suffice alone.

A special phenomenon in the field during the early 1970's was the appearance of Murdo MacLeod's *Spanish Central America: A Socioeconomic History* (1973), which put the historiography of that region on a new and higher level. Clearly affected by Borah and the French school, interested in demography and economics, as well as in society, as the title proclaims, MacLeod nevertheless produced a book which is essentially based on central governmental reports in the institutionalist manner. The focus was changed, but not the method, though much greater sophistication was exercised in interpreting officials' statements than in earlier institutional studies. MacLeod's procedure was fully justified by the need to start from scratch and provide an initial framework in a significant area that had until then been virtually a historiographical vacuum. What he was able to extract from

---

[7]Rae Flory's extensive doctoral dissertation (1978) surveys northeastern Brazilian social types and structures in the late seventeenth and early eighteenth centuries, placing the sugar mill owners in a much wider and more realistic context, on the basis of notarial and other local records. It is lamentable that this fine and innovative study has never been published. An article by Flory and David Grant Smith (1978), using copious individual examples in addition to a statistical overview of the groups' characteristics, shows extensive merchant-planter interpenetration.

the materials he used was primarily a macroeconomic survey of the region over two centuries, no mean achievement, but the internal organization of the main estate types and commercial endeavors remained to be studied, not to speak of society itself in either Spanish or indigenous spheres.

Beyond institutional sources

The inadequacy of a single source for carrying out social-economic investigation gradually became apparent to many scholars; partly for that reason, a search has gone on for other principles of limitation, to restrict the field of vision enough to allow deep exploration in all kinds of sources, yet include a coherent universe. Actually, the documentary base has continued to assert its strength, and most such studies in the end rely mainly on a more or less compact and homogeneous body of documents.

One rather straightforward way to attack the problem is to do a complete anatomy of a small, well defined group of people, both as a random sample of society and as a primary observatory for certain patterns operating at small-group level. By choosing strategically located samples one can achieve results with a broad significance and yet virtually eliminate selectivity. The great trouble is to find a group which includes humble people, yet is well enough documented. So far almost the only such studies are of contingents of conquerors, who started from obscurity but later became associated with wealth and notable deeds, and thus appear with regularity in all kinds of documents.

The first study of this type was the pioneering book of Tomás Thayer Ojeda, *Valdivia y sus compañeros* (1950), which examines the group characteristics of the conquerors of Chile, as to both backgrounds and later careers. Thayer Ojeda had emerged from a quasi-genealogical tradition to produce a monumental collection of biographies of a very large portion of the Spanish Chilean population in the conquest period (1939–41), but lacking statistical compilation or systematic discussion of trends. While he sought his individuals in all known sources, he wrote as a Chilean-Hispanic patriot, and thus de-emphasized artisanry and mercantile activity while rather easily accepting claims of nobility. Out of a lifetime's research and publication he accumulated enough data to put together a list of Chile's first conquerors that seems literally complete, with compilations of vital statistics and career patterns.[8]

Many areas had a larger population than Chile, and it is

---

[8]Eulalia Lobo (1967) carried out a useful social statistical analysis of Thayer's work, but any such attempt must naturally remain the captive of Thayer's outmoded categories and his other distorting tendencies.

An important documentary resource for biographical studies is the large corpus of memorials of services performed (*probanzas de méritos, de servicios*) presented by candidates for honors, titles, grants, or offices. Since they constitute statements by interested parties and are in the form of questionnaires accompanied by duly sworn testimony, they have, as a source, much in common with litigation. Probanzas are extremely easy to misuse; Gardiner, for example, was taken in by his subject Martín López's self-serving probanza campaign. An inflated, unbalanced biographical sketch can be readily concocted merely by rephrasing the questionnaire. Reading a dozen memorials will convince the scholar that all honors seekers claimed to be brave if not heroic, fanatically loyal, of noble birth, and impoverished after having spent their last penny in the service of the crown.

But there is no need to despair; much is still to be learned from probanzas. As incredibly distorted as they often are, they hardly ever contain outright falsehoods. If a person claims presence at a battle, we may assume he was there, though we should not forget that he may have been on the wrong side. A probanza usually gives a usable chronological-geographical framework for a life. Although the language of the genre is inflated, it has its own conventions; the experienced investigator can do quite well at estimating social rank from the convoluted statements. Thus a man described as a "persona honrada y principal, cristiano viejo, temoroso de Dios, hijodalgo," will infallibly prove to have been a rather humble fellow, because if he had been sure of his hidalgo status he would have put it first. Each claimant picked as witnesses his relatives, friends, compatriots, and political allies; witnesses were usually required to give their birthplace. If the researcher has gained any familiarity with the society he is studying, the witness list is pure gold, since it can reveal the claimant's regional, social, and political affiliations with great precision. A careful reading and the comparison of the witnesses' statements will not only tell far more about the claimant than is in the mere questionnaire, but will often unearth as much or more social-biographical information about the witnesses and the whole circle as about the principal figure.

not likely that any large number of scholars will have as many years to devote to preparatory work as Thayer did. Usually there must be a unitary base document which at least establishes the identity of the group. In his *Grupos de conquistadores en Tierra Firme* (1962), Mario Góngora utilized a document which did that and much more. A contemporary survey of the first encomenderos of Panama (found in a residencia, by the way) included not only their names, regional origins, and time of arrival in the Indies, but frank declarations of occupation or of the father's social rank. On the basis of this material, Góngora was able to carry out a sophisticated analysis of the Spanish conqueror as a social type or types. But the Panamanian documentation did not allow construction of further career patterns.

I, too, have attempted this genre in *The Men of Cajamarca*, a study of the 168 Spaniards who seized the Inca emperor at Cajamarca in 1532. Their names all appear on a treasure distribution list preserved because of the enormous amounts involved. Their subsequent eminence makes it possible to trace the lives of most of them, from the Pizarros to the expedition's black crier and piper, and to show the patterns common to them all.

The people taking part up and down this path of conquest from Panama through Peru to Chile were much the same: groups with great internal diversity of social and regional origin, occupation and faction, each expedition an operating microcosm of Spanish society. Their behavior was highly stereotyped. Motives of adventurousness have to be practically eliminated from the reasons underlying their conduct. They acted on a rational view of their own self-interest, all aiming at the same kind of permanent and seigneurial eminence. According to their wealth and social degree, they chose between a governorship, a splendid life in their Spanish birthplace, or an encomienda in the Indies. In any situation that had lasting attraction, they were not easily swept aside, but played an important role in founding a Spanish society and setting social patterns which survived all subsequent governmental and ecclesiastical assaults.

The group anatomy technique could have many fruitful applications, but it has remained and in all probability will remain restricted principally to groups at the higher levels of society, simply because of lack of exhaustive information at the lower levels. Indeed, Schwartz's study of the Relação and Brading's of miners and merchants of Guanajuato involve virtually complete group anatomies. At any rate, any document which gives a complete listing of a group of human beings, whether governmental, residential, or commercial, has immense potential and deserves the close attention of the historian who happens to stumble upon it.

Another approach has been to concentrate on the study of one broad topic, a sector of economic activity or of the population, with well defined limits of time and region in view of the depth and breadth of the reconstruction and the records used. A natural subject for this technique is mining, which is a highly concentrated and profitable activity generating a disproportionate amount of records. Our first close-up portrait of the operation of any branch of Spanish American production or commerce was Robert C. West's study of the Parral mining district of northern Mexico (1949), followed by his treatment of placer mining in New Granada (1952). Because West was a geographer, his work was anything but social history, yet its emphasis was on describing and understanding basic operations rather than on statistics. West's work began a tradition of mining history which has veered more and more toward the social aspect without, as is natural, ever abandoning concern with prices, wages, and production. One such work is Alfredo Castillero Calvo's *Estructuras sociales y económicas de Veragua* (1967),[9] in which the author not only writes the internal history of the Panamanian gold mines, but uses comparisons with West to trace the main lines of a common Spanish American gold mining society, and investigates the lasting consequences of

---

[9]A somewhat related development was the preliminary work of Lewis Hanke, often in collaboration with Gunnar Mendoza, on Potosí, with an emphasis more social than technical. Hanke edited chronicles, described and gave samples of archival materials including notarial records, and provided provisional syntheses. See Hanke 1956, 1965, and Capoche 1959. In later years Peter Bakewell took up the challenge and provided us with two full-scale books (1984, 1988) of primary, socially oriented research on the Potosí mines.

the mines for the towns and farms of western Panama.

A further development came when two Englishmen set about the study of the great Mexican silver mining centers, Zacatecas and Guanajuato. Here the available documentation is far more detailed, varied, and voluminous than for a site like Parral. P. J. Bakewell for his 1971 book on Zacatecas to 1700 worked through an impressive amount of local administrative, judicial, and even notarial records, and wrote a complete set of chapters on varied aspects of Zacatecas industry, agriculture, society, and government. The work was the result of the most complete survey of the local records of a given district, its people, and its economic activity that had been carried out to that time, and it correspondingly gave the fullest and most integrated portrait of a local society and economy, laying bare its basic interlocking processes and their trends over a period of some generations. On the other hand, with such a strong and valuable regional concentration, the interregional connections of the district, especially commercial links with firms in the Mexican capital, went uninvestigated. I have previously mentioned some important substantive conclusions of this study, and I will have occasion to mention others when we come to speak of the hacienda.

David Brading's *Miners and Merchants in Bourbon Mexico* (1971) deals with eighteenth-century Guanajuato on the basis of a survey of local documentation almost as thorough as that of Bakewell, except that he did not make as much use of notarial records. These were substituted in part by a detailed and refined local census. But Brading's is a very different, broader book, starting with government at the national level, proceeding to a thorough investigation of the organization of import-export commerce based in Mexico City, and extending to the silver mines only as a necessary last step. Brading's interest was especially in immigration and the upper levels of mining and commerce. He began systematically to follow careers, families, and important firms, integrating information from wherever he could find it until he had multidimensional portraits of large numbers of important figures. Merchant guild litigation containing inventories and testaments was one crucial source, but there were others. Finding that his people's lives stretched widely over the Mexico of the time, he followed them equally in the archives of Seville, Mexico City, and Guanajuato, and he investigated their connections with the Consulado, the administration, and the nobility. In the end, on the basis of patterns visible in multiple, exhaustively studied examples, Brading succeeded in describing recruitment patterns, social trends, and structure of both mining and international commerce on a countrywide scale, without resorting to impressionism. One of the many social mechanisms he demonstrated is that of the Spanish-born Mexican merchants who hand over their businesses to new immigrants (typically relatives from the hometown, specifically sent for and trained up), while the merchants' landed property and perhaps title go to their creole offspring. Such insights, taken with Brading's previously-mentioned work on creole officeholding, brought a new understanding to replace the old creole-peninsular stereotypes.

Another in this series of works is Enrique Otte's study of Cubagua, the island base of the Caribbean pearl fishery in the first half of the sixteenth century.[10] Otte demonstrates here, as in his many articles, how much coherent social-economic detail exists in the Archive of the Indies, if one is willing to explore the sections Justicia, Contaduría, and Contratación. Otte, like Brading, used the technique of synthesizing careers of many important individuals and firms from widely scattered data. He made particularly enlightening use of private letters, infinitely more frank and revealing than official correspondence.[11] While Cubagua is somewhat peri-

---

[10]Otte's *Perlas del Caribe* was in many ways complete, and I became acquainted with the work, more than a decade before its appearance in 1977.

[11]In the classification of sources above (p. 30) there might logically have been a category "private correspondence," falling just after official correspondence. But the Iberians have never been noted for letter-writing, memoirs, and the like, and what they did write in that style was far more exposed to loss than was more public documentation. The most diligent searches have not to this date unearthed enough coherent collections of private correspondence to serve as the basis for an approach; thus the field was spared an otherwise probably inevitable period of domination by shallow bio-

pheral and hermetic, Otte does full justice to social aspects. The book will stand as a demonstration of what Spaniards would do if put on a desert island. What they did on this one was to concentrate on the primary (and only) export industry and organize a municipality, with the largest investors in the pearl industry on the city council. These quasi-patriarchs started building large urban houses and forming estates, until the pearls gave out and the whole venture was abandoned.

Extractive industries and related commercial activity thus make a very practicable framework for social investigation,

---

graphies of luminaries.

Published collections of letters, even the best, such as Porras Barrenechea's *Cartas del Perú*, or Pérez de Tudela's edition of the Gasca-Pizarro papers, have been mainly official in nature. Any private letters they contain usually proceed from trial records into which transcriptions were introduced as evidence. The archives contain many more such letters, but although they are enormously suggestive, they are so scattered that it is not likely that they can ever be other than welcome windfalls for more broadly-based research projects.

The most consistent correspondents were perhaps the merchants, who were also forever involved in litigation. Some of their letters are almost book-size, and at times they can be found close enough together to be studied systematically. Here Otte has led the way in creating the genre of the article which is part synthesis and comment, part publication of letters (1966b, 1968).

Otte has also discovered and exploited (1969) the letters which New World settlers sent back to relatives in Spain; if the recipients later decided to emigrate, they would present such letters to the officials, causing them to be preserved. Some lots are sufficiently concentrated to serve as the beginning of an extraordinarily intimate, if somewhat impressionistic and one-sided portrait of settler society in a given locality (Otte 1966). In any case, the letters possess remarkable human interest, and the settlers appear in a fresh perspective as immigrants building up their own version of the myth of a new land of opportunity. We also see an aspect of the settlers' vocabulary and conceptual equipment that is otherwise hidden from view.

Feeling the desirability of making a wider public acquainted with these appealing materials and some of their significance, Otte and I published a collection in translation, with extensive comment, in 1976 (*Letters and People of the Spanish Indies*). Much later Otte published a monumental collection of sixteenth-century private letters (1988).

with many implications for the society as a whole. There is no inherent reason why the tracing of lives cannot be extended down at least as far as the ordinary mine workers; even without doing this, Brading and Bakewell have given us a reasonably articulated and realistic picture of that stratum. But for all the importance of mining, it is somewhat detached from the general evolution of society. The same kinds of considerations hold true for import-export commerce, of which these very works of Brading's and Otte's were until recently the principal studies with social content.

Another sector standing out as a distinct unit of study are the Indians. Serious work on postconquest Indians began at almost the same time as mining studies, with Charles Gibson's *Tlaxcala in the Sixteenth Century* (1952). One might expect that there would have been a corpus of anthropological writing on which to build, but such was not the case. Anthropologists had studiously avoided the postconquest period, as if they knew that Gibson would come. Their interest in late pre-Columbian society itself, as opposed to archaeology and artifacts, was slow to develop; they knew approximately as much about this subject as we would know about sixteenth-century colonial society if we had only the *Recopilación de Leyes* and some late chronicles. Therefore Gibson essentially had to start from scratch. His methods and sources (though he was anthropologically well informed) were not those of anthropology, but of Latin American history as it had been developing over the years. His field of interest was wide; nevertheless, in *Tlaxcala*, and even more in his broad-based *Aztecs Under Spanish Rule* (1964), he more than anything did institutional, corporate, jurisdictional history (although at a new level). Such an approach almost imposes itself when a new area of the discipline is being opened up, not to speak of the extraordinary difficulty of getting at the actual lives of Indians.

Thus in one sense Gibson's work had little to do with social history, beyond setting a framework for it. In other ways there were close affinities. If the bulk of Gibson's documentation was in one way or another administrative, it was also very much at a local level, rural in emphasis, and relating to people who if not exactly uniformly humble had at

least, up to that time, been largely left out of historical consideration. Like the social historians, Gibson became an
advanced skeptic about the active powers of the state, and he
produced an account of the evolution of the Indian communities in which broadly sociocultural forces are the active
principle, with formal law only the legitimizing stamp added
after the fact. Above all, Gibson worked at the same level of
profundity as the social historian. Accepting few ready-made
categories, he resynthesized his categories out of the actual
usage of the time. And like the social historian again, Gibson
aimed not so much at "conclusions" as at deep-going analysis
that changed our very way of viewing things. This is the
rationale of Gibson's passion for detail; some of those who do
not understand it would do well to imitate it.

In due course, studies analogous to Gibson's began in Peru.
A strong impetus came from the work of the anthropologist
John Murra. His publication and analysis of amazingly
detailed visitas or inspections of Indian provinces stand
within anthropology's tradition of primary interest in pre-
Columbian times, but the visitas themselves are early postconquest, and they have great potential as a starting place for
intensive local studies, although such have not to date ma-
terialized in the form one might have envisioned.

An important regional study on Peruvian Indians is Karen
Spalding's dissertation "Indian Rural Society in Colonial
Peru: The Example of Huarochirí" (1967). Its scope might be
described as halfway between *Tlaxcala* and *The Aztecs*. With
sources much like Gibson's, it established jurisdictional-
administrative entities and sociopolitical categories and
trends, all in all quite reminiscent of central Mexico. As the
title indicates, one object of the study was to go beyond the
Gibsonian emphasis to concentration on society proper. At
this point sources once again asserted their weight. The
types of documents sufficient for Gibson's purpose were not
necessarily enough to penetrate into the ordinary lives of
rural Indians. In the Huarochirí study, sophisticated use
of "fragments of information included almost unconsciously
by the author of a document" at least made possible the
nearest approach yet. Such a close view showed even greater
change, internal variety, and mobility (especially spatial

mobility) than Gibson's picture, some of which must be attributed to different approaches, some to true differences between the regions. Spalding's approach also revealed somewhat more about both indigenous social organization and the Spanish social-cultural impact on the Indians, whether through migration to cities and mines, or through the presence of a growing Spanish element in the country. However, no records appeared to exist for the Huarochirí district that would yield a truly intimate portrait of indigenous society below the level of the Indian lords.[12]

At times Spalding made skillful, somewhat wistful use of notarial records from the provincial town of Huánuco, which happens not to fall within the Huarochirí district. Apparently we will have to seek meaningful detail on rural Indians wherever we can find it, rather than choose a specific restricted locality for study purely on the basis of intrinsic interest. The most propitious situations often disappoint us. My own first venture in the direction of ethnohistory came in 1969 when I sampled some very complete notarial and judicial documents from the latter sixteenth century in the Mexican provincial center of Toluca, which was then still nominally an Indian town, with an Indian cabildo and a *corregidor de indios.* It soon became apparent, however, that the core of Toluca was occupied by a thriving, dominant Spanish community; both the notarial records and the corregidor's court proceedings mainly concerned that group, and so did the related piece I published subsequently (1975). Such evidence is greatly instructive about the timing and nature of the Hispanization process, but once again the Indians escaped us. It was only later yet that Indian-language records were to open up the central Mexican indigenous world

---

[12]The work I am speaking of here is distinct from Spalding's *Huarochirí: An Andean Society Under Inca and Spanish Rule* (1984), although the latter does originate in the dissertation. The published book manages to approach yet closer to the lives of individual Indians in some respects and shows several kinds of increased sophistication and breadth, yet it also manifests certain problematics that did not attach to the dissertation, and several valuable parts of the earlier work did not find a place in the book, so that one still needs to consult the dissertation for some purposes.

in a quite different way, permitting us to study the structure of these people's lives somewhat as we do with other groups.

In the years when Spalding was working on Indians in Peru, Frederick Bowser was doing the same with blacks in that country in the time from the conquest to 1650, resulting in *The African Slave in Colonial Peru* (1974). Bowser gave us the most complete, reliable, informative book yet to appear on Africans in any Latin American country during the early period. After this work, there could be no doubting the primary attributes of the black population in Spanish American central areas—intensive or skilled work, proximity to Europeans, an intermediate or auxiliary function in the Spanish-Indian context, a slow absorption into the lower levels of Spanish society. Deriving patterns from an over-flowing wealth of individual lives and cases, Bowser demon-strated that it is possible, for early Latin America, to do the social history of a tightly defined and lower-ranking group over a long time span without sacrificing the depth and subtlety of insight that come from large-scale use of freshly synthesized careers. The book almost appears to have been done in two stages; there are large institutional-statistical sections that have relatively little to do with the social core and would seem to have been written earlier, in a different spirit, although ultimately Bowser reinterpreted or dis-counted most of the utterances of officials and interest groups in the light of the social reality he so deeply studied. After all, many of the monuments of this age of miracles in early Latin American social history showed strong signs of the still incomplete transition from institutionalism.

If mining, commerce, and Africans are rather specialized topics, and Indians recalcitrant, the trouble with the great estate as a limiting principle is that it does not limit. It stretches in every direction; its primary function is the connection of city and country, into both of which it looms importantly. Every social type from community Indian to Spanish city council member has some role in it. Thus study concentrating on the more purely agricultural aspects fails to include large and vital segments of the functioning entity.

Perhaps it was then both inevitable and appropriate that the first major studies of the subject should be wide ranging.

Freyre we have already mentioned. A great advance came with François Chevalier's study of the Mexican hacienda in the middle colonial period (1952). In the Marc Bloch tradition, Chevalier brought a far sharper temporal and geographical focus to his work than Freyre; he surveyed a vast amount of relatively direct documentation in the Mexican archives, including provincial ones. Such a wide net caught many of the elements of the broader social-economic pattern, particularly the multi-tiered social structure of the hacienda (although the important temporary laborers eluded his vision). But since he proceeded on such a broad front, Chevalier was not systematic at the local level. No one area was surveyed exhaustively; rarely if ever did Chevalier follow a single family or hacienda through various kinds of sources, nor did he use internal hacienda records, preventing him from approaching closely to the labor question. Thus despite the real gains there remained large lacunae, which Chevalier filled with current stereotypes (such as "debt peonage"), ideas familiar from European history (feudalism, the Spanish national character), or shrewd guesses that could be off the mark when they were made without a sufficient context. Thus it was left for Gibson, not studying the hacienda per se but working far more intensively on a smaller area and using hacienda payroll records, to discover that debt peonage did not live up to its name. Bakewell, merely by virtue of studying Zacatecas closely, saw that Chevalier's idea of ruined miners retiring to their self-sufficient haciendas is highly unlikely. What happened first to the ruined miner was the confiscation and forced sale of his hacienda.

It was obvious that a more intensive type of investigation was called for, concentrating on one locality or subregion at a time. Even projects of this type would be tantamount to the study of the whole region, so that further limitation was necessary. The first important post-Chevalier hacienda research tended to stick close to land tenure. After a large research effort on local land titles, Mario Góngora in his study of the evolution of the hacienda in a Chilean valley (1956) did not proceed far beyond landowning, land use, and markets. The latter aspect, however, showed Spanish estates reacting to markets much more rationally than in Chevalier's picture. Then in his *Encomenderos y estancieros* (1971), following the careers and connections of estate holders through the entire local documentation, Góngora got inside estates, showing their rationale, inner structure including labor, and evolution in form over time responding to changing conditions. In this study, Góngora tied later estates to the encomienda of the conquest period much more meaningfully than Chevalier had managed to do.

William Taylor's *Landlord and Peasant in Colonial Oaxaca* (1972) was also at root a thorough land tenure study, although it involved serious attention to the general history of the region and especially of its Indian population at the corporate level (Taylor was a student of Gibson). Taylor provided an exhaustive series of individual reconstructions of all kinds of estates (including those held by Indians and church entities) over a period of generations up to the end of the colonial period, at least in landholding aspects. He found estate development retarded in comparison with central Mexico. Indian communities and their traditional rulers retained large amounts of land to the end of the colonial period, while Spanish properties were mainly not consolidated or stable. At this point it was not yet clear how much of the deviance of Taylor's findings from those of Chevalier was regional variation, how much actual correction, but Taylor set the field on the road to investigation of both questions, leading eventually to the realization that estates everywhere were more dynamic, volatile, and frequently traded than Chevalier had imagined, yet there was in fact important regional variation as well, estates regularly becoming consolidated earlier where there were more Spaniards and better local markets. Robert Keith's *Conquest and Agrarian Change* (1976), concerning the development of the hacienda system on the Peruvian coast, could be described as mid-way between the methods and outlook of Chevalier and the later more rigorous regional studies. At any rate, it gave a most useful example of the evolution of estate forms from a time of small or medium holdings to larger estates in response to the growing market of Lima.

Another tack was to attempt as complete as possible an investigation of one estate or enterprise. The advantages of this procedure, starting with depth and ending with an easy extension through a long time period, are apparent. Unfortunately, most estates failed to preserve enough records to support such an approach. Hundreds if not thousands of wealthy Latin American families today have what they imagine are colonial hacienda records, but actually, when these are earlier than the nineteenth century, they usually consist only of land titles and litigation papers about land. Virtually all the coherent internal estate records preserved in both Spanish America and Brazil seem to be of Jesuit properties or such oddities as the Cortés estate.

Ward Barrett's study of the Cortés estate's sugar hacienda (1970) covers the whole colonial period, is breathtakingly thorough on many aspects of production and general operation, and is far less purely "geographical" than one might expect from its author's disciplinary affiliation. Even career patterns are not ignored completely, and we learn much about the labor force at all levels. The general impression is of a rational, sophisticated, market-oriented business, very different from Chevalier's view. Barrett believed that the Cortés hacienda was less anomalous from the point of view of technology and management than in many other respects. This strikes me as true, though I would imagine the technology to be yet more standard than the management.

How informative Jesuit estate records can be is seen in the use made of them by Stuart Schwartz (1973) in working out the number and productivity of the tenants of the sugar *fazenda* Sergipe do Conde in the Bahia area over a long time span.[13] Even the tenants' names are given, and Schwartz was able to deduce with reasonable certainty the numbers of slaves they owned. The result was a revolutionarily new view of what a "plantation" really was and what kind of an arena it represented for Portuguese-African interaction. A resource

---

[13]Schwartz's article on *lavradores de cana* was part of a large research project on the Bahia sugar complex, centered on Sergipe do Conde, which led in due course to his *Sugar Plantations in the Formation of Brazilian Society* (1985). Schwartz did so much additional research in so many dimensions that he was largely able to transcend the question of Jesuit peculiarity.

with this much potential could not be ignored. It was clear that we should exploit what the Jesuits have given us, always with an eye to distinguishing what is Jesuit peculiarity and what is more general. Many basic processes must have been the same in a Jesuit enterprise as in any other. Valuable studies of Jesuit estates have continued to appear, and doubtless more will be seen in the future. Still, as a control, detailed internal records of any estate never owned by the Jesuits are worth their weight in gold, whenever and wherever they appear. Even when estate records seem relatively complete, it is important to seek out the personnel in other kinds of documents to do justice to the estate's multiple dimensions and avoid a new formal institutionalism.

The remaining large constituent element of Iberoamerican society that can be studied as a separate unit is the whole broad portion of it that was European or Europeanized at any given time—what the Spaniards called the *república de los españoles*. This entity tends to be roughly identical with the network of Spanish cities and towns, but also includes the Hispanic elements of the estates, plus the rural ecclesiastics and some others. Though unwieldy, it has great internal coherence; the rural members look to the towns, and the towns to the capital. All types and functional groups stand in close relation to each other, so much so that almost all of them need to be seen to make any one of them truly intelligible, while the whole makes a rounded unit.

On the practical side, to take the Hispanic world as one unit recommends itself because the subgroupings within it all appear together in the same collections of records; to investigate any one, the researcher must read the same mountain of papers that is the source for all. This tends to be the case even for a group as distinct as the Africans, who everywhere accompanied the Iberians, so that the study of them by themselves is very arduous and sometimes artificial. The same applies very much to the study of women. As a subject, the Hispanic-urban world—though no more the totality than the other elements—recommends itself for its centrality to the process of social evolution. It is at the center not only physically and demographically but also in the sense that many of the dynamics of change (marginalization, market

formation, etc.) are contained within it. It includes the cutting
edge of cultural interaction: those indigenous people who are
in daily contact with Iberians.

At what order of magnitude should this unit be studied?
The multiplicity of sources tends to put a sharp limit on
extension through time, though the smaller the region one
takes, the longer the time one can cover. In *Spanish Peru*
(1968) I attempted to study the Hispanic society of one major
region for about a generation, the broader conquest period up
to about 1560. The method was essentially to read widely in
many types of sources that reflect the ordinary activity of
people at all visible levels, assembling numerous examples of
careers and contracts, then sorting out the main social types,
processes, and popular concepts. Following individual lives
through all sorts of records was a crucial technique, as with
Brading. Aside from study of governmental records kept on a
countrywide basis, the local documentation of three important centers was surveyed, and much advantage was taken of
the fact that people from all regions were constantly in the
capital.

The totality of the records proved to have coherent detail
on the careers not only of the famous and the wealthy, but of
the obscure and humble, down to artisans, mariners, free
blacks, and urban Indians. Information on the lower groups
tended to come predominantly from notarial records. Indeed,
the social-commercial-economic aspect of private life leaped
out of these documents so strongly as to give me the impression during research that my study rested almost wholly
on the notaries, while the rest was only elaboration and duty.
I would still assert that its public or notarial documents
represent an indispensable, basic, comprehensive tool in
writing the history of any local Hispanic society, but for
discovering the true contours of lives many other sources
must often be added. Any document that places a specific
individual at a specific place at a specific time is grist for the
mill. The biographies I put into *Spanish Peru* as samples of
career patterns contain references to all the various kinds of
sources we have referred to above, as do the files on other
individuals that did not actually enter into the book. Each
source gives a new aspect of the person's life, making possible

a multidimensional, imaginatively reconstructed picture that is still reliable and adds up to one unified pattern.

Particularly important among other types of documents are local trial records.[14] One studies them not to find out who was guilty, but to explore a social milieu. Almost any local trial reveals the internal structure of a whole social circle, often including even servants and children. If you are fortunate enough to locate the same individual in both notarial records and litigation, you have the main elements needed to discover that individual's life pattern and function. If you can find fragments of a dozen other such lives with similar morphology, you have discovered and documented a social type, nearly coterminous with a social subgrouping and a social-economic function.

To indicate in more substantive terms the kind of results one can achieve, I believe that *Spanish Peru* made sense of the Hispanic element of sixteenth-century Spanish American society in the Peruvian (= central or classic) variant by revealing its main constituent types, their functions, and their relation to each other, as well as pointing to the extreme earliness of protonational development, the near irrelevance

---

[14]Visitas and residencias have most of the same characteristics. So do Inquisition trials, with the added advantage of their close attention to the whole life history and even genealogy of the principal figure, a feature not present in much ordinary litigation. Nevertheless, traditional writers on the Inquisition usually read only the trial sentences, or if they went so far as to read the testimony, only employed it to redirect focus on the institution, or at most on certain groups as the objects of persecution. Despite their advantages of richness, intimacy, and frequent concern with humble people, much sophistication is required to put Inquisition records to work for social history. To a very large extent the situations and social types appearing in these records are marginal or abnormal. Often the witnesses are of more interest than the accused. Some authors who have made progress toward social utilization of Inquisition trials are Wiznitzer (1960), Liebman (1970), and most especially Greenleaf (1969). The latter, by not taking the proceedings at face value, using trials to put together meaningful life histories of the principals, and connecting the Inquisition data with data from outside sources, was able to show the political and economic motivation of much Inquisition litigation and to throw light on the overall functioning of early Mexican society.

of administration to that development, and the important role of humble Europeans and others whose existence had hardly been recognized.

As to indigenous people, Spanish local documentation of the conquest period is highly revealing on the subject of urban Indians, and there is enough to show that the main mechanisms of both Hispanization and economic exploitation were established very early indeed. There is, however, distressingly little about rural Indians per se in any of the kinds of documentation used for *Spanish Peru*. But as one comes forward in time, the characteristics of the records change to the degree that Spanish society grows and expands. By the seventeenth century, the Spanish world has extended into distant regions to the extent that a study of it will also include fresh insight into local indigenous society.

With the gains come new difficulties. The sheer volume of records and their geographical dispersion can make the *Spanish Peru* approach impracticable. One must wait longer for the same individuals or firms to reappear. In the seventeenth century a provincial center is usually still easy enough to study; one gets the feel and recognizes some people in a week or two of work. But Mexico City is hard, and the whole is somewhat staggering, as I found out in some preliminary archival surveys in 1969. Away from the Spanish American viceregal capitals, large subregions are still quite practical arenas for this approach in the middle colonial period, as seen in studies by John Super (1973) of the Querétaro region, by Marta Espejo-Ponce Hunt (1974) of Yucatan, and by Rae Flory (1978) of Bahia.[15]

By the eighteenth century, the difficulties have greatly magnified. Paul B. Ganster undertook a social investigation of Lima in the mid-eighteenth century. He encountered a forbidding mass of notarial records and finally decided to limit himself to the secular clergy, producing a study (1974) which combined an analysis of the institutional side of the hierarchy with career pattern information on the clergy at all

---

[15]Summaries of the studies by Super and Hunt later appeared in Altman and Lockhart, eds., *Provinces of Early Mexico* (1976), and an expanded version of Super's work was published in Spanish in 1983.

levels, greatly enriched by his earlier explorations in the
notarial archives and other non-ecclesiastical records, so
that his subjects could be placed in a well understood context
of family and broader society. Eighteenth-century studies
have continued to be thematically restricted in the main, so
that whatever the difficulties, the need for wide-ranging research on the society of that time is as great as ever.[16]

Aspects of biographical technique

Much of the work of Otte, Brading, Schwartz, Bowser,
Bakewell, and myself can hardly be imagined without the use
of a method on the order of multiple or collective biography.
In no case is such the sole technique, and the same procedures
of typification can be applied to objects other than people,
particularly to contracts, popular concepts, and social institutions. But collective biography has been sufficiently
central and distinct to warrant discussion of its special
nature. The effect of following the careers of several apparently similar individuals (usually "ordinary" rather than
famous ones; but it makes no difference) is to reveal and make
intelligible a repeating pattern, one that is usually in the first
instance what was called above a social type, or type of life
history with characteristic contours. The approach aims
directly at understanding a general principle of the operation
and articulation of society, and is thus the opposite of

---

[16]Some years after the time frame covered here, John Kicza
through massive research in notarial and other records, and also
through the courage to be selective once trends were clear, bolstered
further by the denser social statistics that the late period can
generate, produced a general career-pattern survey of Mexico City
society in the last several decades before independence. Most,
though not all, of his work is represented in his 1979 dissertation,
and one large chunk of it was published in 1983 as Colonial Entrepreneurs. The Kicza corpus is a uniquely valuable monument in
eighteenth-century studies and cries out for imitation by those with
large capacities and ambitions. It provides a general framework for a
myriad of more specialized works, often showing that patterns
imagined by their authors to be peculiar to a particular sector in fact
pervaded the whole. It also looks at the country from the center, a
refreshing and necessary perspective after what has now been a
wave of rural and provincial research.

atomistic. Nor is it static. Discovery that training black and Indian helpers is a standard part of the successful Spanish artisan's life is tantamount to putting one's finger on an important element of social dynamics.

Since multiple biography deals with more than one individual, it appears to have a quantitative aspect, and in a sense it does, but not necessarily in the same way as social statistics or demography. The object of attaining redundancy in the biographies is not to survey a certain percentage of all exemplars of the type, but to get a sense of the trend of repetition. The principle is not unlike that of a wind sock, which is reliable although it tests only a millionth part of the air. It is important to understand that collective biography requires neither a complete knowledge of all actual careers, nor completeness within the sample career, to yield significant results. The role of career samples within social history can be compared to that of skeletons in physical anthropology. A dozen career outlines do as much to delineate a social type as two or three skeletons a physical type. What percent of a total prehistoric population a small number of sample skeletons represents is a question we do not ask, nor do we quibble over some missing bones. For many kinds of basic, general, even subtle analysis, a few skeletons are as good as several hundred. For other research, such as range of age and size, a larger sample is needed. In the same way, career samples can give an exact idea of a certain social stratum's general life habits, relation to other groups, and overall function, without always telling us much about the group's absolute numbers or whether its living standard is rising or falling at the moment. The method does give us a good understanding of *why* the group might be of a certain size or have a certain living standard. There is more supplementation than duplication between statistical work on straightforwardly demographic data and a biographical approach, even if the two methods employ many of the same sources. One approach seeks trends by aggregating atomistic data; the other cuts across the data to resynthesize basic units. It is the difference between counting dinosaur finds and reconstructing dinosaurs.

A career outline need not contain every detail of a person's life to be useful. In just such a manner a skeleton reveals little about external characteristics, but has its own individuality and subtlety, and sets certain limits for the other traits. If we have a birthplace and date, a marriage, a property inventory or two, some hint of length of residence, organizational affiliation, and friends, we can carry out many kinds of analysis and correlation, and see how the life hangs together, unhindered by the fact that we do not really know the individual intimately and that much of his or her activity was never reflected in any written document. (A deep study of local litigation will often give the researcher a good sense even of thoughts and events that were not ordinarily recorded.)

While it might appear that career sampling would be difficult or impossible at the lower levels of society, such is generally speaking not the case. Doubtless upper groups are better represented, but much litigation survives in which people as lowly as blacks, Indians, and mariners figure as principals, not to speak of their frequent appearance as witnesses. Many of their apprenticeships, loans, wills, and work contracts are in the notarial records. Their names appear on the lists of sodalities, and on payrolls. The patron-client nature of many types of organization aids research, for inventories and wills of the heads of families and enterprises mention people far down the scale, when it comes to debts and legacies. In short, there is no real difficulty in acquiring a sufficient redundancy of multidimensional career samples for any social type that was in close contact with the Iberoamerican cities and towns, or with any other place that has preserved records of a trial court and a notary. The difficulty is to be encountered not with lower groups as opposed to upper so much as with rural groups as opposed to urban. Nothing but hard work separates us from an excellent structural understanding of the urban and semi-urban poor. It is in the countryside that the records tend to forsake us, often leaving institutionalism, impressionism, analogy, and quantitative extrapolation as the only possible approaches.

The difference in applying biographical technique to upper as contrasted to lower urban-oriented groups is that with the upper groups one can approach near enough to completeness that even ephemeral and external characteristics can be integrated into the picture, and standard quantitative techniques can be used. Even with the lower groups, one can often do much toward measuring relative frequencies and thus change or variation, but far less than for a restricted group like high court judges, holders of entails, or encomenderos. As to intimacy and subtlety, as to that combination of suggestive detail and the eternally human which calls up an almost physical presence, the records of the humble yield little or nothing to those of the prominent. No situation has ever come home to me more than that of eleven-year-old Ana mestiza, who lived in semi-adoption in the house of a poor Spanish woman of Lima in 1560, along with the latter's black slave woman and female Indian servant. All the women were more or less abandoned, and they lived from boarding transients. The grown-ups were often gone in the evening, shopping, gossiping, or prowling, and Ana whiled away the time dancing alone in the empty house until the others returned.[17]

Multiple biography does not involve, as some seem to think, any attempt to prove that property-owning or kinship are the final determinants in human affairs, any more than studying a chess game implies a belief that the pieces make the moves.[18] But people of all types express only a small part

---

[17]Archivo Nacional del Perú (Lima), Real Audiencia, Procedimientos Penales, legajo 1, trial of Isabel Gómez.

Perhaps this is the point at which to insist that women are not only in themselves an essential part of any balanced treatment of social history, but through their presence or absence, their marriages, dowries, activities, and property-owning, are essential to measuring the quality and velocity of general social development, as well as any individual male's rank, prosperity, and affiliation (the converse is also true). Women appear regularly in all the Iberian sources from cedularies to litigation; though their exclusion from most active professions is a handicap, career skeletons and even full, intimate portraits are not much harder to produce for women than for men of the corresponding social categories. Some examples may be seen in Lockhart 1968, pp. 150–70, 197–98, 210–11, 216.

[18]Such suspicions run through Lawrence Stone's 1971 article on prosopography. The differences between the biographical tradition that has grown up in early Latin American historiography and the more established one that Stone describes, mainly for English and classical historiography, are most suggestive. The Latin American work is far more primary, in part no doubt because of the lack of preceding preliminary writings, but with profound effect on the

of what they think; much of what they do express is lost; and even what remains is affected by self-interest and camouflage, so that we must resort to the record of their behavior, however incomplete it is, to deduce what they thought and what their language meant. Such a survey points neither to simple economic determinism nor to blind behaviorism. Instead, it often reveals the force of widely held social conventions and other unexpressed, often subconscious mental constructs.

Some general and theoretical considerations

Having by about 1975 at least sampled most of its known documentary resources, the field was henceforth somewhat freer from documentary determinism; the time since has seen an increasing eclecticism. Still, a very large proportion of recent history in our field, including much research without biographical orientation, can be described as the close study of a certain segment of social reality, with broad documentation, concentrating on categories and types as embodied in specific examples, each of which is seen as an organic entity rather than as an ingredient for aggregate statistics. I have some reflections to offer to both authors and readers of such studies.

For writers, nothing could be more important than to widen the documentary base, not so much in sheer amount as in variety. Each kind of source imposes its own distinct perspective and contains its own distinct subvariety of the

---

quality of the result. The nature of the Latin American (Iberian) documentation is also vastly different, particularly when it comes to lower groups. The Europeanists tend to use "prosopography" for upper groups, statistics for lower groups, whereas several Latin Americanists have managed to synthesize careers from primary data across the board. Many of the weaknesses Stone found in the collective biographical approach come from an attempt to tie surface politics too closely to the social-economic self-interest of the actors, something most of its Latin Americanist practitioners have never tried to do. The two biographical traditions grew up quite separately. I had not heard of Stone until after I had written *Spanish Peru* and *The Men of Cajamarca*, and though I have since become cognizant of his work I have not followed it. The early Latin American biographical tradition since the 1960's is a distinct school with much to contribute to general historiographical method.

general language and conceptual equipment. The reciprocal correction and complementing of the various types bearing in on a single subject matter results in balance, validity, and insight unattainable with a one-source approach. It is obvious that such investigation must be restricted in scope if it is to operate at the necessary depth. Therefore it cannot normally cover whole consecutive centuries or vast regions. Even the totality of such studies, though by now very substantial and ever growing, offers nothing approaching complete "coverage," and perhaps never will. It becomes necessary to give some attention to general strategy in the choice of topics, using a process of triangulation to plot long-term, multiregional developments or patterns of uniformity and variation.

Such work must be read in the same spirit. In the usage of some scholars, any book which is not a general text is called by the slightly pejorative term "monograph"; and any study on a subject ostensibly less inclusive than a national entity through all eternity may be considered a "microhistory." "Microhistories" are deemed to be mere "case studies" that can add up eventually in an almost mechanical way to "macrohistory." Actually this is a thoroughly false perspective. There are general patterns at a local level, and many important general patterns are observable *only* at the local level.

The social historians from Gibson on have often proceeded directly from observation of individual examples to the formation of concepts and categories, whether social types, ideals, concepts embodied in special language, conventions, patterns of behavior, or principles of organization. Such a procedure immediately attains a deeper stratum and a greater universality than either the substantive "idea" or the substantive "generalization." Rather than manipulating concepts, social history has altered them. It gradually became clear that most of the basic categories first used to understand the postconquest centuries were anachronistic and naive projections of a later onto an earlier time: Indian village, plantation, soldier, missionary, debt peonage, and many more. Backward projection of a recent past had resulted in a false impression of extreme rigidity and lack of movement.

Social history together with demography has largely destroyed this picture and has begun to replace it with a reconstruction of secular trends and regional variation in terms of more adequate categories, hoping to do justice to unity without denying complexity.

Such an endeavor implies an accompanying elaboration of theory. In the great scholarly emporia of Europe and North America one can acquire ready-made theories at bargain prices. But personally I have from the beginning been antagonistic to the imposition of concepts from the outside. In the 1960's and 70's such concepts and procedures came primarily from certain of the social sciences—sociology, economics, political science. My objections were not so much humanistic, for I, like the social scientists, want to study broad and general patterns (though seen originally in fleshed-out, living examples), and I believe in the ultimate autonomy of social-cultural evolution as something comparable to and related to the evolution of human language, beyond the conscious planning or even awareness of any individual or set of individuals. But I think that social science brought in rigid concepts from a different context which often corresponded to nothing and impeded a fresh view of historical reality.

The social sciences as we know them arose in industrialized countries in the late nineteenth and twentieth centuries; they often presuppose an easily available, trustworthy informational base, and strong, uniform institutions. Nothing could be further from the early Latin American situation. Ideas from the social sciences can serve to inspire interpreters as well as any others—but no better. Each new external element must be tested critically for applicability; otherwise we are in danger of repeating the mistake made with the anachronistic concepts the field has now overcome. Unsophisticated work on insufficient sources with the newest European methods and concepts is, as Rolando Mellafe (1970) has said, nothing but an amusing intellectual game. In the event, the historians of early Latin America never did become excessively influenced by the social sciences, developing instead their own procedures and ideas, their own tradition, adapted to their topic. A new generation of notions from the outside has arisen, however—from European-based postmodernism, from studies of other areas of European expansion—and the struggle goes on in a different form.

Theoretical and general statements on early Latin American social history, based on the materials and writings of the field itself, have not been entirely lacking. An able first attempt in this direction was made by Lyle McAlister in 1963, before the real onset of the social history movement. His essay may be viewed as essentially a rationalization of social thought articulated by Spaniards of the early period, in legislation, official reports, and travelers' accounts. Interpreted in this fashion, the article is as valuable as ever. As an analysis of actual social organization and dynamics it was understandably overtaken by the subsequent scholarly production that it helped to stimulate. In 1969 I published an article sketching out an interpretation of the Spanish American great estate as a unitary, coherent organizational type characterized by a relatively unchanging social core and overall function, with simple principles of evolution and variation.[19] In the introduction to Altman and Lockhart, *Provinces of Early Mexico* (1976), I expanded on this analysis, introduced the concept of the trunk line, and carried out other types of general analysis of social organization and evolution. Since that time I have gone considerably further in that direction.

Epilogue
(1989)

The present article originally appeared in 1972. It has since become clear that the time around 1965 to 1975 was a golden age of social historiography in the early Latin American field, with the appearance on the scene of Bakewell, Bowser, Brading, Russell-Wood, Schwartz, Spalding, Taylor, and myself, and the publication of major works in new genres with new methods by almost all of this group. Through reading dissertations and still unpublished manuscripts, I was able to catch most of these developments in the original article; now I have made a few additions, bringing the time

---

[19]Now Chapter 1 in this volume.

covered up to about 1975 or 1976. I have also done such re-wording as was appropriate to make 1988–89 the temporal perspective. Portions of the final section were omitted, partly because they contained recommendations for research tied to the period of original composition, and partly because I have since further developed some of the theoretical analysis therein contained (Lockhart 1984, applied extensively in Lockhart and Schwartz 1983).

In the time since 1975, mainline career-pattern, small-entity social history has continued to appear and make its contribution. A great deal of it has taken the form of studies of rural estates. A perhaps even larger stream has been diverted into ethnohistory, done as social history of Indians, but with new methods and perspectives required by the circumstances. A rapprochement with anthropology has taken place in this respect, up to a point, and though there are problems with the relationship it is a much more comfortable and natural one than the earlier interaction with disciplines oriented essentially to Europe and the United States. The time after 1975 saw a rash of eighteenth-century studies, often social-institutional in nature, but this wave seems to be subsiding. An important new development is a greater emphasis on cultural studies, some of it coming from a new and more analytical school of literary history, but much of it growing directly out of the "social" history movement, which was perhaps somewhat misnamed from the beginning. Of the work on Mexican Indians I am presently completing, four of the core chapters are "social," and four appear more "cultural" (though at a deeper level I make little distinction).[20] In a note to the original article, I said the following:

Just as social conventions can be distilled from examples of behavior, popular concepts can be studied in examples of speech. A surprising amount of ordinary usage is contained even in the highly formulized notarial records; but the greatest repository is litigation. Spanish legal clerks came at times amazingly close to capturing the actual word-flow of witnesses deposing before them. The possibilities of such

---

[20]I was speaking of the work later published as *The Nahuas After the Conquest* (1992).

a source are practically unlimited. It seems to give us the means of finding out what key words such as "creole" meant in the ordinary usage of various people at various times. We could then grasp the rhythm and context of the evolution of such terms, which are not at all as they appear in the limited, overdrawn, sometimes uncomprehending statements found in travelers' accounts, chronicles, and legislation, the main source for this kind of intellectual history to date.

Thus if social history is converging with demography and anthropology on the one hand, it is approaching cultural-intellectual history on the other. In both subject matter and source material, socially oriented research is close to giving early Latin American intellectual history a depth and generality that have so far escaped it. There are still major problems of technique. Despite its overall richness, court testimony is a very diluted source; unlike a behavior pattern or a social convention, a concept embodied in a word cannot be seen fully exemplified in a single carrier.

To conclude I will quote a passage from a review I recently wrote:[21]

The category "social history" is no longer generally valid. In certain subfields, the term still has much meaning on the level of conversational usage. Thus in early Latin American history it means specifically work which features fleshed out portraits of actual individuals and organizations and stands in contradistinction to demography; but the sense of the expression varies from field to field. The designation was originally justified in that widespread dissatisfaction with political/administrative/elitist/military/diplomatic history first took the form of an urgent feeling that more people, indeed the entire population, should be included. Far more important, however, was the need to go beyond celebrating events as such and accepting the actors' conscious rationale for their actions. The pursuit of a deeper truth has by now led scholars in a vast number of directions, investigating all the concerns of the humanities and the social sciences in time depth.

---

[21]Lockhart 1987.

3. Letters and People to Spain
(1976)

O NE NOTES gratefully the growing success scholars are having in estimating the numbers, regional origins, and some other characteristics of the emigrants from Spain to America in the sixteenth century. Later emigration stands open to study by the same means—primarily the compilation and analysis of data gathered by governmental agencies of the time. Already we see a movement of truly mass proportions, far more broadly based as to region and social recruitment, far more sustained than we once had reason to think. The implications are both deep and broad, bearing in the most direct way possible on the manner of creation of Spanish America, the main lines of the evolution of early modern Spain, and the general or comparative history of emigration.[1]

Interpreting the movement is no easy matter. One cannot use gross data of the type available for direct measurement of the impact of emigration on either place of origin or point of destination, much less for meaningful discussion of the question of whether emigration was "good" or "bad" for Spain. Aside from some work of an economic and statistical nature, the social history of early modern Spain is virgin territory, far less explored than Spanish America itself; in measuring the effects of emigration the scholar faces the logically contradictory problem of measuring the impact of a loss on a vacuum.

In any case, there is a whole area of interest left untouched by the emigration statistics. What of the emigrants' expectations and motivations?[2] What of contacts preserved with

---

[1] A whole vein of older work drawing conclusions from supposed differences in English and Spanish emigration patterns is now thoroughly outdated. It emerges increasingly that early modern English and Spanish emigration movements were quite similar in kind, and further that the European emigration wave of the nineteenth and twentieth centuries contains practically *nothing* new, i.e., that the entire set of movements represents a single phenomenon.

[2] J. H. Elliott asks such questions in *The Old World and the New, 1492–1650* (1970).

home? These and other matters can never be elucidated with sources and statistical methods proper for the study of the overall trends of migration. What is required to answer such questions is a direct understanding of the processes of migration as they affect individuals. Correlations of emigrant statistics with rising or falling trends of overall population or with differential regional characteristics still do not bring us close enough to that understanding. Two things are needed: study of direct utterances by the individuals involved, if possible at the level of frank, intimate discourse; and work on career patterns, considering the total lives of emigrating and returning individuals, including their position in the society that surrounded them on both sides of the Atlantic. Work on such materials has hardly begun.

Here I wish mainly to bring together some impressions from research done by my colleague Enrique Otte and myself, formulating in more general terms what we have already said in scattered publications. This cannot replace a major research effort, but perhaps it can give some hint of the kinds of results that larger-scale, more concentrated investigation could yield. Like many others, Otte and I have seen the phenomena of emigration only from the edges, as historians of Spanish America. The private letters Otte has worked with were mainly written from the Indies to Spain.[3] So far, few letters sent from Spain to the Indies have appeared. The search should be pressed, for such letters would be even more direct data on the private Spanish image of America than those going in the other direction. My own work on the social history of Spanish America has led me to deal on occasion

---

[3]Otte has published many articles which are part comment and analysis, part publication of letters, and I will have occasion to refer to one or two of them later. The two largest collections, with substantial analysis of many aspects of the letters' significance, are "Cartas privadas de Puebla del siglo XVI" (1966), and "Die europäischen Siedler und die Probleme der neuen Welt" (1969). Otte and I have prepared an English translation and edition of some of these letters along with others both private and public in a volume entitled *Letters and People of the Spanish Indies, Sixteenth Century* (1976). (Much later Otte published a far larger collection in the original Spanish with the title *Cartas privadas de emigrantes a Indias, 1540–1616* [1988].)

with the returnee[4] to Spain as an important element in the cycle, and to study some actual careers, but only as seen in the characteristic sources of the Spanish American historian, on this side of the Atlantic and in Seville's Archive of the Indies.[5] The subject demands study as *Spanish* social history; one wishes for a comprehensive book on a given Spanish city in the sixteenth century, one part of which would deal with returnees, as well as their status in and impact on a community whose structure is well understood.

I will present here some glimpses of three topics touched on in the work I have mentioned above: first, some special characteristics of the stream of emigration as seen in private correspondence; second, the image of the Indies that the settlers presented to Spaniards at home; and third, the role of the returnees, with less emphasis on their direct impact in Spain than on their part in a dialectic of emigration, return, and further involvement brought on by the return. This process established lasting personal-familial-regional relationships between colony and motherland which became an important part of the life of the motherland itself.

In speaking of emigration, I want to give priority to a person of transcendent importance who strongly affected the settlers' manner of depicting the New World, and loomed large in ongoing connections: the nephew. The greatest commerce in Spanish America was the importation of nephews on credit, against promises of favor and fortune. One is tempted to say that the Indies were populated by nephews, sent for by their importunate uncles, pushed out by their hard-pressed fathers. To judge from its reflection in the letters we know, correspondence from Spain to the Indies seems to have been

---

[4]For present purposes let us accept the convention that the English language contains the horrid neologism "returnee," meaning not a person forcibly returned somewhere, but one voluntarily going back to the homeland, usually permanently. "Returner" yields the wrong sense; "repatriate," which I have used before, on the model of "expatriate," strikes most people as an active verb form; *indiano* is a loaded, over-literary, partially anachronistic category.

[5]In my *Spanish Peru, 1532–1560* (1968), and *The Men of Cajamarca: A Social and Biographical Study of the First Conquerors of Peru* (1972).

largely an appeal for money; correspondence from the Indies to Spain sometimes appears as one great appeal for nephews.

An encomendero (holder of a grant of Indian tribute and labor) in Trujillo, Peru:

> What I would need now is what there is too much of there, which is a boy from among those nephews of mine, to ride about on horseback inspecting my properties.[6]

A rich linen-trader in Puebla, Mexico:

> Nephew, you will give me the greatest happiness if you will come here with me; I have no one to give all this to but you.[7]

A petty dealer in Indian goods in Mexico City:

> Now, nephew, I am advanced in years and can no longer take care of all this. I wish, if it please God, that you would come to this land, as I have written you in other letters, so that I could rest and you would remain in the business.[8]

An Augustinian friar and professor of theology in Mexico City:

> And if one of my nephews knew Latin or wanted to be a friar . . .[9]

A priest at the silver mines of Potosí:

> The priests and friars who have a nephew here whom they can trust are very rich.[10]

The rationale of the pattern is not far to seek. To reconstruct an archetypal situation, the oldest son of a family would stay in Spain to take over whatever property or position the family might have, while his younger brother, in his twenties and still unmarried, would leave for the Indies. Even there he would not marry until he had established himself in some way. Once established, he would want trusted subordinates and aides, in a word sons, but since he was newly married, he would have small children or none, and so he would write off to his older brother, who was himself no longer movable but whose sons would now be approaching manhood. Once again a younger son would be chosen, and the cycle was completed.

---

[6]Lockhart and Otte 1976, p. 66.

[7]Ibid., p. 30.

[8]Ibid., p. 145.

[9]Ibid., p. 116.

[10]Ibid., p. 254.

That the operation of the pattern was indeed cyclical and long-continuing can be seen in the work of David Brading on the Spanish merchants of Mexico in the later eighteenth century.[11] Even at that late date, family continuity (and peninsular Spanish management) was often assured by the practice of bringing a young relative from the north Castilian hometown of the merchant; there were large businesses which were handed on in this way two or three times in succession over the period of a century. Nor was the pattern in all probability new in the sixteenth century. In a dissertation on the seventeenth-century Portuguese merchant community, David Smith points to a longstanding migration of this type from certain Portuguese provincial towns toward Lisbon.[12] As Smith himself notes, in migration to America the Indies plays the role traditionally played by the large city.

With this, let us leave the nephew; he can remind us that much of the pressure of the Indies on Spain was that of recruitment, and that much of the lasting connection between Spain and the Indies had a familial substratum. Indeed, in the correspondence, other relatives including women are frequently implored to come. Letters often ask for people with special skills as well, and, out of exuberance or despair, make even wider appeals. But the emphasis is on young unestablished male relatives.

At the same time as the letters triply underline the kinship orientation of migration, they contain resentful mention of others who come without the help of relatives; usually the writers point to them in order to shame the pusillanimous kin who have not yet decided to come. I quote passages from two of the letters cited above:

The encomendero:

> Somehow two thousand paupers manage to get here; they look for a way to come across and finally they find it.

The linen-trader:

> Why, there are others who have the courage without

---

[11]D. A. Brading, *Miners and Merchants in Bourbon Mexico, 1763–1810* (1971).

[12]David G. Smith, "The Mercantile Class of Portugal and Brazil in the Seventeenth Century" (1974).

having any support here, who make the fortunes they can without owing anyone anything.[13]

But even these waifs do not proceed out of nowhere into the unknown. The linen-trader continues, "except for the favor they get for being from that part of the country." Where kinship left off, regionalism took over, and some Spaniards went to the Indies knowing that many from their hometown had gone there already and might give them aid.

As for the image of the Indies that settlers painted for Spaniards at home, it must have been conveyed in two main ways, by people returning and by letters. Not having the returnees' conversation, we must rely on the letters, which we may presume contain much the same picture. We may not, of course, presume that those at home accepted it as the whole truth. There is little need to go into detail about the vision that the letters project, because it is so familiar to us; it is nearly identical with the tales of a land of opportunity and plenty with which immigrants to the United States inundated Europe in the nineteenth and early twentieth centuries. The image has great uniformity, whether coming from the highly placed or the humble, whether from Mexico or Peru. I know of no fuller expression of it than a letter from a tailor in Puebla.[14] There is plenty of work, and it is better paid than in Spain:

> Imagine that if back there we got 8 reales for a coat and
> a short cloak, here they give us 32.

Every Spaniard has a horse to ride. Food is plentiful and cheap. Things from Spain (wine specifically) are expensive, but with so much money from good pay, one thinks little of it and buys what one needs anyway.

This is not El Dorado, not treasure, romance, and gold on the streets. The letters, even from rich encomenderos and miners and even when most enthusiastic, speak not of something for nothing, but of business opportunities, of helping people get started, of a rich reward for a good effort. Those who have made fortunes have done so "by their industry." A minor official of western Mexico wrote his nephew:

---

[13]Lockhart and Otte 1976, pp. 67, 130.

[14]Ibid., pp. 117–19.

> There are many things I could write you about this land, but I will mention only one, which is that here men who know how to work and give themselves to virtue make a living, and those who don't, don't.[15]

Let us compare this picture for a moment with that presented by viceroys and governors during the second half of the sixteenth century, in whose reports Spaniards in the Indies will not work; rebellion is to be expected any moment; Spaniards, mestizos, and blacks should be deported; the silver mines lie in ruin for lack of labor; and even food in the cities is high priced and in desperately short supply.[16] I think it is clear which version is closer to the mark. Unlike the viceroys, the settlers in private correspondence do make qualifications, do mention vagrants and other problems in a realistic perspective; they often come as near to a good general statement as could be expected from people whose business is not disinterested analysis. The letter last quoted (dated 1577) assesses the food situation perfectly:

> Wherever a man goes he will find someone to feed him, though it is true things are getting tighter than they used to be.

Surely such words, uttered between relatives and friends, must have affected the opinions and actions of Spaniards more than overwrought official reports. The private lines of communication that existed between Spain and the Indies are fully as important as the public lines of governors' reports, chronicles, and pamphleteering. The public statement is often a reflex, a secondary comment on and reaction to a primary social-cultural reality better reflected in more private, individual materials.

The letters of viceroys, bishops, friars, and even the public correspondence of encomenderos and miners are thickly populated with Indians; controversies over their treatment and concern over the spread of Christianity among them are very nearly the dominant topics of the whole literature.[17] A

---

[15]Lockhart and Otte 1976, p. 252.

[16]The well known collections of documents relating to the Indies are filled with such letters. A good sample may be seen in *Cartas de Indias* (1877).

[17]Or so it appears superficially. Very often what is going on is a

striking facet of the private correspondence, however, is the
near absence of Indians or worry over their religious welfare.
If such things come up at all, it is usually in passing. The
priest at Potosí writes mainly in order to acquire a nephew to
run a silver-ore refining mill for him, but in deliberating over
whether he might return to Spain or stay in Peru, he says:

> If I decide to stay, I will buy a very good farm or *chá-*
> *cara*, with a vineyard of ten or twelve thousand stocks
> and many trees, Castilian and local, that will support
> me when I want to retire and rest, and not go about
> instructing Indians, which is surely a great travail.[18]

Here the disparity between the two bodies of correspondence is of a different sort. The private letters reveal the
artificiality and one-sidedness of the public ones in this
subject matter as well, but one could not say that Indians were
not in a hundred ways important to the Spaniards, or that the
Spaniards were irreligious, for their letters are dotted with
prayers, preaching, and thanks for divine help. On the basis
of the correspondence, Indians were not much in the forefront
of the settlers' consciousness; they were seen as outside the
private, internal world of Spanish affairs. Certainly neither
Indians nor religious ministry to them plays any discernible
role in the image of the new land which the settlers presented
to those at home. That image, and the type of motivation it
implies for both the settler already in the Indies and the mi-
grant just leaving Spain, are those associated with European
settler colonies in areas where there was little or no indigenous population.

One part of the Spanish image of America emerges clearly
from the settlers' letters, not as anything they are trying to
project, but rather in their replies to what relatives at home
have written them, and in their awareness of what is expected
of them. One of the few known personal letters from a conqueror at the scene of the conquest, addressed from Peru to the
young writer's father in the Basque country, begins:

> Sir: it must be about three years ago that I got a letter
> from you, in which you asked me to send some

---

power struggle among Spaniards, of which the Indians are only the
occasion, or even the pretext.

[18]Lockhart and Otte 1976, p. 255.

money.[19]

To people in Spain, during the conquests and later, the Indies were a place relatives might send money from. The settlers usually sent traveling money to those who were coming to join them, and/or promised payment of debts accumulated on the trip. But beyond this, there was the expectation that they would send something every time they wrote. Hardly a letter fails to contain an apology for not sending money at the moment, with promises to do so in the future—sometimes for dowries for the girls of the family, occasionally to educate the boys, most often without specific mention of purpose. Often enough, instead of apology there was the money itself, a substantial amount of from fifty to several hundred pesos; some settlers sent such amounts repeatedly over the years, whenever they found a carrier to be trusted.

If a new area seems a land of promise, there must be a counterimage of the old country, and so we find it here. The letters cast one aspersion after another on Spain, calling it a "land of scarcity,"[20] referring to the "misery" there (the favorite word), scoffing at the paltriness of Spanish dowries, making fun of Spanish housing ("those little huts they have there").[21]

We have, then, the image of America as a place where there is opportunity and wealth for all who will work; and the people of Spain are prepared to believe it to the extent of investing second sons and hounding the big talkers for money. What role did the returnees play in all this, or rather, since we lack evidence of their sentiments as direct as the correspondence for the settlers, what can we say about the patterns of their activity, about their impact on Spain and the Spain-Indies nexus? Quantitative aspects of the stream of return migration can be studied in the same way as for the original emigration from Spain. We do know that it was a steady, significant movement.[22] For the social history of the

---

[19]Lockhart and Otte 1976, p. 4.

[20]Ibid., p. 86.   [21]Ibid., p. 115.

[22]Theopolis Fair in his doctoral dissertation "The *indiano* during the Spanish Golden Age from 1550–1650" (1972) hardly begins to exploit his announced topic, but does, in estimating the stream of repatriation, give a gross figure of 60,000 for the century between

phenomenon, I will try to draw a few general implications from Peruvian research I have engaged in.

The often harsh treatment that Spanish literary sources give to the *indianos* would make one think that they were rejected in peninsular society;[23] but the unflattering picture may just as well be the expression of resentment over their success. In any case, it is a stereotype beneath which we must search for a social reality if we are to understand either the real role of the returnee or the real meaning of the comment about him. The situation in sixteenth-century Trujillo (Extremadura) can throw light on the picture of the indiano as an uneducated upstart, perhaps rejected, perhaps vaulted into undeserved eminence.[24]

The evidence consists of fairly coherent, if skeletal, career information on one group known in its entirety: the ten first conquerors of Peru, members of Francisco Pizarro's main conquering expedition, who returned rich to their native Trujillo, recruiting point for the expedition's first nucleus. They and their wealth must have jolted the town. As to the property they bought and the marriages they made, only hints are presently available. But we do have information systematic enough to bear analysis when it comes to the Trujillo town council, which they packed shamelessly. By mid-century about half of them were councilmen. These shared several characteristics: they were literate, had been treated with consideration in Peru from the inception of the conquest, and bore the names of known hidalgo families of the town. Of those who were not councilmen, only one or two were literate, and all were of lower stations: a Pizarro steward, a horseshoer, a black crier and piper. They had the wealth and presumably shared the ideal, but never became councilmen.

1550 and 1650 (p. 75). Registers were kept of passengers on returning ships. The average number per ship register can be found and multiplied by the total estimated number of ships to give yearly totals. The method seems sound and capable of considerable refinement, though Fair's averages are based on samples from only five years in the 1570's.

[23]Fair 1972 at times takes this position.

[24]See Lockhart 1972, p. 58, and information scattered through the individual biographies of men from Trujillo.

We do not know, actually, that the plebeians even attempted to gain seats, but one of them at least was dissatisfied, for after years in Trujillo he returned to Peru and there attained a seat on the council of Cuzco. Here, perhaps, is our upstart and rejected indiano.

The Trujillo case shows us that even under what would appear to be a situation uniquely conducive to social revolution—where a dozen returnees came into a small city at the same time, probably tripling or quadrupling the liquid wealth in the local economy—no change of a structural nature took place. By 1550 there were council members who would not have been there but for the upheaval, but they were people of the same type as before. The repercussions were of a lesser magnitude. Personnel was displaced; there must have been severe disappointments, realignment in Trujillo's long-standing familial-political factions or *bandos*, and probably some screaming that the city patrimony was being sold to nobodies, untrue as that was. As for the plebeians, they generally contented themselves with a certain wealth, respect, and fame short of the highest social position. It is my impression that most of them made no move to marry the noble doñas of the town, or to invade the council chambers. Within this framework of accommodation by hidalgo and plebeian, returnee and stay-at-home, one finds a little dissent by commoners who had enough connections or education to feel eligible for higher status, but whose pretensions were rejected because the people at home remembered their beginnings too well and saw the disparities too sharply. These men might become disgruntled, might even return to the Indies.[25] Cases of this kind may have contributed more than their share to the indiano's literary image.

Although I have no other overview of a local situation to compare with Trujillo, this analysis can be generalized at

---

[25]Short of going back to the Indies, one could (though few did) go elsewhere in Spain, where one's wealth and good presence could be seen and one's origins were not known so precisely. In fact, the only plebeian on the Trujillo council was an Alonso Ruiz, born in the kingdom of Leon, who became in Peru the partner of a Trujillan, and on return married his partner's sister and settled in Trujillo. See Lockhart 1972, pp. 343–46.

least for the body of conquerors returning from Peru to Spain in the 1530's and flourishing there through the middle years of the century. Despite their unparalleled wealth, only those who could pass reasonably well for hidalgos by peninsular standards were able to sit on the town councils of their home areas. Others accepted a lesser success, and a few, all of them plebeians, went back to Peru after some years in Spain. Quite possibly the aggregate from all areas of the Indies over a century or two could have been an appreciable element in Spain's internal economy, but that question goes beyond my resources. In the internal social organization of Spain, one might hazard that the returnees caused only a ripple; they were conservative men, whose ambition was to realize conventional ideals through a conventional pattern of activity.[26]

Let me proceed to the somewhat more tangible topic of how the returnees, who appeared to be abandoning the Indies, were actually important in strengthening Spain's involvement there: they made various kinds of interaction with the Indies a normal, almost internal process, establishing traditions and social-economic networks.

If the experience of the first conquerors, along with some other early returnees from Peru, was at all representative, each new arrival from the Indies quickly went to his home area in Spain, bought income properties or annuities, built or bought the largest house he could, either at his very birthplace or in the nearest town of any size, and filled it with as large a following of servants and retainers as he could afford.[27] Often he could afford a substantial establishment, because by the

---

[26]See Lockhart 1972, pp. 54–59 and 63–64.

[27]I do not agree with those who postulate one mentality for "conquerors," another for "settlers." The conquerors' letters read just like those of their successors. Conquerors who could not afford to return home set about exactly the same kind of economic activity as "settlers"; they were in fact the pattern setters for those after them and around them. So many of the first conquerors of Peru returned because they had unparalleled removable assets. "Settlers" who had the same did the same, merchants as well as notaries, artisans, agriculturalists, and others. Comparative analysis shows that the factor determining the rate of return was not mentality but the degree to which position in the Indies could be translated into position at home. The emigrants' letters indicate that practically all settlers

mores of the Indies one went home rich or not at all. Again the example of the first conquerors of Peru: those who returned immediately after the conquest were all in all those with the largest shares of treasure; the others hoped to accumulate more before returning. Again and again in the settlers' letters the writer announces he will be home in two or three years—if he has saved a given amount of money. Sometimes a Spaniard with no position and few prospects would have a windfall and go home with a few hundred pesos.[28] But overall, in early Peru, the returnee was someone who had made a fortune in Spanish peninsular terms without getting hopelessly enmeshed in local affairs, as most did. It is also observable that those returning tended to belong to the upper half of settler society in birth and education.[29]

Whatever the impact of the returnee on Spanish society generally, one effect of his return was to send young men from his own town scrambling for the Indies, generally to the part of the Indies he had come from, to do the same as he had done. As powerful an inducement as letters and money were, the actual presence of the person was more powerful. In working with documents on early Peru, when I saw someone leaving rich, I learned to expect the quick appearance of his relatives. For the first conquerors there are some documented examples,[30] and my impressions tell me the phenomenon went far beyond that. One tends to attribute it to the demonstration effect, but it need not have been that alone. Once home, the man of the Indies could give his relatives and compatriots a much more detailed, convincing account in repeated conversations. Also the returnee, with his wealth, generally became the functioning head of his lineage, and may have used his new authority to send the young men of the family off to do what he felt was best for them. In any case, the effect of the returnees, particularly when a number of them came into a single Spanish community, was to strengthen and deepen the

---

originally intended to return, and that the maximum ambition for all, regardless of how often it could be realized, was a seigneurial existence in Spain.

[28]See Lockhart 1968, pp. 145–46.

[29]See Lockhart 1972, p. 50.

[30]Ibid., various instances.

tie between the community and some part of the Indies, to make the citizens of the Spanish town more knowledgable about the colonial settlement, hastening a second generation of involvement with it, and helping create a cycle and a set of expectations. There was an expectation at certain times and places that when anyone returned from the Indies someone else should be sent to replace him, to take advantage of his connections, and in a sense to inherit his position. A corresponding expectation existed in the Indies. In discussing private letters from Puebla, Otte points to a longstanding association between Puebla and the Castilian town of Brihuega; not only letters and emigrants, but also successful returnees were involved in maintaining the tie.[31] Brading speaks of the same small Castilian towns sending sons to Mexico City generation after generation until the end of the colonial period.

If the returnees were important to the creation of lasting regional ties, they were even more essential in establishing professional networks that spanned the Atlantic and transcended the internal history of either Spain or the Indies, while representing an important part of each. The best developed of these by far were the mercantile networks. Among the merchants we are in a different world. In their letters from the Indies we find no talk of a land of opportunity, no wooing of recruits; the writer is a junior partner addressing his superior, and the man at home knows as much about the Indies as the local representative, probably from having been there.[32] Among merchants, the goal was Seville, because that is where the large companies were based. In fact, it is often inappropriate to speak of merchants leaving anywhere or returning. One could go and come, abandoning nothing, advancing along a single line of promotion within a single family network: first running errands for Father around the docks in Seville; then setting off for Lima as a lad to learn from, help, and tattle on Uncle, the firm's main representative there; perhaps doing a stint taking merchandise to Arequipa and the Potosí mines; then succeeding Uncle when

---

[31]Otte 1966, pp. 10–13.
[32]See for example Lockhart and Otte 1976, pp. 17–38.

he returns to Seville after Father's death; finally returning to Seville and the top position oneself; and eventually sending one's son to Lima in turn. Of course companies or partnerships did not usually last long, and there were disasters of many kinds. Failure for the company or the individual meant that the latter stayed wherever he happened to be at the moment. But the same migration pattern obtained even outside company channels. A young man of merchant family might emigrate as an individual, get a start in Potosí in local commerce, advance to head a medium-sized company of his own in Lima, and then, when he had accumulated enough capital, repeat the process on a large scale in Seville. There may never have been a time when an actual majority of the large exporters of Seville had had beginnings in the Indies, but one could easily get that impression. In a letter of 1553 Francisco de Escobar, long in Peru himself and now head of a large Seville combine trading with Lima, is considering new company arrangements, in the course of which he discusses a number of other exporters to Peru; one name after another goes by, of men once active in Lima or Panama, except for the prior of the Seville Consulado, and even he has sent a son to Lima. For a century or so this inseparable unity of Seville and the Indies continued in commerce, based on economic factors, but maintained in large part by the movement of people back and forth within well defined channels and conventions.[33]

Notaries also showed some of the merchants' tendencies, although the movement was comparatively minor and irregular, and outside any network. In early Peru notaries were among those most likely to return to Spain, and once there they sometimes, though not as invariably as the merchants, continued dealings with the Indies. A notary among the first conquerors of Peru became a solicitor in the Council of the Indies.[34] Juan Franco, once chief notary of Lima, went to Spain and bought one of the notarial offices of Seville; much of his business there concerned the Indies, and the merchant Francisco de Escobar (see just above) issued documents before

---

[33]See Lockhart 1968, pp. 80–81, 87–91, and Lockhart and Otte 1976, pp. 86–113.
[34]Lockhart 1972, p. 264.

Franco in Seville as he had formerly done in Lima.[35]

I do not know of studies about other professions which would permit a full discussion of trends. Mariners moved back and forth more than anyone else, but they were so peripheral in Spain and so scorned in the Indies that they barely belong to the internal history of either area. In church and government, some of the same patterns prevailed as in commerce. The hierarchies embraced both hemispheres, and a number of the most fully successful individuals followed a career pattern which led first to the Indies and then to a high position in Spain. It appears to me, however, that in the upper levels of the church, returning to Spain was always more an exception than a rule, perhaps because of the relatively advanced age of high dignitaries when appointed. On the lower levels, on the other hand, and especially among the loosely supervised secular clergy, many returned, but more in order to retire wealthy, like other returning Spaniards, than as a step in professional advancement. In government, particularly for the judges, one can discern a promotional ladder like the one in commerce: it led from minor Audiencias to those in the viceregal capitals, then to the Council of the Indies or other high posts in Spain. Moreover, the pattern remained valid for a long period of time, and also included the sending back of younger relatives to take one's place. What Audiencia in the Indies was without its Licenciado Altamirano or Doctor Maldonado, appointed through the influence of a relative formerly stationed there and now on the Council? One is left with the feeling, however, that in no other branch of life was the social integration of the two hemispheres as complete as in commerce.

All of these networks met the same fate. At some point the cycle broke down in that most of the successful figures stopped returning and built positions in America instead. The result was two parallel, partially competing entities rather than one integrated one. Partial maturation of the American system would seem to account for the change: the capitals of the Indies became progressively better places in which to retire, the European sector of American life grew too large and com-

---

[35]Lockhart 1968, p. 75.

plex to be managed from outside, and the economy generated enough capital to allow buying from Seville rather than full dependence. The process is not well understood in any of the branches, but one can say a word or two about the broad lines of it in the commercial world. By the seventeenth century the transatlantic companies seem to have split in two. Seville firms generally penetrated only as far as Veracruz and Portobello, where other firms, based in Mexico City and Lima, bought up the shipments wholesale. By the eighteenth century, Brading shows us, the large merchants of Mexico were acquiring titles, lands, and all the appurtenances of a permament position in the Indies. Even so, these merchants were still Spanish-born.[36] The input of nephews long survived the breakdown of full integration, continuing in a now traditional fashion until Spanish American independence and even beyond. At any rate, for many decades before the pattern changed, Spain and the Indies functioned as a unit in various important respects, and some of the most influential people in Spanish life were men made in the Indies.

---

[36]For a view of the evolution based on two additional decades of research on commerce, see "The Merchants of Early Spanish America: Continuity and Change," Chapter 6 in this volume.

4. Double Mistaken Identity: Some Nahua Concepts in Postconquest Guise
(1985, 1993)

F OR A LONG TIME in the mid-twentieth century many people thought that the Spaniards on their arrival in central Mexico, land of the Nahuas, had nearly effaced indigenous culture, quickly replacing it with Spanish structures and patterns. Another school held that the indigenous population lived in relative isolation and that large sectors of its culture had survived quite untouched. Eventually it was seen that neither position was right. The indigenous people of postcontact central Mexico were far less isolated from Spaniards than had been imagined; at the same time, many basic features of preconquest culture survived indefinitely, though often in new forms. By the nineteenth century it would have been hard to find many things in the Nahua way of life that could safely be declared to have been entirely European or entirely indigenous in ultimate origin. The stable forms that emerged in the long run often owed so much to both antecedents, with many elements having been very similar from the beginning and others now interwoven and integrated, that identifying what belonged to which antecedent becomes to a large extent impossible, and even beside the point.[1]

The composite forms arising in postconquest times were made possible in the first place by extensive convergences between European and central Mexican societies, of a type perhaps not so unusual to find between any two sedentary societies worldwide, but remarkable enough considering how long the two sides involved in this case had been out of all contact. Convergence, however, is not identity. The indigenous and Spanish phenomena that both sides saw as similar

---

[1]The much longer historiographical discussion which originally began the article was later incorporated into Lockhart 1992, where it can be seen on pp. 2–5. I do not include references in the present version; the factual aspect rests largely on Lockhart 1991, 1992, and 1993, aside from some things that are general knowledge in the field.

were rarely, indeed never, literally the same. At the heart of cultural interaction was a process I call Double Mistaken Identity, in which each side of the cultural exchange presumes that a given form or concept is functioning in the way familiar within its own tradition and is unaware of or unimpressed by the other side's interpretation.

In the earliest phases, what one often finds is the operation of an indigenous cultural complex under a Spanish-Christian overlay that may be little more than terminological; with time things became more complicated. Also, after an interval, awareness sometimes began to grow, especially on the Spanish side, of the inaptness of the original identification, and the mistake in identity was rectified, though too late to change the direction things had taken. In the present paper I wish to discuss several aspects of postconquest Nahua corporate culture in which indigenous ways of thinking existed under Spanish auspices or put their stamp on ostensibly Spanish-derived forms. In doing so I will try to consider how it was that the different concepts and practices involved somehow intermeshed to give a workable result minimally acceptable to both parties.

A very widely diffused type of organization employed by indigenous peoples in pre-Columbian times, not only in Mesoamerica but in the Andes and elsewhere, could be called cellular, as opposed to a more hierarchical or linear mode. It was characteristic of preconquest Nahua cosmography, land allocation, rhetorical and poetic speech, artistic expression, and even grammar, but let us go straight to some postconquest manifestations regarding the sociopolitical entity that contained Nahua life in the same way that the polis contained the life of the ancient Greeks.

The key Nahua sociopolitical unit in preconquest as well as early postconquest times was a city-state-sized entity, an ethnic state called an *altepetl*, with a well defined territory and constituency, and a dynastic ruler, the *tlatoani*, to whom the whole owed allegiance and paid tribute. This unit presents many analogies to the Hispanic municipality-province. The Spanish entity, though, had a pronounced nucleus and was strongly hierarchical in the sense that organizations of all kinds stretched from a dominant center in the city to subordinate parts in the country, with territorial subdivisions of the entity relatively unimportant, whereas the unit indigenous to central Mexico was divided into a certain number of independent and equal subentities, which we used to feel confident in calling *calpolli*, each with its own sense of separate origins, each a microcosm of the larger whole. The whole functioned by means of each of the parts taking turns with duties to the ruler, each paying its share of the general tribute, providing its allotment of laborers for public works, etc. Rarely were the "calpolli" a miscellaneous, asymmetrical

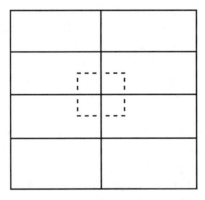

Fig. 1. Schema of an indigenous altepetl with its constituent parts and optional nucleus.

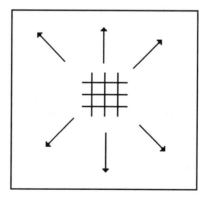

Fig. 2. Schema of a Spanish city-province.

set. Rather they went in pairs, fours, and eights. Uneven sets arose from particular circumstances, but even-numbered symmetry and reciprocity was clearly an ideal pattern.

The Spanish presence was built on the altepetl, preserved in its integrity and functioning much as before. Though the Spaniards recognized, utilized, and tried to reorganize existing indigenous sociopolitical entities (including complex polities as well as simple ones like that seen in the illustration), they did not really understand them. In an altepetl the Spaniards discerned a *cabecera* or head settlement and *sujetos* or subject settlements; in reality, however, the altepetl was the entire group of constituents spread over the entire territory, functioning according to a set rotational order, and did not involve one subunit ruling others. Never did a polity contain a central settlement with a name or identity separate from that of the whole entity.

How did two such different interpretations of the same situation arise? The Spaniards on first arrival in an altepetl would be greeted by its tlatoani and conducted to his palace, one of the largest and most elaborate buildings to be seen anywhere in the area. Nearby would stand the temple of entity's tutelary god; that often huge structure was the very symbol of the entity's sovereignty and power and was built to make a corresponding display. In the vicinity of the palace and temple was the entity's central, largest marketplace, the hub of the trade between the subdivisions. A significant concentration of people would live nearby either temporarily or permanently in connection with the altepetl's three main unifying institutions, rulership, temple, and market. Even after the Spaniards had been present long enough to bring about some significant changes, the situation would retain the same characteristics. A main church, if anything even more dominant than its predecessor, would replace the temple; a municipal building would eventually replace the ruler's palace; the marketplace was likely to remain little changed. Given the way Spanish municipalities were organized, it is truly no wonder that the Spaniards virtually equated Nahua organization with their own; what they saw seemed to confirm it.

Yet their "cabecera" was largely an illusion. If an altepetl had a large settlement cluster in the vicinity of the palace, temple, and market (and not all did) it still did not constitute a corporate entity with its own identity distinct from the rest. It would consist of parts of various subunits like those in the rest of the territory, each taking turns with them and bearing the same relationship to the ruler of the whole. The ruler himself was based in one particular subunit which had its given place in the rotational order and was in every respect on the same footing as the others. Each subunit had its own ruler at that level, who was one of the magnates of the altepetl, and the nobility of the whole larger entity was distributed in the establishments of rulers of subunits. With the larger and more complex states especially, a well organized altepetl with its set of rulers, divisions, and subdivisions might be spread over non-contiguous territory, have no one dominant settlement, and be practically impossible to pinpoint geographically, something the Spaniards never seem to have fully grasped.

Organization by rotating independent parts, as opposed to a ruling settlement with subordinated dependencies, was something the Nahuas held on to tenaciously for centuries. When in the eighteenth century the word "cabecera" had been circulating among the Spaniards for so long that it began to enter the Nahuatl language, it was still taken by some to be identical in meaning with "altepetl," that is, to include the whole entity, not some dominant part of it.

How, then, could things work? The Spaniards somehow succeeded in collecting tribute from the Nahuas, in using them on a massive scale for all sorts of labor (long on an obligatory basis), in creating large supra-altepetl administrative districts among them, and in integrating them into the Christian church, not to speak of obtaining supplies in their markets as individuals. One thing the Spaniards had done; they had correctly identified the operative sovereign unit. They thought of it as a cabecera with its sujetos, and the Nahuas thought of it as an altepetl, but both conceptions embraced exactly the same territory, population, and local figures of authority. The secret of the Spaniards was to leave the internal operation of the altepetl to itself; if Spanish authorities had little grasp of the inner workings of the altepetl, it literally did not matter. They demanded what they wanted first from the traditional ruler and later from his successor the governor, head of the Spanish-style municipal council instituted by then, and he, using the normal internal mechanisms, saw to the rest. If the proper result was not forthcoming, the Spaniards might jail or replace the leading altepetl authorities; there was nothing more they were equipped to do. Usually they got some approximation of what they demanded, though sometimes rather less and often with great delay. In this way they reaped some benefit without investing extremely scarce bureaucratic manpower or having to master the frightful complexities of Nahua organization and language. The Nahuas retained what they wanted most, a large degree of local autonomy.

By the eighteenth century, the Spaniards were speaking less of cabeceras and sujetos and tending to call any discernible indigenous settlement, whether it was a constituent part of another or not, a "pueblo." In a way the change represented an admission of the inappropriateness of the term cabecera, but it was also an adjustment to changing conditions, for the constituent parts of large altepetl were increasingly breaking out of the altepetl confederations and dealing with the Spaniards directly. Such former fragments, however, still had constituent parts and called themselves altepetl. They had come into existence at a time and in a way that was compatible with Spanish interests, to which the payment of tribute and the use of altepetl mechanisms to acquire temporary labor were no longer central. But if that is why the Spaniards allowed it to happen, the Nahuas had different motives, and it was largely at their initiative that the development occurred. They were looking for that small-unit autonomy that had been dear to them from preconquest times and that could be indulged now that the protection and channeling of a larger-scale altepetl was no longer needed. That the small units were viable was the result of traditional cellular organization.

After a first postcontact generation, which I call Stage 1, in which the internal indigenous organizational framework remained largely unchanged, a great wave of reorganization took place at the beginning of what I call Stage 2, from the mid-sixteenth century forward. At this point the analogy that the Spaniards saw between the altepetl and a Spanish municipality resulted in the establishment of a municipal council in each altepetl and the naming of officials with appropriate Spanish titles. Once again, the perceptions of the two sides deviate, but here at least a common vocabulary was used; the Spanish names for the new offices quickly became frequently spoken Nahuatl words. When either a Spaniard or a Nahua spoke of an *alcalde* or a *regidor*, the same word was being used in reference to exactly the same person.

In preconquest times public office was held by nobles of the entity concerned and seen as both burden and honor. The Hispanic conception was very similar, so that a transition to Hispanic-style municipal offices in Nahua altepetl in the course of the sixteenth century was very simple and easy, or so it appeared. At the council level, the offices introduced were those of governor, alcalde (first-instance judge), and regidor (councilman). In addition there was a notary, important to the council's functioning even though not exactly a member. Lower officials, constables, ushers, and the like, with Spanish titles, were established in due course.

The Nahuas immediately equated "governor" with tlatoani as to both recruitment and manner of operation; for quite some time this office tended to dominate local government or even constitute it. By the second and third generations there had come to be a very substantial change, in that several candidates might rotate periodically in the post. Even this was a rechanneling of preconquest dynamics; rather than the victorious new ruler eliminating and exiling his rivals as in the old days, all the credible candidates took turns. In many towns the governorship remained recognizably dynastic over the whole colonial period, and even where it was not dominated by a single family, multigenerational jockeying between two or three rival dynasties was often the pattern.[2]

Thus the largest piece in the Spanish-style municipal governments was an official with a Spanish title and some Spanish attributes but essentially equated by the Nahuas with their traditional ruler. The word "governor," variously spelled and pronounced, quickly became an important Na-

---

[2]See Haskett 1991.

huatl word; at the same time, the Nahuas long continued to call the governor tlatoani, above all in direct address but also in all kinds of more polite, ceremonial speech. From the Spanish side, the governor had never been a pure case of Double Mistaken Identity. A Spanish municipal council's presiding officer had a different title and above all was from the outside. The Spaniards in effect recognized the altepetl's greater degree of autonomy and devised a new kind of more locally based office for the situation.

In preconquest kingdoms the rulers of the constituent parts, each equipped with a special lordly title pertaining to his unit, carried out a multitude of functions among which the judicial aspect was so prominent that some observers have referred to these dignitaries as judges. In any case, officers with the Spanish title of alcalde quickly took hold as judicial, ceremonial and administrative figures, much as in Spanish councils, so we must presume that the Nahuas saw a parallel between the office of alcalde and the preconquest posts.

A town council in Spain, or a Spanish council in the Indies, possessed a corps of perhaps six to ten regidores, representing well known local families, usually holding office for longer terms than the alcaldes, making important decisions and giving the council its institutional continuity. Here the indigenous setup seems to have contained no close parallel. Once having gotten the governor and alcaldes functioning, most Indian towns did name a standard number of yearly rotating regidores to be on the municipal council, but often they seem not to have known what to do with them. In effect, there was no place in a Nahua altepetl for a body of regidores in the Spanish sense, no guiding notion of their function, so that in many cases, across the decades, the regidores tended to wither away or be reduced to adjutants. Here Double Mistaken Identity failed.

An outstanding success was the office of notary. Long before the sixteenth century was out, and usually from the very beginning when the other constituted official was the governor, every altepetl large and small had its municipal notary, recording the acts of the town government and other local legal business in Nahuatl written in the Roman al-

phabet. The person holding the post was standardly a noble;
he might later serve on the council proper. In the aura of his
post as well as in his functions, there was hardly any difference between a Nahua notary and his Spanish counterpart.
Since the precise attributes of the preconquest *amatlacuilo* or
writer are not well known, it is hard to say to what extent the
identity perceived by the Nahuas was mistaken. But surely the
indigenous concept that the writing or painting of records on
paper in the name of the community is a dignified and necessary task gave the post its first impetus. The preconquest
precedent provided not only a general role model but notions
as to how to prepare documents. The importance of received
ideas about writing and writers in Mesoamerica is perhaps
most clearly seen in the contrast with Peru, where notaries
seem to have been late and few and alphabetic writing in
indigenous languages never did become as strong and lasting
a local tradition as it was all the way from the Valley of
Mexico to Guatemala.

The Spanish principle of short-term rotation of at least
some municipal offices made much headway in Nahua towns
during the colonial period, but in the end the indigenous
principles of permanent and collegial office reasserted
themselves in a way at once subtle and blatant. The Nahuas
appeared to rotate properly as governor and alcaldes, and
they adopted the Spanish distinction between present and
past holders, speaking of the *gobernador actual* or *gobernador
pasado, alcalde actual* or *alcalde pasado*. But they made much
more of these terms than the Spaniards did themselves. In
effect, being alcalde pasado was almost another way of being
alcalde. The past and present officials together witnessed
testaments and other solemn acts, signed petitions, and even
on occasion, illegal though it was, jointly issued grants and
orders. By the end of the colonial period the prevailing
system—rule by an informal council of all those who had
rotated as governor, alcalde, and *fiscal* (church steward), with
a negligible role for regidores—still obeyed preconquest
norms as much as it did Spanish ones.

We have hardly touched on the deepest difference between
the Spanish and the Nahua conceptions of the offices we have
been discussing. Both sides would have immediately agreed

that the governor/tlatoani held his position in relation to the whole entity. Beyond that, from the Nahua point of view, the alcaldes, regidores, and even officers like constables each were members and representatives of a particular subunit, where their primary obligation and affiliation lay, whereas in the Spanish scheme these figures too were officers at large of the overarching entity, not associated with some particular subjurisdiction (although they often in effect represented a certain lineage or faction). By Nahua principles, if there were to be two alcaldes, they must rotate around the constituent parts, or even better, the number must be increased until there were as many of them as there were constituents, and things moved quite far in that direction. This sort of distribution of the offices was one thing that helped to make the later fragmentation of the altepetl so readily feasible.

The Spanish name for a municipal council was *cabildo*, and the Spaniards duly so denominated the sets of officers they created in each altepetl in the mid-sixteenth century. The word also made some inroads in Nahuatl, though it did not become as embedded as the words for particular offices, and for good reason. The Spaniards saw the cabildo as a separate entity with its own corporate profile and interests, different from those of the larger municipality which it governed, whereas from the Nahua point of view no such separation existed; the group of representatives of the subunits were not a separate corporation any more than the conglomeration of people in the general vicinity of the ruler, temple, and marketplace was a separate settlement.

The Spaniards soon noticed that Nahua alcaldes and regidores did not act quite like their Spanish counterparts, for example not even attempting to maintain the confidentiality of secret sessions, and making little distinction between themselves and lower officials, who in the Nahua system were persons of great consequence, while in the Spanish they were definitely lesser. Spanish usage gradually moved away from speaking of cabildos among the Nahuas, by mid-seventeenth century settling on the term *oficiales de república*, "officers of the commonwealth." The new wording was actually much more apropos, and perhaps by that time the Spaniards had gained some insight into the differences between their own councils and those that had evolved among the Nahuas.

During a long period of gestation, however, the Spaniards could imagine that they had introduced Hispanic governance with all its paraphernalia of offices, legal procedures, and records, while the Nahuas could imagine that they were the same collection of sovereign local states as before, with the same ruling circles and the same mechanisms of law and officeholding, now somewhat renamed. Neither side would be entirely wrong. We have already seen how it was that the persistent deviances from the Hispanic system were tolerable to Spanish authorities, for the Nahua altepetl ran itself internally. All the viceroy and Royal Audiencia had to do was confirm the elections the Nahuas had made among themselves; they became more directly involved only when factions came from inside the Nahua altepetl complaining of election irregularities and the like, in which case some Spanish adjudication was required.

Let us look at how legitimation or legalization occurred within the altepetl in postconquest times. Europeans and Mesoamericans shared the notion that in addition to inherent rights and properties, individuals and corporations could acquire certain specific rights which neither the generality nor any reasonable individual would contest, and furthermore both civilizations agreed that such rights however acquired passed from the realm of the de facto into that of relative incontestability through the proper performance of ritual. But the content of the ritual differed considerably between the two spheres.

From the mid-sixteenth century forward indigenous central Mexicans adopted the main Spanish instruments of legalization (grants, acts of possession, wills, donations, bills of sale), which were written down in Nahuatl by the notaries of the altepetl. Over time, especially in the larger centers, such documents approached ever closer to the Spanish models on which they were based. But never did they attain identity, always retaining this or that idiosyncrasy above and beyond those occasioned by the language itself. In general, they contain more direct speech than Spanish equivalents, a carryover from the heavily oral tradition of preconquest times.

One pervasive characteristic of Nahuatl legal documents is that they are more broadly witnessed than comparable Spanish documents. To be valid a Spanish public document needed the presence of a notary and three witnesses; a larger number might be listed for extraordinary things such as the testament of an important person, but three was the general rule. Nahuatl documents commonly list more. In fact, many early documents do not descend to name-listing, but say only that a large assemblage of people from the local community was present; it may be further specified that those in attendance gave their assent. Before long, however, the majority of documents came to have a list of witnesses (*testigos*) appended in the Spanish manner. But rather than three random adult males as in Spanish documents, in Nahuatl texts we may see some or all of the highest authorities of the local unit, whether it be the altepetl or a subdivision. Or just as commonly there will be a list of from five to ten or more names, apparently every person present, and standardly including women. In the Spanish tradition, although women could and did issue legal instruments of all kinds and gave testimony in court, one simply does not normally see them among the witnesses to the validity of documents.

Eventually the reader of this documentation comes to grasp that despite having adopted the Spanish term "testigo" the Nahuas did not mean quite the same thing by it as the Spaniards did. The witnesses not only attested to the attaining of a formal legality through the performance of certain acts, but actually assented to the justice of the content of the proceedings. Originally the assenting body was the entire assembled populace of the unit, but the unit's authorities or even that portion of the populace which chanced to be present could represent the whole. The assent given was very broad. In a will, for example, the witnesses apparently authenticated not only the fact that the testator distributed goods in a certain way, but the fact that they were his or her goods in the first place. One consequently finds Nahuas using wills not only against competing heirs but to establish property rights against outside claims. In Spanish law such evidence strictly speaking had no force, yet it appears that Spanish courts were in fact often influenced by it.

It is perhaps in this light that another characteristic of Nahuatl documentation can be interpreted. Public statements of the preconquest period, to judge by the samples in surviving collections, had been full of admonitions, and postconquest Nahuatl documents continue the tradition. After nearly every item in a Nahuatl will there follows "my order is to be obeyed," "no one is to take away what I give him," etc. Such things are lacking in Spanish wills and would be quite beside the point. Nahuatl wills go even further, issuing specific commands to be carried out by third parties and even specifying prices to be paid by them. When an indigenous town council settled a matter, it often not only affirmed the validity of its decision, but set stiff penalties for anyone who should as much as step forward to dispute the ruling (something entirely beyond its power to do, at least in the Spanish scheme of things). And if we look at the so-called "primordial titles," documents quite distant from the Spanish tradition in which Indian towns tried to give a historical justification for their territorial rights, we find that the central content is often the statement of the town's principal representative that "this is my land, my property." In the European tradition we would expect the statement to be made by an outside instance or by the representatives of surrounding towns who were present. It seems, then, that in the old Nahua view a strong statement of fact or recommendation under solemn circumstances, made before a non-demurring audience, had something like binding legal force, and that this view continued to prevail among indigenous people in postconquest times. Moreover, the Nahuas seem to have imagined that it was the same among the Spaniards. Like most altepetl-internal matters, their view did not affect the Spaniards directly or even usually come to their attention, so it was able to persist indefinitely. When this way of looking at the law did impinge on Spanish authorities, as when towns would present their "titles" as evidence of legitimate possession of their lands, it failed resoundingly; in Spanish courts the titles were usually simply ignored, sometimes ridiculed.

To judge from its survivals, an important part of Nahua legalizing ritual was the feast. The Nahuas took quickly to

Spanish ritual, such as pulling twigs and grass and throwing stones in sign of taking possession of land, and they even added their own wrinkles, for example making such gestures in their own traditional four directions, but they did not therefore give up feasting. Many of the "titles" note that after the great original postconquest border survey the local ruler would give a meal (turkey, *atole*, etc.) for both homefolk and the neighboring peoples, after which all would part content. With time, feasting disappeared from Nahuatl documents, but not from Nahua practice, as we can deduce from repeated Spanish complaints to the effect that Indian town officials were worthless drunkards who instead of attending to duties constantly ate and drank with everyone who came to them on business. The feast seems to have had a function like the signature in the Spanish tradition, an indispensable seal and symbol that the action was now irrevocable. And as with the manner of witnessing, here too the Nahua equivalent is more inclusive and public, dramatic rather than written.

The Nahuas thus developed a system within which official documents and ceremonies had substantially different forms, meanings, and functions than in the Spanish world, but at the same time they were in large part modeled on and named after Spanish counterparts, so that the Spaniards could generally accept them as equivalents of their own conventions, smiling a bit at oddities they noticed but mainly knowing and caring very little about how these things actually worked among the Nahuas. On the Nahua side, accordingly as the time was earlier, the setting more provincial, and the writer or official less practiced, the greater was the traditional indigenous cultural content inside the ostensibly Spanish frameworks.[3] But even in the latest, most urbane productions, appearing to approach contemporaneous Spanish standards very closely, strong hints of another origin remained.

---

[3]The titles, a phenomenon of Stage 3, the time after the mid-seventeenth century, and done mainly by unpracticed writers, with their strong deviance from any Hispanic model, appear to go counter to the temporal trend. I think, however, that only their written form was new, and that they are the descendants of earlier popular oral versions even more distant from anything Spanish.

A Nahua realm of great interest to the Spaniards, originally, was religion. Double Mistaken Identity was operative in this area, but in a rather different way than in the world of sociopolitical organization, where perceptions were fully symmetrical (that is, each party took the central sociopolitical institutions and mechanisms of the other to be much like its own). The Spaniards identified traditional Nahua rites not with the mass and the sacraments but with forbidden pagan sacrifices they knew of from scripture and European religious history. They equated the Nahua deities not with the Christian God or even with the gods of Greece and Rome,[4] but with the devils and demons of Christianity, granting them reality while interpreting them as purely evil. As a result they did not attempt reorganization of these aspects of religion; they knocked down the temples, removed the priests, and did their best to eradicate the rites, from human sacrifice on down. The old high priest did not become the local Christian priest as the local ruler became the governor; Spaniards took over priestly duties themselves. Nor was the priest's main assistant, the fiscal, at first a dominant figure chosen from among those of highest rank in the altepetl.

The difference in the ways in which politics and religion were viewed was more on the Spanish side than on the indigenous. The Spaniards lacked a fully unified view not only of Nahua religion but more especially of their own, perhaps as a result of an older case of Double Mistaken Identity associated with the transactions between Christianity and predecessor religions in Europe in late antiquity. A high religion of individual morality and salvation was perceptibly distinct from the popular religion featuring a multitude of different saints with special powers and special iconography, serving to sym-

---

[4]An incipient tendency to identify Mesoamerican religion with Islam, seen in the way the temples were sometimes called mosques, never seemed to take hold. The public practice of traditional rites by the Nahuas was permitted only in the most provisional settings, in contrast to the longer-term toleration of Islam under comparable conditions in medieval Christian Spain. Yet the Moors were the great general precedent in all the Spaniards' early dealings with the indigenous peoples of America, and I imagine they were still somewhere in the mental background.

bolize and heighten sociopolitical identities. At a somewhat more subterranean level, apart from both spheres, uniformly disapproved of by the first and sometimes accepted by the second, was a world of occult curing skills, divination, and witchcraft.

Spanish laymen as well as priests seemed shocked at the manifestations of organized indigenous religion, above all at human sacrifice but also at the temples and the appearance and actions of the priests. Inconsistency showed up only as Christianity was brought among the Nahuas. The mendicants who were mainly in charge of religious matters in the first generation or so after contact wanted an austere religion with emphasis on morality rather than on saints and pomp. If their view had rigorously prevailed, the Nahuas would have had a much harder time finding a foothold for their own notions. But the laity and the secular clergy were much devoted to the saints, their images, and their processions. Also, even the most zealous of the friars had their own attachments to certain saints, and they took it for granted that any consecrated church should have a particular patron saint.

That was all the Nahuas needed. From millenia of wars, migrations, and conquests, they were predisposed to come to terms with the gods of a conquering group. Skepticism about the existence of supernaturals of any kind was not much in evidence. All known peoples had their own gods (remember that the Nahuas constituted many peoples and knew many more); it was not a question of which existed or did not, for they all presumably existed, but of the special attributes of each and their relative efficacy in supplying protection and benefits.

It is well known that the Mesoamericans and among them the Nahuas had a huge pantheon of supernaturals, some of them originating in astronomical phenomena, some in forces of nature, and some in historical figures, while many were mixtures of all three and of yet other things. Like the saints, they had special iconographic attributes and domains of influence, and festivities and processions were devoted to them at particular points in the annual calendar. It is not quite so well known that the specific manifestations of all these divinities were strongly affected by ethnicity and sociopolitical organization. Probably any temple to any supernatural whatever belonged to a particular sociopolitical unit, and the rites and festivities associated with it pertained in the first instance to that unit. Most especially, every altepetl had its tutelary deity who watched over the people and gave them what they had; he was ensconced in a temple that was the unit's largest, most impressive structure (one of the main words for temple meant "god-house"), and his festivity was the greatest occasion of the year.

When the Nahuas saw that Christianity was to be celebrated in and around a large and elaborate building containing the statue of a supernatural who was the patron of the church, gave his (or sometimes her) name to the whole altepetl, and was to be feted in a splendid annual festivity and procession, how could they not identify the church with their traditional temple and the saint with their ethnic god? That is, they may well have felt that a transfer of allegiance had occurred, but they put the new saint and church in the place of the old god and temple in a series of ways. Many of these did not conflict with popular Christianity: the notion that the church and saint symbolized the glory of the sociopolitical entity and were to be maintained in as much splendor as possible; the ostentation and sense of pride associated with the annual festivity; the expectation that the saint could be called upon for help in bad times and especially with certain kinds of disaster that were his or her speciality. Sometimes the lack of complete identity of the two backgrounds could be detected in the result. In preconquest times the gods had given their people the land to use and remained the ultimate owners of it, and the Nahuas tended to transfer this attribute to their saints, so that the patron saint of an altepetl was the residual owner and guarantor of its land, while the saints of the subdivisions had the same role there, and household saints were associated with particular plots at the level of the domestic unit. But why should the Spaniards complain of such an apparently devout way of thinking?

Many of the old ways of celebrating holiness came into the new system, on the presumption of an overall equivalence between the two types of religion. Feathers, flowers, and copal incense were lavished on the saints, and sometimes holy herbs, that is, hallucinogenic materials, were associated with them as well. Sweeping at and around altars, which had been a specifically ritual activity, continued. Traditional ritual dances accompanied festivities, with the singing of texts that probably contained much preconquest religious material. It is notable that the Nahuas did not appear to languish over the loss of extensive sacrificial bloodletting and human sacrifice. Human sacrifice was, I think, primarily a byproduct of endemic warfare in a context of inter-altepetl rivalry, and it quickly faded away along with the whole complex system of military terminology and ranks that had once been so important in Nahua society. New ways of besting the neighboring altepetl were available in superlative churches, elaborate accoutrements, and resplendent processions.

An aspect of Double Mistaken Identity from the Nahua side that had wide-reaching effects was the assumption that all religion was in some sense one, that it was a domain in which various ends—protection, good weather, good health, legitimation of status, identity—could be attained, and various means could be combined for that purpose, from wherever they might come. Shamanism was one of those means in preconquest religion, especially important for health and the assurance of daily routines; it was not radically set off from high religion as in Christianity but invoked the same gods as those in the great temples. Nahuas were slow to realize that they were called upon to relinquish aspects of their tradition entirely and definitively in favor of Christianity. After an inevitable time of transition they largely adopted the Christian forms, strongly colored with their own concepts as we have seen, wherever Christianity offered adequate substitutes, and to every appearance they identified with them deeply, consciously or unconsciously taking them as true equivalents of what they had had before. The new ways seem to have been felt adequate at the level of the church edifice and the saints, the public ceremonies, and the rituals of life represented by the sacraments, in other words across the bulk of the range Christianity covers (with, it seems, less concern for individual morality and eternity, corresponding to the nature of preconquest Mesoamerican religion). But the important part of the spectrum covered in the preconquest system by shamanistic activity found no equivalent in Christianity. The result was that it continued; the Nahuas clearly saw no conflict. In due course they came to realize that Spanish ecclesiastics did not approve, and then such activity went underground, but it did not cease to be practiced, sometimes even by indigenous people in the local political and religious hierarchy.

On the Spanish side, for all their belief that the whole content and practice of Mesoamerican religion was an aberration and a diabolical invention, Spanish clerics without usually admitting it in fact largely equated the two religious systems as functioning organizations. Outside the Spanish cities, they had the new churches built on or near the sites of the old temples, and they used a form of the old temple staff for personnel, now renamed cantors and sacristans to be sure. Yet the word that became definitive for "church" in Nahuatl was *teopan*, one of the names for a preconquest temple precinct, and the personnel were called *teopantlaca*, "church people," just like the staff of the old temples. In due course, by the end of the sixteenth century, the fiscal, starting as the priest's right hand man and not a luminary in himself, evolved into an important figure, well born and well connected, often the second ranking person of the altepetl behind the governor. With this, in a sense the old high priesthood had been partially reconstituted, that is, as a position, for the development seems to have no doctrinal tendency in itself (although it made it more possible for the Nahuas to run Christianity their own way). One can, it is true, ask to what extent the ecclesiastics were aware of such things. Even though they were present more than Spanish governmental officials and knew Nahuatl better than any other Spanish group, I consider it quite likely that the Nahua church personnel developed their indigenous characteristics in the same spontaneous, mainly unintended way as the local municipal officials, abetted by a hands-off policy on the part of the priests, who spent much of their time in Spanish cities in any case.

The questions of just who was making equations and how conscious the process was becomes acute with the form Christian church precincts took in scores, indeed hundreds, of altepetl in central Mexico in the course of the sixteenth century. These elaborate complexes struck the eye as entirely European Christian. No overt preconquest emblems or building types remained. Yet the whole, a towering structure facing onto a huge enclosed patio set up for processions and open-air worship, with a platform in the center of the patio, corresponded to the preconquest model too closely for coincidence. Someone—perhaps on both sides—had consciously or unconsciously equated indigenous and European religious construction and worship patterns and achieved a solution which retained much of the earlier organization of space without leaving substantial evidence of preconquest influence on the surface. The Nahuas could readily feel at home in such a complex, yet there was nothing in it for the most orthodox Spanish Christian to object to. Each group could find its main expectations met.

In general, the fact that Spaniards could inspect Nahua religious art, displayed in a prominent place, without the barrier of language meant that it came much closer to Spanish criteria than the alphabetic texts the Nahuas wrote or the Spanish-style church and governmental organizations they operated. At times there was room for some play at the edges. In the frescoes of the Augustinian establishment at Malinalco,[5] done in the third quarter of the sixteenth century, the friars had laid out the outline of a garden apparently representing paradise, dominated by Christian monograms, with some other major Christian themes, and apparently left the rest to be filled in by the Nahua artists with appropriate birds, animals, foliage, and grotesquerie. Into this space the indigenous artists put, along with much Christian European material, depictions not only of highly prized indigenous plants and flowers, but also of stylized birds and bees that in preconquest lore specifically represented fortunate souls in the afterlife. They had understood the theme and had equated their own tradition with that of the Spaniards. A Nahua could read much meaning into what a Spaniard looking at the same composition would see as idyllic trivia.

As so often in these matters, it is hard or impossible to penetrate the subjective understanding of the Nahuas who

---

[5]See Peterson 1993.

were involved. Yes, they had in some fashion equated the Christian and the indigenous afterlife. Did they still imagine the Christian heaven as on the indigenous model? Or were they using a familiar vocabulary as a means of expression of something new, consonant with all the Christian devices in the composition?[6] And were the Spanish friars who organized the project aware of the non-Christian religious content of some of the motifs? I would tend to think they were not. The meaning of the traditional material is forever ambiguous, but almost precisely for that reason, it having been reduced to a secondary position, the Spaniards could tolerate it while the Nahuas appreciated it in another way.

As time went on the Spanish clergy's attitude toward the Nahuas' adaptations changed and developed. At first, at least in their public statements, the friars were overwhelmed with the favorable indigenous reaction, the eagerness to be baptized, the enthusiasm for building churches and taking part in all the ceremonies. By the last third of the sixteenth century they were seeing things with different eyes. They had learned Nahuatl and studied preconquest religion quite deeply, and now they knew that sweeping before the altar was not merely a touching demonstration of Christian faith, that the Nahuas' dances were full of pagan elements, that their understanding of everything about Christianity deviated from that of the Spaniards. Even so, the clerics largely accepted the compromise. Then in the eighteenth century a new wave of representatives of enlightened orthodoxy coming from Europe took yet another look, and the now well established compromises were declared to be pagan abominations, leading to attempts (not usually successful in the long run) to abolish many of the practices of Nahua Christianity.

It would be interesting to see how Double Mistaken Identity functioned in the third great realm of Nahua corporate life, the marketplace, but at present our knowledge is not nearly sufficient. My impression is that here Spanish and Nahua

---

[6]Analagous questions need to be asked in all the numerous cases where a Nahuatl word came to be the approximate equivalent of one in Spanish, or where a Spanish word came into Nahuatl (often developing meanings beyond those in the original language).

practices were very similar indeed, and that the role of reciprocal misunderstanding was less. Perhaps in coming years we will find sources good enough to prove that I am wrong.

I trust that I have made clear that my emphasis here on the continuing indigenous substratum of Spanish introductions as the sine qua non of their success among the native population at large by no means implies that no alteration of the original patterns took place. On the contrary, among the Nahuas the only thing as rare as the utter displacement of indigenous elements was their survival in completely unadulterated form. As we have seen, a number of Spanish words, concepts, and forms, however reinterpreted, entered so deeply into Nahua life that the Nahuas themselves no longer considered them in any way foreign or imposed. Across the generations, with constantly renewed and increased contact between Hispanic and indigenous populations, many "introductions" which at first were only the roughest equivalent of the Hispanic forms approached progressively closer to the original Spanish intention. In the matter of language this is particularly clear. The first Spanish loanwords in the sixteenth century were pronounced without the voiced stops and other sounds which Nahuatl lacked. Then over the centuries Nahuatl speakers mastered all of the special sounds of Spanish. And so it went with Spanish documentary genres too. On the other hand, some indigenous variants could remain strong or undergo recrudescence, as we have noted in matters of officeholding. There is every reason to believe that in the following centuries, as many once fully Nahua communities became Spanish-speaking and on the surface Hispanic in general culture, they retained numerous structures and patterns which were at least partially indigenous in origin, and retain them to this day. These developments would never have taken place (and on the periphery of the Spanish occupation in fact did not) had it not been for a whole range of phenomena in the cultural encounter similar enough that each party could operate for centuries on the unexamined, often quite false assumption that it was walking on familiar ground.

5. Trunk Lines and Feeder Lines: The Spanish Reaction to American Resources

(1991)

I T MAY SEEM strange to speak of sixteenth-century Spanish American behavior in the language of nineteenth- and twentieth-century railroads. But despite the anachronism, the terms have the right flavor of economically rational action working itself out in a context of markets, populations, raw and manufactured materials, and geographical realities. In a way we must account it a shame that Latin American history got its start with the extravagant language and often chimerical notions of the Italian Columbus. Actually, a strong realism, an active search for and exploitation of every economic possibility, were the norm for the Spaniards, and no less the Portuguese, though the latter were mainly employed elsewhere for most of the sixteenth century.

The Spaniards were far more pragmatic and quick to adjust to the new situation not only than Columbus himself but than the Italians in general, who remained centered in the Mediterranean and Europe. This was in fact a rational use of resources given Italian location, strengths, and possibilities. The Genoese (main Italian representatives in matters concerning America) were wedded to a set of procedures that had proved markedly successful from the eastern Mediterranean to West Africa and which they were not prepared to change. In fact, as they saw what was involved in America they increasingly pulled back to financing and indirect participation (it would probably be too much to say that the Spaniards pushed them out).[1] Much of the pragmatism and flexibility of the Spaniards had to do with the fact that, relatively speaking, from a very early time large numbers of them came, forming a whole sector in effect irrevocably committed to the new situation, devising its own solutions on the spot, beginning to build up its own traditions and techniques even if these were originally but variants of European models.

---

[1] Compare Verlinden 1970 and Pike 1966.

Our topic being resources, let us stop for a moment to consider what resources are. In a certain time and place certain raw materials, natural species, human populations, and climatic conditions either exist or they do not in a very unconditional way, but often that is not the decisive factor. First these things have to be recognized to exist. Then they must pass through technological, cultural, and economic filters before they can be considered meaningful resources for a given society at a given time. The indigenous societies are of course highly relevant in this respect, but from the point of view of colonization the society that comes directly into question is the European, specifically the Spanish, and most especially that segment of the Spanish population that was already in the Indies. Though differential immigration directly from Spain to various specific American regions was a crucial factor in the overall ensemble, it was determined not so much through weighing and sifting by Spaniards at home as through the differential success of the settlers, who called to their relatives and neighbors to come only where they had had good luck and could use them.

What resources mattered, then, depended in the first instance on who the immigrants were and what were their goals and needs. Almost from the beginning the immigrants were a broad selection of ordinary Spaniards from many occupations, ranks, and regions, increasingly including Spanish women as well. Their maximum goal, in many cases, was sooner or later to return wealthy to Spain. In fact, rarely did return prove possible, and the alternate goal was to live in the New World fully in the style of a high-ranking Spaniard.[2] In either case, the Spaniards of the Indies somehow had to gain leverage on the European economy, sending to Europe items which could be converted into large amounts of currency; to be spent directly in Spain if they were able to return, or to import European products which would make a Spanish lifestyle possible if they had to remain in the Indies. Let us not blame them for not producing everything they needed in the New World itself. The ever increasing but still

---

[2]See Lockhart and Otte 1976; Lockhart, "Letters and People to Spain," Chapter 3 in this volume; and Lockhart 1972.

limited number of local Spaniards contained only an insignificant fraction of the persons with relevant skills back in Europe, nor were the materials available identical, nor could the still nascent local market support the requisite specialization even when the skills and materials were available. The indigenous population was numerous, but it neither required that type of goods nor could pay for them in ways that would meaningfully reward the settlers.

To home in on what drove the conquerors and immigrants (for the two groups are one), what they were looking for, we need to look at what did *not* drive them. Popular stereotypes on exotic topics are not only as pernicious as weeds, they are as hardy, and must be combated anew each season. The Spaniards were not impelled by any light-hearted or reckless sense of adventure leading them to ignore the solid benefits of a given situation and strike out for wider spaces and fresh challenges. Those who were established stayed where they were; those who went on were the newly arrived and unestablished who had no choice. Even in recent and reputable works the group of men who went with Francisco Pizarro to conquer Peru can still be found called "adventurers," but quite some time ago I wrote a book demonstrating that they were no such thing.[3]

Because of the later prominence of these individuals, their lives can be traced, and I was ultimately able to track down the fates of the great majority. Those who were senior and best connected received the greatest monetary rewards and promptly went home therewith to create establishments. Most of the rest, junior or less well connected, stayed in Peru and did the same there, receiving the best encomiendas and becoming the leading citizens of the major Peruvian cities. Few indeed went anywhere else in the Indies. But a few did. Surely here would be some adventurers. In fact, however, certain major leaders who were serious rivals of the Pizarros (Hernando de Soto, Sebastián de Benalcázar) were pushed off to find their own areas to dominate, where they would be no threat to Pizarro hegemony. Practically all others who left central Peru for Chile or other destinations in the Indies were

---

[3]I refer to Lockhart, *The Men of Cajamarca* (1972).

regional compatriots and close allies of the Pizarros' greatest enemies, knowing full well that they would not receive good treatment, perhaps not even be tolerated, in Peru itself. We do find one person from Pizarro's homeland, with an impressive family name, Ulloa, who nevertheless went to Chile with Almagro. Here then, we might say, must be at least one adventurer among 167 pragmatists. But looking at the list of the division of gold and silver among the conquerors, we find that the wretched Ulloa received hardly a token share, far the smallest among the whole group. He lacked enough money to go home to Spain, was for whatever reason clearly in disgrace with the Pizarros, and did well to take his chances in Chile.

Nor were the Spaniards avid explorers intent on advancing world geographical knowledge and mapping. The best pilots among them were usually Italians, other Mediterraneans, Portuguese, or at least Basques and mariners, and if there was anything Spaniards held in lower esteem than a foreigner it was a sailor. Let me tell the story of my encounter many years ago now with the editors of *World Book Encyclopedia* over Vasco Núñez de Balboa. The encyclopedia had Balboa down as an explorer pure and simple, who allegedly sat at his doorstep as a child peering into the distance and dreaming of new discoveries in far lands. In the new article I wrote for them I called Balboa a conqueror rather than an explorer, which brought on stout resistance, and finally I had to compromise on "conqueror and explorer." No one ever deserved the epithet explorer less. Balboa probably never gave a thought to distant lands until internal family politics demanded that someone seek his fortune away from home. On the Caribbean coast of Tierra Firme he was long concerned with assigning encomiendas to his men and using the Indians to mine gold. The indigenous people virtually tugged at the hems of his clothing telling him that not far away was another vast ocean, on whose shores pearls were to be found, but as long as the Caribbean coast economy held up, he shrugged them off. When the population and the gold fields declined, he finally, in effect, asked the Indians "Where's this ocean you've been talking about?" They thereupon led him and a group of Spaniards a short distance along a trail well known to them, until approaching a large hill they said that the great sea on the other side could be seen from the top of it. Then in a staged performance the group in general was held back while Balboa went up to look first, followed by others in the order of seniority, each recorded in turn by a notary. Never was there a more unlikely explorer.[4] But Soto on the Florida expedition of 1539–42, or Gonzalo Pizarro on the Amazonian expedition of 1541–42, were no different; any new geographical knowledge was the lightly regarded byproduct of a pragmatic effort to find a good way to make a living, tantamount under the conditions to finding the combination of precious metal deposits and sedentary Indians.

Nor were the Spaniards excessively swayed by myths, whether ancient, medieval, or newly coined. Yes, the Amazons, El Dorado, the Land of Cinnamon, the Land of Seven Cities, and the Fountain of Youth do turn up. But we must keep things in proportion. Such legends were used to help justify to neophytes ultimately unsuccessful ventures off the main track *after* nearby major areas of interest had already been conquered and opened up, ventures of whose hopelessness those most in the know were already convinced, being not a whit deterred from the activities they had already undertaken in proven areas. They sometimes helped finance these "romantic" *entradas* precisely in the hope that the ignorant, newly arrived malcontents going on them would never come back. The romanticism grew in retrospect. The very late writer Bernal Díaz del Castillo says for the public that in the conquest of Mexico he was once reminded of the stories of Amadís of Gaul, the hero of chivalric novels,[5] but one can read ad infinitum in the contemporary reports of conquerors and early governors, or the private letters of early settlers, and find nothing of the sort. It was above all the Europeans back home, and among them above all non-Spaniards, who projected a whole series of stereotypes of the unknown and exotic onto America; those directly involved were far more realistic, though they too could speak the language of legend and turn it to their advantage.

It is hardly necessary to say that the Spaniards were not

[4]See Sauer 1966, chapter 11, especially p. 233.
[5]Díaz del Castillo 1947, p. 82.

distracted from resource exploitation by any military orientation. The conquerors were not professional or permanent soldiers by any means, and even in the heat of conquest they were business-minded and concerned above all with resources in the sense already explained. Nor was there any appreciable element of ideological or religious protest among them. A manifestation such as the half-demented Lope de Aguirre (on an Amazonian expedition of 1560) insulting the crown was the greatest rarity, something to be expected at most in an ultimately marginal situation, very late and very far from the centers.[6] The settler "rebellions" which took place in Peru were fights between interest groups (based mainly on Spanish regional affiliation and time of arrival in the new country) over the allocation of resources, all parties staying within the same framework of justification and basic allegiance. Except for some rather deeply submerged members of Jewish and Moorish minorities, I think the settlers were nearly one hundred percent loyal Spaniards and orthodox Christians, so that there was no inclination to accept, in the name of a cause, hardships and changes in material culture and general way of life, as may have been the case in some of the English colonies. In the Spanish Indies everyone wanted the same thing, and the settlers were distributed strictly according to who arrived first, who had the right skills and connections, and how much opportunity there was in a given place.

But if nearly all were true believers, was religious fervor a factor seriously affecting the utilization of resources? Surely not. Though the conquerors in their reports to the crown sometimes emphasized the great service they were performing in providing so many new candidates for Christianity, in the private letters which survive from them and other settlers, concern about the conversion of the Indians is conspicuously absent.[7] The settlers seem to have thought of their Christianity as they thought of their Spanishness, as a facet of their obviously superior culture, not something easily

---

[6]Compare Lockhart 1994, p. 162.

[7]See Lockhart and Otte 1976 and other letters Otte has published, referred to in the bibliography there.

imparted to anyone else or which they even expected to impart, nor something which was in the forefront of their minds. In their correspondence the divinity appears on every page, but almost always, even in the letters of clerics, it is in the hope that he will provide a safe journey, good health, many children, or a profitable business venture, meanwhile fending off calamities. A student of mine working with this literature once said that the Spaniards' concept of God seemed to be equivalent to good and bad luck. The religious beliefs of the majority, then, however pervasive, in no way impeded or even affected their economic activity.

When it comes to the clerics, especially in their corporate manifestation, things may seem different, but effects on the direction of the economy are hard to detect. The organized church presence was a function of the general Spanish presence. Bishoprics and provinces of the orders were established first and in greatest strength in precisely those areas where the lay Spaniards had already gone in greatest numbers for broadly economic reasons.[8] The organizations fed off and were fitted into that economy. Clerics often served as encomienda administrators and took part in much other business, including mining, as entrepreneurs and lenders. Donations from wealthy laymen, directly out of the local economy, were an important factor in the establishment of church organizations, often in conjunction with already existing or newly arranged kinship ties between clerics and local lay Spaniards.

We must, of course, consider the noisy campaigns carried on mainly by clerics to reorganize or weaken the encomienda and other labor devices, with great possible repercussions on the mining industry and its support system. These were to an extent internal church disputes. Those who arrived earlier cooperated and received rewards; those who arrived later received little and wanted to bring about changes to their own benefit, not unlike the lay Spaniards who arrived too late to receive encomiendas. And in fact, it was only where the existence of many lay Spaniards wanting access to resources created competition and pressures that changes urged on

---

[8]See A. C. van Oss 1978.

humanitarian/religious grounds by the more radical of the churchmen took effect. Indian slavery was abolished and the encomienda as the main vehicle of temporary labor procurement was gradually replaced in the course of the sixteenth century in central Mexico and many parts of Peru, where they were no longer adapted to the then existing economic and demographic conditions, but despite the campaigns these institutions held on for generations in a multitude of peripheral regions where they still represented an efficient way for thin local Spanish populations to utilize the resources available there. Doctrinal considerations on the part of the clergy were one element entering into political, social, and economic struggles concerning Spanish resource utilization, but in truth, one can predict the outcomes just as well without even including them in the calculations.

Nor did any severely anticommercial spirit or overemphasis on nobility keep the Spaniards from seeing and using the resources available to them. By the time they came to the Indies, the Spaniards had learned all the commercial lessons the Genoese had to teach them, and indeed I think they had understood and practiced most of this lore for a long time. Not only were there numerous professional merchants in the Indies representing transatlantic combines based in Spain, and other merchants starting out on their own, but commercialism had permeated the entire conqueror and settler population. Ordinary Spaniards knew all about credit operations whether lending, borrowing, or buying on credit; they constantly made various kinds of partnerships among themselves, whether for conquest, mining, or other ventures.

The Spanish urge for prominence definitely included a strong striving for nobility or *hidalguía*, and in both hemispheres we find what by the standards of some other European countries could be considered an inordinate number of people claiming to be and being accepted as nobles (*hidalgos*). But this was not incompatible with a thorough-going exploitation of local resources; indeed, standard expectations concerning hidalgo status fomented certain kinds of development. Whatever else we have been told at various times, the hidalgo was above all one who was wealthy in a very permanent and stable way. The hidalgo was expected to be the head of an estate and an establishment. At its core was the family or lineage, but that was no impediment to business. The family was precisely the best way of doing business then known, and the professional merchants themselves made it one of their primary organizing devices. It provided relatively trustworthy subordinates, even at a distance, and a natural chain of command. Since the Spanish family with its illegitimate members and poor relatives existed at several levels at once, there was a role for everyone and someone for all the roles, including managers, collectors, labor bosses, messenger boys and other underlings. The family's often extensive ties with other ranking families were extremely important for business purposes, not least in acquiring credit. The establishment also included servants and slaves, with emphasis on their permanent membership in the entourage. In the Indies, not only Africans but especially indigenous people were quickly pressed into this role, serving as intermediaries who were in intimate contact with every aspect of the local scene, giving the Spanish presence a dimension and ubiquitousness it would otherwise not have had. It is said that it was a permanent Indian employee of a Spaniard, a *yanacona*, who discovered the silver deposits of Potosí.[9]

In both Spain and America the strategy of the estate was to maintain permanence, security, integration, and perhaps a degree of dominance by involving itself in every locally profitable branch of endeavor currently in existence. In Spain, stockraising and agriculture were very important, because they were equally important in the economy generally, but ventures did not stop there, extending to urban real estate, investment in craft and mercantile enterprises, and ownership of government annuities. Holding vast amounts of land was not per se the emphasis; often stock and grazing rights were more valuable and central than land. It was simply a function of what yielded the best long-term revenue. In the New World, then, far less was there any pervasive greed for land as long as the local Hispanic market was severely restricted. Enough land was taken over to supply the Spaniards of the cities and mines with Spanish foods, but that

---

[9]Lockhart 1994, p. 249.

required only a tiny percent of the available usable land and yielded only a relatively modest profit, so that land and farming/ranching did not yet dominate Spanish estates of the conquest period. The emphasis was where it might well be, on mines when possible, either owning and running them, or backing them indirectly. But whereas merchants specialized in dealings permitting liquidity because they had to return the profits to the head of the firm in Seville, and persons of low rank, with few possibilities, were forced into specializing in transport, a truck garden, or a craft, estate owners at the higher rank invariably diversified, scouring the local situation for every potentially profitable opportunity.

I have previously used the example of the southern Peruvian encomendero Gerónimo de Villegas, who in addition to supplying the mines of Potosí worked others in the area of his encomienda grant, raised stock there for the Arequipa market, sold whatever he could directly to his Indians, speculated in urban real estate, maintained a company for ocean fishing and supply between his encomienda and Arequipa, and took part in the import-export trade, partly through his merchant-majordomo.[10] Villegas was unusual only in having left such a full record of his activity. Efraín Trelles has since shown that the Spaniard who both preceded and followed Villegas as holder of the encomienda did exactly the same things.[11]

Not all regions were as well endowed as southern Peru, however, and in these situations—the majority—the diversification emphasis in Spanish estate formation really came into its own, leading to a very broad and systematic search for every conceivable way of making money directly or indirectly. This took place within the already explained framework of looking for either an export product or something to sell to those who were already profiting from export products, but even so the surveys were broad, and indigenous products were not overlooked, nor even indigenous consumers, wherever they participated enough in the export economy to be able to pay cash. Murdo MacLeod has portrayed the

[10]Lockhart 1994, pp. 29–36.
[11]Trelles Aréstegui 1982.

process for Guatemala and the surrounding region, which after the exhaustion of precious metals and slave export involved balsam, wax, incense, cañafístula, sarsparilla, and other unlikely medicines, herbs, and resins before cacao, at first primarily for central Mexican Indian consumers, became the solution—for a while.[12] As MacLeod sees, the search went on in the same terms from the first moment the Spaniards arrived, with no change of mentalities or methods from conqueror to settler. Similar tales could be told of somewhat similarly situated Ecuador and northern Peru.

Iberian family/estate structure, always the same at the core, could be and readily was adapted to a thousand purposes depending on the local conditions; it appears in enterprises as exotic as growing coca, selling *chuñu* (Andean dried potatoes), or diving for pearls. The classic adaptation of the conquest period, however, was one in which the estate expanded to include vast numbers of unskilled temporary laborers—unskilled, that is, in the specific techniques of the enterprise, though skilled in their own often parallel enterprises, accustomed to the tasks of sedentary life, and available through existing mechanisms of indigenous government. A limited number of Spaniards of high or highish rank, with a full grasp of the whole enterprise and its social-economic-political context, owned and directed it; an almost equally limited number of lower-ranking Spaniards, non-Spanish Europeans, Africans, and permanently employed Indians beginning to feel the impact of Spanish culture had useful but partial expertise, serving as technicians, foremen, and cadre; and a mass of indigenous workers performed basic labor under close supervision on a temporary basis, not becoming a permanent part of the structure.

Population loss, changes in local markets, and growing technical demands gradually changed the proportions, but meanwhile organizations of this type gave impressive results, especially in mining for precious metals and in city construction. The system worked best when the tasks at the base were straightforward, uniform, and intensive rather than spread over the whole year, so that skill, responsibility, and perma-

---

[12]MacLeod, *Spanish Central America* (1973).

nence could be concentrated at the upper levels, in the still restricted sector of Hispanic and Hispanized people. If the operation was profitable enough (usually tantamount to being close to the export sector), and concentrated enough, the structure could do without the numerous lower level altogether. What it had the hardest time adapting to, even when considerable wealth was involved, was a situation where profit was not intensive per unit, yet great skill, spread over large parts of the year, was required by large numbers of people at the base of the process. Things were all the more difficult when the special technology involved was indigenous. In Mexico, cochineal production and chinampa agriculture (mud farming at the edge of a lake) are good examples of profitable activities highly resistant to Spanish estate organization.[13] For the Andes, scholarship has not yet delivered specific relevant studies. Spaniards entered directly into coca production, while raising highland crops and animals remained primarily in the hands of indigenous Andeans. Coca was the most profitable, but the highland food and animal complex also had economic potential, and it may be that the nature and locus of the related activities represented a considerable barrier to Spanish enterprise.

Spanish values, habits, and concepts, then, not only were generally compatible with a rational exploitation of the economic resources of the New World, but specifically led in that direction and contained organizational devices highly appropriate for the purpose. I wish to expatiate a bit more, however, on two false notions that show particular tenacity in the public mind: that the Spaniards had some special obsession with precious metals, a "lust for gold," and that they had an unhealthy preoccupation with goods of specifically Spanish or European origin.

Now as to gold, in the first place, the Spaniards were soon to give overwhelming emphasis to silver, because there was infinitely more of it. But even in the initial stages in many areas, when the reliance indeed was on gold, there was no obsession with it in the sense of wanting to keep it, rub it, gaze at it; rather it was treated simply as money and an export

---

[13]See Hamnett 1971 and Gibson 1964, pp. 320–21.

product. The initial impetus toward it was neither a medieval admiration of the metal nor a reconquest concern for "booty," but the fact that of all the things the indigenous population in the Antilles and Tierra Firme knew and valued, this was the only one to the purpose. If any further conceptual framework was needed, it was provided by the analogy with Africa, which Columbus with his African experience, not to speak of any other Italians and Portuguese present, immediately brought to bear. The export products that the West African coast had supplied the Portuguese were gold, slaves, and exotic items such as tropical woods and ivory. The Spaniards gave them all a try, but the woods of the Caribbean islands were mainly not suitable, and the Indians died from lack of immunities to European disease before they could be transported back to Spain for sale as slaves (one important reason why it was possible within a generation or two to abolish Indian slavery in the central areas of the Indies). Gold was a big success, and it required relatively little capital investment together with a relatively small amount of expertise. Even Peru and Mexico were to rely ephemerally on gold until their silver mines could be developed.

But gold *was* an industrial enterprise. In Africa the Portuguese merely traded with the local population for the metal; the Africans carried on quite intensive production themselves. In the Caribbean and other American placer-mining areas, current indigenous production was slight, and on the other hand, the Spaniards were able to occupy the entire area, came in greater numbers, and had a greater need. They were in effect forced into a direct involvement with production; but they were up to the challenge. The yield paid their debts, rewarded them, and attracted many new immigrants from Spain before exhaustion of the deposits. The Spaniards must have done a reasonable job of exploitation, since the fields they abandoned were rarely to be worked again in succeeding centuries.

And if gold mining was already production rather than extraction, silver mining was a full-scale industry. It was highly technical, it required a great deal of machinery together with sophisticated experimentation and adaptation, and it involved a complex sequence of separate processes. It was large-scale and long lasting at the same site. It called for extensive systematic prospecting and expert assaying; most of the Mexican industry was located far away from the centers of indigenous population at sites not previously worked or even known. Even in Peru the greatest site had not been worked by the Incas. Silver mining demanded great amounts of capital investment far in advance of a return, and the investment was forthcoming, since there was the legitimate expectation of a vast profit. Improvements needed could be projects as huge as the *socovones* or adit tunnels cut into hillsides to intersect with vertical shafts, and they could affect the whole landscape, like the dams, reservoirs, and aqueducts making it possible for Potosí to use water power in its stamp mills.[14] The final product, nearly as negotiable as money, deserves a better name than "raw material," and silver was indeed being minted in both Peru and Mexico long before the end of the sixteenth century.

We might ask if sugar was not a realistic alternative or complement. Although a different order of activity, that is, one neither using an indigenous raw material nor practiced among the indigenous people, sugar production was an important part of the Portuguese West African complex that served as the immediate precedent for the exploitation of the Indies; indeed, it was on its way to becoming the *most* important part. Subsequent centuries have shown that the Antilles are a quite decent place to grow sugar, and the seaside location was also favorable. Cane fields and sugar mills did make their appearance in the Caribbean phase, often with the help and participation of the Genoese, long the main spreaders of the sugar industry.[15] But as an export enterprise sugar did not flourish; sugar production in the Spanish Indies was to be primarily for internal markets generated by silver, as with the sugar grown on the northern coast of Peru.

I attribute this result above all to the prior existence of a viable Portuguese industry on the islands off Africa, already adequately supplying the then small demand for sugar in

---

[14]See Bakewell 1984a, pp. 110–13.
[15]See Otte 1965 and Pike 1966.

Europe.[16] The Portuguese had a lead in techniques, plant, market contacts, and all the rest. At the time, the Portuguese were also closer to the market (after the creation of the Brazilian industry in the late sixteenth century this would no longer be true). In the Caribbean, the reputation of the Indies was just getting established, sufficient lines of credit were not available, and a low-investment business like gold was much more attractive than a notably high-investment enterprise like sugar. Later, capital was in some sense available, but it was already being poured with excellent results into the silver industry; furthermore, in sugar one still faced a formidable established competitor, in silver none at all. Location alone precluded the export of sugar from Peru in the sixteenth century, and the inland producing areas of Mexico were in the same situation. Thus the Spaniards within hardly two generations after their first glimpse of the New World had discovered the dimensions of its primary, indeed essentially only great export resource for sixteenth-century Europe and created a complex major industry which successfully exploited it.

Turning to the question of the preference of the Spaniards in the Indies for European imports, I reiterate that the accumulation of experience all over Europe, the availability of long used and tried materials, together with the size of the European market and the great pool of people with expertise, inevitably meant that European-style goods produced in Europe would be more varied and of higher quality than those that local Spaniards tried to produce for themselves. In many cases it would simply prove impossible to produce close equivalents. Some crucial raw materials were entirely lacking, such as iron, not then known to exist in the hemisphere. Local Spaniards did what they could, manufacturing many items from imported or used iron rather than importing finished products, as well as tailoring imported fine cloths locally. We must remember how different the situation was than in many struggling settlements Europeans would later establish in other parts of the world; the Spaniards of the

---

[16]Compare Stuart B. Schwartz, *Sugar Plantations in the Formation of Brazilian Society* (1985), pp. 3–27.

central regions of the Indies, because of their spectacularly successful export industry, had the purchasing power to import relatively large amounts of high-quality European goods. Few settlers elsewhere were to have such possibilities.

Some goods, too perishable or too bulky, proved impractical to import from Europe into Spanish America. In such cases the Spanish reaction was to produce the item in the Indies rather than to resort to use of the closest indigenous equivalent. Eating maize or wearing items of indigenous clothing were emergency measures. Foods were the main item affected, and the production of European meat, grain, vegetables and fruits became an essential branch of the economy, not for export of course, which would have been even more impossible than import, but to supply local Spaniards who could pay from the profits of export. A cultural criterion is clearly at work here rather than what one could call a purely economic one, yet cultural criteria determine value and price in all economies, including ours, especially when it comes to food and dress. The Indians too were slow to change in these respects.[17] The resource in these cases is an environment where the European plant or animal variety can successfully reproduce, and the Spaniards with a great deal of active searching and experimentation found such environments somewhere in the general vicinity of each of the two great central areas. The products aroused no complaint in the consumers. Buildings could not be imported either, nor on the west coast ships, so that local production soon began to flourish in both these major branches of the economy.

When something could be imported but was too expensive for the generality of the settlers or for everyday use by the wealthy, the solution was to import as much as could be afforded and seek to produce local surrogates for the rest of the need. This led by the second generation to textile works called *obrajes*, mainly using locally produced European wool, supplying the lower end of the Indies market. The same thing happened with wine; in due course Arequipa and Chile were producing wines which could not compete directly with the Spanish originals but found sales nevertheless. One could

---

[17]Compare Super 1988.

discuss whether to call wine a product, a value, a habit, or a need, but by all the evidence of history it takes time to develop a distinguished wine and also a palate for it, and I think that both the Castilians' preference for their own sherries and their valiant efforts to duplicate them meet general world standards very well. Above I said that the holders of great estates could be counted on to involve themselves to some extent in everything remotely profitable in a given region, so they are indeed found participating in the import-substitution business, but the latter was the special province of those of lesser standing, with less capital, education, and connections, or those located in out-of-the-way areas, who were not well placed to take a direct part in the import-export economy and thus sought to profit from it indirectly.

Spanish society in the Indies was import-export oriented at the very base and in every aspect. The silver industry was the ultimate source of economic wellbeing of most of the Spaniards, whose whole distribution across two continents makes sense only in terms of location with respect to silver deposits. Production for local consumption ultimately depended on what was too expensive or too bulky to import from Europe. One can only smile at the naiveté of those who debate over whether to put the entry of Latin America into the world import-export market in the late nineteenth century or in the twentieth.

It may be that what we sometimes call "values" are ordered in the same sense as logical or linguistic processes, that without one being exactly more important than another, some apply earlier, some later. For the development of the Indies the value that came first was to establish one's family permanently in the most solid way possible in the normal Spanish fashion, if possible in one's hometown in Spain, or if not then in a major center of the Indies. To do so required money, and that required finding and exploiting the assets with leverage on Europe of which we have already spoken. As Bakewell has pointed out, this drive goes far to explain the incredibly rapid Spanish expansion over so much of two continents.[18]

---

[18]Bakewell 1984a, p. 108.

I would go even further than Bakewell does when he speaks of the Spaniards' occupation of their portion of the New World. The Spaniards in fact quickly surveyed the entire hemisphere for areas with the requisite qualities and more or less consciously left to whoever wanted them those parts found lacking, that is, without any apparent major export product or facilities for supplying an export-producing region. Spaniards went to wealthy areas and avoided poor ones, which was possible and natural because immigration was primarily spontaneous, by family and region of origin. The government had little to do with the content and direction of the flow. If we want to see what happened when it did occasionally intervene, we can look at the attempt inspired by fray Bartolomé de las Casas to get Spaniards to go to be small farmers in the hopeless fringe area of Venezuela, which was not only not well located with respect to markets (in sixteenth-century terms) but had a mobile and hostile Indian population, so that the spontaneous stream of Spanish immigration largely bypassed the region. Few recruits signed up; of those a large proportion deserted in Santo Domingo on being apprised of some of the realities of the Indies, and the rest left after finding out the unviability of the enterprise in situ.[19]

Some of the values imagined to conflict with resource exploitation really did not exist (love of adventure and exploration), others surely did exist in small measure or large, but they literally did not affect the basic process. Following the nexus of personal-familial ambition and money, the Spaniards went to certain places, not to others, and carried out certain economic activities, not others; additional factors came into play only in that context, in those places, and concerning that activity. Whatever importance one may give to controversies over religious indoctrination, the encomienda, or mining labor, they are all in this sense secondary, as they show by invariably lagging chronologically in any given area. And they are only partial expressions, one group taking a position against something in

---

[19]See Lewis Hanke, *The Spanish Struggle for Justice* (1949), Chapter 5, and Enrique Otte, *Las perlas del Caribe* (1977), pp. 184–85, 276.

self-interest, another supporting it for the same reason. Thus encomenderos can appear anticommercial despite their own extensive commercial activity because they as principal consumers often tried to set low prices for the merchants and artisans who supplied them.

A crucial resource not yet fully taken into account here is the indigenous population, which is a large topic in itself and one on which I have spent most of my waking hours for many years. We have already seen that Indians could not be exported to Europe as slaves in the manner of Africans, at root because of their low survival rate. Although they were a primary determinant of what the Spaniards could and could not do and a very important factor in attracting or deterring immigration and in determining the Spanish settlement pattern, in the Spanish resource perspective they were secondary. Hardly any of their products were exportable, and even in the case of the one that was, precious metals, their procedures unchanged would not sustain an adequate level of production. This was true even in Upper Peru, where Indians contributed mightily to mining techniques in the early period. If we had only the Peruvian example, we might tend to believe that the silver industry could not have operated without Indian inputs of technology and manpower. The Mexican example, on the other hand, inclines one to think that the Spaniards could and would have mined silver using only themselves, their own methods, and imported laborers, as the Portuguese did in the Brazilian sugar industry.

As it happened, the silver deposits were located in the general vicinity of the areas of the densest, most highly organized and most sedentary Indian populations, which thereby came to be a basic, integral part of the general complex in both cases. Though Mexican mine workers of the sixteenth century left their homes, towns, and many of their organizational devices and techniques behind them in central Mexico, it was still central Mexican Indians who provided the base of the mining labor force. Peruvian Indians did the same without abandoning their homes or political units permanently (some, it is true, became full-time miners). In both cases the area of sedentary indigenous settlement provided an environment in which to establish a series of Hispanic cities as the permanent base of the bulk of the Spaniards who in one way or another lived from the silver industry.

The various cultivated plants developed over the centuries by the indigenous societies were an enormous potential resource. Many varieties had unique properties, and the agriculture of Mexico and Peru has been judged among the most productive in the world. From the point of view of affecting colonization, however, indigenous crops became important only to the extent that there was a market for them in Europe, or as a second best a market among local Spaniards, or failing that, enough Indians participating in the silver economy and wanting the product that they became a viable market in that particular case. Actually, the process usually started with the last possibility and gradually led, if at all, to the others. Since preconquest times both the Andes and Mexico had known, in addition to their staples, certain crops and goods which were in special demand because they were not available in all regions or took special skills to produce; complex systems of regional exchange had evolved. Although some products, such as warrior outfits or jaguar skins, quickly faded out after the conquest, others, such as cacao, pulque, and cotton cloth in Mexico, and coca and textiles in the Andes, remained important to indigenous life. Indigenous people who worked for Spaniards, whether in the mines or elsewhere, or sold things to them, thereby acquiring money, spent it above all on such items. As more and more of the indigenous population came into direct contact with the Spanish economy, money began to circulate in indigenous society generally (we find cash sale in local indigenous markets of Mexico before 1550),[20] so that even Indians not directly touched by the Spanish economy could pay cash for certain things.

Spaniards were quick to see the possibilities. The Indians of central Mexico were the principal market for the cotton *mantas* (cloaks, lengths of cloth) sent from Yucatan and the cacao sent from Guatemala, produced in the traditional fashion and acquired through tribute, so that it was the central Mexican Indians who were sustaining the encomenderos of those marginal regions, as well as some lower-

---

[20]See Anderson, Berdan, and Lockhart 1976, pp. 138–49, 208–13.

ranking Spaniards from central Mexico who became traders in the items. The greatest bonanza of this type, though, was in Peru. There, because of the relative closeness of the silver deposits to the bulk of the indigenous population, combined with the concentrated nature of the deposits, very large numbers of Indians moved in and out of a single site and had access to meaningful amounts of silver, creating a powerful secondary market not only for indigenous prestige items (coca and textiles), but for ordinary provisions including dried potatoes and other Andean foods. As in Mexico, encomenderos and lowly traders both entered the trade, but with more spectacular results, including the creation of some true fortunes, and consequently there was an earlier attempt on the part of the Spaniards to intervene in production, especially with coca, where Spanish enterprises arose, owned by encomenderos and others, combining indigenous technical lore with European organizational principles.[21] Thus though Spanish enterprises generally aimed at Spaniards as consumers, this was only because they had more money, and when Indians had sufficient, the process was the same even though Spaniards might have no direct interest at all in the product, as was the case with coca through the whole colonial period.

When, however, local Spaniards took to using a given indigenous product, Spanish economic interest in it rose accordingly. They never did warm to maize or potatoes, unless highly doctored in specialty dishes, but at some unidentified point they became convinced, the Mexican Spaniards first, of the virtues of cacao. The result was the development of Spanish-style cacao-growing estates, first in Venezuela and ultimately in Guayaquil, producing primarily for the Spanish Mexican market.

With that foothold, cacao then later won over the European market, becoming a viable primary export product. But for better or worse, Europe long remained oblivious of or resistant to the merits of New World crops. It was not yet the time when the tomato would revolutionize Italian cooking, the potato would become a staple food in Ireland and Poland, and maize would feed the world's meat animals. Perhaps the

---

[21]See Lockhart 1994, pp. 27–28.

Spaniards of the Indies were remiss in not campaigning more actively, distributing brochures and free samples all over Europe. But such was not the way of the age, and in any case, the American Spaniards lacked motivation. These great contributions were to be simple donations, from which the Indies would profit not a whit, because the crops involved were untransportable or lacked the specific value to repay transport, and in any case they could be grown in Europe. If anything of this nature was to be sold to Europe it must not only be wanted there, it must have high specific value and not be produceable there. In the sixteenth century only Mexican cochineal, a quasi-agricultural product and useful textile dye, came close to filling the bill, but the truly great interest in textile dyes was to come in later centuries, and the process was so labor-intensive and environment-specific that it resisted Spanish estate organization; production remained mainly in the hands of Indians, and Spaniards acquired the dye through purchase or demanding it as tribute.[22]

We now come at last to the phenomena mentioned in my title. As the result of spontaneous immigration for economic reasons, the primacy of silver, and the very strong secondary pull of the sedentary indigenous groups, those regions which combined silver and sedentary Indians quickly became what I have elsewhere called simply the central areas of Spanish occupation, with all else constituting a fringe.[23] When we look closely, however, we see a division within the central areas themselves. The great majority of the Spaniards in the Indies were distributed along two lines—one for each central area—leading from an Atlantic port to the silver deposits, what I call the trunk lines,[24] and Spaniards who were anywhere else were there more or less by mistake and from lack of choice,

---

[22]For some facets of the industry see Hamnett 1971.

[23]The concepts and their application are explained in some detail in Lockhart, "Social Organization and Social Change in Colonial Spanish America" (1984), and used as basic principles in Lockhart and Schwartz, *Early Latin America* (1983).

[24]I first used this term in the introduction to Ida Altman and James Lockhart, eds., *Provinces of Early Mexico* (1976), p. 7 (also p. 5). In Lockhart and Schwartz 1983, the concept is central and copiously illustrated, but the term is not much used.

having wrongly thought that other regions would prove as advantageous and then being left stranded, or arriving late, without connections or skills, and being pushed off to the edges.

The trunk lines do not, however, follow the straightest possible route to the mines, but take into consideration the good lands of sedentary indigenous settlement, in or around which is found a capital city acting as the hub of the route and of the whole Spanish presence. The silver sites did not themselves become the capitals despite having relative permanence because they were in inhospitable locations and at the end of the line, whereas a central, amenable location was what was required as a headquarters on many counts—for conquerors, encomenderos, and entrepreneurs who wanted to establish permanent family estates; for merchants who needed to be in touch with their superiors and source of supply in Spain; for the providers of services from craftsmen to lawyers, who needed to be located where they would be available to the whole system. Once the Spanish population and especially the wealthiest portion of it was concentrating in the two capitals, the main market for goods and services was there even though it was ultimately sustained by the silver mines.[25] Governmental and church organizations naturally followed suit in the location of their headquarters, for reasons too numerous to detail here; let it be clear that

---

[25]A market in the sense I mean here is determined by the ability to pay in silver, not by the number of people wanting the goods or services. Sometimes modern economists are shocked at what a small percentage of overall economic activity had to do with import-export and trunk line activity, and are inclined to downgrade its importance or say it affected only a small minority of upper-ranking Spaniards. On the contrary, it affected everyone everywhere. As we have seen, indigenous people in and near Mexico City, Lima, and Potosí were a coveted market for Spaniards in far distant areas, who employed a significant part of the population there in the attempt to supply them, because they could pay in silver. Likewise the indigenous people on the trunk line paid higher taxes than those off it. Even on insignificant-looking, unprosperous spurs of the trunk line, social, economic, political, ethnic, and religious affairs were different than for more isolated neighboring districts (see Chapter 11 in this volume, pp. 318–20).

they were attracted to the trunk line centers after the latter had already taken shape, not the other way around. The conquerors and other immigrants for their own reasons had already made Lima and Mexico City their principal seats before the arrival of Audiencias, viceroys, and archbishops.

Indeed, these trunk line complexes responding spontaneously to social and economic imperatives were the framework and partial determinant of everything else the Spaniards did; when the first universities, printing presses, or theaters appear, we know exactly where to expect them. It has been shown that the earliest cathedrals completed were regularly along the trunk line.[26] The effect of liquid wealth flowing back and forth along an extended line was to draw organizations of all kinds more tightly together across great distances than would happen in other regions. Elsewhere I have referred to this phenomenon as "major consolidation."[27] Communications were better; hierarchies of all kinds, commercial or institutional, stiffened, always being concentrated in the capital, and family connections too were stronger and intermarriages more frequent across distance, everyone aiming for a foothold in the capital.[28] The great

---

[26]Van Oss 1978 (The fact is shown but not fully comprehended).

[27]Lockhart 1984, p. 311.

[28]See Bronner 1977 and Davies 1984 for illustrations of this phenomenon.

The capital can seem to dominate the scene overwhelmingly, drawing all our attention, but we should not forget that major consolidation is a phenomenon affecting a macroregion as a whole. The leading city was surely a hub, but it would have been quite insignificant without the ties that ran from it and through it to all parts of the system. Appearing dominant, it was also dependent, for people, for supplies, for bullion, and even for secondary markets important to many of its citizens. It sent representatives out to do its bidding in the provinces, but successful people from the provinces were forever coming to the capital and reaching the top. When a vast area by means of the trunk line attained major consolidation, the flow back and forth that characterized any normal provincial city jurisdiction and made it a functioning unit, and not just a rural district being acted on by a city, came to operate country-wide, creating the same sort of indivisibility at that level. Marginalization and attraction, the great processes creating regional ties and differentiation at all levels, operated over the entire Indies centered on

wealth flowing along the trunk line, created by silver production, Europe's interest in the silver, and the local Spanish
population's need for the things of Europe, was thus a powerful force for concentration, consolidation, unification. When
wealth and production were less, concentration was less, as
with the gold fields of New Granada, where the complex never
developed a single overwhelmingly predominant route or
central city.

Those who ended up off the trunk line, since they were not
members of an explorers' club or worshippers of the simple
life, did their best to participate in trunk line activity and the
flow of silver there by selling whatever they could to the
people on the main line and using the profits to buy European
goods, sometimes directly from Spain, sometimes from firms
based on the trunk line. In Mexico the line ran through
Veracruz, Puebla, Mexico City, and on to the mines of the
north, of which there were several districts, with Zacatecas
long leading. The already mentioned orientation of Yucatan
and Guatemala toward central Mexico through the sale of
indigenous goods gave rise to typical feeder lines.[29] Yucatan
and Guatemala, though well populated at contact, with highly
organized, easily utilized indigenous societies, attracted a
relatively modest flow of Spanish immigration in view of
their disadvantageous location with respect to the silver line,
but they did have the advantage that because of geographical
differences their areas had products in demand by the
indigenous population of the trunk line area.

Oaxaca, on the other hand, was a fertile temperate region
hardly any different from Puebla or the Valley of Mexico and
hence had nothing to sell to either the Spaniards or the
Indians there. From a very humble start, Puebla, straddling
the trunk line half way between the port and the capital,

---

the trunk lines in all their extension and not just the capitals. (See
Lockhart 1984, p. 304.)

[29]I recognize that here the analogy is not complete. A feeder line
in the usual sense would send traffic into the entire larger system,
whereas in this case goods and people coming in on the secondary
routes typically go no farther than the nearest center of consumption, usually mining districts, the two capitals, or other major urban
centers located on the trunk line.

became a metropolis at times almost rivaling Mexico City,[30] whereas Oaxaca, far off the line, stagnated until enlarged European demand created a cochineal boom in the eighteenth century. From the point of view of Spanish colonization, immigration and economic development in Oaxaca were long minimal. From the indigenous point of view, lands, autonomy, structures and patterns of all kinds were preserved longer than in central Mexico, and so it went in general everywhere off the trunk line. William Taylor has shown us many dimensions of the greater and earlier impact of Spanish life on the indigenous population in central Mexico than in Oaxaca,[31] the whole difference being ultimately attributable to the trunk line. The trunk line effect developed also in new areas, where Spaniards and sedentary Indians were moving into previously thinly settled spots and starting fresh. By the seventeenth and eighteenth centuries in northwestern Mexico, where by then a branch of the trunk line went to the mines of Durango and Parral, parishes were more populous and more closely spaced, and personal mobility greater, on the line than off it.[32]

The Peruvian trunk line was somewhat more complex than the Mexican. Its "Atlantic port" was a combination of Cartagena and Panamá, neither anywhere near Peru and one not even facing the Atlantic, and its capital was Lima, not in the center of the sedentary lands where we might expect it to be, but the Peruvian system did have a more satisfactory terminus than the Mexican, ending resoundingly and unambiguously at Potosí. Andean geography, both the high altitude of the interior and the difficulty of land travel there, induced the Spaniards to abandon their original inclination to put their capital in Cuzco or Jauja and establish themselves on the

---

[30]Both great capitals were able to maintain their position from the early sixteenth century until today. In the seventeenth century, though, Puebla gave Mexico City a run for its money for a while, for it had much the same characteristics as to climate, indigenous population, and agricultural supply, and it was closer to the port. Had it won out, little would have changed in the system as a whole.

[31]William B. Taylor, *Drinking, Homicide and Rebellion* (1979), and *Landlord and Peasant in Colonial Oaxaca* (1972).

[32]Swann 1982.

coast instead. Thus the trunk line was to bypass a great portion of the central Andean indigenous population, most of
which was to be in a situation more like Oaxaca and Guatemala than like the Valley of Mexico and the Puebla region.

A serious but not uncommon misconception about the Peruvian system is that the main route from Lima to Potosí
went inland straight through Cuzco. Actually, from the first
the main route went south from Lima by sea, then inland
through Arequipa and La Paz; later, a good portion of the
traffic was diverted even farther south by sea before going
across land to Potosí. Huancavelica as the producer of mercury (needed in refining) was practically an adjunct of the
silver industry and the trunk line, but generally speaking the
Peruvian inland, including Cuzco, resorted to typical feeder
line activity. As mentioned before, the rewards of such activity under the southern Peruvian circumstances could be large,
but the effects of this trade could not transform the basic
situation. If the trunk line had really gone directly through
Cuzco, that city would have moved a great deal further in the
direction of Puebla than it did. Quito, not only off the trunk
line but far removed from both capital and mines, lived an
existence closely comparable to the far south of the Mexican
sphere.

The facts of Peruvian geography had large implications for
surrounding regions. Not enough areas close to Potosí were
propitious for European livestock and temperate crops, so the
opportunity existed for a relatively intense development of
otherwise unremarkable Tucumán off to the southeast on the
basis of cattle, mules, and artisan products. Lima lacked an
adequate agricultural hinterland, so that eventually Chile,
far away but reachable by sea, took up the slack in wheat
production.[33] We see here that though indigenous products are
perhaps typically the basis of feeder line activity, such is not
necessarily the case. Both Peruvian and Mexican systems,
then, eventually included feeder lines extending long distances across both land and sea, carrying both Spanish-style
and indigenous products, making possible Spanish coloni-

---

[33]Borde and Góngora, *Evolución de la propiedad rural en el Valle
del Puangue* (1956).

zation of a type that could have been sustained in the peripheral regions in no other way.[34]

Turning now briefly to the historiography of these matters, I will concentrate on the sixteenth century, not only because it is on the early period that the weight of attention falls in the present article, but because it is the epoch of the greatest historiographical need. We know enough by now to realize that there is a continuous social and economic history leading from the first moments of the arrival of Spaniards among Indians unbroken into the following centuries: in estate history, mining, commerce, crafts, in everything. Those first moments and decades cannot be said to have determined what happened later, but they shaped and gave precedent for later developments and in that sense have and always will have a kind of primacy. Moreover, it is already clear that the deeds of the conquest period, on both Spanish and indigenous sides, were carried out in the same spirit as the more obviously routine activities of later generations.[35] Yet realistic, adequate studies concentrate overwhelmingly on later times. When some years ago Ida Altman and I were putting together an anthology of original pieces on regions of Mexico in the postconquest centuries,[36] we discovered that we had not a single contribution on the conquest period. Despite some back-

---

[34] A sort of back-door trunk line developed from Buenos Aires in the direction of Potosí in the middle colonial period, bringing slaves from Africa and allowing the Portuguese to participate in trade with the silver mines. In the late eighteenth century, beyond the temporal scope of this article, the Buenos Aires route became, because of changes in sea transportation technology, the main outlet for silver, and at that point a full-scale trunk line, very much like the earlier ones centered on Mexico and Peru, promptly began to develop.

[35] For the illustration of this point in the area of estate organization, see my "Encomienda and Hacienda," Chapter 1 in this volume. (My "The Merchants of Early Spanish America: Continuity and Change," written later and also included here, as Chapter 6, does somewhat the same for aspects of commerce. My *We People Here* [1993] begins to make the same kind of points for the indigenous world of central Mexico.)

[36] Altman and Lockhart 1976. At that time, not enough regionally oriented studies existed for Peru to make a comparable volume feasible for that country, but things have changed, and it would be highly desirable for one to be organized.

ground discussions, none of the studies involved primary research on any time before about 1570 or 1580. The picture for Peru is similar, but with several notable exceptions. The historiographical break is not so much between sixteenth and seventeenth centuries as between the conquest period going up to perhaps 1560, '70, or '80 depending on the place, and the mature period beginning thereafter. Peter Bakewell and Steve Stern, for example, have made large contributions to the socioeconomic history of early Spanish America, writing books on Peruvian and Mexican topics which go chronologically from the beginning into the seventeenth century, but those books begin to become noticeably more thick, original, and close to the data around the time of which I speak.[37]

Never was Charles Gibson, whom I greatly admire, so wrong as in his belief that the history of the conquest period was virtually exhausted. The historical literature on the topic is mainly written some generations ago, or in that manner, consisting of conquest narrative and history of church and governmental activity. To one side is a body of writing mainly by anthropologists, touching the conquest period but mainly concerned with preconquest indigenous antiquities; this genre has been meaningfully renovated in recent years with new approaches and sources but has tended to retain its preconquest emphasis and exclusively indigenist focus.[38] Not only is the more Spanish-oriented part of the existing historical literature (Prescott, Aiton, Ricard, etc.)[39] often naive and unanalytical and in need of redoing on that score, but it leaves nearly the whole social and economic dimension out of

---

[37]I refer to Stern's *Peru's Indian Peoples and the Challenge of Spanish Conquest: Huamanga to 1640* (1982), and Bakewell's *Silver Mining and Society in Colonial Mexico: Zacatecas, 1546–1700* (1971), and *Miners of the Red Mountain: Indian Labor in Potosí, 1545–1650* (1984).

[38]Leaders in the renovation, to mention only two, have been John Murra for the Andes and Pedro Carrasco for Mesoamerica.

[39]I refer, as the experienced reader will already have recognized, to William Prescott's famous histories of the conquests of Mexico and Peru, Arthur Aiton's biography of Mexican viceroy don Antonio de Mendoza, and Robert Ricard's work on mendicant activity in Mexico. The older literature devotes far more attention to Mexico than to Peru.

consideration. There are some works of an aggregate statistical nature: Chaunu on shipping and Boyd-Bowman on emigration from Spain (note that statistical demography of Indians becomes something approaching an exact science only for the time after the conquest period). Trends in absolute amounts are an important part of the whole picture, but not only are the figures given highly fragmentary, they do not touch on and do not replace an understanding of structures, organizations, operating concepts, practices, and lives. Consider the heroic but somewhat less than satisfactory attempt of Lyle McAlister to write the social and economic history of the immigrants on the basis of Boyd-Bowman alone.

The corpus of work in the Spanish American field which takes the whole range of activity of the conquest period as its scope and studies it as it actually was is very small. There is Enrique Otte with his many articles on commercial activity in the early Caribbean, and especially his book showing even the ephemeral and apparently exotic pearl industry of Cubagua to be a perfect illustration of all the patterns I have beendiscussing.[40] There is José Miranda on economic activity of encomenderos in early Mexico on the basis of notarial records.[41] There is the work of Mario Góngora on early Panama and his book studying the landholdings and enterprises of encomenderos and others in Chile, especially important for showing the gradual rise of later estate forms out of patterns of the conquest period.[42] I have worked, quite a while back now, on the society and economy set up by the Spaniards in

[40]Otte 1977 and 1967 and Lockhart and Otte 1976 contain bibliographical references which will lead the reader to his extensive article production. (Since this was written, a large part of Otte's accomplishment has been incorporated and summarized in his *Sevilla y sus mercaderes a fines de la Edad Media* [1996]).

[41]José Miranda, *La función económica del encomendero en los orígenes del régimen colonial. Nueva España (1525–1531)* (1965).

[42]Góngora, *Los grupos de conquistadores en Tierra Firme (1509–1530)* (1962), and *Encomenderos y estancieros: estudios acerca de la constitución social aristocrática de Chile después de la Conquista, 1580–1660* (1971). The latter deals primarily with a time well after the conquest period proper, but in Chile as in comparable areas phenomena of that period extend forward in time further and with a less sharp distinction of epochs than in central areas.

Peru in the first thirty years after arrival.[43] One should not forget Richard Greenleaf's research related to the early Mexican Inquisition, which though it seems so different from the rest manages, through using specific litigation, to get at the level of actual individuals and the political, social, and economic factors affecting inquisitory action.[44]

To this by now basic corpus there have been some recent important additions. One is a study by Robert Himmerich y Valencia of the holders of encomiendas in New Spain to the 1550's.[45] Another is a work by Keith Davies on the history of

---

[43]Lockhart, *Spanish Peru* (1968, 1994); *The Men of Cajamarca* (1972).

[44]Richard E. Greenleaf, *The Mexican Inquisition of the Sixteenth Century* (1969), and other books.

[45]Himmerich's "The Encomenderos of New Spain" (1983) was later published as *The Encomenderos of New Spain, 1521–1555* (1991). In view of the nature of the volume for which this article was originally written, I have given preference to Peruvianist works in my historiographical discussions in the text proper, but it seems appropriate to describe Himmerich's study at some length in this note because it would be highly desirable to have a similar work for early Peru.

One thing that one could reasonably expect to have been done long since by way of filling a great gap is a Mexican equivalent of my work on Peru, that is, a general survey of conquest society in Mexico. This Himmerich set out to do, but came up against the fact that because of some seventeenth-century fires in Mexico City, mundane documentation of the first generation is, contrary to expectations, actually scarcer in Mexico than in Peru. Instead, Himmerich concentrated on the encomienda, giving as complete as possible an account of all encomenderos and encomiendas for what amounts to a generation and a half. The first thing to emerge was the quick consolidation of the core of the encomendero group (despite their loud complaints that they were losing everything). Some families which were high ranking from the beginning kept, extended, and diversified their holdings, dominating local political office in Mexico City and beginning to intermarry, often giving local alliances precedence over possible matches with regional compatriots in Spanish terms. All Mexico was treated as one unit. Important people got encomiendas near Mexico City, others elsewhere. Especially noteworthy was the pattern of multiple encomienda holding. The great of the land usually had more than one grant, one in the vicinity of Mexico City, or sometimes Puebla, where they would make their establishments, and others in the outlying provinces, which stew-

estates in the Arequipa region to 1650.[46] Davies gives the conquest period the full treatment, showing a detailed knowledge of the membership of all the local encomendero families and then following them over three or four succeeding generations. Over this span, with additions and losses, they and their heirs, relatives, and associates became the owners of Arequipa's wine-producing estates, which were the area's adaptation to its distance from Potosí and its lack of sufficient indigenous products for sale, on the order of Cuzco's example. The relative position and goals of the Arequipa families remained constant throughout. They were always on the lookout for alliances with families of Lima, though by no means always successful in obtaining them. By following the entire group and its holdings over a length of time, Davies is able to make sense of developments whose significance eluded previous investigators. One way to handle the question of land tenure stability has been to count the number of properties against the number of sales, which, however, often gives an illusory impression of instability and lack of orientation on the part of the owners. Davies keeps track of a family's entire holdings and the relative position of family members. He can thus see, for example, that some sales represent not loss to a family but a minor heir reconsolidating an estate by selling his part of the inheritance back to the principal heir. Families and branches of families had their ups and downs, but they were managing a whole set of diversified interests as part of an overall family strategy; their rationale becomes clearer than before and the degree of continuity between conquest period and later is seen to be very high indeed. Davies has given us a valuable case study of an area located near the trunk line but without other apparent economic

---

ards would manage for them. These new insights are a valuable extension of our understanding of the operation of the trunk line and major consolidation near the time of their origin.

It should be mentioned in this connection that Ida Altman has produced a substantial, invaluable article on Mexican conquest society on the basis of published notarial records, "Spanish Society in Mexico City After the Conquest" (1991).

[46]Davies, *Landowners in Colonial Peru* (1984). Ramírez 1986, dealing with north Peruvian estates, is somewhat comparable.

assets until local Spaniards developed an industry appropriate to the situation.

Efraín Trelles has worked on the same area, confining himself in much of his research to the life, holdings, and economic activity of one important encomendero of Arequipa in the conquest period, but following that individual and all aspects of his estate through every imaginable kind of record, leading to an extremely solid exemplification of all the main trends and a greater integration of the characteristics and interests of the indigenous groups in the encomienda than had been possible previously.[47]

In much of what I said above it is clear how basic transportation was to the whole question of colonization and resources. If a product would pay the transportation costs to Spain from the Indies, or to the trunk line from the fringes, then that product became a resource, and colonization gained momentum. Yet ironically, at least on the surface, transportation was neither especially profitable nor prestigious. On land, muleteers and carters were illiterate lower commoners with little capital or connections, ranking nearly as low as any Spaniard could, and on the sea the mariners were considered to be of yet baser sort, as the Spaniards said (*de baja suerte*); even the masters and pilots had much the same social profile and enjoyed little esteem among landsmen. Ships were less valuable than their cargo, and merchants avoided full ownership of them. There has been little study of the transportation business on land or sea. Some older studies touching on carting, roads, and the like rely on such sources as official reports, ordinances, and travelers' accounts.[48] Only research at the level of specific individuals and

---

[47]Trelles, *Lucas Martínez Vegazo* (1982).

[48]The anthropologist Ross Hassig has published a book, *Trade, Tribute and Transportation* (1985) dealing with transportation and other matters of economic relevance in central Mexico before and after the conquest. For the preconquest, sources hardly exist, so the treatment there is skeletal, hypothetical, definitional, though often very enlightening; for the postconquest there are so many sources that Hassig has used only one manageable portion, restrictive legislation on transport. The book should certainly be read, but it contributes relatively little to the matters of interest here

enterprises, based on working records in which those individuals and entities appear, holds out hope of integrating transport into the larger picture.

In Peru, Luis Miguel Glave is far advanced toward a book in this vein on roads, *tambos* or inns, and *trajines* or transport convoys in the central Andes up to the seventeenth century, digging deeply into muleteers' contracts, litigation by Indian groups involved with tambos, and other documents at the local level.[49] The gradual transformation of the Inca system, with many continuities, and the active participation of the indigenous people for their own purposes are among the trends clearly emerging. The transportation business and petty feeder-line trade, ranking low in the Spanish scheme, represented an early opportunity for indigenous participation in the Spanish economy in independent roles, and hence they also present a historiographical opportunity, if one is willing to go into difficult and miscellaneous local sources.

The ready positive reaction of the sedentary indigenous peoples to opportunities existing for European-style economic activity has now been noticed in many contexts (not least Potosí and the Huancavelica mercury mines).[50] But we have not yet demythologized Indian economic activity to the extent that we have Spanish. Every Indian adaptation to the Spanish economy tends to be seen as some sort of miracle. I am convinced that it is rather the result of deep and wide similarities already existing between two types of sedentary societies, the European and the indigenous. In central Mexico, Indian-language documents show that the indigenous people of that area knew the trading and sale of land among individuals, the concept of hiring labor, currencies, specialized

---

beyond showing how frequently the Spaniards built on indigenous patterns or used them to achieve transitions. Despite the laudable inclusion of pre- and postconquest periods in a single framework and the establishment of many continuities across the break, Hassig remains more interested in and knowledgeable about the preconquest side. He is unaware of the trunk line or of the social and economic ranking of the transportation industry.

[49]The work was afterward completed and published as *Trajinantes: caminos indígenas en la sociedad colonial* (1989).

[50]Bakewell 1984, Stern 1982.

production for interregional trade, and many other economic practices which with minimal change could function within the Spanish system (although the differences which existed would also persist indefinitely).[51] As with the Spaniards, the biggest gap, and the hardest to fill, remains the conquest period itself, before the Indians had learned to write their language in the Roman alphabet. I might add that it now begins to appear that Peru was not as devoid of indigenous-language documentation as has been thought, and the approach through this avenue may be viable there as well.[52] We must not, of course, take it for granted that the Andean situation will match the central Mexican in every respect; recent work by Susan Ramírez on early wills issued by Indians in northern Peru shows them apparently not treating their land as inheritable individual property.[53]

The first or contact generation is without doubt the most difficult in many ways, starting with the simple greater difficulty of reading the writing the further back one goes, and the much greater volume and systematic nature of the sources in the second half of the sixteenth century. There has also been the deterrent represented by the older literature itself;

---

[51]My research on these matters is related to a long-term project on indigenous central Mexican society and culture in the centuries after the conquest on the basis of indigenous-language sources (since published as *The Nahuas After the Conquest*, 1992).

[52]George Urioste has in his possession copies of some most interesting mundane documents in Quechua from the central Andes in the seventeenth century, closely parallel in several ways to what exists in Nahuatl and implying possibly widespread recordkeeping in Quechua by indigenous people. (See Chapter 8 here.)

[53]Susan Ramírez, "Indian and Spanish Conceptions of Land Tenure in Peru," paper given at the 1988 conference of the American Historical Association. As interesting as Ramírez's conclusions are, we must keep in mind that this type of research is barely beginning in the Andean field, and that relevant documents in indigenous languages are so far lacking. Through the language barrier, I think it is difficult to be sure that reference to a *chácara* necessarily involves only the improvements and crop, not also the land (the Nahuas of central Mexico used their word for "field," *milli*, to mean the land as well). Moreover, most of the cases come from coastal areas where water, not land itself, was the main source of value. It is to be hoped that parallel research can be done on Andean highland areas.

scholars entering the field have often felt on the one hand that everything was already done, while on the other hand they have accepted the predominant tone of the writing as the tone of the actuality and avoided what appeared to be a swashbuckling, sensational, over-ideological topic. (This indeed is the sentiment that David Brading expressed to me when I first met him, as justification for concentrating on the eighteenth century.)

Nevertheless, much can be done with known sources, and the discovery of new ones has not yet halted. In the cyclical evolution of historical research, I think I can detect a renewed interest among some current students in the very early period. And in any case, a trickle of progressive new work devoted to early Peru especially has never halted. Although the early time can hardly claim an absolute priority, it is a period of extraordinary interest about which despite the appearances far too little is yet known, and it should be built into research involving any part of the sixteenth or early seventeenth centuries. Statistics on absolute quantities (prices, tonnage, number of sales, size of production, acreage) will be to the good, but what the documentation lends itself to, and what is even more needed, is the kind of study that looks at a whole situation in terms of specific individuals, families, entities, procedures, and concepts embedded in currently used vocabulary. Broadness at the local level is crucial because everything affects everything else and many patterns pervade the overall situation; it is efficient because even if one is doing a narrower topic one must look at all the local records in any case.

It is also advisable that the loci of studies be chosen and viewed within a wider context. We need close surveys of some centers off the trunk line, together with their trunk line ties. We need studies running along the trunk line, catching for example commercial firms in both Lima and Potosí, both Mexico City and Zacatecas, rather than concentrating almost exclusively on one regional center as has become the general practice (and one with many advantages, to be sure). We need more studies carefully following families, towns, or enterprises forward from the first generation in the manner of Davies. The work of Himmerich, Trelles, and Glave also pro-

vides useful models. Since Spain is so important as a source of
immigration, a headquarters of Indies commercial firms, a
market, a precedent, and in other ways, we need studies that
will treat both sides of the Atlantic as a unit, following
families or firms in both spheres. This is a difficult but not
impossible undertaking. Ida Altman has recently published a
substantial book on Extremadura and America in the sixteenth century.[54] One of several significant results is documentation of the extent to which the economic attitudes and
procedures of the Spaniards in the Indies replicated those at
home. It remains true that the social-economic history of
early Spanish America is generally more advanced, comprehensive, and sophisticated than that of early modern
Spain; the difference has diminished considerably in recent
years, but it must be erased if we are ever to acquire the right
long-range perspective on the phenomena.

Since what a resource is is so largely determined in Europe,
and not just in Spain, studies connecting broader European
prices, techniques, and demands with the phenomena of the
Indies would be highly desirable, though I do not know how
feasible. Problems of feasibility also adhere to studies concentrating narrowly on specific resources. There is no doubt
that the highly technical physical and chemical properties of
specific items were crucial to the overall operation of the
economy, and that historians are not doing justice to these
facets of the historical process. Yet despite occasional windfalls, information on anything of this nature is generally
speaking spread thinly across the sources and does not reward
the intensive searcher for a single technical aspect alone.
Moreover, without acquiring a host of archival and linguistic
skills, as well as a broad grasp of the overall context in
specific times and places, one will not be able to recognize

---

[54]Altman, *Emigrants and Society: Extremadura and Spanish
America in the Sixteenth Century* (1989). For a summary of some
central points within a broad context, see Altman's article "Emigrants and Society: An Approach to the Background of Colonial
Spanish America" (1988). Since the main thrust of emigration from
the Cáceres-Trujillo region, Altman's Spanish reference point, was
toward Peru, the book contains much material of specific interest to
Peruvianists.

such data as the records really contain, much less interpret them correctly. Better let historians pursue their broad studies, interested in everything, and bring any technical tidbits to technicians when they happen to come upon them. It is true that through certain kinds of research a historian sometimes gradually gains a practical grasp of a good deal of arcane and technical material, as can be seen for example with the historians of mining. We should make the most of such opportunities.

At times those with a narrow technical interest have the vision and ability to ground technical research in the broader context. Thus a recent work by Michael Murphy on irrigation in the Mexican Bajío[55] goes far beyond waterworks proper to carry out a thorough, many-dimensional investigation of estates in specific localities, reaching a series of valuable conclusions with wide implications. Murphy's example is worth emulating for other regions and other technical topics, agricultural and non-agricultural.

Here I will stop, knowing that scholars will in any case follow their own preferences, but I do hope that they will do so in the expectation of finding patterned, in its own context rational, economic activity on the part of both Spaniards and Indians in the sixteenth-century Indies.

---

[55]Michael E. Murphy, *Irrigation in the Bajío Region of Colonial Mexico* (1986).

6. The Merchants of Early Spanish America: Continuity and Change
(1994)

FOR ONE whose primary frame of reference is mainland Spanish America, and above all Mexico and Peru, from conquest to independence, it seems prima facie that the overall social and economic position and reputation of the Hispanic American merchant underwent a vast transformation over the stretch of nearly three centuries. No single area is thoroughly studied from beginning to end of the epoch, but if we put together what we know of both of the great central regions, we will come to the conclusion that the import-export merchant on the local scene, from having been at first a mere transient, concerned with liquidity alone, a subordinate part of an international network, determined to return to Spain, virtually without rank, possessions, or social roots in the local scene, gradually became by the eve of independence a towering figure of local society, dominating a very different kind of company structure, permanently rooted, possessing large local investments and high honors. The early and late phases of the process have been open to view for quite a few years; more recently, an important work by Louisa Hoberman on the merchants of Mexico, 1594–1660, has gone far toward filling in the middle period, in fact showing an intermediary stage in the process and making the notion of a long-term Hispanic American reevaluation of the role of the merchant all the more tempting.

Yet Mexico and Peru do not stand alone and cannot be seen in isolation. Over the years valuable studies have appeared on other areas at various points in time, throwing a very different light on the matter. The picture is still highly fragmentary, too much so, I imagine, for the tastes of a systematic student of mercantile organization, but I as an amateur will proceed undeterred to carry out at least a rudimentary survey and make some preliminary observations. I propose first to rehearse the trends for the central areas, as illustrated in a series of well known works, and then look elsewhere—first at early Seville and the Caribbean with Enrique Otte and after that at the late Plata region with Susan Socolow.

The merchants of Mexico have been admirably studied, except for the bulk of the sixteenth century. The merchants of Peru, on the other hand, are studied almost only for the first generation. Despite the apparent non sequitur, I will tell a mixed story, inserting a Peruvian beginning into an otherwise Mexican sequence, relying on the many structural and chronological similarities between the two regions and looking forward to the day when the scholarship will be more comprehensive and even. The Peruvian episode, of course, comes from the study of early Peruvian society that I did many years ago.[1]

During the military phase of the Peruvian conquest and for a few years thereafter, commerce was a chaotic world in which captains, officials, and unconnected, poorly trained traders competed quite successfully with professional merchants tied to transatlantic networks. But by the early 1540's things had settled down in a form they were to retain for some decades. The professional merchants connected with Seville thoroughly dominated the country's strictly commercial life. Companies with senior partners in Seville, maintaining junior partners or employees (often their younger relatives or compatriots) in Lima and Panama, did the most importation of European goods and got the most silver back. They were both wholesalers and retailers. Partnerships were for relatively short terms, and the same individual might be involved in several of them at the same time, working toward a certain independence within the supporting network.

Peruvian-based companies had less capital and were clearly secondary, operating with smaller volumes and mainly buying their goods in Panama or Lima from combines based in Seville. Arrangements at all levels were fluid, and personnel were highly mobile. If a local company did strike it rich, its senior partner would normally migrate to Spain. Peruvian partners of transatlantic companies aimed not to

---

[1] I will not give detailed references on the early Peruvian situation, they being surely unnecessary. The material comes from Chapter 5 of my *Spanish Peru, 1532–1560* (1968, or preferably the second edition of 1994).

settle where they were but to advance a rung on the company ladder and eventually make it to Seville.

As a result of the overall structure, merchants did not cut much of a figure in Peruvian society. It was largely their own doing. Since they hoped to advance to posts elsewhere, they did not normally marry locally, remaining perpetual outsiders. With an emphasis on liquidity and the quick return of bullion to Seville, they shied away from any investment in the local economy. Most would not even buy a house for a residence and shop. If a Peruvian representative of a firm in Seville attempted to make local investments, he would soon attract unfavorable notice from his superiors at home. Local society, in turn, drew the proper conclusions. For many years merchants were not called citizens (*vecinos*) of the Peruvian cities even if they were quite long-term residents and maintained significant establishments. Above all, they were not eligible for the key position in Spanish Peruvian society, that of encomendero. The epithet *mercader* was incompatible with the receipt of an encomienda grant. It is true that some merchants became encomenderos anyway, but they did so by abandoning the merchant label and membership in transatlantic combines, at the same time entering fully into the local society and economy. Treasury officials were also sometimes merchants, but in disguise. The only hint of honorific treatment of declared merchants was their frequent employment as stewards for religious corporations.

It was at the lower levels of commercial organization that identification with the local scene began to show itself. Of the secondary importers, those who were based in Lima or other Peruvian cities and lacked a headquarters in Seville, but bought shipments in Panama or Lima from Seville-based combines, only a minority ever achieved the kind of success allowing them to graduate to Seville themselves. Despairing of Spain, they were inclined after a time to reconcile themselves to permanent local residence, buying a house, marrying, investing part of their capital in mining, transportation, or even local products for local consumption, and seeking local honors. But since their connections were not of the highest and their capital not the greatest, their successes were at first not very impressive.

Our view now shifts to Mexico. Louisa Hoberman's work on the merchants of New Spain, 1590–1660, is one of the largest contributions anyone has made to the commercial history of the Indies in many a year, and virtually the only major, up-to-date source for the seventeenth century anywhere.[2] The picture Hoberman shows us contains much that is familiar from the conquest generation. The great majority of the wholesale merchants of Mexico were still born in Spain; over half were from Spanish merchant families, and family ties were still the building blocks of commercial combines. Sometimes an older relative was based in Seville, with one or two younger ones in or around Mexico, and at times a younger relative returned to Seville to replace the senior figure at his death. Some of these relationships were expressed formally as transatlantic partnerships.[3]

But what had once been the dominant pattern had now receded to the status of a minority phenomenon. Most of the largest merchants now lived out their lives in Mexico City, expressing at the individual level what had been expressed corporately by the creation of a Consulado in Mexico City toward the end of the sixteenth century—that the Mexican merchant community had become relatively autonomous and localized. As a result, almost all important local merchants married in Mexico as their careers were gaining momentum, almost always to Mexican-born women (virtually the only ones present). The marriages were vital to their mercantile careers, for whether they married the daughters of senior merchants, of families with a commercial tradition, or of notables of other types, they received dowries usually equalling or surpassing their own assets at the time and elevating their business to a new level. With marriage came ownership of a substantial residence and place of business in Mexico City.[4] As permanent and wealthy residents, they sought the advantages of officeholding; some of the most eminent of them obtained middle-level posts, often connected with fiscal matters, in addition to taking an active role in tax

---

[2]Louisa Schell Hoberman, *Mexico's Merchant Elite, 1590–1660* (1991).

[3]Hoberman 1991, pp. 41–48.   [4]Ibid., pp. 64–68, 139.

farming and the bonding of government officials. They also appeared at times on the Mexico City cabildo. The one place (a highly strategic one) where they were clearly dominant was among the officials of the Mexico City mint.[5] Merchants also began to seek other local honors, and some of them (especially the childless) made quite stunning local ecclesiastical endowments.[6]

Investment was still overwhelmingly in imported merchandise and credit operations, with emphasis on liquidity.[7] But even the large merchants of the first half of the seventeenth century were deeply involved in the local economy, especially (though not exclusively) the sectors with export potential. They rarely owned silver mines or produced cochineal themselves, but through financing and advancing goods they became an indispensable part of the operations of those industries.[8] It was they almost alone who carried out the last step in silver production, the minting of coin.[9] With sugar production in the Cuernavaca region for Mexico City consumption, they went beyond financing to become administrators and even owners of a significant portion of the mills.[10] All of these activities have to do with eminently salable products fitting easily within the classic definition of long-distance commerce, but some of the Mexico City merchants of this time also moved in the direction of acquiring assets of the type used by aristocratic families to buttress their wealth over generations: urban real estate and large landed properties or haciendas. The haciendas were not the very largest complexes, and only a minority of merchants made such acquisitions, but owning urban rental property was more widespread.[11]

Thus by the first half of the seventeenth century the merchants of Mexico had moved a long way toward the until recently better known situation existing in the late eighteenth century and early nineteenth. Higher honors and even greater involvement with the general economy were yet to come, but

---

[5]Ibid., pp. 83–85, 149–82.   [6]Ibid., pp. 236–38.
[7]Ibid., p. 54, with statement of the share of different types of investment by percentage.
[8]Ibid., pp. 82, 124.   [9]Ibid., pp. 83–86.
[10]Ibid., pp. 98–99.   [11]Ibid., pp. 111–17, 140.

most of the phenomena of localization as known in the later period had already taken shape. The structure of import-export firms, however, was still in a transitional phase. It does not appear that we can presume that the clear general Mexico City dominance of local commerce, so characteristic of the later period, had formed by this time. It is true that Mexico City merchants headed the combines operating the Philippines trade in full independence of Seville, as, if nothing else, the Seville Consulado's determined opposition to the trade tells us.[12] But as mentioned above, some older-style Seville-dominated transatlantic partnerships still existed. And above all, Hoberman demonstrates that commission agents, called encomenderos (not to be confused with the recipients of grants of Indian tribute and labor), played a significant and ever-increasing role.[13]

Earlier, a young man beginning a high-level mercantile career in the Indies trade would typically have started out (after the apprenticeship stage, at least) as the junior partner or factor/employee of a Seville-based firm. Now he was likely to begin as a commission agent for merchants of Seville, using his 4 or 5 percent earnings as a means to become independent later. The change in structure implies that the two sectors, Spanish and Mexican, had grown apart and were no longer fully integrated, but still maintained close relations. The necessity and importance of this sort of arrangement is seen in the fact that working on commission was by no means only for relative neophytes. Established merchants of Mexico City continued to act as commission agents, and some of the largest dealers did the bulk of their shipping on that basis. Most of the transatlantic trade was being handled on commission. The overall structure was still in the process of rapid change. Hoberman shows that in the period 1614–1639, commission activity rose from 39.8 percent of the value of total shipping to 76.7 percent, while partnership activity fell from 19.4 to 1.0 percent.[14]

---

[12]Ibid., p. 216.   [13]Ibid., pp. 48–50.

[14]Ibid., p. 49, table 6. Hoberman's data seem to reflect primarily exports to Spain (including bullion) rather than imports, but since the two aspects must have corresponded to each other closely, her results are highly significant. None of the other works discussed

Even Mexico, blessed as it is with studies, cannot provide us with a book for each successive half-century. It is not until the second half of the eighteenth century that we again have recent accounts of the Mexican commercial world detailed enough to be held up against Hoberman's picture. First David Brading provided the broad outlines (the nominal dates of the book are 1763–1810), then Christiana Borchart did a thorough study of the activities of the Consulado membership in the years 1759–1778, and subsequently John Kicza produced an equally thorough treatment of the organization of all levels of Mexico City commerce in the time slot of approximately 1770–1821.[15] Since none of the three studies is, naturally enough, identical in procedures, sources, focus, and coverage, it is hard to be certain that some apparent differences between them represent actual chronological change over the years 1759 to 1821. I will treat the late period generally as a single block, dealing with a few aspects of possible evolution within those years as a side issue.

As in the other time periods, merchants involved in the import-export trade (now called usually *comerciantes*, not *mercaderes* as before) were overwhelmingly born in Spain, by now mainly the north of Spain.[16] The pattern whereby a

---

(with the exception of Enrique Otte's *Perlas del Caribe*, which deals with a rather more limited situation) are able to speak in terms of the percent of the overall trade that certain kinds of merchants or types of transactions accounted for.

[15]D. A. Brading, *Miners and Merchants in Bourbon Mexico, 1763–1810* (1971); Christiana Renate Moreno geb. Borchart (who now writes as Christiana Borchart de Moreno), "Kaufmannschaft und Handelskapitalismus in der Stadt Mexico (1759–1778)" (1976); John E. Kicza, *Colonial Entrepreneurs: Families and Business in Bourbon Mexico City* (1983).

[16]Borchart 1976, pp. 23, 26, 91; Kicza 1983, pp. 101, 265. One must at least consider the possibility that changes in terms for designating merchants correspond to changes in the organization and conceptualization of commercial activity. In Spain and all over the Indies in the sixteenth century, professionals in long-distance trade were regularly called *mercader*. In the Indies, the term applied equally to transatlantic importer-exporters and to those who merely retailed imported goods. Traders in local goods were sharply subordinate; in Peru and some other areas they were called *tratantes*. In Mexico up to 1660 as studied by Hoberman, terminology seems

nephew or other young relative or associate from the older merchant's home region in Spain succeeded to the top position in his Mexican business seems if anything more dominant than earlier.[17] Large Mexico City commercial houses, however, were now even more autonomous than in the seventeenth century. The Mexican capital was the center of the business activity of the largest traders. Some were capable of financing themselves, and the greatest source of financing in general was the membership of the Mexico City Consulado. Mexico City houses sent purchasing agents to the ports and even sometimes maintained them there permanently.[18] They occasionally became even more active, sending a ship and a partner to Spain to buy goods.[19]

By now a full Mexico-City-centric system of commerce had matured. Wholesalers of the capital, and even some of the larger retailers, owned retail outlets throughout the provinces, especially in the northern mining areas, operated by either junior partners or employees, who were likely to be their relatives or at least associates from the Mexico City house. Successful managers were likely to be promoted eventually to Mexico City. A company arrangement was likely to include as principal investor a large wholesaler based in the capital, a second partner acting as general

---

not to have changed, although there were now some terms specifically designating retailers (*dueño de tienda, cajonero*; p. 19). By the mid-eighteenth century, however, the predominant term was *comerciante* or *del comercio*. Other terms designated lesser traders. *Mercader* seems to have passed virtually out of use. Large import-export wholesalers were often called *almacenero*, but apparently not with much consistency (Borchart and Kicza, ibid.). In the Plata region, Socolow describes a more consistent system: *comerciante* for wholesalers, *mercader* for retailer of imported goods, and a set of other terms for lesser traders of various kinds (Susan Migden Socolow, *The Merchants of Buenos Aires, 1778–1810: Family and Commerce* [1978], pp. 12, 108–9). The changes do seem to betray a certain long-term tendency to increase the distinction between wholesalers and retailers. Nevertheless, some successful retailers continued to move into wholesaling, and virtually all wholesalers retailed.

[17]Brading 1971, pp. 112–13; Borchart 1976, pp. 256–58; Kicza 1983, pp. 136–45.

[18]Borchart 1976, p. 90; Kicza 1983, pp. 64–65.

[19]Kicza 1983, p. 65.

manager, also there, and a third partner in a mining camp (but coming from the capital). The two senior partners would likely participate in a number of such deals. Wholesale houses also had longstanding arrangements to sell goods on credit to more independent provincial traders, who nevertheless in the end were often quite dependent; they traveled frequently to the capital to make purchases and settle accounts. The most successful of them were likely to migrate there, becoming senior partner of a company trading with the area just abandoned and leaving behind a representative who might follow later himself.[20] In a word, the system had practically all the same elements as transatlantic trade in sixteenth-century Peru, except for a change of locus, Mexico City having taken the place of Seville, and everything else having shifted correspondingly. Many parts of the system had already existed in the seventeenth century, but now it had jelled.

This is not to say that all vestiges of the earlier trans-atlantic ties of local houses had disappeared. Borchart found one—but only one—case in which a large Mexico City mer-chant had a partnership with a merchant based in Spain. Working on commission was more frequent, and some Mexico City merchants repeatedly did commission importing for the same Cádiz firm. Yet they normally had their own business as well as being commission agents. Borchart found only one Consulado member who worked exclusively on commis-sion.[21] Kicza, whose study goes thirty years past the end date of Borchart's, hardly mentions foreign commissions. Pos-sibly commission deals by Mexico City importers reached an apogee in or slightly after Hoberman's time and were in the last stages of decline in Borchart's, virtually disappearing in Kicza's. It is also entirely possible, however, that Borchart and Kicza's slightly different research paths led to slightly different views of the same situation. Kicza does find that some of the largest traders in Mexico City were somehow affiliated with merchants of Cádiz, normally their relatives, but the nature of the connection remains obscure. It is even within the realm of possibility that the active or senior

---

[20]Borchart 1976, pp. 103–17, 121; Kicza 1983, pp. 77–84.
[21]Borchart 1976, p. 78.

member in some of these relationships was in Mexico City.[22] The record shows that in the free trade period, Mexico City houses did sometimes place agents or junior partners in north Spanish ports. As Kicza says, on the basis of what we presently know it seems that Spanish merchant houses were still somehow significant, but definitely not dominant, in the operations of Mexico-City-based firms.[23]

As in Hoberman's time, the large merchants of Mexico City, Spanish-born though they mainly were, entered fully and permanently into local society, marrying locally born women. The marriages were still of the same type, to relatives of more senior merchants or other locally prominent, wealthy people, and they were still extremely important for business success. It may be that in general the dowry as such was becoming an ever smaller and less essential part of the arrangement. Both Borchart and Kicza find that the dowry was no longer universal in merchant marriages. Examples of dowries given by Borchart are still very substantial, varying with the capital of the merchant; Kicza gives several examples in which the merchant's capital far exceeds the dowry. If this is a progressive change during the period, it is not one of great significance; apparently an understanding of what the wife's future inheritance would be was still quite crucial to negotiations.[24]

Borchart and Kicza do not mention the middle-level governmental positions which play a large part in Hoberman's portrayal. The most important posts, those at the Mexico City mint, had apparently been precluded when in 1729 the crown appointed salaried officials there and began to operate the mint directly.[25] If the wholesale merchants had lost something here (and it cannot be taken as absolutely proven that they had), they had made up for it by the fact that several of the most prominent of them held officerships in the recently bolstered militia.[26] Participation in the Mexico City cabildo continued much as before, with quite frequent appearance of

---

[22]Kicza 1983, pp. 61–62.   [23]Ibid., pp. 151–52.

[24]Borchart 1976, pp. 260–62; Kicza 1983, pp. 161–63.

[25]Brading 1971, p. 143. Such action would not, of course, necessarily eliminate merchants' participation.

[26]Borchart 1976, pp. 62–63; Kicza 1983, p. 173.

the larger merchants, but nothing approaching dominance. Kicza notes that merchants had more success as alcaldes than as permanent regidores, the latter being mainly of older families.[27] In the matter of honors, the Consulado merchants—not all of them, naturally, but a few of the highest ranking and best established in every respect—had reached the pinnacle. Over the years perhaps as many as twenty entered the military orders, and twelve acquired titles of high nobility as count or marquis, associated with entails for their heirs.[28]

The titles rested on a base of social acceptance at the very highest level; that in turn reflected an economic position including not only great liquid wealth but the large-scale ownership of landed property. Even now not every Consulado member owned an hacienda; Borchart finds that about one in four did so during the time she studied. A majority of the properties were still in the Valley of Mexico and surrounding regions. But the scale of ownership by those most involved had increased greatly. Some wholesalers acquired strings of large properties, and by Borchart's calculations, Consulado merchants at times owned 20 percent of all the haciendas in the Valley of Mexico. Despite the fact that most large merchants did not have one, acquiring an hacienda was part of the general pattern of local merchant ambitions at this time. As Borchart points out, wholesalers in the early and middle stages of their careers had to concentrate all their assets on increasing the volume of their imports; only later, when fully established, could they afford to go into landownership (which was, nevertheless, entered into on a profit-making basis, not for mere prestige). Kicza adds another perspective. Substantial retailers who had little hope of ever reaching the Consulado level had less reason to hold back from landownership, so that almost all of them possessed a rural estate of some kind.[29] The picture with urban real estate was similar; only a few commercial people were heavily

---

[27]Kicza 1983, p. 178.

[28]Brading 1971, p. 105; Borchart 1976, pp. 231, 263–70; Kicza 1983, pp. 173–77; the accounts of the latter two as to the noble orders differ somewhat.

[29]Borchart 1976, pp. 162–88, 199–211; Kicza 1983, pp. 167–69.

involved, but the value of the assets of those few was high.[30]

Merchant involvement in sugar and cochineal production was much as it had been in Hoberman's time,[31] but direct investment in silver mining was much higher, especially from the last quarter of the eighteenth century forward. Ownership often came through an increase of the traditional merchant activity in supply and loans (avío), and sometimes involuntarily, through foreclosure. An administrator, receiving a share as a partner, would normally see to mining operations, leaving the merchant free to continue in commerce, as he usually (but not always) did. From about the 1780's, wholesale merchants took to banding together in what amounted to joint stock companies to supply sometimes vast amounts of capital for mining.[32]

Some difference of opinion exists as to the degree of change brought on by the free trade decree of 1778 and the larger volume of imports associated with it. Brading has seen the effects as quite radical, with the Mexico City wholesalers losing much of their advantage. Independent merchants of Veracruz obtained import goods on credit from Spanish shippers and supplied the provinces directly, causing many Mexico City merchants to abandon commerce for mining and landowning.[33] That some did so is established. But on the one hand Borchart shows that large-scale landholding became part of the normal procedure of the wealthiest merchants well before free trade.[34] On the other, Kicza shows that Mexico City wholesalers retained their dominance (though no longer monopoly) in the provinces for decades after the decree.[35] He also sees mine ownership as an integral part of commerce in late eighteenth-century conditions (involving greater silver production, a larger scale of operations, and greater need for investment funds than ever before),[36] but since most of his examples are from after free trade, and Borchart seems to

---

[30]Borchart 1976, pp. 214–23; Kicza 1983, p. 172.

[31]Borchart 1976, pp. 122–26, 195–96; Kicza 1983, pp. 71–73.

[32]Brading 1971, pp. 178, 192; Borchart 1976, pp. 246–52; Kicza 1983, pp. 85–88. Many more examples could be adduced from Brading.

[33]Brading 1971, pp. 115–16.   [34]Borchart 1976, p. 162.

[35]Kicza 1983, p. 63 et al.   [36]Ibid., p. 85.

have found relatively little mine owning in the period before,[37] the point remains to be established (note, however,
that some of Brading's examples antedate free trade).

At any rate, from having been transient figures representing Spanish interests, the import-export merchants of
Mexico had bit by bit over more than two and a half centuries
become deeply embedded in Spanish Mexican society, directly
involved in all the more profitable aspects of its economy,
while their leaders occupied a social position equal to any.
What we have seen above is a very clear progression. But is it a
change in principle, in the place occupied by a profession
within Hispanic culture? I believe not, and the best way to
demonstrate it is to return to the role of merchants in Seville
and the Caribbean in the first decades of Spanish activity in
the Indies.

The work of Enrique Otte can quickly tell us nearly all we
need to know. The mechanisms of commerce in Seville in the
late fifteenth and early sixteenth centuries were much the
same as they would continue to be over the entire time and
space that interest us here. The partnership or *compañia* was
the most important form. Often built, as everywhere, on
kinship and regional ties, with senior partners stationed at
the headquarters and junior members traveling or established at lesser branches, it readily took different shapes. It
might be fully authenticated in documentary form, or it might
rest on unwritten agreement. Within a longstanding, often
implicit relationship between close associates (usually relatives), the individual members of the group might enter for
various purposes into a flurry of short-term companies
with varying personnel and terms of investment.[38] There
were investing partners, partners who supplied work rather
than capital, and simple factor/employees, a fluid continuum. The system, if one can call it that, was supremely
adaptable. Merchants who were not relatives or compatriots
were brought into partnerships as appropriate, and some
investors were not even professional merchants. Company

---

[37]Borchart 1973, p. 246.

[38]Otte, "Träger und Formen der wirtschaftlichen Erschließung
Lateinamerikas im 16. Jahrhundert" (1967), pp. 229–30, 238–39.

operations could go beyond commerce proper to various kinds of production.[39]

If the partnership was the most important commercial form, acting through commission agents was a significant supplemental device.[40] The two forms were not in direct competition; through a commission agent, an investor could take advantage of a fleeting or marginal opportunity not appropriate for a full-scale company, and the agent could in this way work his way toward independence and partner status, or expand his activity beyond partnerships to which he might already belong.

In the fifteenth century Seville was commercially much like the Lima or Mexico City of the sixteenth century. The largest mercantile houses were based elsewhere (above all and increasingly in Genoa); their senior partners were in foreign countries or distant regions, and their local personnel were quite transient. Localization was found mainly among traders of the second rank and less. Not until 1543 did Seville acquire a Consulado. But as the city gained greater commercial importance, its commercial sector grew more independent; firms came to be locally based, and their senior figures made new kinds of investments. The foreigners over time partly localized, partly retired from the arena, supplying rather than directing Seville's commerce. A new wave of companies was based in Seville itself.[41] All this represents an anticipation of the same process we have observed in Mexico over the seventeenth and eighteenth centuries.

Already in the fifteenth century, the *traperos* of Seville, who were both producers of cloth and merchants, had begun to achieve a certain local prominence. They are seen as *jurados* and even as majordomos of the municipality, in addition to acting as tax farmers and bondsmen.[42] These entrepreneurs were from the very beginning closely linked to cloth production, and some of them also became involved in aspects of leather processing, entering into contracts to

---

[39]Ibid., pp. 242, 246–47.   [40]Ibid., pp. 230–31.

[41]Ibid., passim.

[42]Otte, "Wirtschaftskräfte Andalusiens an der Schwelle der Neuzeit: die 'traperos'" (1978), pp. 297–98.

purchase the entire hide output of a given town.[43]

In the first generation or two of the Indies trade, the merchants of Seville went further along the same path. The most prominent were now engaged in transatlantic trade and often had been in the Indies themselves, but their ultimate identification with Seville grew stronger, and their position there continued to rise. The largest traders often became jurados, and they farmed the customs revenues of Seville; they built impressive town houses, purchased rural properties, and made large ecclesiastical donations. Juan de la Barrera bought olive orchards and grazing land, not to speak of entering into a company to operate alum mines in Aragon. He lived next to a *veinticuatro* of Seville, to whom he married his daughter doña Ana (and in these years the "doña" still meant a great deal).[44] Diego Caballero, the prince of the lot, acquired the title of Marshal, himself became a veinticuatro, bought rural properties including olive groves, the basis of a lasting entail, and had a splendid family chapel erected in the Seville cathedral.[45] The eighteenth-century merchant-counts of Mexico were no different.

What strikes one about the activities of the Seville merchants in the Caribbean in the first three or four decades of the sixteenth century is that the distinctive pattern of sixteenth-century Peru and Mexico had not yet taken shape. That pattern, to repeat, involved a well defined hierarchy with the sharp subordination of personnel in the Indies to senior partners in Seville; the avoidance of local investment, especially of a long-term nature; and the inability (as well as disinclination) to acquire offices and honors in the new areas. One accustomed to the mores of sixteenth-century Peru must blink in disbelief upon reading that Alvaro de Briones was Seville's largest shipper to the Indies in 1509, became a jurado of Seville in 1511, and *went to Santo Domingo* in 1512, maintaining a full-scale establishment there and staying at least well into 1514. He then spent some years in Seville, but

---

[43]Ibid., p. 299.

[44]Otte, "Los mercaderes transatlánticos bajo Carlos V" (1990), p. 104.

[45]Ibid., p. 107.

in 1521 went back to the Caribbean for seven years or more before finally returning to Seville definitively.[46] The great merchant Juan de la Barrera (fairly early in his career, it is true) lived for three years in a stone house he built on the island of Cubagua, supervising the production of pearls.[47] The largest of the pearl producers and the most prominent members of the cabildo of Nueva Cádiz de Cubagua during the apogee of the pearl trade in the 1520's and 1530's were merchants with connections in Seville.[48] Merchants of Seville got involved in Caribbean sugar production, and it was not only the misguided Genoese who did so.[49] The famous Diego Caballero was royal treasurer and regidor in Santo Domingo. Though his older brother Alonso, at first in Santo Domingo with him, preceded him to Seville in the normal pattern for sixteenth-century Peru, Diego stayed on for a total of twenty-six years, attaining vast wealth and high eminence before returning to Seville himself.

In the long run the most successful merchants of the early Caribbean usually ended their lives in Seville, in considerable glory, but in several ways commercial life in that time and place resembled eighteenth-century Mexico more than sixteenth-century Peru. Precedent may have been part of the reason. As Otte shows, commercial combines (often foreign owned) trading with the Canaries, Madeira, and the Azores had been drawn deeply into the production process.[50] But the decisive reason for the difference was no doubt the structure of the respective situations. Outside the city of Santo Domingo, and surely in the pearl fishing region, the Caribbean was a very weak consumer market, and export of produced materials or objects offered the only hope of major profits. The importance of production in the overall scheme would tend to keep more senior people directly involved on the local scene. Mexico and Peru, in contrast, soon contained a numerous Spanish population representing an excellent market, from

---

[46]Ibid., pp. 100–1.   [47]Ibid., p. 102.

[48]Otte 1967, pp. 243, 247. The message is expounded more thoroughly, of course, throughout Otte's *Perlas del Caribe: Nueva Cádiz de Cubagua* (1977).

[49]Otte 1990, p. 98.

[50]Otte 1967, p. 231.

whom a large profit could be skimmed with less risk, trouble, and delay than from production.[51] Travel and communication possibilities may also have weighed in the equation. It was far easier to travel from Seville to the Caribbean islands than to inland Mexico City, much less Lima, and once there, it was easier to stay in touch with events in Seville.

The research of Susan Socolow on the merchants of Buenos Aires in the years 1778–1810 allows us to take a look beyond Mexico-Peru not only at the beginning of our period, but at its end.[52] The Plata region was at the forefront of important changes occurring in transatlantic commerce at the time: a transportation revolution, with the rerouting of Potosí's silver, and the beginning of the transition from precious metals and exotic crops to bulk products of a more ordinary nature and lower specific value, in this case above all hides. Buenos Aires was new as a true urban society, and large-scale import-export commerce was equally new in the region (the city's Consulado was established only in 1794). The overall result was a quite mixed situation, not exactly like any other we have reviewed, but not falling out of the general range, and in several ways more like Peru in the sixteenth century or Mexico in the seventeenth than the Mexico of its own time.

As to the mechanisms of trade, we already know them. Fluid partnerships, with the usual emphasis on kinship, regional ties, and marrying in, were the universal framework, supplemented by dealings through commission agents. Wholesale import-export merchants often tended perhaps to a certain branch of the trade or to dealing with a certain region, but always diversified their business and never aimed for strict specialization; they did some retailing themselves and dealt with retailers of every description.[53]

---

[51]Let me here offer the suspicion, based on scattered impressions and no doubt premature, that early Mexico, though a great deal like Peru, had a bit more of the Caribbean about it—that merchants were less separate from other segments of the population, that hier-archies were less well defined. If this is so, the reasons may be on the one hand the fact that Mexico was closer to the Caribbean in time and space, and on the other that Mexico was at first not as rich in bullion, and hence not as good a market, as Peru.

[52]Socolow 1978.   [53]Ibid., pp. 14, 57–58.

We by now expect the bulk of the larger merchants in any Spanish American region at any time before independence to be Spanish-born, and that holds true for pre-independence Buenos Aires as well. Most came from the Basque region and other parts of northern Spain, just as in contemporary Mexico.[54] What stands out in strong contrast to the mode of operation of their Mexican-based cousins is how much more closely they were integrated with Spanish mercantile houses. It appears to have been the norm that young merchants coming to Buenos Aires had already worked for or had some connection with a Spanish firm. In some cases peninsular merchants specifically sent their sons to Buenos Aires to work with merchants there who were their former associates, perpetuating transatlantic commercial ties beyond a single generation. The local wholesalers with the most associates in Spain (Madrid, Cádiz, Seville, Bilbao) tended to have the most influence in Buenos Aires.[55] At the top, apparently, were merchants who rather than rising through a long process of local apprenticeship and later intermarriage came to Buenos Aires directly as the representative of a Spanish mercantile firm.[56] Personnel were forever traveling to Spain and back for business purposes.[57] The transfer of goods might occur through partnership, commission, or sale on credit, the actual effect not always differing as much as the form. Sometimes we see the sixteenth-century Peruvian pattern in all its purity. Socolow gives the example of a Buenos Aires merchant who returned to Cádiz, became an exporter, and established a long-term relationship in which, through various kinds of transactions, he sent goods to an old associate who stayed behind in Buenos Aires.[58]

In general, things would seem to have been at a stage intermediate between sixteenth-century Peru and seventeenth-century Mexico. Buenos Aires merchants were jealous of their independence, aiming to deal with various Spanish suppliers and not fall under the dominance of any one of them.[59] Above all, the size of the trade and the nature of the growing city had

---

[54]Socolow 1978, pp. 16–18.

[56]Ibid., p. 24.

[58]Ibid., pp. 152–53.

[55]Ibid., pp. 55, 58.

[57]Ibid., p. 86.

[59]Ibid., p. 7.

induced importers to make a permanent commitment to the area, and they had come to form a cohesive community. Many planned to return to their place of birth, and some favored group activities and churches in their home region more than those in Buenos Aires, but in the end very few ever left.[60]

Established wholesalers owned large amounts of urban real estate, retail shops to rent out as well as their own homes, which were among the city's largest and most elegant.[61] Marriage to local women was the norm, and two-thirds of the wives were daughters of other local merchants, very often the grooms' senior partners or associates. As in Mexico, a good local marriage was a virtually indispensable ingredient of a successful local career; the son-in-law often if not usually succeeded eventually to the father-in-law's business position. The social and business connections were generally more important than the immediate capital infusion; as with Kicza and Borchart's studies of eighteenth-century Mexico, Socolow finds the dowry not essential in many cases (a fourth of the merchants did entirely without dowries, another fourth received under 2,500 pesos).[62]

In matters of the local economy, the merchants of Buenos Aires lacked the multidimensional involvements of their Mexican contemporaries. They had little to do with financing the silver mines of Potosí,[63] perhaps because of the distance, perhaps because financial mechanisms had matured before the change to the Atlantic route. Sugar and cochineal production were missing from the Plata economy. Even that sector of the merchant group exporting an increasing number of hides seems to have operated primarily through simple purchase of the product for resale. The bulk of the Buenos Aires merchants lacked substantial rural properties of any kind, most owning at the maximum a suburban garden and retreat.[64] The reason for the situation with hides and landed properties is not far to seek. Buenos Aires was such a recent formation as a meaningful urban entity and market that neither landed estates nor an established landholding group

---

[60]Socolow 1978, pp. 87, 90, 113.   [61]Ibid., pp. 62–63, 71–72.
[62]Ibid., pp. 37–52.   [63]Ibid., p. 66.
[64]Ibid., pp. 64–65.

yet existed; there were no estates to buy, no one to buy them from. The Buenos Aires traders did have a clientele of retailers in the inland provinces and the silver mining area. The connections have not been systematically studied, but the network appears to have been much less impressive than that of Mexico, relying more on credit sale and agents, less on partnerships.[65] All in all, the wholesalers of the Plata region were much less wealthy than those of Mexico. The largest estates left by merchants of Buenos Aires were worth some 100,000 to 120,000 pesos,[66] whereas in Mexico the corresponding figure was often 500,000 and in the maximum cases much higher.[67]

Rooted in the community as they were, the Buenos Aires wholesalers were well on the way in the matter of acquiring local honors and offices. They were majordomos of local religious organizations, on the governing board of the principal charitable brotherhood, and endowers of altarpieces and chaplaincies, albeit on a somewhat modest scale.[68] They often served as officers in the militia, much as in Mexico at the same time.[69] They held several significant middle-level offices in the local royal government, including administrator of the mails, assayer, and military supplier,[70] and the children of some prominent merchants married into high-ranking governmental and military families.[71] Perhaps their most striking success was that large merchants dominated the Buenos Aires cabildo over most of the time Socolow studies, not only serving as alcaldes but providing the vast majority of the regidores, turning the body into what Socolow calls a "merchant council."[72] In this respect the performance was much stronger than in Mexico, clearly because there was no entrenched native-born upper group to contend with, and the entire local economy was based on commerce. Perhaps the council of the early Nueva Cádiz de Cubagua represents something comparable. In other respects, in a sense because of insufficient passage of time, but more directly because of the

---

[65]See Socolow 1978, pp. 9, 56, 68, 155.   [66]Ibid., p. 30.
[67]Kicza 1983, p. 17 and passim.   [68]Socolow 1978, pp. 90–102.
[69]Ibid., pp. 114–18.   [70]Ibid., p. 61.
[71]Ibid., p. 172.   [72]Ibid., pp. 121–22.

lack of landed estates and great fortunes in the local economy, eighteenth-century merchants of the Plata region fell short of those of Mexico. No merchant became a count or marquis or established an entail (nor did anyone else in Buenos Aires), and only three entered the military orders.[73]

Nothing in the commerce of Buenos Aires, then, was without ample precedent in the history of transatlantic trade; it is often precisely to earlier times, and not to the obvious example of contemporary Mexico, that we must look for parallels. Even the trade in hides, which was admittedly to transform the situation a few years later, had familiar dynamics. Again and again over the centuries, those with less capital, fewer connections, and less elaborate training were left out of the business of importing European merchandise in return for bullion and forced into dealing in one way or another with local products. Already in the early Caribbean phase, hide export was one of several possible alternatives (most of which had limited success at that time) that merchants hit upon as they were casting about for something to compensate for the dwindling gold supply. The late Plata region was little different; those who could manage it concentrated on European imports for silver, avoiding and looking down on the hides business, and those involved in that branch were originally lesser figures lacking in commercial connections, however much some of them may have eventually profited.[74]

The study of early Hispanic American commerce is closely related to, or even a part of, the history of migration. A succession of regional groups dominated transatlantic trade, and the bulk of the larger traders were first-generation immigrants in all known times and places from conquest to independence. The Genoese of Seville and then the "merchants of Burgos" or north Castilian traders were quickly succeeded by Andalusians, who had a much longer reign, giving way, however, to Basques and northern Spaniards again before the eighteenth century.[75] The northerners of that

---

[73]Socolow 1978, pp. 32, 173.

[74]Ibid., pp. 55, 153, 172.

[75]Hoberman finds the Andalusians were still the largest single

time provided both the leading firms and the great majority of the personnel in import-export commerce at all levels from one end of the Indies to the other.[76] These trends have to do sometimes more with the international European business and financial structure (the case with the quick fading of the Genoese), sometimes more with Spanish demography (the apparent case with the northern predominance of the eighteenth century). They do not seem to have affected the form and substance of commerce. Each group behaved very much like the others at any given time and place, and we have virtually no reason to take regional origin into account when plotting the development of commercial organization, progressive localization, etc. It is not to be forgotten, of course, that merchants always dealt preferentially with others of their own group, and that the groups showed a certain corporate solidarity at times, but these things are equally true of all of them.

The continuing predominance of first-generation immigrants calls for some consideration. As long as the largest houses were based in Spain, with revolving personnel, it is self-explanatory. Many of the same factors, and especially the crucial nature of personal transatlantic contacts, would still have operated when most importing was done on a commission basis, as appears to have been happening in the Mexico of Hoberman's time, even if most of the migrating merchants now settled in the new country permanently. Nor do we have reason to puzzle over such a new and transitional situation as pre-independence Buenos Aires. But how is it that most important merchants were still immigrants in late eighteenth-century Mexico, long after the largest local firms had attained commercial and financial independence and were deeply embedded in the local society and economy?

I dismiss the notion that peninsular Spaniards were more industrious and economically motivated or capable. Kicza has shown us that of the great fortunes of Mexico, only a few

---

regional group among Mexican wholesalers in her epoch, with 35 percent from Seville-Cádiz-Huelva, but even so, a greater number already came from the central and northern provinces (1991, p. 41).

[76]For Mexico, Borchart 1976, pp. 37–39; for Buenos Aires, Socolow 1978, p. 18.

belonged to peninsular merchants, and that at any given time a certain number of the greatest merchants were in fact locally born.[77] A possible part of the explanation is that in some way as yet unclear, local firms may have been dependent on merchants in Spain after all.[78] Another explanatory factor, to which the writers on these subjects have given relatively little emphasis, is the age structure of the migration cycle. Each new immigrant, though usually arriving young, spent years in establishing himself, hence waited ten years or more before marrying. After marriage, he soon began to feel the need of assistants. Nephews, younger brothers, and other unattached young fellows from home were splendid candidates; dependent as they were on the established merchant, otherwise unconnected locally, he could do with them as he pleased, send them where he wished.[79] But a large part of the reason for his choice of a peninsular relative was surely that his own children were babies. By the time of the merchant's death or retirement, the nephew was an experienced, connected, trusted associate, who ended up with the bulk of the business, while the sons were still wet behind the ears. Possibly the relatively few prominent locally-born merchants were sons of fathers who married unusually early or lived unusually long.

We tend to view the merchant migration question as part of relations between a motherland and its colonies. We may not be right in doing so. The patterns of migration and succession that we see in Mexico City or Buenos Aires had longstanding antecedents within Iberia. Otte shows that as early as the first half of the sixteenth century, many of the Andalusian mer-

---

[77]Kicza 1983, pp. 16–18, 25–26, 41.

[78]Studies of commercial activity and organization of many kinds are still needed, including research on the periphery of the Indies, on Mexico in the sixteenth century, and on Peru after that time. But the type of work most likely to bring new perspectives and deeper understanding is research like that of Otte (or that of Ida Altman on transatlantic migrants) for later time periods, that is, studies which begin with Spain or at least embrace both sides of the Atlantic equally. Apart from Otte, the best research has been done from a western-shore perspective.

[79]See Kicza 1983, p. 152, on the advantages of young relatives from the outside.

chants of Seville, very much including those involved in transatlantic trade, were not from the city itself but from surrounding provincial areas.[80] He gives us the example of clans from the Huelva region that maintained themselves in Seville by continuing to recruit younger relatives from the home area.[81] The most fully worked out study of a mercantile community renewing itself by the recruitment of relatives from home concerns Lisbon and hamlets in the Portuguese hinterland in the seventeenth century.[82] Socolow finds that many of the merchants who later came to Buenos Aires first migrated from some rural setting to join older relatives in some major Spanish center.[83] Mexico City thus succeeded to a role in which Seville had preceded it. Rather than seeing dominant peninsular Spaniards taking over a sector of a colonial region, we are justified in seeing Mexico City as a metropolitan center to which humble people from poor rural areas in Spain were repeatedly attracted. Parts of the north of Spain were in some senses a hinterland of Mexico City; Mexico City was using the area as little more than a nursery.

In general, it seems to me that the impressive shifts to be found in the commerce of Hispanic America in the three centuries or so after its inception took place within a framework of commercial devices and social practices present from the very beginning. Changes apply primarily to regional origin of personnel and the location of various phenomena as new parts of the transatlantic system localize and hive off. Each time and place is unique in containing a special combination of the common elements. It is no part of my intention to imply that organization was unduly static, that any other framework should have been adopted or would have

---

[80]Otte 1967, p. 236. I too found that Andalusian merchants in early Peru tended not to originate in Seville proper (Lockhart 1994, p. 90).

[81]Otte 1990, pp. 95–98, 101–5.

[82]David Grant Smith, "The Mercantile Class of Portugal and Brazil in the Seventeenth Century: A Socio-Economic Study of the Merchants of Lisbon and Bahia, 1620–1690" (1975). See especially chapter 2. I do not here enter into the Portuguese sphere, but I am sure it would fit well within the range of phenomena I discuss.

[83]Socolow 1978, p. 19.

brought on different kinds of developments. As Otte has noted, the flexibility inherent in *compañía* arrangements made it possible to use them for an incredible variety of undertakings in the transatlantic world of the sixteenth century.[84] In eighteenth-century Mexico equally, Kicza has shown us that it would have been impossible to find a type of economic activity, whether commercial or productive, that was not normally regulated by some kind of partnership agreement, usually distinguishing between investor and active manager.[85] The diversification or lack of specialization accompanying fluid partnerships was fully appropriate to the overall situation existing through our entire period, characterized by limited markets, relatively slow transportation devices, and huge risk in any one kind of enterprise.

---

[84]Otte 1967, pp. 229–30, 237–41, 252–56, and passim.

[85]Kicza 1983, p. 135, and see under "Companies" in his index. The several-man partnerships that Mexican merchants used to muster large-scale investment in silver mining in the late eighteenth century (Kicza 1983, p. 88) might seem new, but merchants had long joined together for large enterprises, as when twelve merchants shared the customs farm of Seville in 1530 (Otte 1990, pp. 98–99).

7. A Double Tradition: Editing Book Twelve of the Florentine Codex

(1995)

WHEN THE Europeans first came on the scene, most or all of the peoples of the Western Hemisphere possessed a well developed, multifaceted cultural lore and elaborate forms for expressing that lore. Few indeed, however, had writing traditions. Only the Mesoamericans, the peoples essentially of what is now central and southern Mexico and Guatemala, put records on paper with ink. Of these, only the lowland Maya had ever reproduced whole running sentences of inflected words, and it appears that by the sixteenth century even they no longer practiced the art to the extent they had in earlier times. In the great majority of culture areas on both American continents, not only was there no indigenous mechanism for preserving genres, content, and perspectives beyond the spoken word, but the peoples involved, lacking a tradition of writing, did not readily take to the European version of it, and produced no writings after contact; if a few groups did produce some, it was not during the time when unaltered cultural elements and the experiences of first contact were still in the general consciousness, and rarely indeed was it in their own language.

In Mesoamerica, however, members of most of the major language groups—probably it will turn out to be virtually all when we have explored the matter fully—learned alphabetic writing in the Spanish manner in about a generation and began to use the technique to produce records of various kinds in their own tongues, some in preconquest genres, some in Spanish-style genres much affected by their own traditions. Among these groups the Nahuas of central Mexico stand out, not because their writing tradition had more affinities with Spanish writing than the rest, for the opposite was true, but because they were the most numerous and dominant language group of the whole macroregion and received a corresponding amount of attention from Spaniards of all types.

Spanish ecclesiastics took the lead in introducing European-style writing among the Nahuas. We have only posterior and romanticized accounts of the process, so we must judge primarily from the artifacts produced. Even with such apt students, success was not instantaneous. No dated Nahuatl text is earlier than the mid-1540's (the conquest proper of central Mexico having taken place in 1519–21), and for the few early undated examples, no serious recent estimates antedate the later 1530's. Meanwhile the ecclesiastics, mainly mendicants and among them predominantly Franciscans, had been gaining competence in the language, devising an orthography, and working out genres of expression. They operated within Renaissance humanism, following particularly the precedent set by Antonio de Nebrija's Latinate Spanish grammar and dictionary, as well as the tradition of polyglot editions of biblical and other texts.

But the clerics were not alone in the enterprise, and indeed it is doubtful that unaided they could have had the success that they did. From an early time they took in classes of boys to indoctrinate in Christianity and expose to Hispanic culture in a depth beyond that attainable by the populace in general. A few of the most gifted became the friars' aides and protegés; they often received instruction in Spanish and even in Latin, and in return, in a sense, they were the instructors of the friars in Nahuatl. These aides were the first Nahuas who learned to write their language alphabetically; as they matured and gained seniority, their influence grew. They became not only amanuenses—virtually none of the corpus of older Nahuatl documentation is in the hand of a Spaniard, even if the Spaniard is in some sense the director or author— but coauthors. They were responsible for assuring that material such as catechisms, confessionals, and hymns were cast in an idiomatic, socioculturally correct Nahuatl. They provided the Nahuatl glosses that went into lexicons (dominated by the great vocabulary of fray Alonso de Molina, with a first edition in the 1550's and a definitive one in 1571) and the phrases that illustrated the friars' Nahuatl grammars. They may not have devised the original orthographic canon to be employed in transcribing Nahuatl, but in their hands that canon was used quite differently than it would have been by Europeans. Almost immediately, Nahuas instructed by the friars branched off to produce documents on their own, sometimes as the clerk-notaries of the new Spanish-style municipal councils set up in most of the local ethnic states of central Mexico in the period 1540–55, using primarily genres of Spanish origin, and sometimes operating even more independently, creating alphabetic (as well as pictorial) versions of their own traditional genres, especially historical annals.[1]

In several instances the friars went beyond the business of replicating Christian doctrinal material in Nahuatl to promoting the production of traditional indigenous lore, primarily with the intention of learning what deviltries they were combating, but with time also motivated in part by simple enthusiastic interest in the topic. The deservedly most famous of those working in this vein was the Franciscan fray Bernardino de Sahagún, active in central Mexico from 1529 to 1590.

By the 1540's Sahagún had conceived the project of a general encyclopedic history of preconquest Nahua culture, written in Nahuatl under his direction by his indigenous aides on the basis of information systematically acquired from Nahua informants, usually senior and influential. The corpus of material thus created was variously revised, expanded, and reorganized over the decades, until by the late 1560's it began to assume the fully elaborated, twelve-book form of the work known sometimes as the General History of the Things of New Spain, or more often as the Florentine Codex, from the best and only reasonably complete manuscript that has come down to us. The Codex itself is a product of the end of the 1570's, and it was not until that point that Sahagún's Spanish translation of the Nahuatl was prepared; the original and the translation run through the entire work in facing columns, both written by Nahua copyists.[2]

The main thrust of the enterprise had little to do with the Spanish conquest, at least in any direct way. But from the

---

[1] For a more detailed discussion of the matter of the preceding two paragraphs, see Lockhart 1992, chapter 8.

[2] For a detailed history of the General History and the Florentine Codex, see Charles Dibble's article in Sahagún 1950–82, Part 1, pp. 9–23.

1550's, or conceivably earlier, Sahagún had been using the same team and the same methods to concoct a narrative of the conquest of central Mexico or, as it turned out, of that portion of it of interest to his informants, who in this case were the people of Tlatelolco, the junior partner of Tenochtitlan at the center of what we often know as the "Aztec Empire." We cannot be certain that the conquest narrative was originally meant to be part of the general cultural and historical survey, but in the end it was incorporated into it as the last of the General History's twelve books.[3] Book Twelve, on which I focus here, thus shares the genesis and principal characteristics of the General History and must be seen in that context.

The history of editing the Florentine Codex bifurcates according to the Spanish and Nahuatl columns of the original. For a wider audience, the immediately comprehensible Spanish part was the whole work; hence it has been published without the Nahuatl several times (though the Spanish has not been translated). The deviant spellings and usage of the Spanish version were immediately apparent to prospective editors, who viewed these features purely as errors or defects, and all had recourse to the so-called Tolosa Manuscript, a posterior copy made in Spain, in which the copyist regularized the orthography and grammar by his own lights, making the text more acceptable to a general readership. Editors have further modernized and standardized following their own tastes.[4] While the bulk of Sahagún's message and even of his Spanish survives these procedures quite handily, the interesting traces of the role of the Nahua copyists who produced the extant original are lost or submerged.

More serious attempts have been made to deal with the Nahuatl. Sahaguntine scholarship really begins with the work of the German anthropologist Eduard Seler in the early part of the twentieth century.[5] Although ultimately more concerned with the substance of the Sahaguntine corpus and its interpretation than with editing it, Seler published German translations and transcriptions of portions of the Nahuatl of the Florentine Codex, including Book Twelve. Both his ed-

---

[3] See ibid., pp. 10, 13.   [4] Ibid., pp. 21–23.

[5] Much of Seler's philological work is in Seler 1927.

itorial practices and his translations are worthy of respect, but I will refrain from discussing them because they bear a generic similarity to the work of his most important successors, Arthur Anderson and Charles Dibble, who through three decades (1950's–1970's) published a complete edition of the Florentine Codex, a book at a time, with transcriptions and translations of the Nahuatl column.[6] The Spanish was extensively used as a source of inspiration for translation, and many passages are quoted for their relevance, but the Spanish column as a whole was not reproduced or translated. Below I will have more to say about Anderson and Dibble's work. Suffice it for now to assert that their splendid transcription of the Nahuatl is more than adequate for most scholarly purposes; their translation is intentionally quite literal, but useful for that very reason, and it remains as a resource that future translators will survey as carefully as the contemporary translation of Sahagún himself.

The Mexican scholar Angel María Garibay, who worked on Sahagún contemporaneously with Anderson and Dibble, had come on the scene a bit earlier but involved himself above all in the philology of Nahuatl song. His main activity with the Sahagún corpus was to publish the Florentine Codex in Spanish, unaccompanied by the Nahuatl, as has been the practice.[7] Cognizant, however, that Sahagún had only paraphrased many sections of the Nahuatl of Book Twelve, and omitted some altogether, Garibay proceeded differently with that book, adding his own new translation to Sahagún's Spanish version; he provided no transcription of the Nahuatl. When Garibay did his translation of Book Twelve, Anderson and Dibble's Florentine Codex project was already under way. Garibay was a highly intelligent, intuitive, but also arbitrary translator; despite flashes of insight and occasional spectacular, half-intentional mistakes, his translations were overall approximately as literal as Anderson and Dibble's.

---

[6] Sahagún 1950–82. The general volume of 1982 (Part 1) followed the rest by several years, and indeed, some of the volumes of the body had seen a second revised edition before that time.

[7] Sahagún 1975.

To date, no general edition combining the two streams, the Spanish and the Nahuatl, has seen the light. As volume after volume of the Anderson and Dibble edition came out, the late Howard Cline began to make transcriptions and translations of the Spanish, hoping eventually to produce a full edition combining his own work with Anderson and Dibble's, so that for the first time both the Spanish and the Nahuatl would be reproduced in the same volume, in facing format, with translations of both. Cline did a great deal of work, but the plan never came to fruition. I have profited from his transcription and translation of the Spanish of Book Twelve, graciously made available to me by his daughter.[8] The transcription is fully diplomatic, as it should be, and the translation is perfectly adequate (translation is in any case a much less crucial matter with the Spanish than with the Nahuatl).

My own undertaking, a volume of the *Repertorium Columbianum*,[9] includes several Nahuatl conquest accounts, but all of the others together fade in significance and bulk compared with Book Twelve of the Florentine Codex. My one obvious innovation was to carry out, with at least one book of the Codex, a plan like that envisioned by Howard Cline, with the Nahuatl, the Spanish, and new English translations of both all facing. In the following, I discuss aspects of transcription, translation, and the treatment of illustrations as encountered in work on Book Twelve, but also in the broader context of Nahuatl philology.

Nahuatl orthography as employed in the sixteenth through eighteenth centuries was based squarely on Spanish values, with the addition of some conventions for sounds not present in sixteenth-century Spanish (*tz, tl,* an intermittent *h* for glottal stop). Despite an underlying uniformity and ready mutual intelligibility, the various subtraditions that were present from the beginning never coalesced entirely into a single orthographic standard, not even among the Spanish ecclesiastics who originated the system, and far less among

---

[8]S. L. Cline, active in the philology of both mundane Nahuatl texts and Sahagún (Cline and León-Portilla 1984, Sahagún 1989).

[9]Lockhart, ed., 1993. The introduction and notes to that book deal in greater depth with many of the matters discussed in this paper; it is also true that I address several themes more directly here.

the Nahuas who mainly practiced it. Spelling often followed pronunciation closely; thus one will find evidence of such things as lenition (*meztli* instead of *metztli*, "month," indicating the weakening of an affricate to a sibilant before a consonant), assimilation (*huelloquichiuh* instead of *huel oquichiuh* for "he really did it," indicating the incorporation of the word *huel* into the nuclear phrase), and variant word forms (*chipochitl* instead of *ichpochtli*, "maiden"). Examples like these tell us much about speech, syntax, and regional variation.

Moreover, change in the system took place across time. At first, the main representations of prevocalic [w] were *u* and *v*, with *hu* as a relatively little used third possibility. By the late sixteenth century, *hu* had displaced the others, to the point that later writers sometimes failed to understand the intention of earlier *u* and *v*, making serious errors of transcription in dealing with texts containing them. Thus on the one hand there is no dominant canon which present-day readers would understand better than any other and which therefore would have priority as a basis for modern transcriptions, and on the other hand a strictly diplomatic transcription contains essential clues about a given text's dating, regional origin, and intellectual lineage.

Nevertheless, the transcriptions made by modern scholars, especially in Mexico where the most was being done until recent decades, were at first usually standardized in a method based on modern Spanish orthography. The main features varying from original practice were the use of *z* before back vowels instead of the original *ç* (and the *s* which succeeded it in the eighteenth century) and a uniform *hu* for prevocalic [w], although vowels were also standardized, and other liberties were taken. This system became orthodox in Mexico with the work of Garibay and was followed by Miguel León-Portilla and Fernando Horcasitas.[10] During the 1980's, the philosophy of transcription among the Mexicans, perhaps affected by the work of Anderson and Dibble, whom I will discuss next,

---

[10]As in Garibay 1964–68, León-Portilla 1956, and Horcasitas 1974. The latter, however, is laudably inconsistent; Horcasitas left many especially interesting deviant forms as they are in the original.

began to veer in the direction of a more exact reproduction of the original; the transcription in León-Portilla's edition of Sahagún's *Coloquios*, for example, is fully diplomatic.[11]

Anderson and Dibble went over to reproducing all letters and diacritics as exactly as typographic techniques will permit, and their policy has gradually become the normal one for scholars working with older Nahuatl texts. It is also my own practice. Here I wish to discuss briefly some of the implications and ambiguities involved with transcribing the Nahuatl of Book Twelve in particular.

Sixteenth-century Spanish calligraphy as done by ecclesiastics used a set of diacritics on *q*, well known to those who work with late medieval and early modern Latin, to indicate *qui*, *que*, and *qua*; among secular writers, the only such sign in common use was a more cursive version of the one for *que*. In time, the same came to be true of writing by Nahuatl speakers, but since the first-generation writers were mainly trained by Spanish ecclesiastics, the *q* diacritics tend to be prominent in the texts they produced. These signs are thus a prime measure of the proximity or distance of ecclesiastical influence. Not even all the ecclesiastics used the diacritics in the same way. Thus the aides of Sahagún, in whom he instilled a uniform canon, hardly used the *qua* sign at all. Some writers in the Tlaxcalan region at the same time, however, made very liberal use of it. The differences reveal the existence of and even, to an extent, delineate subtraditions and regional schools; hence the original marking must be carefully preserved in an edition.

A major diagnostic characteristic of Sahagún's system in contradistinction to all others is the use of *o* and *ho* for [w] in preference to the other variants (though they appear too). It is especially important, then, to reproduce these quasi-deviant *o*'s, but it becomes rather difficult because in both Sahagún's

---

[11]Sahagún 1986. It is interesting that although Luis Reyes, a giant of Nahuatl philology, is highly progressive and greatly concerned with approaching ever closer to an appreciation of the originals in every way, he and his followers have retained elements of the older policy. (He uses *z* in the orthodox Mexican fashion; he has changed *hu*, but standardizes with *u* instead.) See Kirchhoff, Güemes, and Reyes García 1976 and Celestino Solís et al. 1985.

system and in Nahuatl phonology a clear difference between the value and function of *o*, *u*, and *v* is lacking, leading the copyists to merge them visually to the point of indistinguishability, especially *o* and *v*. Many cases are uncontroversial, but at a certain point, arbitrary decisions become necessary; direct representation reaches its limits, and only by comments in the apparatus can one apprise the reader of important surface aspects of the original.

Much the same thing happens with punctuation. In many Nahuatl texts, punctuation is so sparse that one must seriously suspect a punctuation-like mark of being an error, and transcriptions of mundane documents often, without notable loss, ignore punctuation altogether. Not so in texts produced under the auspices of Spanish ecclesiastics, who set value on punctuation, although their practices were loose and not those of today, and their students seem not to have fully understood their instruction in this respect in any case. The particular way of using punctuation in a text of this type is a clue to its provenience and tradition, as well as to the divisions of Nahuatl syntax. The distinctions between comma, semicolon, colon, and period seem to have sat lightly on the Nahuas (and even on their instructors); all of the marks appear to have the same primary function, that of indicating the beginning and end of phonological phrases. As a result, the writers were not much concerned with externally distinguishing a comma from a period, or a semicolon from a colon; arbitrariness and commentary again become necessary.[12]

In general, then, I advocate following the original as closely as is possible in a printed book, trying to avoid the loss of distinctions of great potential use to research in

---

[12]A special problem is a mark in Book Twelve looking rather like a question mark, a theory confirmed by the fact that it often coincides with the end of a direct question. It also appears in connection with indirect questions, however, and more notably, with statements of the kind associated with exclamation marks and with other sentences where its presence is rather hard to explain except by the presumption that the writer thought of it as something like quotation marks, to be used with any direct speech by the characters. In the end I used question marks except for the cases where exclamation marks seemed more appropriate, explaining myself in the apparatus.

various kinds of cultural and linguistic history. The one area where I have departed from that principle is in the spacing of letters on the page. In my edition (as in similar publications I have been involved in) I respaced everything into words by modern grammatical criteria. Such has come to be the general practice in reproducing older Nahuatl, on the grounds that it is empirically virtually impossible to distinguish spaced from connected elements. Spaces in any case are better called gaps or intervals; the *space* as we know it in a printed book or a typed page was not a part of the calligraphy of most sixteenth-century writers, any more than it was of the practice in Roman inscriptions. Ecclesiastical writers, however, did tend to leave a discernible and meaningful space between words, and some of their Nahua students at first did somewhat the same, although the entity comparable to the word in European languages is rather larger, more flexible, and more complex. In the Florentine Codex, spaces are exceptionally regular and potentially significant (articles and some small particles are often integrated spatially into the larger word). Nevertheless, the system falls far short of consistency, and above all, no hyphens were placed at the ends of lines, so that deciding between a space and a continuation at the thousands of line breaks occurring in a small-column format is entirely arbitrary. Anderson and Dibble followed the apparent spacing closely, making their own deductions at line breaks and arbitrarily separating articles and the like from larger words. Their procedure is very reasonable, but since the user of their edition would still have to consult a facsimile to ascertain the full details of the original spacing, I decided to respace even in this auspicious environment.

One must also consider the matter of spacing larger elements. The Florentine Codex in general and Book Twelve specifically are divided into titled and numbered chapters. Although it is clear that the chapter division is posterior to the generation of the Nahuatl text, it seems better to leave the chapters as they are than to attempt the tricky business of establishing prior units. The chapters are essentially undivided internally in both Spanish and Nahuatl, except for gaps made necessary by pictures or by differences in the length of the two columns. On purely intellectual grounds, there is no doubt that the surface unity of the chapters should be retained. In fact, however, the modern reader is extraordinarily unhappy with such a solution. Using introductory particles and speaker changes as clues, as have my predecessors, I divided the chapters into paragraph-sized chunks in both Nahuatl and Spanish, loudly warning the reader in the apparatus that these divisions are for convenience only and do not correspond to the original. Perhaps future editors of such materials will have the courage I lacked and will let chapters run on undivided.

The existence of a facsimile thus becomes a prime desideratum even though one does everything in an edition to make consulting it unnecessary. A marvelous color facsimile of the Florentine Codex was published some years back, and serious scholars will consult it regularly over and above any edition.[13] The kind of fidelity on the printed page that I have been advocating, however, is not rendered superfluous by a fine facsimile; printed pages with the relevant details scan far more readily than the originals, not only for neophytes but for trained and experienced scholars, and work with a whole corpus of texts becomes nearly impossible without sophisticated editions at once following and clarifying the originals.

I have been speaking primarily of the Nahuatl text. The transcription of the Spanish text obeys the same imperatives, and is all in all markedly less problematic. One does, however, face the matter of the notable deviance from normal Spanish orthography and even style caused by the fact that the copyists were native speakers of Nahuatl, not Spanish. I never had any doubt that the deviance, being among the most interesting and significant features of the Spanish text, should be preserved (though some Romance philologists apprised of the project were initially of the opinion that standard forms should be inserted in brackets, with the odd forms relegated to notes). The question was not so much the reproduction as the explanation of the phenomena, in order to avoid the impression, dominant until now, that the Spanish text of Book Twelve (and of the whole Florentine

---

[13]Sahagún 1979.

Codex) was simply an inferior and erroneous version.

The orthographic deviances are of two types, visual and aural. The latter are more common and perhaps more informative , but the former have their interest as well. We can tell that a deviance is visual when there is no similarity between the sounds represented by the standard letter and the one which has been substituted, with the similar appearance of the letters on a written page remaining as the explanation. Thus the copyist of the Spanish once put "se desperauā" where the original intention, reflected in the Nahuatl, was clearly "se despeñauā," "they hurled themselves off." The repetition of such examples (there are perhaps a dozen in the manuscript) first tells us that the Spanish of the Florentine Codex as we know it rests on a previous written version, not directly on Sahagún's dictation (which still remains the most likely ultimate origin), and second it shows us the limits of the copyist's comprehension of Spanish, thereby measuring one aspect of indigenous acculturation.

More frequent in Book Twelve are phonologically based letter substitutions, depending on the similarity of a sound in Spanish to one in Nahuatl. These tell us of how the copyist, and presumably his peers, pronounced Spanish; we can deduce from the relatively frequent substitutions that he had made little if any phonological adjustment to Spanish, using the closest Nahuatl equivalent where a Spanish sound was missing in his mother tongue. Nahuatl lacked voiced stops, thus Nahuas often substituted the corresponding unvoiced stop; lacking [r], they substituted [l], and their lack of a distinction between [o] and [u] led to the merging of those Spanish sounds; the same happened with unstressed [e] and [i]. Since the Nahuas perceived no difference between these pairs of sounds, on the written page they engaged not only in primary substitution, such as *p* (labial unvoiced stop) for *b* (labial voiced stop), but also in hypercorrection, as in *b* for *p*. These phenomena are well attested in the mundane Nahuatl documentation of the time.[14] The bulk of the "misspellings" in Book Twelve are expectable substitutions for the time when they were written, and they betray the fact that even the

---

[14]See Lockhart 1992, chapters 7 and 8.

highly educated aides of Sahagún did not escape the general processes of language evolution. The following table of examples from Book Twelve can illustrate:

Letter Substitutions
in the Spanish of the Florentine Codex, Book Twelve

normal substitutions

p for b	supita	for	subita (súbita) "sudden, unexpected"
t for d	moternas		modernas "modern"
c for g	delcadas		delgadas "slim"

hypercorrections

b for p	bueblo	pueblo "settlement"
d for t	desde	deste "of this"
r for l	abrir	abril "April"

o and u

o for u	arcaboceros	arcabuceros "harquebusiers"
	yocatan	yucatan "Yucatan"
u for o	su pena	so pena "under penalty"
	estamus	estamos "we are"

e and i (unstressed)

e for i	se rendieron	se rindieron "they surrendered"
i for e	los siguian	los seguian "they followed them"

Not all of the oddities of the Spanish are phonological. One will notice that in the great majority of cases, the copyist writes *los* for the plural indirect object as well as for the direct object. Here we have not a merging of the sounds [o] and [e] but a reflection of the fact that Nahuatl makes no distinction between direct and indirect objects, and there are some other traces in the text of Nahuatl grammar carried into Spanish. Again, the indicated treatment is not to banish these manifestations from the text, but to explain their significance to the reader in the apparatus.

Moving now beyond matters of transcription, let me say that any translation of a complex text in older Nahuatl done at the present time is inevitably provisional, not merely in the sense that any translation whatever is always in some way for that occasion and purpose only, but in the sense that rather substantial alteration of substance and tone is likely in the future. Precision of translation gains with the increasing size of the corpus being translated and the number of generations spent on the enterprise. The corpus of older Nahuatl—that is, the known and available corpus—is still growing apace, and although a few items are now being translated for the third or fourth time, many more are receiving their first translation, and much of the corpus, including some monuments and even whole genres, remains untranslated.

The main precedents for translating the Nahuatl of Book Twelve are first Sahagún himself as represented in the Spanish column and second Anderson and Dibble (for they have substantially incorporated the translations of Seler and Garibay). The two are very different. Sahagún as the director of the whole original project was in a unique position to understand the Nahuatl text and even to ask his aides when he did not; he also had a deserved reputation as one of the two Spaniards in Mexico who knew Nahuatl best. He did not aim, however, at a full rendering, but as with most Spanish translators of his time, produced something more on the order of a paraphrase, sometimes with his own commentary. The Spanish is usually much shorter than the Nahuatl (the difference being filled with illustrations), and a few whole sections of the Nahuatl lack any Spanish equivalent at all. Even when translating fairly closely, Sahagún tended (for he was far from consistent) to favor a pithy idiomatic translation over a longer and more literal one. So far did he go in this direction that the wave of translators beginning with Seler often failed to see the connection between the Spanish and the Nahuatl and produced a semantically less accurate literal translation in its stead. Recently we have gained even more respect for Sahagún, recognizing some of his faithful renderings of obscure idioms. Doubtless more remain to be discovered, one reason among others why it is desirable to have his Spanish available in facing format when studying the Nahuatl.

As the first English translators of the Florentine Codex, Anderson and Dibble almost inevitably hewed to highly literalistic procedures; moreover, they were encouraged in that direction by the project's original sponsors.[15] A literal translation always has pedagogical value, and all the more so with discourse as complex and metaphorical as was common in older Nahuatl rhetorical practice. By giving element-by-element equivalents of the Nahuatl, it also informs us of the often (apparently) poetic elements that go into stock phrases, of double structures, of the elaborateness and indirection of many statements in a way that cannot be incorporated into a pragmatic translation. As translators of Nahuatl have moved more in the direction of emphasizing the intention, pragmatics, or sense of the text, they have still felt the need for a more literal component in some of their editions. Some editions, in fact, have included two complete translations, one more literal and the other more pragmatic.[16] A good deal of Book Twelve is in straightforward language that will not look very different in translation no matter who the translator or what the premises. Also, with four facing columns already, there was no place in my edition for another translation of the Nahuatl. My translation of the Nahuatl of Book Twelve thus stands in a quite permanent complementary relationship to that of Anderson and Dibble, and students may find it advantageous to have both at hand in working on the text.

As mentioned above, Anderson and Dibble undertook their translation under certain general instructions, including the prescription that the language should be archaic, in the fashion of the King James Bible. They complied, with some private misgivings, silently resisting in some subtle ways, such as often using the past tense instead of the present because older and newer English coincide better there.[17] This rather superficial feature of their edition detracts little if at all from its basic value. Anderson and Dibble actually published another version of Book Twelve, without the Nahuatl but with more illustrations, in modern English.[18] The basic

---

[15]See Anderson's discussion of the beginning stages of the enterprise in Sahagún 1950–82, Part 1, p. 4.

[16]For example, Karttunen and Lockhart 1987. The idea is not new; see Tezozomoc 1949 and Garibay 1943.

[17]Sahagún 1950–82, Part 1, pp. 4, 6.

[18]Sahagún 1978.

nature of the translation remained little altered. In general, a formal, weighty tone is entirely appropriate to portions of the Florentine Codex, but not necessarily to all of it. My own intention was to retain an elevated tone where appropriate, but not to aim for archaisms and not to neglect the original's occasional strong colloquialism and down-to-earth vocabulary. The tone of each translation, of course, is its own, and not an important part of any general trend of the field. I fully expect that many will find my translation of Book Twelve too colloquial.

To attempt to illustrate the relation of Anderson and Dibble's translation to mine, I will include here a perhaps not entirely unrepresentative passage with the two renderings.[19]

> in iuh quima, in iuh moma, ca iehoatl in topiltzin Quetzalcoatl in oquiçaco: ca iuh catca iniollo in çan oallaz, in çan quiçaquiuh, quioalmatiz in ipetl, in icpal: ipampa ca vmitztia, in iquac ia. Auh in quimioa macuiltin, in quinamiquitivi, in quitlamamacativi: in teiacantia Teuoa, in itecutoca, in ipiltoca Ioalli ichan.

Anderson and Dibble:

> Thus he thought—thus was it thought—that this was Topiltzin Quetzalcoatl who had come to land. For it was in their hearts that he would come, that he would come to land, just to find his mat, his seat. For he had traveled there [eastward] when he departed. And [Moctezuma] sent five [emissaries] to go to meet him, to go to give him gifts. The first was the teohua, whose lordly name, whose princely name was Yoalli ichan.

My translation:

> He thought and believed that it was Topiltzin Quetzalcoatl who had landed. For they were of the opinion that he would return, that he would come to land, that he would come back to his seat of authority, since he had gone in that direction [eastward] when he left. And [Moteucçoma] sent five [people] to go to meet him and give him things. The leader had the official title of Teohua [custodian of the god] and the personal name of Yohualli ichan.

---

[19]The Anderson and Dibble translation may be seen in Sahagún 1950–82, Book 12 (Part 13) (2d edition, 1975), pp. 9–10; my translation is in Lockhart, ed., 1993, p. 62. Both have transcriptions.

Most of the progress recently made in translating Nahuatl has to do on the one hand with a growing stock of well understood set phrases and idiomatic usages, many of them first elucidated in work on mundane documents, and on the other with a better grasp of syntax, much of it the result of a new generation of studies inspired to a large extent by the work of the seventeenth-century Jesuit grammarian Horacio Carochi. Little advance has been seen in the interpretation of individual Nahuatl words referring to concrete things. With the many puzzling terms of this nature in Book Twelve, I relied primarily on Anderson and Dibble, who searched many obscure modern works of reference and also brought to bear explanations in various parts of the Sahaguntine corpus that are not found in any dictionary. The state of knowledge about the vocabulary of material culture is far from satisfactory, and improvement will be hard to achieve. Perhaps systematic lexical work with modern spoken Nahuatl can provide additional meanings.

This is not the place to discuss my more specific strategies of translation. I will, however, mention two salient aspects. The first relates to a single key term, *altepetl*, referring to a type of local ethnic state, usually of modest size, that was the framework of Nahua sociopolitical organization and indeed of Nahua culture in general. The discovery and increasing comprehension of the altepetl has been crucial to recent developments in central Mexican ethnohistory. No one English translation will cover all cases of the word's occurrence, or even most of them; yet a single rendering is necessary if the reader of the translation is to be able to appreciate the role of the entity and the contours of the concept. Despite my general striving after simplicity and readability, I decided to leave the term untranslated in the English version, hoping to naturalize it at least for those who are interested in early Mexico (and indeed, the word is already beginning to achieve that status in the ethnohistorical literature). The same treatment, after all, has long since been accorded in early Spanish American history to an equally crucial, idiosyncratic, and even related institution, the encomienda, or grant to a Spaniard of rights to an indigenous entity (i.e., in central Mexico an altepetl).

A second noteworthy feature of my experience in translating the Nahuatl of Book Twelve does not in the end surface unambiguously in the translation itself. The original falls into two distinct parts stylistically, a fact that no one seems to have commented on before my edition. The first, a section concerning the activity of the Spaniards before they reached Mexico City for the first time, is in a rather elevated, highly repetitive style peculiar to the Sahaguntine corpus. The second, the bulk of the narrative, concerning events taking place in the immediate vicinity of the informants, is much more straightforward, colloquial, and action-oriented. Comparing Book Twelve with other conquest accounts, I found that the first section has no close parallel there. I deduced that the first part, which has been virtually the only source for the general view of the initial reaction of the Nahuas to the Spanish presence, was in origin posterior to the rest by at least a generation, with all that that implies. The difference is much less apparent in the translation than in the original. Yet I deemed it to be something the reader must know about, and I felt that a detailed discussion of the stylistic-linguistic facts and their substantive implications was a necessary part of the introductory apparatus.

The Florentine Codex and Book Twelve along with it are blessed with a large amount of accompanying pictorial material. I do not immediately say illustrative material, because in the preconquest Nahua tradition, the most basic elements of a presentation were conveyed in pictorial-glyphic form, and an oral recital (the origin of the alphabetic text written down after the conquest) was an elaboration upon it; thus the pictorial element was much more than mere illustration. The question that arises is whether or not the pictures accompanying Book Twelve retain the traditional role. Apparently they do not. Much of the narrative itself is highly visual and episodic, and in some cases, as with the elaborate costumes said to have been presented to Hernando Cortés, the text doubtless describes a pictorial original. Yet those pictures are no longer present in the form of Book Twelve that we know. An earlier, all-Nahuatl version has no pictures at all, and the ones in Book Twelve in the Codex seem to have been reinvented, inspired by the narrative, thus approximating

European illustrations after all. As I mentioned earlier, their most obvious function is to fill in empty space left by the circumstance that the Nahuatl is much longer than the Spanish. The illustrations, for with this background we may call them that, are done in predominantly European style, at least superficially, although elements of the indigenous tradition, even at times full-scale glyphs, are ubiquitous. It was apparent to me from the beginning that the pictorial element should be fully integrated into the edition, as it should be with any early Nahuatl text, in view of the preconquest tradition. The very fact that the old pictorial primacy was giving way to secondary status for the pictorial component as simple illustration is of the highest interest for Nahua cultural history. Because of early deadlines and, even more basically, because of my lack of adequate training in preconquest art history, I was not able to do justice to this aspect. I did manage to get good reproductions of the pictures into the edition,[20] distributed in positions quite closely corresponding to the original, and I supplied rudimentary legends, as well as a brief general discussion of the nature of the pictorial material in the introduction. I lament, however, not having been able to do more, and I hope that future editors of this type of material will bring a higher degree of art historical expertise to the enterprise of publishing Nahuatl documents. Simply consulting art historians is not likely to do the trick; it is necessary that someone get a mastery of both Nahuatl philology and Mesoamerican art history of the preconquest and early postconquest periods.[21]

In summary, transcriptions and translations of older Nahuatl are to an extent for different audiences. There is no large group of people who by virtue of their general education can both read the originals and appreciate the translations.

---

[20]To do so would have been impossible without the kind help of the University of Utah Press, which lent out excellent photographs of all the illustrations without charge. Many of them had been included in Sahagún 1978.

[21]Dana Leibsohn, formerly a doctoral student in art history at UCLA and now at Smith College, who is doing interesting work on the Historia Tolteca-Chichimeca, is such a person. (See Leibsohn 1993.)

Transcriptions are research tools much needed by a very active but still small group of Nahuatl scholars; translations
are partly for that group too, but above all are the only avenue
through which a wider scholarly circle can have access to the
materials.

A strictly diplomatic transcription serves best. All the elements of the orthography have European histories, but they
cannot be treated as though they were directly in that tradition. No dominant orthographic canon of Nahuatl that
readers would be familiar with exists; only the highly qualified will be attempting to read the transcriptions at all. In the
special case of Spanish texts copied by Nahuas, not a common
occurrence outside the Florentine Codex until a much later
time, one might think that they could be treated in the normal
manner of early modern Romance philology. But we have seen
that the Nahua writer's distinct culture shows through in his
"mistakes." In a well established tradition, one can confidently note the intention of a slip or deviance. Here it is by no
means clear what the intention is, or whose intention should
count. Two different intentions are involved, that of Sahagún
and that of the Nahua amanuensis. For me, the latter must
take precedence. Ideally, one would make separate versions,
or at least annotate extensively, trying to divine Sahagún's
intent. I have not gone that far in my edition, and not only for
practical reasons or because of my own interests. Sahagún's
exact orthography is beyond reconstruction (and indeed, with
Sahagún's shaky hand, the original was probably dictated to
a Nahua secretary in the first place). Since the syntax and
usage are at least ninety percent consonant with normal
sixteenth-century Spanish practice, the lay reader of Spanish
can approximate Sahagún's phrasing as well as anyone else.
The apparent errors in this material need interpretation in
the edition itself; hardly anyone can be expected to understand the interference of the Nahuatl substratum. It is only
from large-scale, close linguistic analysis of the corpus of
mundane Nahuatl texts that we can recognize the patterns.

In matters of translation, the trend has been from pragmatic with the sixteenth-century Spanish friars to literal
with the first modern translators, then back to pragmatic and
colloquial more recently. There is some need for double

versions with many texts, especially since very few readers can recognize words (drowned in affixes) in the original. True puzzles are left after even the most assiduous translation process. Open questions and mysteries must be tolerated. (A copy editor, feeling that my question marks in the translation were excessive, turned them into angular brackets; I would have preferred question marks.) In most serious translations from European languages, there are few enough questions about the primary semantic thrust that those instances can be discussed in all detail, with all possible alternatives. With a complicated older Nahuatl text, in the present decade and any decade in the near future, this procedure would lead to an apparatus the size of the Bible, dwarfing the text. Furthermore, a good deal of its contents would be pure expression of mystification or desperate speculation rather than informed weighing of realistic alternatives. Translating the Spanish of the time, however, even when copied and somewhat transformed by Nahuas, presents relatively few problems.

The edition of older Nahuatl texts is and needs to be a relatively autonomous subfield. Translation and even transcription are an inseparable part of a larger process of opening up Nahuatl texts, very much including mundane documents that might seem superficially to have no relation at all to things like the Florentine Codex. No truly definitive editions are possible or should be aimed for until the process is much further along than it is at present. And yet a very considerable apparatus of commentary is called for because of the extreme rarity of the contextual knowledge required to make certain important interpretive decisions. Ultimately, the entire enterprise of understanding older Nahuatl texts, from the most mundane to the most elevated, is a single campaign. None of the material can receive fully adequate editions until all of it has been worked through as a unit.

8. Three Experiences of Culture Contact: Nahua, Maya, and Quechua[1]

(1998)

I N THE CONTACT episodes between peoples of the Western Hemisphere and Europeans, the nature and rate of cultural change on the indigenous side (change which does not usually preclude survival and continuity) seems to depend primarily on two things. The first is the degree of similarity, that is, convergence between the two cultures involved. The second is the type and extent of contact between the bearers of the two cultures, for cultures can meet only through the medium of living, breathing individuals. This second element is actually dependent in part on the first. Without a quite strong convergence, there can be little normal, peaceful, mutually meaningful contact between the members of two separate societies. Cultural convergence is also an element in the attraction of outsiders, bringing in larger numbers of Europeans and intensifying contact. Europeans could build on societies structured somewhat similarly to their own and hence draw greater economic benefit from them. Economic benefit, especially leverage on the economy of Europe, was the motor of Iberian emigration, so that the characteristics of indigenous populations were by no means the only factor causing the Europeans to crowd into some regions and avoid others. As it happened, silver and similarity coincided reasonably well; until the late eighteenth century, the great bulk of Spanish immigration (which was at the same time the majority of total European immigration) went to Mexico and the central Andes. It is the experience of this core, the central areas per se, where the most Europeans confronted the largest indigenous populations and where elements of convergence were strongest, with which I am concerned.

I am not, of course, the first or the last with such an interest, which has long dominated and continues to dominate

---

[1] I wish to express my thanks to Kimberly Gauderman, who joined me in studying Quechua and was instrumental in procuring and copying dictionaries and grammars.

the more or less Latin Americanist ethnohistorical literature. My particular angle has to do with identifying, analyzing, and following the evolution of a people's concepts and basic structures across a broad spectrum, not so much in their conscious statements on such matters as through the many types of records, often mundane, in which they use their vocabulary and reveal their thoughts more unselfconsciously. Such work naturally requires records done in the languages of the people involved at the time and place of interest. I have worked for years with the Nahuas less because of their centrality than because they have left us a large corpus of alphabetic texts in Nahuatl, written by themselves in every nook and cranny of central Mexico from around 1540 to the late eighteenth century. In searching for cases to be used for comparison with the Nahuas—and that is the enterprise toward which I am gradually turning—I again must follow the trail of language; this time, for practical reasons, with more attention to the existence of scholarship which can guide me.

Yucatan and Yucatecan Maya leap out of the crowd of non-Nahua Mesoamerican languages and peoples. All the Mesoamerican groups shared in the region's preconquest writing traditions, and all took up alphabetic writing after the conquest to some extent or other; Kevin Terraciano has located and worked with a mass of documents in Mixtec, for example.[2] The Yucatecans' Mayan cousins in Guatemala may

---

[2]Terraciano, a doctoral student in history at UCLA, is far advanced on a dissertation which amounts to a general cultural and social history of the Mixtec region across the postconquest centuries, based primarily on sources in Mixtec discovered by himself. Terraciano is going into language contact phenomena quite deeply; shortly we should be able to add the Mixtec example to the others.

(In due course Terraciano completed the dissertation, "Ñudzahui History: Mixtec Writing and Culture in Colonial Oaxaca" [UCLA, 1994], before this piece was published but after its first writing and presentation in 1992. Briefly, Terraciano shows a process resembling that of the Nahuas in its shape more than the Maya example does, but with its own distinct profile. For one thing, the Mixtecs bordered the Nahuas and had their first experience of linguistic contact phenomena in Nahuatl, which many of the nobles knew. The general process runs similarly to that seen among the Nahuas, not only in content but in rhythm and chronology, a

equal them in the size of the raw documentary heritage—
though Matthew Restall (1992, 1997) is finding Yucatan apparently as thickly documented through indigenous texts as
the Nahua world—but they lack Yucatan's philological and
linguistic tradition, stretching from Ralph Roys (1939) to
Victoria Bricker (1981) and Frances Karttunen (1985).

The third most accessible language of the sedentary peoples, at the moment, is Quechua. George Urioste (1983), now
joined by Frank Salomon (Salomon and Urioste 1991), has
edited the legends of Huarochirí, and Urioste has made the
Quechua in Huaman Poma's chronicle available (Guaman
Poma 1980), while Bruce Mannheim (1991) has discussed the
whole available corpus, drawing many linguistic and other
conclusions from it. What is mainly absent from the known
writings in Quechua is the large body of mundane documents
in Nahuatl and Yucatecan Maya written by native speakers
for other native speakers and not done under Spanish auspices. Little or none of the material studied to date has that
character, and without it many things that are an open book
in Mesoamerica can never be known.

The situation may change, however, and in a certain sense
has already begun to. George Urioste has in his possession
photocopies of some twenty pages of mundane Quechua of
unknown archival provenience but undoubted authenticity,
done by a clerk of the indigenous town of Chuschi in the
central Peruvian highlands in 1679, consisting of complaints
about the parish priest and extracts from local church or
municipal records. The hand, tone, and language are very
comparable with those of Mesoamerican records of the same
genre and time. I will not be able to analyze these papers in
appropriate detail here, not only because of my still small
competence in Quechua, but because, though Urioste gave me a
copy of the materials a few years back, I do not feel that I have
the right to make extensive public use of them. I will only

---

generation or so behind Nahuatl. But the stages are not so distinct,
and there appears to have been greater regional variation; one could
argue over whether the full equivalent of Stage 3 was achieved during
the time of production of Mixtec documents or not. All this is much
what we would expect in an area further from the center of the
Spanish presence than the Nahuas but not as far as the Maya.)

mention an interesting detail or two and carry out some general comparisons with better known, if more rarefied, Quechua writings. The implications of the existence of the Chuschi papers, however, are enormous. The documents are in a practiced hand and follow mature conventions; the only conclusion one can draw is that this indigenous writer had long been in the habit of putting municipal and other records on paper in Quechua, and further that he cannot have been operating in a vacuum. There must have been others, in other places and times. We have every reason to think that a large mundane Quechua documentation existed in the seventeenth century and perhaps earlier and later. What can have come of it is another matter, and the fact that so little has surfaced after so much searching is not a cause for optimism.

Though chosen for pragmatic reasons of linguistic accessibility, Yucatan and the central Andes make an excellent counterweight to central Mexico on other grounds as well, not only because they have been much and well studied on the basis of Spanish materials, but because Yucatan can legitimately represent the south of Mexico, culturally distinct from the center in several ways and less directly affected by Spaniards than either central Mexico or Peru, while the Andes represent an entirely different culture area, the other half of the world of Western-Hemisphere high civilizations.

The Nahua case

I will not enter into any detail here, because, on the one hand, I have been expounding the evolution of the Nahuas for a few years now, and have done so at length in a pair of books I published not long ago (Lockhart 1991, 1992), so that the essence of the matter may well already have reached the ears of the reader; and on the other hand, a full analysis would be far too lengthy.

In brief, Nahua reactions or adaptations to the Spanish presence have the character of a broad, semi-autonomous, in large part subconscious process in which the Nahua component is as important as the Hispanic component—we are not dealing with simple imposition, and absolutely not with imposition by fiat. The process advances across the entire cultural spectrum in a parallel, often reciprocally reinforcing

Table: The Three Stages among the Nahuas, and some of their implications

	1 1519 to ca. 1545–50	2 ca. 1545–50 to ca. 1640–50	3 1640–50 to 1800, in many cases until today
Language	Essentially no change	Noun borrowing, no other change	Full range of phenomena of bilingualism
Temporary labor mechanisms	Encomienda (whole indigenous state assigned long-term to one Spaniard)	Repartimiento (small parties divided among Spaniards for short periods of time)	Informal, individual arrangements between Spaniards and Indians
Government of the local states	Tlatoani (king) and nobles as always	Hispanic-style town council, cabildo (manned by tlatoani and nobles)	Fragmentation of local states and more idiosyncratic forms of officeholding
Terminology of noble rank	No change	Applied to members of the cabildo	Disappears, replaced by ↓
Naming patterns	Christian (first) names	Complex stepped naming system gradually develops	Mature naming system, precisely locating every individual in society by rank
Kinship	No change	Marriage concepts and terminology adopted	Terms for siblings, cousins, nephews/nieces, and in-laws change to conform with Sp.
Songs	?	Genre mixed preconquest-postconquest in content, preconquest in form, with verses indicated by vocables, pairing of verses, and symmetrical arrangement of pairs	Rhyme, meter, line length, indefinitely continuing set of verses with no numerical pattern
History	?	Annals divided equally between pre- and postconquest	Annals almost exclusively postconquest. Syncretizing, atemporal legends called "titles" are written down.
Records	Pictorial/ideographic-oral (latter dominant)	Pictorial/ideographic-alphabetic	Primarily alphabetic
Art and Architecture	?	Great idiosyncratic monastery complexes built; frescoes and decorative carving in mixed Hispanic-indigenous idiom	Small Spanish-style parish churches built; art mainly European in style
Religion	God, baptism	Saints proliferate, one per sociopolitical unit	One saint, Guadalupe, takes on national significance

Source: James Lockhart, *The Nahuas After the Conquest*, p. 428.

fashion. Over the postconquest centuries, three stages emerge quite sharply: Stage 1, a generation of little cultural change; Stage 2, about a hundred years from around 1540–50 to 1640–50, a time when change affected predominantly corporations, and Hispanic elements entered Nahua frameworks as discrete items; and Stage 3, after 1650 until today, a time of personal interpenetration of the two societies and more intimate, structure-altering change. The accompanying table, from my book *The Nahuas After the Conquest* (1992), can give some notion of the nature and scope of the phenomenon.

Language was crucial both to the investigation of the process and to its inner development. It was in the language of the texts the Nahuas wrote that the stages first showed themselves, and it is perhaps there that they can be seen most clearly. Structural changes in various realms of life manifested themselves to a large extent in altered concepts embodied in new or adjusted vocabulary. Thus my comparative undertaking must begin with language, and I will minimally characterize the linguistic aspect of the stages. Stage 1 involves describing introduced phenomena with the resources of native vocabulary and naming mechanisms, resulting in extensions and neologisms rather than loans (other than the borrowing of proper names). Stage 2 involves massive borrowing of Spanish vocabulary in the areas of new species and items, role definitions, economic, political, and religious concepts and procedures, and measurements of all kinds. But virtually all loans were grammatically nouns. Loans were naturalized phonologically and to an extent semantically; grammar and syntax could hardly be said to have changed. In Stage 3, as the result of large-scale bilingualism, Spanish verbs and particles were borrowed; idioms were translated, with some Nahuatl words becoming automatic equivalents of Spanish words in the process; Spanish sounds were acquired; new types of nouns were borrowed, including words for blood relatives and terms for which close equivalents already existed.

As I say, across the centuries adjustments in a large array of cultural realms ran parallel to those in language. Let us take just one example, of special interest because the phenomenon projects partly into the Hispanic world and can be detected even in situations where we have no access to indigenous-language sources—Spanish procurement of temporary indigenous labor. In Stage 1, the central Mexican encomienda (grant of the tribute and labor of an Indian group to a Spaniard) was in a monopoly position in this respect, diverting the indigenous *coatequitl* or draft rotary labor to the purposes of the encomendero through the authority of the ruler of the local ethnic state, the *altepetl*. At the beginning of Stage 2, the encomienda per se lost its labor rights, and in a system called the *repartimiento*, indigenous workers channeled through the coatequitl were assigned ad hoc for brief periods to any Spaniard showing need for them. Close to the time of Stage 3, the repartimiento collapsed in turn, and Spanish employers and indigenous temporary workers negotiated as individuals, outside the corporate framework. The complementary nature of the language and labor developments will be readily seen. For example, Nahuas of Stage 2, who understood a number of common Spanish terms, were more ready for contact with a broader range of Spanish employers in smaller groups, with less elaborate indigenous supervision; conversely, the change in the type of contact involved in the repartimiento caused more Nahuas to hear Spanish in everyday life, reinforcing Stage 2 linguistic developments and pointing toward Stage 3. Thus a thick web of reciprocally reinforcing phenomena helped the process along at any given point.

The logic of the stages

The three stages among the Nahuas have sufficient clarity, breadth of spectrum, and cross-regional uniformity to suggest that they might represent a universal aspect of the contact of cultures, at least on the indigenous side of large-scale conquests or intrusions, as with the Gauls and the Romans, or the Anglo-Saxons and the Norman French. If so, why has such a thing not been frequently noticed? One possible reason is that the vast majority of cases of culture contact occur between peoples who already know each other or at least know similar peoples, who have already made adjustments and even belong within a single overarching cultural framework, depriving the process of the distinct starting point and sharp focus it possesses when two peoples meet who have been entirely out of touch, whether directly or indirectly, for many millenia. (Surely many of the peoples of Asia, Africa, and Europe were foreign to one another, even unknown to one another, but they shared things as basic as iron, the horse, and disease microbes, and however distant they might be, a continuum of social and cultural contact across the whole vast expanse of the Old World had existed unbroken from prehistoric times.)

Something a bit similar to the Nahua stages is reported from North America, involving a different European nationality and indigenous groups very differently constituted indeed from the Nahuas. On the basis of work with dictionaries, the historian James Axtell (in a lecture given at the University of North Carolina, Chapel Hill, in June 1992) reports a difference in the linguistic reaction of the Iroquois, located inland, and the more coastal peoples. The Iroquois handled European introductions through descriptions using native vocabulary, whereas the others borrowed many English words (often phonologically and morphologically assimilated). That is, by the time dictionaries were being made, the isolated Iroquois were still in Stage 1, while the coastal peoples, who had had much more massive contact with the English, were in Stage 2 (presumably having been in Stage 1 earlier).

Let us examine, then, the logic of the Nahua stages to see if there is anything about them that would distinguish the process in principle from a seamless continuum. If we take the stages as corresponding to degrees of contact (contact being defined as routine, peaceful personal interaction), we can say that, in addition to a general increase over the entire centuries-long process, Stage 1 corresponds to essentially no contact, Stage 2 to contact through formal corporate groups, and Stage 3 to contact through individuals. The same distinctions can be made in terms of language: in Stage 1, the Nahuas, even when thrown together with the Spaniards, only saw them or perhaps heard the sounds from their mouths, but did not understand what they were saying; in Stage 2, they understood largely through intermediaries and translators; in Stage 3, they understood directly—Stage 3 is the time of substantial bilingualism. In cultural phenomena more generally, Stage 1 represents no change (that is, no structural mental/cultural adjustment, however great the transformation of the external facts of the overall system). Stage 2 represents above all corporate change, with political, religious, and economic institutions coming to terms with Hispanic culture; during this time, indigenous corporations generally flourished. Usually, Hispanic elements were placed within a little-changed indigenous framework. Stage 3 represents change above all at the level of the individual; indigenous corporations experienced stress and fragmentation, and newly incorporated Hispanic elements began to alter the indigenous cultural framework itself. Clearly the entire process can be imagined as an unbroken continuum or progression, and even in the Nahua case there are plenty of long transitions from one phase to another, as well as different tempi in different realms of life. But the three stages do have enough of a basis in logical, expectable distinctions that one is moved at least to look for them elsewhere. One might expect, as indeed I still do, that variants of them will reappear in various situations, hastened by the presence of large numbers of Europeans and slowed by the opposite, more distinct or less depending on local factors such as the geographical distribution of the two parties in the area and their relative cultural constitution.

The Maya of Yucatan

Many of the relevant linguistic facts for Yucatan have already been worked out by Frances Karttunen in her *Nahuatl and Maya in Contact with Spanish* (1985). I myself have intermittently pored over Roys's *Titles of Ebtun* (1939) across the years, and I have profited from the document collection, transcription, and study of loanwords carried out recently by Matthew Restall in his dissertation work (1992).[3]

What we might expect, at least to the extent of testing it, is that Yucatecan Maya would go through a process closely analogous to that seen in Nahuatl but later or more slowly in view of the smaller relative presence of Spaniards. To a great extent, this expectation is borne out. The significant body of

---

[3]The dissertation has since led to a book, *The Maya World: Yucatec Culture and Society, 1550–1850* (1997).

loanwords entering Maya from the sixteenth through the eighteenth centuries was constituted very much like Stage 2 loans in Nahuatl and included a great many of the very same words (Karttunen 1985, pp. 51–58). Loans were assimilated phonologically in exactly the same manner as in Nahuatl (Karttunen 1985, pp. 57–58). Particles and verbs were borrowed only later, just as in Nahuatl, and they are not found, it appears, until well into the eighteenth century, a hundred years or so later than in Nahuatl texts (Karttunen 1985, pp. 59–61). Among the particles, *hasta*, "until, as far as," was prominent as it was in Nahuatl (Karttunen 1985, p. 65). Verbs were borrowed using the infinitive as an invariant nominal stem, to which an indigenous verbalizer was added, plus normal inflectional endings, again just as in Nahuatl (Karttunen 1985, p. 59). In Maya too, Spanish sounds were gradually acquired in the late period. (For many of the above points see also Restall 1992, pp. 410–21, 505–12.)

If we look for differences in the process, however, they are not lacking, in some cases perhaps only apparent, attributable to the nature of the evidence, but in others surely involving substance. So far there is little sign of a distinct Stage 1. The first known documents in Maya are already in the equivalent of Stage 2. It is true that a word such as *tzimin*, "tapir," for "horse," puts us in mind of Nahuatl *maçatl*, "deer," for the same animal, a prominent feature of Stage 1 among the Nahuas (Lockhart 1992, pp. 270–72). The retention of *tzimin* over centuries (see Restall 1992, p. 419) might be seen as consonant with generally slower movement in the Maya sphere, but I would not make too much of such a notion, since Nahuatl retained several Stage 1 expressions for European animals indefinitely even though it did soon go over to a loanword for horse. Since early documentation and lexical work are much scarcer for Maya than for Nahuatl, it could be that a fully developed Stage 1 in Maya would simply escape our notice.

It must give us pause, however, to note that although not very numerous, alphabetic documents in Maya are extant from the third quarter of the sixteenth century, polished in calligraphy, conventions, and vocabulary, with all the diagnostic traits of Nahuatl Stage 2. Thus Maya would appear to have reached a crucial phase right on the heels of Nahuatl, and in relative terms actually earlier, since the whole Yucatecan experience with the Spaniards got off to a perceptibly later start. A very short time indeed would be left for a Stage 1 a la Nahuatl.

Here we see the first of several indications that although there was a progression and sequence over the centuries in contact phenomena in the Maya language, and the thrust and content of that progression was much as in Nahuatl, the stages were not as distinct. In view of the relative paucity of sixteenth-century Maya writing and at the same time its advanced and polished nature, one is nearly forced to imagine that the Stage 2 culture reflected in it initially affected only some people in some places, leaving others in something perhaps like Stage 1 for an unknown stretch of time.[4] In that case, the two stages would be in large measure simultaneous, lacking the impressive uniform, region-wide sequence of the Nahua world, where developments varied by region hardly as much as a decade, and relatively humble people in remote corners were quite au courant. Indeed, under the hypothesized conditions among the Maya, it would be artificial to speak of stages at all.

Extant Maya documents of the sixteenth and seventeenth centuries, much of the eighteenth, and even to a large extent the early nineteenth century are, however, fully described by the characteristics of Nahuatl's Stage 2 (see Restall 1992, pp. 411–18 and text examples in ibid., pp. 448–64 and in Roys 1939). At the same time, such noteworthy stability represents another important difference between the two evolutions. Nahua documents can be dated fairly well (not that there is generally a need to do so) by stylistic and linguistic criteria even within Stage 2, which is barely a hundred years. Maya documents tend to have a notable sameness of vocabulary and documentary conventions over a very long period of time. The

---

[4]Nancy Farriss has tellingly suggested that climatic conditions probably account for the relative lack of sixteenth-century texts (most of those known to exist are preserved in Spain). The corpus could thus once have been much larger. Restall (1992, p. 414) speculates that almost all legal, religious, and political terminology was adopted before 1600.

main trend one notices is a certain evolution in calligraphy and orthography (less, however, than among the Nahuas). If there was change during this time, it must have been more diffusion than progression. Essentially, the long stable period, except for its early start, does tend to confirm one's expectation of slower movement and later development in Yucatan.

Eventually, as I have already mentioned, the symptoms of Nahuatl's Stage 3—loan verbs and particles, and phonological change—do make their appearance; the new loans surface around mid-eighteenth century, as I understand Karttunen. The timing, some hundred years later than with Nahuatl, fits well with the notion of a similar process in both culture areas, expectably delayed in the case of Yucatan. But the manner in which the change took place is very different. Though Nahuatl's transition from Stage 2 to Stage 3 can be seen as stretching over thirty or forty years in the middle of the seventeenth century, by the end of that time the language was strongly affected in every dimension across the entire macro-region. Among the Maya, on the other hand, phenomena of the new type are found scattered here and there in relative isolation, temporally and spatially, with most texts still hardly changed from the long stable period. Even the quite numerous texts of the first decade of the nineteenth century can hardly be assigned to the equivalent of Stage 3. Restall, who has compiled a loanword list from what is doubtless the most extensive exploration among mundane postconquest Maya documents to date, reports in all the texts he has covered no particles at all and a loan verb or two only in the infinitive, used nominally (this quite early; Restall 1992, p. 414). The texts of the Cruzob, later into the nineteenth century, do have more of a Stage 3 feel (Bricker 1981, appendix), and today Maya fully meets the requirements of Stage 3. A hundred years or more of transition from the second to the third phase again raises the likelihood of numbers of people at a different point in the process simultaneously, for an extended period of time, and once more highlights the differences between the clear stages of the Nahuas and the Maya experience.

Just above I said that Maya shows close equivalents of the

Nahua Stage 3 phenomena, as indeed it does, but our evidence on one important aspect, the calques by which the Nahuas translated Spanish idioms, is so slight as to make us wonder if they were lacking, at least until recently. There are some hints, such as the phrase *calle chumuc*, the equivalent of *calle en medio*, "across the street" (some examples in Restall 1992, p. 333) Perhaps closer examination will find more idiom translation than is immediately obvious. But even today, Maya seems to indicate possession in traditional ways, remaining without a full equivalent of Spanish *tener*, "to have," whereas Nahuatl, starting early in Stage 2, developed its verb *pia*, "to guard, have custody, hold," first to mean simply possession and then in Stage 3 to take on all the other meanings and uses of *tener*.

I will devote only a few words to the broader cultural picture; some of the relevant developments are just beginning to be studied, and I am at the present moment not fully conversant with all the studies that *have* been done (a lack I hope to remedy with time). Given that the documentary corpus in Maya tends to show the language in a state closely comparable to Nahuatl's Stage 2 from the second half of the sixteenth century all the way through the eighteenth, one could look for a similar longevity of other traits associated with Stage 2 in central Mexico. Both Nancy Farriss (1984) and Marta Hunt (1974, 1976) have already pointed out the tendency of Yucatan to retain certain characteristics longer than central Mexico.

The encomienda lasted as a meaningful institution into the late eighteenth century in Yucatan, far longer than in central Mexico, where it faded drastically well before the onset of Stage 3 in the mid-seventeenth century. The labor picture is not yet clear to me. The Yucatecan encomienda lost its labor power, but I have not been able to determine when (see Farriss 1984, pp. 47–56). Over most of the stretch of time involved, a system of draft labor comparable to the central Mexican repartimiento persisted, as one would expect in a Stage 2. But labor for Spaniards was far less basic than in central Mexico, and the production of tribute goods far more. Given the different nature of the two economies, the long-lasting tribute goods obligation is perhaps the true Yucatecan parallel to the Stage 2 labor repartimiento among the Nahuas.

Maya municipalities did not noticeably fragment in our time period as their Nahua equivalents did in Stage 3, nor did personal names evolve into a complex system involving elements of Spanish origin (instead staying as Nahua names had been in early Stage 2 or even Stage 1). Some Spanish kinship terms were borrowed, but one does not see the transformation of same-generation terms found in Nahuatl sources. More or less historical writing in Maya continued to be in close contact with the preconquest legacy, in this like Nahua annals of Stage 2, not Stage 3, and songs were written down in the eighteenth century, a practice which halted among the Nahuas in mid-Stage 2. The large monastery churches of Yucatan were apparently not supplemented by a plethora of sub-parish churches as in Nahua Stage 3. No Virgin of Guadalupe seems to have appeared on the horizon (if the movement of the Cruzob is any parallel, it came only later, into the nineteenth century). We have, then, a reasonable list of close parallels to the Nahuas' Stage 2 over the long time during which the language continued to show Stage 2 traits, suggesting the same interrelation and congruence across the board as with the Nahuas.

Some of these traits, however, have little or nothing to do with any cultural progression or sequence; they follow rather from the nature of Maya sociocultural organization. The Yucatecan Maya polities failed to fragment not merely because the conditions for a Stage 3 were not met, but because the *cah*, the equivalent of the altepetl, lacked the clearly organized territorial and ethnic subunits that made the altepetl a fragmentation bomb waiting to explode. (The safety valve of the bordering region of Yucatan not under Spanish rule no doubt also had its effect.) The same aspect of cah structure explains the lack of a push for additional small churches inside the unit. The emphasis among the Maya on named lineages, absent among the Nahuas, made it virtually impossible for them to give up indigenous surnames, no matter what the overall cultural context. Even so, the general lines of a picture familiar from the Nahuas' Stage 2 can be discerned; if we can ever trace the probably gradual movement toward something more or less equivalent to a Stage 3 in the nineteenth and twentieth centuries, we will be able to judge better what might be sequential, what a persistent Maya-internal pattern.

The Quechua speakers

The central Andes had the same combination of a large sedentary population and vast silver deposits as the Mexican region, so a closely comparable European influx took place. As we have seen, the process was highly uneven in Meso-america, varying sharply between central Mexico and the south, and the impact varied within the Andes region as well. Communication difficulties and other hardships (for Euro-peans) presented by the Andean highlands meant that the Spanish occupation, in contrast to the Mexican experience, was far more intensive on the coast than in the interior. Since the Quechua world had been highland-oriented from the beginning, and the coastal peoples, like others in such loca-tions, diminished quickly and drastically after contact, Greater Peru began to take on the aspect of a Spanish/African coast and an indigenous interior. It is true that a substantial Spanish presence was required at the silver mining sites of Charcas, in the area of the mercury mines of Huancavelica, along routes to these places, and at such a major highland center as Cuzco. Nevertheless, the centers and the overall distribution patterns of the two populations were distinct, unlike the central Mexican case, where in macroregional terms the patterns were identical, the Spaniards having simply fastened on the Nahua settlement pattern. In Peru, the two populations lived in relative isolation from each other, much as in southern Mesoamerica and even, one might judge impressionistically, more so.

Since contact propels the process of cultural change, my original expectation was that the Quechua speakers of the central Andean highlands would remain in the earlier stages, linguistically and otherwise, at least as long as the Maya of Yucatan. Such linguistic evidence as we have, however, turns out not to point in that direction at all. Looking at texts produced by Quechua speakers—the Huarochirí manuscript, the Quechua passages produced by Huaman Poma, and the Chuschi papers—we find all in agreement on the essentials.

Judging by these materials alone, Quechua did experience Spanish influence very similar to what was seen with Nahuatl and Yucatecan Maya, but rather than a lag, comparable with Yucatan or greater, we see the opposite; all these texts are in most respects already in the equivalent of Stage 3. The Chuschi papers of 1679 fall within the time of Nahuatl's Stage 3, but the other two sets come from the first two decades of the seventeenth century and would put Quechua well ahead of Nahuatl chronologically—by thirty or forty years in absolute time and by even more relative to the beginning of the Spanish occupation in the area.

The only text which I have yet found opportunity to survey systematically is that of the Huarochirí legends. We may not know just where the writer of the manuscript was from, but the Quechua interference in his Spanish chapter titles and the letter substitutions in his versions of Spanish words leave no doubt that he was a native speaker of Quechua, or at the very least an indigenous person and not a native Spanish speaker. The text contains an impressive number of loans and is even more impressive for the number that are not nouns, compared to Nahuatl texts even of Stage 3. I have (see the appendix to the chapter) counted 103 nouns, 8 adjectives some of which could be interpreted as nouns, 7 particles, and no less than 24 inflected verbs; there are also 14 phrases and what might be called universal proper names approximating generic nouns.

To find 24 verbs in a corpus of this size is stunning. Years of combing through Nahuatl texts has hardly brought the total of attested loan verbs from conquest to independence to fifty (though given the nature of the texts we can be certain the number borrowed in actual speech was greater).[5] A fully consistent convention for incorporating Spanish verbs exists in the Huarochirí text, to that extent like Nahuatl and ultimately Maya, but very different in the nature of the stem used. Both Nahuatl and Maya used the nominal infinitive in its entirety as a base for derivational and inflectional suffixes. The Hua-

---

[5]Barry Sell, in his doctoral dissertation research on ecclesiastical imprints in Nahuatl, found well over a hundred loan verbs given in one way or another in the published writings of an eighteenth-century priest and Nahuatl grammarian working in the Guadalajara region.

rochirí manuscript (and Quechua in general) adopts a simpler and more radical solution (radical also in the literal sense), taking the actual Spanish stem (the infinitive minus -r, the same as the third person singular of the present in many cases)[6] as the basis of a verb that is structured like any Quechua verb (sometimes the stem turns out to have the shape consonant-vowel-consonant-vowel like many verb stems in Quechua), as in *pasa-* from *pasar*, "to pass," thus *pasanqui*, "you pass."

Since the Huarochirí manuscript is the oldest known

---

[6]One is tempted to think that the third person singular present-tense form, as doubtless the most frequently heard, provided the actual origin of the Quechua stem. The loan stems in the Huarochirí text, however, do not evince the vowel changes seen in the third person form of many irregular verbs. Moreover, they seem to retain the final vowel of the infinitive rather than the final vowel of the third person form, where the two differ. Thus we see *servi-* (as in Urioste 1983, p. 182) rather than *sirve-*, *destrui-* (p. 32) rather than *destruye-*, and *reduci-* (p. 48) rather than *reduce-*. It is nearly impossible to extract certainty from such examples, however, for the writer, like many other Quechua speakers, tended to merge *e* and *i*. Although *servi-* is the majority variant, *sirvi-* also appears at times (as p. 146). *Prometi-* (p. 42) clearly involves *i* and *e* merging, since *i* would not appear in any form in Spanish. *Perdi-* (p. 182) is similar, but contains perhaps the most definite indication that we are dealing with a form of the infinitive, not the third person present, since the diphthong *ie* of *pierde*, the third person form, would not be subject to the same kind of merging.

From this evidence, it would seem that the Quechua loan stem derives from the infinitive (minus *r*) after all. The likelihood is increased by the exceptional, doubtless early *casara-* stem (see below).

Yet modern loan stems put the matter in doubt once again. In one modern grammar, the stems regularly show third person vowel shifts whenever they occur in the Spanish verb itself: *cuenta-*, *entiende-*, *piensa-*, (Bills et al. 1969, pp. 441, 443, 445). Another grammar, though it attempts to deemphasize loan verbs, nevertheless confirms *entiende-* and has in addition the strange form *truequa-*, presumably affected by *trueca*, the third person form of *trocar* (Grondín N. 1971, pp. 209, 316). At the same time, the final stem vowel is that of the infinitive, not the third person present, and here there can be no doubt of confusion because of merging: *bati-*, *escribi-* (Bills et al. 1969, pp. 440, 441). All in all, perhaps the most likely analysis is infinitive origin with influence from the third person present.

major all-Quechua running text by a Quechua speaker, we
have no direct evidence that there was any time lag between
noun and verb loans at all.[7] There is, however, a hint or two of
an earlier mechanism for borrowing verbs, one more like
those found in Nahuatl and Maya, for the loan verb from
Spanish *casar*, "to marry," has as a stem not *casa-* but *casa-
ra-*, which I take to be the infinitive plus an epenthetic *a* added
to give it the final vowel typical of a Quechua verb stem. This
form is no vagary of the Huarochirí text, since, to anticipate,
it is found in the Chuschi papers, in Huaman Poma (Guaman
Poma 1950, p. 420), in González Holguín's dictionary (Gonçalez Holguin 1952, p. 51),[8] and in modern spoken Quechua from
Bolivia to Ecuador. The Chuschi papers also have *pagara-*
from *pagar* "to pay," and this too is confirmed in modern
grammars.[9] I deduce that there was a time when Quechua
toyed with the infinitive like the other languages, and that
these two verbs were among the first borrowed, retaining what
became an archaic form after the definitive strategy of incorporating verbs evolved. "To marry" by Christian rites and "to
pay" money are indeed among the most likely candidates for
the first Spanish verbs to enter the language on the grounds of

---

[7]Bruce Mannheim tells me of some notarial documents he has
found in Cuzco, from an earlier time, apparently done by an indigenous person in both Quechua and Spanish. These texts may
contain invaluable clues on the early period, and I look forward to
their publication. Frank Salomon has also informed me of two letters
in Quechua between Andean lords, which at present I have not yet
had the opportunity to inspect. Any older text in Quechua that
should come to light, however short, fragmentary, or uninteresting in
its ostensible subject matter, has vast potential for delineating postconquest Andean cultural history.

[8]Although *casara-* appears prominently in the Quechua to
Spanish section, the older forms used by Santo Tomás dominate the
corresponding part of the Spanish to Quechua section (p. 449). The
form *casada* there is presumably a loan noun.

[9]The confirmation is admittedly a bit indirect. Bills et al. 1969
gives *paga-* as the main form, illustrated in examples of actual usage
(pp. 122, 202, 213, 445). Nevertheless, *pagara-* is found in the phrase
Dios pagarasunqui, "thank you" (literally, "God will pay you"). The
identical phrase is given by Grondín N. 1971 (pp. 60, 311). I presume
that *pagara-* was once the normal form, more recently assimilating
to the general tendency while the yet more basic *casara-* resisted.

being markedly new and at the same time basic to the post-conquest situation.

Although mundane sixteenth-century texts in Quechua are not available to me, one can inspect the work of the pioneer fray Domingo de Santo Tomás, whose grammar and dictionary appeared in 1560. In a quick check, I have detected no loan verbs in the Santo Tomás corpus, and the dictionary certainly has neither *casara-* nor *pagara-*. Under words related to marriage, the dictionary gives expressions having to do with taking a man or a woman (Santo Tomás 1951a, pp. 73–74). In his grammar, Santo Tomás includes a model speech or sermon in which the relatively few loanwords are all nouns: *Dios*, "God," used repeatedly, and *ángel*, "angel," *caballo*, "horse," *cristiano*, "Christian," and *diablo*, "devil"; the last is specifically referred to as a foreign word and explained (Santo Tomás 1951, pp. 189–207). *Caballo* also appears in the dictionary (Santo Tomás 1951a, p. 253).

We have some reason to think, then, that loan verbs were rather more problematic than nouns and came after a time of hesitance, resistance, or experimentation, but on the basis of the known texts, the interval was not nearly as great as with Nahuatl, much less Maya. The Huarochirí document's loan verbs include the somewhat technical type predominant in Nahuatl but have a distinctly broader semantic and pragmatic scope.

Loan particles are prominent in the Huarochirí manuscript, chief among them the expected *hasta*. As happened with some words in Nahuatl too, usually as a transitional measure, *hasta* is always accompanied by a native equivalent, *-cama*. Again, the same word and the same construction are found in the other texts and in spoken Quechua today. Very striking in the Huarochirí text is the frequent use of the conjunctions *y*, "and," and *o*, "or" (the latter often accompanied by the indigenous *-pas*), even when no Spanish vocabulary is involved. The particles are all more or less on the same order as those seen in Nahuatl except for a *-mente* adverb of manner, *heréticamente* "in a heretical fashion."

Further work will be required to settle the issue, but I have the impression that the text includes some calques on Spanish phrases. Its loan nouns include the types familiar in

Nahuatl's Stage 2, but also embrace words for indigenous items or concepts already apparently well covered by native vocabulary, another sign of Nahuatl Stage 3. Indeed, the manuscript shows all of the diagnostic traits of Nahuatl Stage 3 except the phonological aspect, for judging by the orthography it does not appear that the writer had securely acquired any of the Spanish sounds lacking in or different from Quechua pronunciation.[10]

With the other two texts, I must for the moment rely on impressions. In a word, they have all the same signs and much of the same loan vocabulary, confirming that the writer of the Huarochirí manuscript was not alone in his tendencies. Such agreement is significant enough when found in the writings of Huaman Poma, in time very close to the Huarochirí legends and in genre and auspices also somewhat allied, but it is even more striking when seen in everyday working documents done some sixty years later in a highland location. All three texts are more or less central Peruvian in provenience, but still there is a considerable breadth, especially considering Huaman Poma's catholicity. Not only do the Chuschi texts have the same tendencies as the Huarochirí manuscript, those tendencies are more pronounced. I have not made a quantitative survey, nor even a transcription, but it is already clear that loanwords are even thicker and verbs even more frequent. The contact phenomena of the three seventeenth-century sets agree closely not only with one another but with the situation reflected in modern dictionaries and grammars, so there is every reason to imagine that we are dealing with real speech of native speakers and not some artificial idiom.

What to make of the overall situation of the Quechua speakers, then? It goes against every intuition to presume that the majority of Quechua speakers across the vast and remote Andean highlands shared the idiom, bearing strong traces of bilingualism, of the writers of the three texts. Bruce Mann-

---

[10]The topic awaits closer study. It appears to me at present that the primary deviance from normal Spanish orthography has to do with vowels and to a lesser extent with sibilants. A preliminary search has revealed none of the expected merging of letters for voiced and unvoiced stops.

heim has reported a marked difference between urban and rural Quechua today. That difference is probably not new. To explain the Andean situation, I hypothesize a bifurcation, much deeper and starker than that I have imagined in Yucatan. Greater Peru received a strong flow of Spanish immigration, but as I have said, it tended to concentrate on the coast, precisely the area where the indigenous population threatened to diminish to the disappearing point. In the Peruvian coastal region at any time after mid-sixteenth century, the proportion of Spanish speakers to speakers of indigenous languages exceeded not only that seen in Yucatan but anything seen in any part of central Mexico, including the main urban centers of Mexico City and Puebla. As I found in my research years ago on early postconquest Peru, many of the Quechua speakers on the coast were displaced highlanders in the employ of Spaniards and highly open to all kinds of cultural influence (Lockhart 1994, p. 246). It would not be unexpected that coastal-urban Quechua should have reached something like Nahuatl's Stage 3 even earlier than Nahuatl. Quechua speakers who were employed by Spaniards—*yana-conas*, ecclesiastical and governmental aides—circulated widely across the hinterland, as the example of Huaman Poma shows. Such people could easily have spread a Stage 3 Quechua to mining regions, larger urban centers, and even to the local indigenous ruling groups who had to deal with Spaniards on an almost daily basis. Most of the highland population could have remained in something more like Stage 1 or Stage 2 indefinitely. I suspect, however, that certain high-frequency items such as *casara-*, *pagara-*, and *hasta* achieved wide currency in the general population from a relatively early time. At any rate, we have again a situation in which no clear progression of stages can be detected. On their first appearance, Quechua texts are already in a full equivalent of Stage 3; only hints of an earlier progression are seen, and any such evolution must have taken place with lightning rapidity, if there was a progression at all.

Looking about for broader cultural phenomena that might throw light on the Andean situation, I find relatively little that is unambiguous, partly because of the lack of the large corpus of mundane indigenous texts that is most revealing for the Nahuas and the Yucatecans, and partly because of my present rustiness with the Peruvian historical and anthropological literature. In the realm of temporary labor, we find some initial similarities with central Mexico, followed by very long term stability at Stage 2. Temporary labor rights originally belonged to the encomienda alone, then before the end of the sixteenth century were channeled through the Peruvian equivalent of the repartimiento, the *mita*. To this point, the pattern and relative chronology of Peru and central Mexico ran reasonably close, but thereafter the mita remained strong and quite central to the economy virtually to independence, showing an even more marked and prolonged "Stage 2" aspect than in Yucatan. It must be remembered, however, that the Andes of all the regions of America had the strongest tradition of draft rotary labor from the beginning, involving the longest work periods and the greatest distances traveled, and it was no accident that the repartimiento here took on a Quechua name.

In other realms, comparability is hard to find.[11] Indigenous municipal corporations much like those in central Mexico and Yucatan were formed in the later sixteenth century, bringing the Andean region in that respect into Stage 2. Instead of a rotating "governor," though, as among the Nahuas in Stage 2 and later, the undisguised preconquest local ruler, with full dynastic trappings, held forth (called *cacique* by the Spaniards and *curaca* by the Quechua speakers), more as in Stage 1 with the Nahuas. (Yucatan was half way between the two; the presiding officer was usually called a *batab*, using the indigenous term for local ruler, and held office for a long period of time—perhaps ideally twenty years— but was not strictly dynastic and was tightly integrated with the cabildo, often not the case in Peru [Restall 1992, pp. 150– 55].) The secular trend for sociopolitical entities was neither the unilinear fragmentation process of the Nahuas nor the stasis of the Yucatecans, but a wave of consolidation at-

---

[11]In the following, I rely in part on my own Peruvianist work and direct knowledge, but also, in a general way, on Bakewell 1984a, N. Cook 1981, Frazer 1989, Spalding 1967 and 1984, Stern 1982, Wethey 1949, and Wightman 1990.

tempted by the Spaniards, followed by a redispersal which may have tended to reestablish something like the original pattern.

As to the indicator of church building, large ecclesiastical structures were hardly built in the Andean countryside in the sixteenth century; the affiliations of later structures are not yet clear to me. The reason for the difference is not primarily the place of the Andean region in any sequence at any particular time, but the lack in the Andean highlands of the strong Mesoamerican tradition wherein a splendid stone temple was the primary symbol of the sociopolitical unit. Likewise, aspects of the stages having to do with writing and written genres cannot be applied readily to the Andes because of the lack of the Mesoamerican writing traditions that prepared the Mesoamericans for the full-scale incorporation and adaptation of European-style writing in their own languages by a single generation after contact. I will leave it to others to say whether the Virgin of Copacabana or the Señor de los Milagros compares in any way to the Virgin of Guadalupe as a Stage 3 symbol of a new protonational entity transcending the individual indigenous corporations and embracing both Spaniards and non-Spaniards. Parts of the Andes, through the seventeenth century and perhaps longer, were maintaining Christianity and indigenous religion as separate, relatively unintegrated cults, a situation not seen in a large way in central Mexico after Stage 1 (something of the kind did hang on longer in Yucatan and other peripheral areas).

Whereas with Yucatan I imagine I can see enough to satisfy myself that the region long remained in a perhaps ill defined but recognizable Stage 2, generally as well as in language, only certain aspects of the Andean picture over the postconquest centuries are reminiscent of Stage 2; others point to an even earlier phase, while some elements of the sequence seen in Mesoamerica are missing because of pronounced differences in Mesoamerican and Andean culture. It would probably take much more in the way of indigenous-language sources to detect any Stage 3 traits beyond those already seen in language itself; so far, none are evident. The Andean example, as I provisionally glimpse it, does not seem to manifest even the rough simultaneity and congruence across many realms seen in Yucatan. Such a state of things would be compatible with the bifurcation (perhaps multifurcation) that I postulated above in speaking of the language situation.

In general, the nature and sequence of certain cultural developments in the postcontact period is much the same wherever we look, although clearly it is by no means inevitable that a certain point in the sequence should ever be reached unless local conditions are favorable. Under the right conditions, even a reversal of the sequence is imaginable. In two of the three examples, there is a broad congruence and relative simultaneity of certain phenomena both linguistic and nonlinguistic; in the third example, the Andean region, that does not presently appear to be the case. If, however, with further research two or more separate spheres can be identified and characterized, a greater congruence in each may yet emerge.

The clear three stages of the Nahuas do not appear in the other two examples. If Yucatan were more fully understood from the moment of contact until today, I think the three stages would be more recognizable than they are at the moment, but they will never have the clarity and relative uniformity of the Nahua case. I provisionally attribute the well defined stratification of the Nahua experience to two factors: first, the fact that here alone did a large immigrant population meet a large indigenous population head on, and second, that the Nahuas appear to have had more cultural common ground with the Europeans than any other indigenous group, making it possible for them to build their adjustments on their own traditions in virtually every sphere and leading to a tightly interlocking system that tended to evolve as a unit. So I hardly expect more examples of a fully developed three-stage sequence. Nevertheless, every indigenous society coming into contact with Europeans went through a somewhat related experience, and proceeding from the better known cases to the less known, we should be able to identify universals and come to understand much more than we do now about the principles of variation.

Appendix to Chapter 8: Words and phrases
of Spanish origin in the Huarochirí legends*

Nouns: abuela, abuelo, aguinaldo, alcalde, andas, ánima, animal, año, aposento, araña, arco, brazo, brujo, caballo, calle, campana, cantarillo, cañaveral, capítulo, caracol, cielo, cofre, conde, corregimiento, costumbre, cristiano, cruz, cuerpo, cuidado, cuñada, diluvio, dios, doctor, doctrina, don, doncella, enemigo, esquina, fanega, fe, fiesta, forastero, frezada, frontera, fuente, garabato, iglesia, indio, junio, juramento, latín, maestro, manga, marzo, mayo, media (fanega), mesa, mestizo, milagro, misterio, mortero, muchacho, mundo, noviembre, oficio, oración, oveja, padre, parte, pascua, patio, peligro, perdón, platero, plato, plaza, predicación, procesión, provincia, punta, real, reducción, romano, rosario, sabio, sacerdote, sarampión, señal, señor, señora, sobra, sobrino, teniente, tiempo, tijeras, trabajo, traición, trompetero, ventura, vestido, virgen, víspera, zarcillo – 103

Verbs: casar (casara-), confesar, conquistar, convidar, destruir, enamorar, envidiar, gastar, heredar, juntar, menospreciar, ofrecer, pasar, perder, perdonar, pintar, prometir, reducir, renovar, rezar, sentenciar, señalar, servir, visitar – 24

Particles: hasta (and hasta que), heréticamente, o, porque, si, sino, y – 7

Adjectives: azul, blanco (?), crespo, entero, loco, mayor, rico, segundo (a) – 8

Phrases, proper names: Ave María, Cabrillas, cara a cara, Cieneguillas (a place or settlement), Corpus Christi, quiere decir cuatro, digo, espíritu santo, gato montés, Jesucristo, Lima, padre nuestro, Santa María, Todos Santos – 14

---

*I have used the 1983 Urioste edition. Words in the chapter headings in Spanish, though generated by the same writer, were of course not included. The present list should be considered provisional. Though I surveyed the text carefully and checked my findings more than once, my experience with similar work on Nahuatl sources leads me to believe that lists like this one need to evolve for several years before they reach final form, because of inadvertent omissions and problems of analysis. I have adopted modern Spanish spellings and have used the citation form, including the full infinitive of verbs (in texts, the *r* would be missing in all cases except with *casar*).

9. Between the Lines

What you call social history can't be taught.
Perhaps it can be imparted.

Amos Funkenstein to Jim Lockhart, mid-1970's*

F OR MANY YEARS, starting in the late 1960's, I taught early Spanish American paleography to small groups of graduate students, usually on an informal basis, at first using mainly reproductions of documents from Peru in the conquest generation, acquired in the course of my Peruvian research. The samples were horribly difficult to read, and with the added problem of all the extraneous marks coming not only from the original but from the first photography and from subsequent recopying, they were next to impossible. I put considerable effort into erasing and whiting out the smudges, and also, to tell the truth, darkening faint lines and redrawing ones that were no longer there, then recopying and working on the copies all over again until the result was quite abstract, though not inaccurate. I also prepared drawings of common abbreviations and signs. In a word, I gave great attention to the extremely convoluted external form of the documents, which seemed to be the primary obstacle to understanding them.

In due course I was disabused of the notion of the primacy of the outer appearance. I found that native speakers of Spanish and others who knew older Spanish well could fly right along in material of which they could visually read only perhaps a third, because that third implied most of the rest for one who was in tune with the flow of the language and content. From then on I added typed versions of standard documents, complete with all their formula, to the curriculum, to be if not memorized then in some fashion absorbed, so that one would know what to expect, and I found this method had a greater effect than concentrating on how certain letters were written.

Even so, I was often disappointed with the results. With

---

*Amos Funkenstein was a distinguished intellectual historian of Europe and the Judaic tradition, active at UCLA, Stanford, the University of California, Berkeley, and in Israel.

rare exceptions, the students, smart though they were, saw little *meaning* in the documents. It was natural enough. They lacked the context which gave life and significance to so many passages in the texts, and they were not used to examining the implications of every detail of fact and expression. I began expounding on many things other than the written characters before us, with, it seemed, better results. The skill we were working on we called (and we were surely not the only ones to do so) reading between the lines. Through a combination of close observation, imagination, the drawing of parallels and distinctions, and the exercise of memory, it produces a wealth of reliable, often new, otherwise undiscoverable information about social and cultural facts and categories.

The present piece is a gesture toward laying bare the method involved. I include in their entirety three documents, one in Spanish, two in Nahuatl, with transcriptions, translations, and commentary, presented section by section.[1] These particular texts are unusually rich and revealing, but the same principles obtain in working with any text as a social-cultural document, and marvels often lurk in the briefest, most perfunctory example.

Our first text, which is actually two closely related ones, came into being as a result of the hanging of a prominent Peruvian encomendero for defection from the rebellion headed by Gonzalo Pizarro in 1544.[2]

Sepan quantos esta carta de testamento vieren como nos Antonio de Robles vecino desta cibdad de los Reyes e yo Juan de Ribas vecino de la cibdad del Cuzco de las provincias del Peru en nombre del capitan Martin de Florencia vecino que fue de la cibdad del Cuzco ya defunto

---

[1] For the present purpose I have kept my usual principles of transcription to the extent of reproducing the original orthography in general, adding no punctuation, and respacing words, but I have resolved the abbreviations and have capitalized proper names, things which under other circumstances I would not recommend.

[2] The document is in Biblioteca Nacional del Perú, Lima, A33, f. 279. I will not give references for the many points of fact and interpretation that I will be adding here, for the procedure is what is important in the present context. Much of the background of this text, properly documented, can be found by seeking Martín de Florencia in the index of my *The Men of Cajamarca* (1972) and reading more broadly in my *Spanish Peru* (preferably the 1994 edition).

e por virtud del poder que del para lo de yuso contenido tenemos que paso ante el escriuano publico yuso escrito su tenor del qual es este que se sigue

Know all who see this letter of testament how we, Antonio de Robles, citizen of this City of the Kings and I, Juan de Ribas, citizen of the city of Cuzco, of the provinces of Peru, in the name of Captain Martín de Florencia, late citizen of the city of Cuzco, now deceased, by virtue of the power we have from him for what is contained below, the tenor of which is as follows:

Martín de Florencia was from the kingdom of Aragon, important in the Iberian peninsula but not a major source of immigrants to the Indies in the sixteenth century. The few Aragonese present stuck closely together. Florencia's executors include one of his fellow countrymen, Juan de Ribas; I am not sure of the origin of the other, Antonio de Robles, and as we will see, some other mysteries surround him. One executor is based in each of Spanish Peru's main cities, Lima (always styled the City of the Kings in the headings of documents) and Cuzco, which was also Florencia's seat. All three men are styled *vecino*, which in the Peru of the conquest generation often meant encomendero, as it does here, although it was also used from an early time for other citizens who owned urban property and maintained establishments.

En el termino de la cibdad de los Reyes veintedos dias del mes de octubre de mill e quinientos e quarenta e quatro años en presencia de mi Diego Gutierrez escriuano publico e del concesjo de la cibdad de los Reyes estando el capitan Martin de Florencia vecino de la cibdad del Cusco preso por mandado del muy magnifico señor Francisco de Carvajal maestre de campo del exercito del muy ilustre señor capitan Gonçalo Piçarro e a punto para lo ahorcar por su mandado parescio el dicho capitan Martin de Florencia e por estar a punto de muerte dio poder para hazer su testamento a Juan de Ribas e a Diego de Narbaez vecinos del Cusco e a Bernaldo Ruiz vecino de la cibdad de los Reyes ynsolidun

In the jurisdiction of the City of the Kings, the 22nd day of the month of October of the year of 1544, in presence of me, Diego Gutiérrez, notary public and notary of the council of the City of the Kings, with Captain Martín de Florencia, citizen of the city of Cuzco, a prisoner by order of the very magnificent lord Francisco de Carvajal, field-master of the army of the very illustrious lord Captain Gonzalo Pizarro and about to be hanged by his order, the said Captain Martín de Florencia appeared before me and being at the point of death gave power to make his testament to Juan de Ribas and Diego de Narváez, citizens of Cuzco, and to Bernaldo Ruiz, citizen of the City of the Kings, each separately.

Now comes a copy of the original statement empowering the executors. Martín de Florencia had been among the Spaniards who captured the Inca emperor Atahuallpa in 1532, already then a crossbowman and artillery expert, and so a person who might be sought out for participation in wars and rebellions. He had headed contingents of men in battle ever since the early moments of the conquest, but this is the only time I have seen him styled captain (which meant officer or leader of a group in a very general way, and was not as today a position between lieutenant and major). When the great Gonzalo Pizarro rebellion was taking shape in Cuzco in 1544, Florencia was drawn in as a prominent participant, but before long he (like others) defected, fleeing to Lima and going into hiding there. As the document is written, the rebels, who are now in charge of the country, have found him and are about to hang him as an example.

Here Florencia names as his executors Juan de Ribas, whom we have already seen acting for him later; Bernaldo Ruiz, an encomendero of Lima who was also from Aragon; and Diego de Narváez, who though not Aragonese was from an equally remote and marginal land, bordering Aragon, namely Navarre, and was closely associated with Florencia. Later he too was to die opposing Gonzalo Pizarro. That Narváez and Ruiz do not appear in the later enabling document could be attributed to any number of reasons. What is not clear is why the other person issuing the later document, Antonio de Robles, is not mentioned here. I will discuss this point when his name appears below.

declaro que dexa en la cibdad del Cusco e en sus terminos en la cibdad del Cusco e en su casa en una camarica encerradas dos mill pesos que sabe do esta un yndio suyo que se dize Callaquiz e en casa de Domingo el sastre en Lima dexo en su poder del dicho Domingo una esmeralda engastada en una sierpe e unos paños de la tierra e mando que le paguen lo que el jurare que se le debe

He declared that he is leaving in the city of Cuzco and its jurisdiction [the following]: in the city of Cuzco, in his house, locked in a small room, 2,000 pesos; his Indian called Callaquiz knows where it is; and in the house of Domingo the tailor in Lima he left in the custody of the said Domingo an emerald set in a serpent and some textiles of this land, and he ordered that they should pay him what he should swear is owed him.

Departing now from the world of high politics, treason, and defection, we are suddenly immersed in intimate personal details. Florencia has an indigenous servant, probably his permanent personal employee rather than just someone doing encomienda duty, whom he has trusted to the extent of letting him know the hiding place of 2,000 pesos, only a fraction of Florencia's estate but a fair fortune in itself. Although this person, Callaquiz, seems to be in charge of Florencia's main house in Cuzco, or at least in a position of great responsibility there, we can tell from his name that he is not yet baptized, not yet even nominally Christian.

Domingo the tailor is Domingo de Destre,[3] an established tailor of Lima, who though industrious and solid held a social rank far below that of an encomendero. Yet he was Aragonese, and on the basis of that Florencia and Destre have become close. Destre is keeping some of Florencia's valuables, has been carrying out dealings of some kind for him, and has his trust. The valuables are interesting in themselves, indigenous in style: a jeweled ring in which a snake of some precious metal forms the ring, and native textiles of llama or alpaca wool, probably with complex designs.

One might easily miss a very important item here. I mentioned before that Lima was referred to as the City of the Kings (ciudad de los Reyes) in formal contexts. So true was this that in months of research I had never seen it called anything else and had begun to feel that the present name must have originated later. But here, in an extreme situation, doubtless reflecting what Florencia himself originally said, the word "Lima" comes out. So it was there all along, underneath the formulaic expression. In due course I found some other examples like this one and got a sense of its commonness in everyday speech. But had I never seen another attestation, this one would have made the main point.

/ declaro que tiene en los Charcas unas casas e minas y las del Cusco e que las casas de Candia del Cusco heran suyas e sobre ellas se le deben mill pesos poco menos declaro que en un corral de ovejas

---

[3] A biography of Destre is in Lockhart 1994, pp. 125–28.

en Tambo do estuvo escondido dexo enterrado fuera del corral junto
a un arroyo orilla del dos tejuelos de oro que valdran mill pesos poco
mas o menos

He declared that he has in Charcas a house and some mines as well
as those of Cuzco, and the house of Candía in Cuzco is his, and he is
owed a thousand pesos on it or a little less. He declared that in a
sheep pen in Tambo where he was hiding he left buried, outside the
pen next to a brook, at its bank, two ingots of gold that must be worth
a thousand pesos more or less.

Charcas was approximately the area of present highland
Bolivia, occupied in a movement of expansion from Cuzco
southward, in which Florencia clearly took part. Its attraction was that it was far richer in silver than any other part of
Greater Peru. During a transitional period, before encomenderos of the Charcas region gained total dominance, encomenderos of Cuzco participated in silver mining there without abandoning their base in Cuzco. Florencia is an example.

"Those of Cuzco" probably means his main residence there;
a large or complex house was usually referred to in the plural.
"Candía" is Pedro de Candía, a Greek artilleryman who had
been in Italy, then Spain, and was at Cajamarca along with
Florencia. The two were drawn together by their foreignness
as well as by their trade; Florencia was not only from half-
foreign Aragon but was of Italian parentage, Florentine as his
name conveys. They both became encomenderos of Cuzco, and
are found associated repeatedly. By this time, Candía had long
since met a fate very similar to Florencia's, and Florencia
had come into possession of his house, whether through inheritance or purchase.

"Tambo" was a generic word for inns along Andean roads,
but here we are talking about a specific place, apparently the
main settlement of Florencia's encomienda, on which he has
fallen back to weather troubles he has met in the Spanish
world. The sheep mentioned are llamas. Florencia must have
hidden here just after defecting from the Pizarrists, before
going on to Lima. The gold ingots are doubtless from his gold
mining enterprise in Carabaya, of which we will hear more.
Once the background is understood, we see that much of this
material is quite spectacular, almost cinematic, and we can
fall to imagining the hidden gold at the side of the brook next
to the llama corral, but the document is not therefore a whit

less informative about important mundane aspects of life and
speech in the Peru of that time generally.

*- mas declaro que dexo en las minas de Caravaya lo que sacaren y
tenian sacado sus indios e Antonio de Torres questa con ellos*
*- declaro que el dicho Antonio de Torres barbero le debe mill pesos
por una escritura*

- In addition he declared that he left in the mines of Carabaya what
his Indians, and Antonio de Torres, who is with them, should extract
or already have extracted.
- He declared that the said Antonio de Torres, barber, owes him a
thousand pesos by virtue of a notarial document.

Around this time, with the Peruvian silver mining industry not yet well established, the Spaniards were still very
much involved in the placer gold mining that had accompanied the Spanish conquests ever since the Caribbean island
phase. Within the Cuzco jurisdiction was the wet lowland
pocket of Carabaya, and there a gold rush went on for a while.
Here we see Florencia taking part. He has sent the Indians of
his encomienda, presumably in fulfilment of their labor duty
to him, to Carabaya to extract gold under the direction of the
Spaniard Antonio de Torres.

It is of interest that Torres is a barber, not a professional
miner or metalworker, confirming our general notion that
placer mining for gold was a rough and ready business. From
the large amount of money Florencia has lent or advanced
Torres, he seems as much a business partner as an employee.

*- declaro que sus yndios del Tambo le tienen cierta cantydad de ropa
que tiene oro texido en ella*

- He declared that his Indians of Tambo are keeping for him a certain
quantity of cloth with gold woven in it.

Once again we see Florencia acquiring indigenous luxury
goods from his encomienda, whether in the name of tribute or
not we cannot know, and entrusting the Indians with valuable
goods that he claims.

*- declaro que dexa en las mynas y en el Cuzco seys negros llamados
Diego al qual ahorro e dixo que dexaba horro e libre de cabtiberio por
buenos serbicios que le hizo / mas dixo que dexa por sus esclabos a
los dichos cinco negros restantes Anton Barba e Diaguito e Juan
Gilof e Juan Grande e otro Bartolome e otro negro que lo tiene el
capitan Vergara en los Bracamoros e una negra que se llama Ana e
otros bienes*

- He declared that he is leaving in the mines and in Cuzco six blacks, one named Diego, whom he freed and said that he left free and exempt from captivity for good services that he has performed for him; in addition he said that he is leaving as his slaves the other five blacks, Antón Barba, Dieguito, Juan Jelof, Juan Grande, Bartolomé, and another black that Captain Vergara has in the Bracamoros, and a black woman called Ana, and other property.

It was not uncommon for a testator to free a slave who had been his personal servant or the head of his staff. These are typical slave names for the time and place; Jelof refers to an African ethnicity, and Barba is probably a variant of another. Some of the African slaves are being used in the Carabaya gold mining, but since they are few, four or five at most, and the encomienda Indians are many, they must be serving as intermediaries between Torres the general supervisor and the main indigenous work force. Several men and one woman is what we usually see when the intention is mining.

The connection with Vergara, to whom Florencia has lent a slave, is that Vergara is also an artilleryman; he is presently on a rather hopeless expedition sent into the wet tropical Bra-camoros region.

Even when you get very acclimated to the time and know what to expect, a phrase such as "and other property" as used here can surprise you and set you to thinking.

- *declaro que tiene en sus yndios muchos puercos e ovejas en sus indios*

- He declared that he has among his Indians many pigs and sheep.

The sheep are llamas again, but the pigs are the European animal. Florencia is well on the way to maintaining a ranch, what the Spaniards then called an *estancia*, in the area of his encomienda, a strong pattern in the conquest period and after.

- *declaro que Juan Batista le debe las casas de su morada*

- He declared that Juan Bautista owes him the house where he is living.

Florencia is in the real estate business, renting, leasing, or selling a house, probably in Cuzco, to another Spaniard, pos-sibly also of Italian background, for the name Juan Bautista has that flavor.

- mando a Luis e Pedro de Florencia e Isabelica questa en el cacique sus hijos que por tales los reconoscio que dixo ser hijos de Ysabel y Tocto sus indias para con que se alimenten a cada uno mill pesos

- He bequeathed a thousand pesos each for their sustenance to Luis and Pedro de Florencia, and Isabelica, who is at the cacique's, his children, for as such he recognized them and said they were children of Isabel and Tocto, his Indian women.

Now our persistence is being rewarded. You may not care when Lima started being called Lima, or how an encomendero chose associates from his own region and trade, or how he managed his affairs, but almost anyone will be interested in his racially mixed children. Here they are, hidden in the middle of the document. Many notarial documents consist primarily of formula, and with little risk you can skip from the substantive beginning to the signatures and dates at the end. A will must be read all the way through.

Florencia's three children have two mothers, whom he calls his Indian women. They likely belonged to the group that constituted Florencia's encomienda, but we have no way of being sure. From their names we know that one, Isabel, is baptized, but the other, Tocto, is not. For a Spaniard of the conquest period, especially an important one, to have two or even several servant-concubines at the same time was by no means unusual. Sometimes the mistresses went well beyond the category of servant, being of high lineage, connected with the ruler of the encomienda group. Such women were usually quickly baptized and given the title "doña," which is missing here, so Isabel and Tocto are probably not of notably high rank. The fact that Isabel not only has a Christian name but is mentioned first makes one suspect that she has a more general precedence over Tocto, probably having been with Florencia longer and possibly outranking her socially. Presumably the two would ordinarily be in Florencia's company in Cuzco. Where they are right now is not entirely clear. Florencia says nothing on the point, nor does he leave the women anything or say what is to become of them. Mathematics tells us that one woman must be the mother of two of the children, the other of one of them. Isabelica would doubtless be the daughter of Isabel; as the probably senior, Isabel was likely the mother of one of the boys too.

All three children have Christian names and must have been baptized. The two boys, Luis and Pedro, bear Florencia's surname. Isabelica is mentioned separately without it, which might or might not put her in a lower category, that is, she might indeed not have a speech right to the surname, or it could have been simply omitted here, as it often was in giving the names of girls and women at all levels of Spanish society.

We are told that Isabelica is at the encomienda, where her mother Isabel, then, most likely is also staying. Just as with the surnames, we are left short of certainty on the question of whether the information about whereabouts applies to all the children. We could read this as implying that the boys are in Cuzco, perhaps receiving more attention, with only Isabelica out in the country. But when considering that the children are probably with their mothers, and Isabel is likely the mother of two of the children, it seems at least possible that both mothers and all three children are now at the encomienda by way of refuge in troubled times. Yet see the wording used below by the executors, reinforcing the notion of Isabelica's distinctness as to both naming and location.

Florencia's way of saying "at the encomienda" is of considerable interest. The phrase is "en el cacique," literally "in or at the cacique," that being the word the Spaniards used everywhere for indigenous rulers. When I first read this passage I thought the phrase very strange, and I was even somewhat unsure of the meaning. Later it turned up several other times, mainly in informal contexts. On reflection the implication is quite clear. Back in the Caribbean phase of the Spanish occupation, encomienda grants had given a Spaniard a certain "cacique and his Indians," because no one had much grasp yet of the nature and extent of the unit the cacique ruled, and everything would have to be channeled through him as intermediary. The same must still have been true in the Peru of the 1540's, at least for the bulk of the Spaniards, including many encomenderos.

Returning to the children, we notice that Florencia specifically recognizes them as his own, which he might not have been so quick to do had he had a legitimate heir, and he leaves them a thousand pesos each. It was not the same as leaving them his fortune, but each was allotted a very considerable sum, the annual income of a small encomienda or several years' salary for an unskilled Spaniard. Note that here the genders are equal; we were not sure whether the girl used the family surname or whether she was in the same place as the boys, but we know that she received the same bequest. If she actually got it and lived to adulthood, it probably would have provided a dowry allowing her to make a modest marriage in the Spanish world. The boys could expect to find some middling position among Spaniards, perhaps as a skilled artisan, a steward, or a small trader and entrepreneur, and possibly better, if Florencia's friends and allies flourished and kept a strong memory of him after the end of the rebellion.

The children were of course what we today call mestizos. Their mixed parentage is in no way hidden. Yet though the word "mestizo" was already in the vocabulary of the Indies at this time, note that it is not used in this case. It was applied mainly to the abandoned, destitute, and disadvantaged, and above all to one's enemies. When children of mixed parentage were recognized and endowed in this way, they were often taken away from their mothers, but the mothers would receive rather careful treatment in view of their offspring. Here, however, not a word is said; there was clearly much more concern about the children than about their mothers.

- *declaro que Guaman un indio tuerto questa en Lima le dexo una cadena e otras cosas de oro / mando que dello se pague lo que se debe en Lima*

- He declared that he left a chain and other things of gold with Huaman, a one-eyed Indian who is in Lima, and he ordered that what he owes in Lima be paid from it.

Here is almost the same story as with Callaquiz above, an unbaptized, highly trusted Indian. Rather than acting as a steward like Callaquiz, Huaman seems to be Florencia's personal servant and travels with him, even under extreme conditions. Once again items of great value are left in the custody of an indigenous person. (Actually, a word [con or a, with or to] seems to be missing in the original; as it stands, the sentence should mean that Huaman left the things to Florencia. The logic of the situation and the parallel examples of Callaquiz and the encomienda Indians keeping valuables for Florencia allow us to reverse the sense with confidence.)

- *declaro que debe el canonigo Loçano una mula de que le debe ciento e treynta pesos*

- He declared that Canon Lozano owes him for a mule, on which he owes him 130 pesos.

The translation shows my sense of the meaning of this passage, but lacking other evidence I am not entirely sure that what was intended was not the reverse, so I would not for example make much of Florencia selling mules to ecclesiastics. One of the primary skills of the document detective is to feel when one is on unsure ground and step back. This passage, however, whatever it means, allows one to assert that a business transaction (often the external sign of a more complex relationship) took place between Florencia and Canon Lozano.

- *declaro que dexo en el cacique un caballo e una yegua e un potrillo y la yegua es blanca*

- He declared that he left at the cacique's a horse, a mare, and a little colt, and the mare is white.

Here we are shown that the significant phrase "en el cacique" was no fluke. The horse breeding at the encomienda makes Florencia's stock activity there look even more like an estancia than it did above. I never read the words "y la yegua es blanca," "and the mare is white," without some thrill of felt reality shooting through me.

- *dexo para hazer su testamento e para cumplir lo aqui contenido a Antonio de Robles vecino de los Reyes al qual dio poder ynsolidun con los demas a los quales dio poder cumplido*

- He left to make his testament and to fulfill what is contained here Antonio de Robles, citizen of the City of the Kings, to whom he gave separate power along with the rest, to whom he gave full power.

The problem here is why Antonio de Robles did not appear with the executors Florencia named above, all fellow Aragonese or close to it, whereas here Robles alone is actually named. Possibly in the absence of the others, Robles was added because someone based in Lima was needed. Equally possibly, the Pizarrists insisted on Robles if they were going to allow Florencia to make a will at all. To the distant observer, it is remarkable, despite many contrary examples, how often the Spaniards were willing to let defeated enemies retain some or all of their private property. Whatever Robles' role, nothing is done in the present document against Martín de Florencia's interests. If Robles was from Aragon, we could be quite sure that Florencia himself did the choosing, but I never established his origin. Indeed, I never made any further progress in the matter of Robles. It is after all quite tangential to the substantial topics covered in the document, and we mustn't get derailed by mere curiosity. The final judgments in early Spanish American lawsuits and criminal trials are missing as often as not; it hardly matters.

- *dexo por heredera complido el dicho testamento y lo aqui contenido / a Maria Leonarda de Santangel vecina de la cibdad de Balbastro en el reino de Aragon para que herede todos los bienes suyos de lo que restare cumplido lo susodicho*

- He left as heiress, when the said testament has been fulfilled and the here contained carried out, María Leonarda de Santángel, citizen of the city of Balbastro in the kingdom of Aragon, to inherit all of his property that should remain when the aforesaid is fulfilled.

If we didn't already know something of Florencia's place of origin (and when I first read this document I did not), we would now begin to operate on the presumption that he was from Balbastro in Aragon, and we would be correct. We could also begin to suspect that he was of ultimately Italian, probably specifically Florentine origin. We have seen him consorting with foreigners like Pedro de Candía; his surname means "of Florence"; and now we see that his mother's second name is Leonarda, rare in Spain and common in Italy. Florencia begins to look like a second-generation Florentine, and the rest of his record confirms it. One scholar has suspected that Florencia was of Jewish descent; after surveying the evidence I am still not sure, and will not go into the matter here, but it is true that his mother's surname, Santángel, although apparently also Italian, is compatible with Jewish ancestry, for many converted Jews were given Christian religious surnames, which might be retained for several generations. By making his mother his residual heir, Florencia tells us that his father is dead and that he himself is not married.

The name of Florencia's mother is not adorned with the "doña." In the 1530's and 40's the doña was still used quite conservatively in Spain, and though the mothers of the higher ranking nobles bore it, the mothers of many well authenticated but more modest hidalgos did not. So María Leonarda's lack of title does not tell us much beyond excluding Florencia from the highest rank, where as a crossbowman and artilleryman with foreign connections we would not be inclined to put him in the first place. Another, lurid fact further strengthens the supposition that Florencia was of modest social origins: he was hanged, and hidalgos were usually beheaded instead.

- *mando que un testamento que dexo cerrado en el Cusco que sy paresciere se rijan por el quitando e ponyendo como a los dichos a quien a dado el dicho poder para hazer su testamento les paresciere e por esto no lo revoco para que lo que ellos rebocaren e quytaren e acrescentaren sea quitado e rebocado e // acrecentado // e firmolo de su nombre e dexo por albaceas para todo a los arriba contenidos a quien da el poder testigos el capitan Manuel de Estacio e Duarte Borges e Juan Nieto e Rodrigo de Cevera e Juan Enriquez estantes en la dicha cibdad Martin de Florencia*

- He ordered that if a testament he left sealed in Cuzco should be found, they should be governed by it, adding and taking away as those to whom he has given power to make his testament should deem best, and for that reason he did not revoke it, so that what they may revoke, remove, and add should be revoked, removed, and added; and he signed his name and left as executors of everything the above-mentioned, to whom he gives power. Witnesses Captain Manuel de Estacio, Duarte Borges, Juan Nieto, Rodrigo de Cevera, and Juan Enríquez, present in the said city. Martín de Florencia.

The part about the other testament is self-explanatory. At the end of documents one's ears prick up; the signatures and the witness list are often most revealing. What we have here, incorporated in another document, is only a copy, so it is not possible to judge the quality of Florencia's signature, often the best evidence we ever get about the nature of someone's education, but at least we know that he signed, and not merely a rubric, but some form of his name, which alone puts him in perhaps the upper two thirds of Spaniards in the country at the time.

The witnesses to a document, whether perfunctory or extraordinary, were often close associates of the person issuing it and thus prime evidence in reconstructing that person's circle and general standing. But often they included one or more people employed by the notary, sometimes the very one who did the writing; working through a series of items will soon tell us who they are (for it is never said specifically). In this unusual case, no friends of Florencia seem to have been present. Most of the names are unknown to me. Estacio was a prominent captain on the rebel side, probably in charge of the impending execution. Juan Enríquez turns up several times in the chronicles of early Peru as a public executioner.

otorgamos e conoscemos que hazemos e otorgamos el testamento del dicho capitan Martin de Florencia e las mandas e legatos e pias causas en el contenidas segund lo que con nosotros dexo comunicado en la forma y horden siguiente
- primeramente encomendamos su anima a Dios nuestro senor que la crio e redimyo por su muy preciosa sangre y su cuerpo mandamos a la tierra donde fue formado
- otrosi mandamos que el cuerpo del dicho Martin de Florencia sea sepultado y este en la iglesia mayor desta cibdad donde esta enterrado porque a nuestro pedimento por virtud del dicho poder en confianza deste dicho testamento se sepulto y enterro donde esta y de sus bienes mandamos se pague el dicho enterramiento

therefore we grant and acknowledge that we make and issue the testament of the said Captain Martín de Florencia and the orders, bequests, and pious acts therein contained, as he had informed us, in the following form and order:
- first we commend his soul to God our lord who created and redeemed it by his very precious blood, and his body we commend to the earth of which it was formed.
- Further we order that the body of the said Martín de Florencia be buried and remain in the principal church of this city, where it is buried, because at our request by virtue of the said power, in expectation of this said testament, it was given burial where it is, and we order that the said burial be paid from his estate.

The document issued later in Lima by the executors now resumes. The first clause is standard and invariable. The second, in which the executors cover themselves for the expenses of the funeral and burial they have already carried out, betrays the extraordinary circumstances.

- otrosi dezimos que por quanto por virtud del dicho poder nosotros hezimos y mandamos decir al dicho Martin de Florencia por su anima ciertas misas e otras obsequias en la yglesia mayor desta cibdad mandamos que todo lo que en su enterramiento por honra de su cuerpo y por bien de su anima se hubiere hecho se pague de sus bienes del dicho Martin de Florencia

- otrosi mandamos que en la dicha yglesia mayor se digan por el anima del dicho Martin de Florencia las treze misas de la luz y se paguen de los bienes del dicho Martin de Florencia
- otrosi mandamos que se digan en el monesterio del señor Santo Domingo desta cibdad e en el altar del Santisimo Sacramento en cuya cofradia del dicho monesterio le metemos e hazemos cofadre veinte misas reçadas porque goze de los perdones e yndulugencias misas y sacreficios de la dicha cofadria y que los otros hermanos cofadres que en ella entran gozan e deben gozar e porque se le digan las misas e sacreficios que a los otros cofadres difuntos se les deben e suelen dezir e mandamos que se de e pague de sus bienes del dicho Martin de Florencia la entrada que se deve por tal cofrade e la limosna de las dichas misas e la cera que en ella se gasta
- otrosi mandamos que se diga por el anima del dicho Martin de Florencia en el monesterio de Nuestra Señora de la Merced desta cibdad otras veynte misas reçadas ofrendadas de cera e se les pague la limosna acostumbrada

- Further we say that since by virtue of the said power we had certain masses and other obsequies performed for the soul of the said Martín de Florencia in the principal church of this city, we order that all the expenses incurred in his burial for the honor of his body and the good of his soul be paid from the estate of the said Martín de Florencia.
- Further we order that in the said principal church the thirteen masses of the light be said for the soul of the said Martín de Florencia and be paid for from the estate of the said Martín de Florencia.
- Further we order that twenty low masses be said in the monastery of Santo Domingo of this city at the altar of the Most Holy Sacrament, in the sodality (cofradía) of which in the said monastery we put him and make him a member, so that he will enjoy the pardons and indulgences, masses and sacrifices of the said sodality and that the other brothers who enter the sodality as members enjoy and so that the masses and sacrifices which are accustomed and obliged to be said for other deceased members be said for him, and we order that the entrance fee owed for such a member and the donations for the said masses and candles that should be used in them be paid from the estate of the said Martín de Florencia.
- Further we order that there be said for the soul of the said Martín de Florencia in the monastery of Our Lady of Mercy of this city another twenty low masses, with candles, and the customary donation be paid.

Again the executors legitimate things that they have already done. To order masses said for one's soul was a normal part of a Spanish testament. The degree of the testator's religiosity or concern for the afterlife cannot, however, be deduced straightforwardly from the number of masses, for experience shows that the number varies primarily with the wealth and importance of the testator and increases with the lack of eligible heirs. The masses requested here exceed what is seen with the average Spaniard in Peru, but are not beyond what one could expect for a prominent encomendero.

It does seem likely that the observances specified reflect the wishes of Florencia and are not just what the executors thought proper. He has sets of masses said in the three principal ecclesiastical establishments of Lima, the main church (which was soon to be and already in effect was a cathedral), the Dominican monastery, and the Mercedarian monastery (the Franciscans at this time were not yet much heard of). It is quite rare for masses with a specific dedication to be requested, so the thirteen Masses of the Light stand out. One scholar has suggested that they point to a Judaic background, a matter on which I take no position.

The three churchly establishments are treated about equally as to masses, as if Florencia were covering all the bases. The Dominican monastery receives special recognition in that Florencia is made a posthumous member of a lay sodality there, in itself an act so common as hardly to call for comment, but surely Florencia made his choice because it was among the Dominicans that he had been hiding before the Pizarrists caught him.

- *otrosi mandamos por el descargo del anima del dicho capitan Martin de Florencia y por que Dios aya merito de su anima que se den en limosna a Marina Vernaldez hija legitima de Gonzalo Paez vecino que fue de la villa de Huelva en España difunto y de Catalina Vernaldez su legitima muger que al presente esta en esta cibdad en poder de la dicha su madre que la dicha Mari Vernaldez sera de hedad de diezeocho años ciento y cinquenta pesos de buen oro e justo peso para ayuda a su casamiento los quales mandamos que se le den de los bienes del dicho capitan Martin de Florencia el dia que se desposare y nosotros por ser para tan buena obra y que tanto agrada a Nuestra Señora nos constituymos para deposytarios de los dichos ciento e cinquenta pesos y nos obligamos de los dar pagar y entregar a la dicha Marina Vernaldez o a quien por ella los obiere de aver al dicho tiempo y para ayuda al dicho su casamiento*

- Further we order that for the unburdening of the soul of the said Captain Martín de Florencia and so that God should give credit to his soul there be given to Marina Bernáldez, legitimate daughter of Gonzalo Páez, deceased, late citizen of the town of Huelva in Spain, and of Catalina Bernáldez his legitimate wife, who at present is in this city in custody of her said mother, and the said Mari Bernáldez must be eighteen years old, 150 pesos of good gold and proper weight to aid in her marriage, which we order be given her from the estate of the said Captain Martín de Florencia on the day she should contract marriage. And since it is such a good deed and so pleasing to Our Lady, we constitute ourselves depositaries of the said 150 pesos and oblige ourselves to pay and deliver them to the said Marina Bernáldez or to whoever should receive them for her at the said time to aid with her said marriage.

When a man left a bequest in his testament to an unrelated young woman, it was clear enough, in early modern Spain and Spanish America, that they had had an intimate relationship, and when we read of the man's satisfying his conscience through the bequest, no doubt is left at all, even if the finding would not stand up in court. Since Florencia had been living in distant Cuzco not long before, and Marina Bernáldez had probably recently arrived in Peru, the likelihood is that their affair took place while he was in hiding in Lima.

It was common enough in Spain for impecunious parents, and all the more common for a widowed mother, to take a daughter or daughters to the Indies in the hope of a good marriage. Florencia would have been just the person. Marina Bernáldez was a serious candidate for a reasonably good marriage in early Spanish Peru, simply on the strength of being a young Spanish woman and legitimate; the presence of her mother added an aura of respectability. But her hometown, Huelva, was known for humble seafaring folk more than for nobility, and she lacked the doña. The hidalgos and indeed many others among the encomenderos of Peru were beginning to marry exclusively doñas by the 1540's, leaving only some encomenderos of rather marginal social and regional origins, among whom we are perhaps justified in counting Florencia, ready to marry women without the title. Florencia would have been at the upper end of the range of possibilities for Marina. Perhaps there were negotiations in which marriage was discussed, even planned; or perhaps Florencia had set his sights higher, and the Bernáldez women, with the mother probably making the final decisions (note how the text speaks of Marina being in Catalina's custody), were willing to settle for an informal connection with a wealthy man prominent in his way on the local scene.

Money for a dowry in this kind of situation was a standard gesture. The 150 pesos here is meaningful, but not enough to assure Marina much of a marriage. To have a marked impact it would have had to be at least two or three times as large.

I never found any other record of the children Florencia recognized in his will, Luis, Pedro, and Isabel. But twenty-odd years later his son Martín de Florencia got married in Lima. Conceivably Luis or Pedro had been renamed in his father's honor, but it seems even more likely that they were dead and that this Martín was the son of Marina Bernáldez, born after his father's death.

- *otrosi mandamos que en fin del año del enterramiento del dicho Martin de Florencia se le hagan sus honras y cabo daño en la yglesia mayor desta cibdad como se acostumbra hazer y se pague la limosna acostumbrada de los bienes del dicho Martin de Florencia*

- *otrosi mandamos quel dia de Todos Santos primero que verna o despues cada e quando que nos paresciere se hagan y digan por el anima del dicho Martin de Florencia en la dicha yglesia mayor sus honras de enterramiento diziendo una misa cantada con su vigilia e letania ofrendada de pan e bino e cera segund se suele dezir e hazer por semejantes personas en su enterramiento e se pague la limosna acostunbrada de los bienes del dicho Martin de Florencia*

- *otrosi mandamos que se digan en la yglesia mayor desta cibdad o a donde a qualquiera de nosotros paresciere veynte misas por las animas de purgatorio las quales digan las diez misas el bachiller Corral y las otras el padre Canpo clerigos questan en esta cibdad e se les paguen la limosna acostunbrada saliendo con sus responsos sobre la sepultura del dicho difunto*

- Further we order that at the end of a year after the burial of the said Martín de Florencia his honors and end-of-the-year ceremonies be carried out in the principal church of this city as is customarily done and that they be paid for from the estate of the said Martín de Florencia.

- Further we order that on the first day of All Saints that comes or thereafter whenever we should deem fit, his burial honors be performed for the soul of the said Martín de Florencia in the said principal church, saying a high mass with its vigil and litany, bread, wine, and candles, as is customarily done for such persons at their burial, and the customary donation be paid from the estate of the said Martín de Florencia.

- Further we order that there be said in the principal church of this city or wherever any one of us should think best twenty masses for the souls of purgatory, of which ten are to be said by Bachiller Corral and the others by Father Campo, secular priests, who are in this city, saying prayers over the grave of the said deceased person, and they are to be paid the customary donation.

Here the ecclesiastical bequests continue in the same vein: surely quite elaborate, but not out of keeping for a person of Florencia's prominence, wealth, and position. The spirit of the thing is caught in the phrase "as is customarily done for such persons." The policy of spreading the benefits among the entire local clergy continues, with masses assigned to secular priests apparently without steady posts at the moment.

- *otrosi mandamos que todo lo que paresciere que el dicho defunto debe de diez pesos avajo con juramento que hagan que les son devidos se les paguen de los bienes del dicho Martin de Florencia*

- Further we order that everything that it should appear that the said deceased person owes in the amount of ten pesos or below be paid from the estate of the said Martín de Florencia if those owed swear to the debt.

Paying of a testator's debts beneath a certain amount with no questions asked, to save trouble, was a standard feature of Spanish wills, and we can deduce nothing about Florencia or the executors from the presence of such a clause. The amount, however, says something. Even in rich Peru, many Spaniards would have gulped for a moment at ten pesos, a month's pay for some of them. We have here another indication of Florencia's very substantial wealth.

- *otrosi mandamos a la Santa Cruzada e a Nuestra Senora de Guada-lupe y a las otras mandas forzosas y acostunbradas a cada una dos tomines de los bienes del dicho Martin de Florencia*

- Further we assign to the Holy Crusade and Our Lady of Guadalupe and other obligatory and customary bequests two tomines each from the estate of the said Martín de Florencia.

A tomín was the same as a real, one eighth of a peso, so these bequests are miserly. As just above, however, nothing particular is indicated about Florencia and the executors. The funds from obligatory religious bequests had become a source of patronage for royal court favorites and the like, and even the most devout usually gave them nominal amounts.

- *otrosi mandamos a Luis y Pedro de Florencia e a Ysabelica hijos de Ysabel y Tocto sus yndias que la dicha Ysabelica esta en su cacique*

que a cada uno dellos mill pesos que el dicho su padre les mando al tiempo de su muerte y antes con nos dejo comunicados que les queria mandar y mandava y que nosotros les mandasemos para con que se alimenten y crien y dotrinen los quales mandamos que se enpleen en bacas y en yeguas y en cabras de los primeros dineros que de los bienes que por fin e muerte del dicho Martin de Florencia quedaron se sacaren

- Further we assign to Luis and Pedro de Florencia and Isabelica, children of Isabel and Tocto, his Indian women, and the said Isabelica is at his cacique's, to each one a thousand pesos that their said father left them at the time of his death and before that had informed us that he wanted to leave them and left them so that they would be fed, brought up, and indoctrinated, which funds we order to be invested in cows, mares, and goats from the first money that should be taken from the property left by the death of the said Martín de Florencia.

This clause for the most part merely repeats things that were already said in Florencia's instructions above. It adds another example of not giving Isabelica a surname, in contrast to the boys, and considering her, unlike them, to be on the encomienda. The investment of bequests like this in livestock was common, often specifically requested by the testator. At the time, European livestock were scarce, in great demand, and of very high value.

- otrosi mandamos que con toda brevedad se haga inbentario de todos los bienes que por fin e muerte del dicho Martin de Florencia quedaron por ante escriuano y por escusar riesgo se vendan y el dinero dellos se ponga con los demas para cumplimiento del anima y voluntad del dicho testador

- otrosi dezimos que por quanto el dicho Martin de Florencia por el dicho poder que nos da dize aver hecho otro testamento y tenerlo en el Cuzco que por virtud de la facultad que nos da para quitar e poner e rebocar y añadir hallandose el dicho testamento e porque hasta ver sy paresce el dicho testamento o no cumplidamente no podemos hazer el dicho testamento por tanto que reservamos en nos a su tiempo y lugar conforme a la dicha facultad y por virtud del dicho poder y della para que visto el dicho testamento o no lo pudiendo hallar acabar de hacer este dicho testamento o declarar averse acabado con lo aqui contenido asi por via de testamento o por via de codecilio o como de derecho mejor lugar aya

- Further we order that with all brevity an inventory be made before a notary of all the property left by the death of the said Martín de Florencia, and to avoid risk, it be sold and the money from it be put with the rest to satisfy the soul and will of the said testator.

- Further we say that inasmuch as the said Captain Martín de Florencia in the said power that he gives us says that he made another testament which is in Cuzco, by virtue of the faculty he gives us to remove, add, and revoke if the said testament is found and since until we see if the said testament should appear we cannot make the said testament completely, therefore we reserve in ourselves for its proper time and place the said faculty by virtue of the said power so that once the said testament has been seen or not been able to be found we would finish making this testament or declare that it is completed with the herein contained whether by way of testament or by way of codicil or whatever means should be most appropriate in law.

The sale of the entire estate may strike us as a drastic measure, but in the absence of an adult heir on the scene, or a very capable and trusted full-time manager, it was frequently resorted to. Liquidation would make things easier for the executors or the rebel authorities to make subtractions, but we have no particular reason to think that that was the intention. The existence of the missing testament in Cuzco presents a similar problem and opportunity. It was not the executors' fault, for Florencia had mentioned the will in his instructions, and they have done the only thing they could, but as a result whatever they do is provisional and open to challenge.

- otrosi dezimos que si en el poder y declaracion que el dicho capitan Martin de Florencia hizo al tiempo de su fin e muerte o en este testamento ay he se contienen algunas clausula o clausulas o mandas inciertas o a que por qualquier causa o razon la Santa Cruzada o Su Santidad o Su Majestad o otra qualquier persona particular o universidad tenga recurso o derecho a las dichas manda o mandas ynciertas o a los bienes del dicho defunto o parte dellos por la presente rebocamos las dichas mandas ynciertas o por donde se les adquiera el dicho derecho o accion e mandamos que vuelvan a los herederos del dicho Martin de Florencia y se conviertan en su pro e su utilidad asi como si las tales mandas o clausulas no se hubieren hecho e otorgado

- Further we say that if in the power and declaration that the said Captain Martín de Florencia made at the time of his death or in this testament there should be contained some dubious clause or clauses or bequests or if for whatever cause or reason the Holy Crusade or His Holiness or His Majesty or any other person or corporation should have access and rights to the said dubious bequest or bequests or to the property of the said deceased person or to some part of it, by the present document we revoke the said dubious bequests or whatever means by which they acquire the said rights, and we order that the property affected revert to the heirs of the said Martín de

Florencia and be converted into their assets as if such bequests or clauses had not been made and issued.

Probably because of the extremely unusual circumstances and the still unseen testament in Cuzco, the executors are here trying to ward off the effects of any irregularity they may have unwittingly committed, saying that whatever is found illegal is canceled. Such attempts at insurance are often found in Spanish dealings. A bill of sale may acknowledge full payment so that the seller has no right to reclaim the purchase, and then the next document in the volume will be the buyer's acknowledgment in turn, despite what was just said, of a debt for the entire amount. My impression is that such finagling did little good.

- dexamos por albaceas y herederos a las personas quel dicho Martin de Florencia por el dicho testamento nombra a los dichos albaceas por tales y a Maria Leonarda de Santangel madre del dicho Martin de Florencia por su legitima e universal heredera de todos sus bienes muebles e rayzes e se movientes derechos e abciones que por su fyn e muerte quedaron y restaron cumplido e pagado este dicho testamento y el que nos en su nombre hizieramos y lo que asi el dejo mandado por el dicho poder y declaracion que hizo al tiempo de su fyn e muerte

- We leave as executors and heirs the persons whom the said Martín de Florencia names in the said testament: the executors as such and María Leonarda de Santángel, mother of the said Martín de Florencia, as his legitimate and universal heir of all his property, movable, immovable, and self-moving, and rights that should remain and be left when this said testament and the one we should make in his name and what he left ordered by the said power and declaration that he made at the time of his death is fulfilled and paid for.

This clause tells us little new, but it does tend to imply that the two other executors Florencia originally named have not been banished from favor by the Pizarrists, but are merely absent. A universal heir was not necessarily overwhelmed with bounty; often the naming of such an heir was simply a device to make sure there was a recipient for any crumbs left after nearly all the substance of the inheritance had gone into specific bequests. Here, however, if Florencia was as wealthy as he seems to have been, the mother stood to receive a great fortune if it could be conveyed through the troubles of war and the dangers of the sea.

- por esta presente carta reserbando en nos el hacer acrecentar y
quitar deste dicho testamento y del otro quel dicho defunto declara
que deja en el Cuzco rebocamos e damos por ningunos e de ningun
valor e efeto otros qualesquier testamentos codecilios e mandas que
antes deste y del que asi el dicho defunto dize que otorgo el el Cuzco
el dicho defunto haya hecho e otorgado para que no balgan ni hagan
fee ni tengan fuerza ni bigor en juizio ni fuera del salbo este e el que
mas asi si fuere necesario atento lo en este testamento contenido
hizieremos e otorgaremos al qual e los demas que asi hizieremos y
fuere necesario y se hiziere mandamos que balgan por testamento e
por codicilio e por escritura publica o por aquella via e forma que de
derecho mas puede e deve valer porque esta es la hultima e
postrimera voluntad del dicho Martin de Florencia en testimonio de
lo qual otorgamos la presente carta ante el escriuano publico e
testigos yusoescritos en el registro de la qual firmamos nuestros
nombres que fue hecha e otorgada en la dicha cibdad de los Reyes
veynte e siete dias del mes de octubre ano del nascimiento de
Nuestro Senor Jesucristo de mill e quinientos e quarenta e quatro
años a lo qual todo que dicho es fueron presentes por testigos Pedro
de Villasaña e Pedro Cordero e Andres Duran e Rodrigo Albarez e
Francisco Duran estantes en esta ciudad e yo el presente escriuano
doy fee que conozco a los dichos otorgantes

paso ante mi Diego Gutierrez   *Juan de Ribas*
escriuano publico   *Antonio de Robles*

- By this present document, reserving in ourselves the right to add to
and subtract from this said testament and from the other that the
said deceased person declares that he left in Cuzco, we revoke and
declare null and of no value and effect whatever other testaments,
codicils, and bequests that the said deceased person should have
made and issued before this one and the one that he says that he
issued in Cuzco so that they will not be valid nor credible nor have
force in law or outside it other than this one or the additional one if it
were necessary in view of what is contained in this testament that we
might make and issue and others that we might make and deem
necessary, of which we order that they should be valid as testament,
codicil, or public instrument in the way that can and should be most
valid in law, because this is the last and final will of the said Martín
de Florencia, in testimony of which we issue the present document
before the notary public and witnesses written below in the register,
to which we sign our names. Done and issued in the said City of the
Kings, 27th day of the month of October, year of the birth of our lord
Jesus Christ 1544. In all of what has been said there were present as
witnesses Pedro de Villasaña, Pedro Cordero, Andrés Durán, Rodrigo
Alvarez, and Francisco Durán, present (estantes) in this city, and I
the present notary attest that I know the said issuers of the document.

Done before me, Diego Gutiérrez,   Juan de Ribas.
                notary public.   Antonio de Robles.

Revoking all previous testaments is a standard measure, here vitiated by the existence of the one still to be consulted in Cuzco. The place and date of a document should always be written down so that its position in a possible future series can be determined. Here we notice that five days have passed since the date of the incorporated document, the day of Florencia's execution. Witness lists are always of potential interest, as I have said above, and all the more so with anything like a will. The presence of six persons rather than the three employed in most everyday transactions, and the fact that this document is prepared under somewhat more normal circumstances than the other one, implies that an effort has been made to collect friends of Florencia, probably from Aragon. In the event I was never able to identify further a single one of the witnesses here. It is of interest that there are two people surnamed Durán; also that not a one of these witnesses served in that capacity with the other document.

The term *estantes* should not go unnoted. At a given time and place, notarial convention always made a distinction between full permanent citizens and transients. These people are not called vecinos, so we may assume that they are neither encomenderos of Lima nor maintain any impressive establishment there. The term *morador*, inhabitant, was just coming into use locally for those who did not head an establishment but were permanent residents. "Estante" is lowest on the scale, implying that the person so denominated is not a permanent part of the local scene. The vocabulary for these matters varies from place to place and also evolves over time, but the terms are always very informative once understood.

Diego Gutiérrez was at this time the secretary of the cabildo of Lima and the city's premier notary. He did a good deal of his own writing, more than many notaries; even so, his hand was among the most inelegant I have seen (the present document is in the hand of an amanuensis). The two executors produced fluent signatures implying full literacy and a knowledge of affairs.

Now that we have gone through this document with a fine tooth comb and pulled out much (by no means all, surely) of its half-hidden meaning and pattern, you may say that what is going on here is hardly reading between the lines, that much of it depends on crossreference with outside sources of information. I would reply first that much of it does not. Callaquiz, Huaman, and Tocto, for example, are not seen outside this very document. We can begin to build up a sense of some patterns in relations between an encomendero and indigenous Andeans from this text alone.

Of course crossreference must be used, and it is very important indeed. Do not imagine, though, that the kinds of information and background used in interpreting Martín de Florencia's will can be found in reference books, and certainly not when I was first working on the text. The specific information about individuals came from a large number of documents comparable to this one, if less spectacular (many of them not seen until later), and mainly had to be extracted by the same means, often ignoring the main ostensible thrust of the text to notice every detail and even the absence of features, taking notes on everything of interest and, without a doubt, retaining much of it in the memory so that a light of recognition goes on when you see something related, even weeks or months later. Background information is simply the accumulation in the mind, on paper, or on a computer of regularities in the totality of the individual examples. It is in that way that one discovers that most well born encomenderos were marrying doñas, or that a bequest to a young woman usually meant an intimate involvement.

Systematic compilation of crucial information about individuals is an inestimable aid in this kind of work. I would have been severely handicapped in writing *Spanish Peru* and *The Men of Cajamarca* if I had not kept a general file giving the regional origin of all Spanish men and women I had found in whatever source, for regional ties and antagonisms determined behavior in politics, war, business, and family life. Keeping a record of all known occupations of individuals was nearly as important. Such files work in two directions, on the one hand helping in the interpretation of specific documents, as here, and on the other representing the beginning of tables that can throw light on the broader picture in terms of absolute numbers and proportions. I do not say that regional ties and occupations of individuals will be either crucial or discoverable in all situations. In a given set of records from a given time and place, one needs first to spend a time simply being immersed in the material, with all antennae active, until one gets a sense of what is new or unexpected and hence probably significant, and what repeats and hence can be studied.

In the work I have done about people in Hispanic society, I have usually found individuals reappearing often enough that the sort of accumulation and crossreference seen in the case of Martín de Florencia produces a large proportion of the results in terms of insights about concepts and patterns. When I came to study the Nahuas of central Mexico, I was rarely able to see the same individual a second time. Yet things proved far from hopeless. Here is a Nahuatl testament from Culhuacan, just south of Mexico City (now part of it), done in 1581 in a time of epidemics.[4] Not a one of the people mentioned in it are known to appear in any other document except the notary who wrote it and some of the officials mentioned among the witnesses.

- *Ma quimatican yn ixquichtin yn quittazque yn quipohuazque amatl yn queni nehuatl Juan de Sanct Pedro notlaxillacaltia Sanct Pedro Çacapan maçonellihui y ninococohua yeçe yn noyollia naniman amo quen catqui yhuan huel mellahuac ynnic nicnoneltoquitia sanctissima drinidad tetatzin tepiltzin dios Espiritu Santo yhuan mochi nicneltoca yn ixquich quimoneltoquitia yn Sancta Yglesia de Roma auh yeyca yn axcan yn ica ynotzalloca ytlatlauhtilloca yn totecuiyo dios nicchihuah nictecpana yn notestamento*

- Know all who see and read this document that I, Juan de San Pedro, of the district of San Pedro Çacaapan, even though I am ill, nevertheless my spirit and soul are undisturbed; and I truly believe in the Most Holy Trinity, Father, Child, and God the Holy Spirit. And I believe all that the Holy Church of Rome believes. Therefore now with invocation and supplication of God our lord I make and order my testament.

---

[4]The document was published in Cline and León-Portilla 1984 as document 48; I got to know it as general editor of the series in which the book appeared. Cline uses it several times in her book of 1986, and I refer to it more than once in mine of 1992, making Juan de San Pedro's establishment the archetype of a Nahua household (see the respective indexes). Because of differing conventions and a few new discoveries, I have made some changes in the translation.

The Spanish testamentary form was brought into Nahuatl, where it flourished, unchanged in its framework and in many particulars. Nearly all of the first paragraph reads like a translation of the beginning of a normal Spanish will. Some of the changes are the result of differences in the two languages and probably have no further significance, religious or otherwise, in this context. In Nahuatl the gender of a younger relative is not normally specified, so that whereas in European languages Jesus Christ is called "the son," in Nahuatl he normally and inevitably appears as "the child."

Several Christian concepts, for reasons too complex and too little understood to go into here, did not usually get translated at all, in a sense. Instead, as Nahuatl began borrowing Spanish words after 1540 or 45, a series of Spanish religious words and phrases came into the language quite unchanged, here "Most Holy Trinity," "God," "Holy Spirit," "Holy Church of Rome," and "soul." The last is accompanied by a Nahuatl synonym, -yolia, one's means of living, vital force, which may or may not have been a neologism invented to explain the Spanish ánima. The word for testament is also from Spanish. All of these expressions, and the whole way of writing the first paragraph, were quite standard for the time, though each locality and each notary might do them a bit differently.

Formula of this type belongs to the writer, not the testator. This will is in what originally was a book with many others from the same time and place, a large number of them by this same notary, with nearly identical first paragraphs and other formulaic sections.

Spanish wills in America usually locate the testator as a citizen or resident of a particular city or large jurisdiction but do not go into further detail. Nahuatl wills generally name the altepetl, the local ethnic state which is now reorganized somewhat as a municipality, and then go on to specify the district within the larger entity, for Nahua polities had well defined independent constituent parts (tlaxilacalli, calpolli) that were functioning microcosms of the larger whole. In the Culhuacan wills the larger entity, Culhuacan itself, is mostly taken for granted, but the constituent part is carefully specified. Here it is Çacaapan, a preconquest entity judging by the Nahuatl locative word ("Where there is grass in the water") which names it. Çacaapan has received in addition the name of San Pedro, who we can take it is now the patron saint of the district.

The testator's name is given as Juan de San Pedro. By this time and long before, all Nahuas had the Spanish version of Christian names. Gradually more and more of them took on Spanish-style second names as well, which were of many types and continued to evolve in a way that often allows us to deduce a great deal about the person by the name alone. Juan, one of the most popular names (probably *the* most popular) among Nahuas as among Spaniards of all ranks, tells us little. The rest is more suggestive, though still ambiguous. The most common way to add a second Spanish-style element to a person's name was to use a saint's name. Simple Pedro would become Pedro de San Francisco, or Pedro de Santo Domingo, etc. Before long such appellations became so routine that they were shortened to Pedro Francisco, Pedro Domingo, and so on, with the "de San" being saved for more formal occasions, or for a person of a bit higher rank. In Culhuacan around 1580 the process of abbreviation was only beginning to take shape, so we cannot make much of the unabbreviated form in a given case. Such names did not usually serve as stable surnames for whole family lines, nor do they here. No one else in the will is surnamed "de San Pedro."

The outstanding thing about Juan's second name, as you may have already noticed, is that it is taken from the district saint. Often a large proportion of the population of the district would take the saint's name, nearly losing an individual flavor in order to express district affiliation. Many Nahuas in everyday life went without any surname at all, and when they got into a situation calling for one would conjure up the saint's name ad hoc. That could have happened here, though we can't be sure. The upshot is that though Juan's name is interesting we do not learn too much about him from that alone.

- Ynic çentlamantli niquitohua y noyollia naniman yçenmactzinco nocontlallia yn totecuiyo Dios yehica ca oquimochihuilli oquimo-maquixtillitzinno yca yn itlaçoezçotzin y nican tlalticpac auh yn nonacayo nicmaca yn tla[lli] yeica ca tlalli ytech oquiz

- First I declare that I place my spirit and soul entirely in the hands of God our lord because he made it and redeemed it with his precious blood here on earth. And my body I give to the earth because from earth it came.

This clause comes in the same place as in a Spanish will and says the same things almost word for word.

- *No yhuan niquitohua yn nocal ynn oncan nihuetztoc yn tonatiuh ycallaquiyanpa ytzticac niquinmaca yn nopilhuan Maria Tiacapan yhuan yn Augustin ypampa yn iuh niquitohua yn ynic niquinmaca yn nopilhuan canel notelpochcal ca oc nitelpochtli yn nicquetz calli cayamo ninonamictia auh yeicah yn iuh niquitohua çan oncan moyetztiyezque yn nopilhuantzitzin yn imeyxtin yntla mohuapaltizque ca onpa tepaltzinco monoltitoc yn Sanct Juan Xaltilolcoh ayac tle quimixtoquilliz*

- And I declare that I give the house where I lie, which faces west, to my children María Tiacapan and Agustín. The reason I say that I give it to my children is that it is my "young man's house," because I was still a young man when I built the house, not yet married. Therefore I declare that all three of my children are to be there if they grow to be adults, for they are dwelling in the house of other people in San Juan Xaltilolco. No one is to claim any of it from them.

The formulaic part is now over, and from here on the words are more likely to have been uttered by the testator himself. Juan de San Pedro lies sick in a house facing west (more literally, toward where the sun goes down). When I first saw such passages, I would take it that what was meant was a house off by itself with its main entry to the west. By reading many of these texts, finding the houses occasionally abutting on each other, with a patio mentioned now and then, I finally grasped that the "house" was a usually one-room structure with one door opening onto a central patio, often one of three, four, or even more similar structures surrounding the patio. The truth was not quick in coming, for the word for house (*calli*) was also used for the whole complex. Saying that a building faces in a certain direction was the Nahua way of saying that it is on the opposite side of the patio. If Juan's house faces west, it is on the east side.

Juan uses the special term *telpochcalli*, "youth house" or "young man's house," to characterize the building in question. Special terminology is the very stuff of analysis, so we pay full attention. This word happens to be quite famous in the older literature dealing with the preconquest Nahuas, in the meaning of an establishment where youths were brought together to be educated. It would have been easy to get altogether on the wrong track here if Juan had not been so good as to define the term as a structure built for a young man to live in before marriage (though possibly already with an eye to marriage). The fact that a special word is needed for a house destined for a single person tells us something very important, that a residential structure inside a house complex normally holds a nuclear family.

The house having been built by himself for himself, Juan feels free to leave it to his children, and he wants them to live there as they grow up. They are not there now, however, but at someone else's house. We can deduce that Juan's wife, the mother of the children, died before he did, possibly in the same epidemic; that the children are too young to take care of themselves; and that during Juan's illness they have been staying with relatives of Juan's wife, likely their grandparents. Apparently Juan had married a woman outside his own district, in San Juan Xaltilolco. We are not able to say for sure just who is taking care of the children, but we cannot fail to draw the conclusion that families are spreading out beyond a single district.

Juan speaks of three children but names only two. Likely the third is an infant, or perhaps some mistake has been made; the discrepancy should not occupy us unduly. The first mentioned of the children, hence probably the eldest, is a girl, María Tiacapan. She lacks a Spanish second name, and we will see that that was true of many females of the time. As we continue to read, we can be left with no doubt that in the Culhuacan of around 1580 more males than females had Spanish-style second names. The patterns had differed even before the Spaniards came, with men's names much more varied. Women often had order names, and in fact Tiacapan means "eldest" (eldest of the daughters being understood). The boy Agustín, however, is given no second name at all, perhaps because of his youth, perhaps in haste, or perhaps he was growing up without a second name, as it is just possible that his father did too; the preconquest Nahuas had generally had only one name.

Juan reinforces his bequest with a final admonition, "no one is to claim any of it from them." Nothing of the kind was seen in the sometimes elaborate Spanish testamentary documents concerning Martín de Florencia above, nor in comparable texts, but such passages are rife in Nahuatl wills, and they accompany many of Juan's bequests. They remind us that there must have been some sort of preconquest Nahua testamentary convention, an oral procedure in which the testator speaks to a surrounding group that will be responsible for enforcement. That tradition is still alive, here in this document and in the whole Nahuatl testament genre.

- *yhuan niquitohua y nocal yn caltitlan ycac tonatiuh yquiçayanpa ytzticac yn quinn oticquetzca tonehuan nonamic niquitohu[a] nicneltillia yn iuh quitotiuh noteicauh Parbara Tiacapan yn quitemacatiuh quauhtectli matlactetl quimacatiuh yn inamic Luys Perez yhuan yn icompadre Diego de Tabian ychan Sanct Ana Tetlan mani no x tetl yhuan yn nahuitzin Ana Xoco no quimacatiuh v tetl ycc onaçi yn xx ommacuili quixitinizque yehuatl quimomamacazque amo ytlacahuiz yn itlatol yn noteicauh Barpara canel ye oquiteaxcatitia ayac quimixtoquilliz no nehuatl niquitohu[a]*

- And I declare concerning my house [next to the main house?] that faces east, that we two, my wife and I, built later, I say that I am carrying out what my younger sibling Bárbara Tiacapan said, that she gave the [firewood, leftover wood] to others; she gave ten [piles] to her husband Luis Pérez, and ten also to her compadre Diego Tapia, whose home is Santa Ana Tetla; and she also gave five to my aunt Ana Xoco, with which it comes to 25; [the house] is to be knocked down and [the wood] distributed to them. The words of my younger sibling Bárbara are not to be violated, because she already made it their property; no one is to claim it from them, and I also say it.

Since the building mentioned here faces east ("where the sun rises"), it is on the west side of the common patio. Juan calls it his and says that he and his wife built it, but the resident must have been Bárbara Tiacapan, who has already arranged for the house to be demolished and part of it distributed among others, and Juan respects her wishes, whether willingly or reluctantly we cannot say. (At times I have thought I sensed reluctance, that Juan really thought he should have been the one to dispose of the house, but is not going to go against a fait accompli.) Bárbara must have died recently, presumably without a formal will, probably of the effects of the same epidemic. If she had been living in the house, then her husband Luis Pérez must have come there to live with her. We see in the examples of Juan and Bárbara that a couple might reside at the childhood home of either spouse, depending on the conditions.

It may seem extreme to tear down a house at the occupant's death, but though it by no means always happened, it was a common practice. In many cases most of the materials were rough, light wood of the kind that as here might reasonably be destined for firewood. Often only larger beams, the foundations, and finished pieces like doors had permanent value, as we will shortly see.

The Nahuatl word *caltitlan* as used here remains puzzling to me. It means literally "next to a house or houses," but it is hard to see what house is meant; not Juan's, which is on the other side of the patio. Perhaps the original main house, which as we will see was on the north side. More likely, this phrase has an idiomatic meaning I have not yet encountered in a context where it is clear, and whenever I run onto *caltitlan* in a text I think back to this passage and try to see if the new example sheds any light on the old. So far I have had no results, but it is by keeping a file of mysteries in one's head that one eventually solves some of them. Meanwhile, the fact that one word is ununderstood does not detract from the things we are sure of and can use to deduce from.

The name of Juan's younger sister, Bárbara Tiacapan, is on the same plan as that of his daughter: one Christian and one Nahuatl name, which not only designates a birth order but is literally the same name, Tiacapan, eldest, because she too is the first-born daughter. Another character is introduced, Ana Xoco, Juan and Bárbara's aunt, of whom we will hear more. Her name too is of the same type; Xoco means youngest. The names of Ana's husband, Luis Pérez, and her compadre, or ritual kinsman through godparenthood, Diego [de] Tapia, are for the time and place of a high category, of a type that a Spaniard might well bear, and they imply that the family of Juan de San Pedro, though without any very impressive names, may have been quite well connected. That the compadre is from yet another district again shows us cross-district mobility in terms of intimate relationships.

- *No yhuan yn iapecho mochiuhtoc yn itetocayo onicteneuh calli oncan pohuiz yn ichantzinco totlaçotatzin Sanct Pedro canah oncan monequiz auh yn itlaquetzallo mochiuhtimani ome nicmaca yn nahuitzin Ana Xoco auh yn itlayxquayo mochiuhtoc monamacaz yhuan yn çempantli quauhtectli yn no xxv li notech pohuiz yhuan yn tetl huel çenmatl yn onicnotlatlapihuilli mochi monamacaz yhuan acalhuapalli monamacaz x tetl ye içoltic yhuan v tetl yntech pohuiz yn nopilhuan auh yntla omonamacac acalhuapalçolli x tetl aço huell açiz ontetl missa yc tipallehuilozque yn ixpantzinco dios yn tonehuan nonamictzin*

- In addition, the platform in the water which forms the stone foundation of the said house will belong to the home [church] of our dear father San Pedro [of Çacaapan], it will be used in some part of it. And the two wooden pillars of [the house] I give to my aunt Ana Xoco. And its lintel will be sold and a row of [the firewood, kindling], also 25 [piles], will belong to me, and also the stone, one full unit of measure of it that I have accumulated, is all to be sold. And the ten used boat planks are to be sold, and [the proceeds of] five will belong to my children. When they are sold, the ten old boat planks, perhaps [the money] will be enough for two masses with which we will be aided before God, my wife and I.

Juan, asserting his residual ownership, now proceeds to dispose of the parts of his sister's house that she has not already given away. The "platform in the water" reminds us that Culhuacan was in lowlying swamp and lake territory, full of canals and ditches, and the most productive farming was done on chinampas, strips of earth and refuse built up in shallow water so that they perpetually had water all around them.

The stone of the foundation, which may be carefully cut and in any case is quite rare in the immediate area, is donated to the district church for construction purposes; the church is dedicated to San Pedro, the patron of the district and the source of Juan's surname. The preconquest word for temple was *teocalli*, "god-house," and the Christian church in the same fashion was often conceived, as here, as the home of the saint to whom it was dedicated and whose image was its most prominent internal feature.

The larger wooden beams from the house, too valuable to go for firewood, are to be bequeathed and sold for future use in their present function. Juan now begins to go beyond the remains of his sister's house to ask for odd items around the place to be sold, partly for his children and partly to pay for the mass or more that he hopes can be performed for himself and his wife, who since no mass has yet been said for her probably died only recently in the epidemic, as we half suspected before. (The word for mass is a Spanish loanword, as always.) The modesty of the items makes us suspect that despite the family's good connections it is quite poor even by indigenous standards. The things contain some implications for how Juan makes a living. His accumulation of stone might be no more than what any householder would engage in, but when we remember the bequest of stone for church construction, it seems possible that Juan is doing something fairly serious in the way of stonemasonry. The boat planks point to aquatic activities, of which we will see more.

The unit of length by which Juan measures the stone he has collected is the *matl*, often on the order of seven to ten feet, used above all in measuring land, and so variable from place to place that one cannot be very precise.

- *yhuan niquitohua y nechcahuillitiuh notatzin catca calli Xochmilcopa ytzticac nicmaca y nahuitzin Ana Xoco ypampa y nicmaca çenca ye nechmocuitlahuia ye nechtequipanohua yn ipampa cocolliztli ypampa yn iuh niquitohua nicaxcatia ayac quenmaniyan quixtoquilliz*

- And I say that my late father left me a house facing toward Xochimilco; I give it to my aunt, Ana Xoco; the reason why I give it to her is that she has been taking much care of me and serving me in my illness. For this reason I say that I make it her property; no one is ever to claim it from her.

Juan now comes at last to the third house in the complex, which belonged first to his father and now to him; this was doubtless where he lived while he was growing up, before he added the "young man's house" that became the residence of his own nuclear family. The structure is described as facing Xochimilco, which was to the south of Culhuacan, so the meaning in effect is "facing south." The Nahuas consistently spoke of the solar directions east and west in general terms but most often used ad hoc expressions for north and south. As we have learned, if the house faces south, it is on the north side of the patio.

We now have a classic situation for a Nahua household. The first house was built on the north, with its face in the full sun. The next two were built on the east and west sides, getting direct sun part of the day. As quite often happened, no house stood on the south side (the door of a house in that position would never get the sun); the entryway/exit would have been there.

Juan leaves the house to his aunt Ana Xoco, no doubt the younger sister of his late father. Note that both Juan and his sister Bárbara have left firewood to Ana, not to mention her having been present to care for Juan in his illness. I deduce that Ana has been living in the complex all along, probably in the original house belonging to Juan's father, which she continued to occupy after his death. That was why Juan and his family failed to move in there when he inherited it, as one might have expected.

The reason Juan gives for leaving the original house to his aunt is gratitude. I do not doubt him; but who else is there to leave it to, or more to the point, who else is there to take care of the place? Juan's children seem hardly out of infancy. If the household is to be maintained at all, Ana Xoco must do it. Juan seems to hope that as the children get a little older they will live there under Ana's care, and that eventually she will leave everything to them.

- No yhuan niquitohua yn metlatl e iii çan mochi yntech pohuiz yn nopilhuan ayac quimixtoquilliz ca ymaxca yhuan yn iatentlallo nocal yhuan yn iquiyahuac temi vii tetl Domingo Tlacatecuhtli yhuan ynn onpa Tecuitlaapan no v tetl çeçenpohualhuiyac onmamacuilli çan mochi yntech pohui yn nopilhuan ayac quimixtoquilliz ca ymaxcah

- Also I declare that all three metates will belong to my children. No one is to claim them from them, because they are their property. And the land at the edge of the water that goes with my house, and seven [chinampas] that are outside the place of Domingo Tlacateuctli, and also the five [chinampas] in Tecuitlaapan, each one 25 [units of measure] long, all belong to my children. No one is to claim it from them, because it is their property.

The metate, a shaped stone for grinding maize, was most often left to a female, but since Juan has three, he leaves one to each child. The chinampas naturally also go to the children. One group is attached to the household complex, forming an integral part of it, a strong Nahua tendency, and others are at a distance, also conforming to the Nahua pattern, for when anyone had very much land, it would be scattered. In two cases Juan specifies the number of chinampas or strips in a certain holding; one is seven, the other five. From that alone we could deduce nothing, but in the larger collection of which this will is a part, chinampa sets are mentioned repeatedly, and the standard number proves to be seven; they must have been laid out in sevens from the beginning. Juan's holdings are not negligible, but many other Culhuacan testators, and not only the nobles and officeholders, had much more.

- *yhuan ynn acaltzintli çentetl çanno yntech pohuiz yn nopil-huantzitzin quitetlaneuhtizque oncan neçiz yn intech monequi yn quimoqualtizqueh yhuan matlatl quinn oniquehuaya ye çenvara ynic huiyac çan mochi yntech pohui yn nopilhuantzitzin ayac tle huel quimixtoquiliz*

- And a boat is also to belong to my children. They are to rent it to people, and from that they will get what they need to eat. And the net which I was just making, that is now one yard long, all of it belongs to my children. No one can claim any of it from them.

Now Juan proves to own a boat of such good quality that he hopes to get substantial income for the children from having it rented out. He has been making a fishing net. Perhaps he made much of his living fishing and boating. We cannot be sure; in Culhuacan everyone had boats and went out on the lake. A "yard" is the Spanish loanword *vara*, which bit by bit encroached on the indigenous measurement words.

- *ye ixquich y niquitohua notlatol macayac tle quitoz yn iquac oninomiquilli ayac tle nicpiyellia ma ytla Ymixpan omochiuh tla-xillacaleque Domingo Tlacatecuihtli Pedro de Sanct Nicollas yhua depodados Augusti Vazquez Miguel Joseph Diego Ellias axcan jueues yc xvi de março de mill quiniyentos y ochenta y vn anos*

- That is all of my statement that I declare; let no one make any objections when I have died. I owe nothing to anyone, absolutely nothing. Done before the district heads Domingo Tlacateuctli and Pedro de San Nicolás and the deputies Agustín Vásquez, Miguel Josef, and Diego Elías. Today, the 16th of March of the year 1581.

A Nahuatl will is in many respects oratory, and the statement proper of the testator usually ends with *ye ixquich*, "that is all," something without a parallel in Spanish testaments.

From the Spanish point of view, much of the reason for issuing a testament was to clear up the status of all debts, and something of that rationale carried over into the Nahuatl counterpart even though the notion of owing money was new to the Nahuas. By the late sixteenth century they were evolving ways to speak of owing; here the verb is *pialia*, literally "to keep something for someone." By the early seventeenth century *pialia* was giving way to a very similarly constituted verb, *huiquilia*. It is only by noting attestations like the present one that we can detect and confirm such trends in language and thought.

The witnessing of Nahuatl documents differed from that of Spanish equivalents. Among Spaniards, the essence of the matter was to have three adult males to attest to the authenticity of the signature of the person issuing the document. Among Nahuas, the purpose was to have auditors who approved the whole proceeding as representatives of the community and would enforce the provisions made. Two types of groups could fill the function, a large assembly of neighbors (usually including women) or a contingent of officials of the entity. The first is the more quintessentially Nahua, but here we have the second. The first two named are elders or officials of the district of San Pedro Çacaapan; the other three are from the larger unit, the altepetl. Here called deputies, they counted among their functions to be present at the issuing of wills and assist in carrying them out. It is typical that the deputies, at the higher level, are called by a loanword, while the word for the local officials is traditional indigenous vocabulary. The altepetl officials all have Spanish second names, whereas the second name of one of the local officials is indigenous. It is of the type that might have been retained at this point in time by a person of any rank, however, for Tlacateuctli (literally "people-lord") was often the title of prestigious rulerships.

Almost all of the words giving the day and date here are Spanish loans, and indeed the last ten words are simply in Spanish. Although this case is just a bit extreme, expression of dates was a point of maximum Spanish linguistic influence, probably because of the lack of common denominators in the indigenous and the Spanish calendars.

- auh yn nehuatl Miguel Jacobo de Maldonado escriuano della yglesia niquitohua ca qualli ca mellahuac ynic oquitlalli ytestamento yn yehuatl Juan de Sanct Pedro ychan Sanct Pedro Çacapan yhuan nehuatl oniquicuillo nican nictlallia notoca nofirma ynic neltitiyez
Miguel Jacobo de Maldonado nonbrado

- And I, Miguel Jacobo de Maldonado, notary of the church, say that Juan de San Pedro, whose home is San Pedro Çacaapan, ordered his testament well and truly, and I wrote it, and to verify it I place here my name and signature.

Miguel Jacobo de Maldonado, appointed notary.

Miguel Jacobo de Maldonado, who here calls himself notary of the church (in Spanish) was also often notary of the municipal council of Culhuacan and may have held that office at this very moment; it is not clear that the two posts were kept separate. Maldonado was at one point removed from office for malfeasance, accused of having taken wills out of the collection in order to rob the testators, although he later occupied municipal posts again.[5] In any case, this will remained; it mentions nothing very tempting.

The Spanish loanword *firma*, "signature," is here paired with the native word for name.

Tracing the details of this document and working out their implications has gradually given us a picture of all the typical elements of a Nahua household of the time, of its organization, and how flexible it was, in this case going from a single dwelling to two and then three as the children married, then shrinking again as a result of the epidemic. The household is an entity and functions as one in many respects, yet its members have their own property within the complex, which they leave to other members or outsiders with much freedom.

The various traces of language contact between Nahuatl and Spanish that have been seen here may give little more than flavor in the context of a single document, but when the effect is compounded, significant findings result. The totality of loans in the Culhuacan testaments has been compiled and tabulated, putting the Culhuacan of ca. 1580 in perspective within the Nahua world.[6] Following such phenomena in such sources on a larger scale resulted in a picture of general Nahua linguistic and cultural evolution, giving the framework in which the snapshot of Culhuacan is meaningful.[7]

Let us look at one more Nahuatl document, this time with a woman as principal. It is the will of Bárbara Agustina, done at

---

[5]Cline and León-Portilla 1984, p. 5.

[6]Cline 1986, pp. 177–81, and Lockhart 1992, p. 290.

[7]Lockhart 1992, pp. 261–325.

Chiucnauhapan in the large altepetl of Coyoacan, just southwest of Mexico City, in 1608.[8] The document is unusual for a
Nahuatl testament in not specifying either the altepetl or the
district within it.

*Ynca ytoncantzin Dios detantzin Dios depiltzin Dios Espiritum
Santon no yehua cemicac ychpochtli Santa Maria dontepantlato-
cantzin ynic nopam motladoltintzinnoz yntla nechmonequiltin-
tzinnoz y notlaçotantzin Dios ca ycemactzinco nicahuan y naniman
y nehuatl nodocan Barbara Agostina nican nictlallia notestameton
axcan martes i de jullios i608 años*
*- ynic ce tlamatli ytla nechmopolhuiz y notlaçomahuiztantçin Dios
tzinlliniz capanan ynic quimatizque yn christianome nictlallia hue-
tzintli — i tomin*

In the name of God the Father, God the Child, and God the Holy
Spirit, and also the eternal virgin Saint Mary our intercessor to speak
on my behalf; if my dear father God requires me, I, named Bárbara
Agustina, leave my soul entirely in his hands. Here I order my testament, today, Tuesday, 1st of July, year of 1608.
- First, if my dear honored father God effaces me, the bell is to be
rung so that Christians will know it. I place an offering of 1 tomín.

The first parts of this will are much like the corresponding
sections of Juan de San Pedro's. But the Coyoacan conventions are somewhat different in detail from those of Culhuacan. Here the Virgin Mary is mentioned along with the
Trinity. The offering and request for the bells to be rung in
one's honor is something I have seen mainly in Coyoacan.

*- ynic otlamatli y nosepoltora ça bar amor de Dios nicnochihuilia ca
ninenecatzintli*

- Second, I make my tomb only by charity, for I am a poor wanderer.

This clause leaves an impression of great poverty, but let us
reserve judgment. The word for tomb is from Spanish, and so
is "bar amor de Dios," a garbled form of "por amor de Dios,"
"for the love of God," "free." This is a case of what we call an
unanalyzed phrase. The Spanish words *por*, "for," and *de*,
"of," have not really been taken into Nahuatl here; rather the
whole phrase is treated as a single string of sounds with a

_____

[8]Karttunen and Lockhart 1976, pp. 98–100, has a transcription
and translation of the document, along with the location of the
original and some mainly linguistic commentary. The text is mentioned in both Lockhart 1992 and Horn 1997; see Bárbara Agustina
in the respective indexes.

known overall meaning. But we can tell that the Nahuas are
hearing and to some extent understanding Spanish conversation by this time.

The word translated as "poor wanderer" comes from a verb
meaning to go about, travel; it could as well have been poor
traveler or pilgrim, and it was probably conventionally used
to express poverty.

- *yniquetlamatlin yn iquac nech[ma]nilliquihui y notlaçopilhuatzin-*
tzin teopantlacan cecan niquinotlatlauhtillia niquinomaquillia na-
hui tomitzin — 4 tomi

- Third, at that time my dear children the church attendants are to
come to take me; I urgently request it of them. I give them 4 tomines.

The *teopantlaca* ("church people"), the indigenous attendants, employees, or staff of a certain church, can nearly be
equated with the cantors or choir members. Their attendance
and performance at funerals was universally desired and
from the sixteenth through the eighteenth centuries usually
received the same remuneration, half a peso for the group.

- *yn iquac ayamo motocan notlalnacayo nopan mitoz vigillia niqui-*
nomaquillia nahui tomitzin — 4 tomi

- Before my earthly body is buried a vigil is to be said for me; I give
them 4 tomines.

Rarely does a testator settle for something short of a mass
on the occasion of a funeral. Failure to request a mass is usually a sign of penury; but again, let us reserve judgment.

- *yhua yntechcopan nitlatohua yn caltzintli nicahuillitiuh y noch-*
pontzin yntocan Juanna Orsolan vca yez ayac quitlacoz y notlatol

- And concerning the house I declare that I am bequeathing it to my
daughter named Juana Ursula. She is to be there; no one is to violate
my word.

Bárbara now proves to have a house, as well as a daughter
to whom, as normal, she leaves it. She fails to mention the
land it stands on, usually a significant farmable plot in the
Nahua scheme of things. The lack of reference to any such
holding leads us to think that perhaps Bárbara owns the
house only and not the land it stands on. As we will see, she
owns no other land either. The implications of relative
poverty continue.

Juana Ursula, Bárbara's daughter, is her *ichpochtli*, a word that when not possessed means a female who has attained puberty and is not yet married. When possessed it means someone's daughter, but still with the implication that she has at least reached puberty. Juana Ursula appears not to be married and to be living with her mother in the house she is inheriting and where she will continue to live. The statement "she is to be there" is not only a sort of command; said in this absolute fashion before the surrounding witnesses, it implies everyone's agreement that it shall be so.

- *yhua monamacaz ycpatl yamaqui onictetencac nohuipil vyezquia mochi ocan yn ipacyo [. . .] mocuiz chiquace tomi — 6 tomin*

- And the soft yarn is to be sold, that I put on the loom and that was going to be my blouse; all the yarn for it is there. Six tomines are to be taken for it.

Bárbara Agustina has been weaving a blouse (*huipilli,* in Spanish *huipil*) to wear, which shows that like nearly all Nahua women of the time she dressed in a style depending strongly on indigenous tradition, and that she wove her own garments on a traditional hand loom. The "soft yarn" probably has a more technical meaning than we can easily divine from texts alone (work on present-day weaving materials and techniques is beginning to make it possible to understand such terms better), but at least the yarn must be of cotton, not the rougher fiber of maguey.

From the one example we cannot know whether Bárbara normally made garments for sale to others or not; many indigenous women did. At least she is aware of the value of her half-finished product, ordering it to be sold. What is more, she dictates how much it is to be sold for, which might seem not for her to say, but from having seen many such passages, sometimes with a later note that the item was actually sold for the mentioned price, I have come to the conclusion that the amount mentioned in these broad commands is the consensus of the audience on what the value is. We will see other examples of dictated prices of future sales below.

- *yhuan ce machon tliltic cepohualli yhua gastolli pesos onicmacac çan itentzinco pohuiz yn totlaçonatzin nicnopiellia ça quitlayecoltiz catelan xochitzintli copaltzintli yc mocouhtiaz y quinextiz yehuatl quinemiltiz nopillotzin Juan Pedro quipiez*

- And a black male mule that I gave 35 pesos for is to belong to the [image of] our dear mother that I have; it is to work for her. Candles, flowers, and incense are to go along being bought with what it earns. My nephew Juan Pedro is to maintain and keep it.

With this clause, our developing assessment of Bárbara's economic situation is revolutionized. She owns a mule. Very few indigenous people of her time owned even a horse; a mule was still more expensive. Many a Nahua family would hardly have seen the 35 pesos Bárbara claims to have paid for it (and the price is credible by the standards of the time) over two or three years, much less ever have had that much cash together at one time. Mules were mainly for pack trains, for the transport of commercial goods, and most of the Nahuas who owned one or more were involved in some sort of inter-regional trade, at least between several markets in a local subregion. We must now begin to suspect that Bárbara is a trader of some kind.

The other outstanding feature of this clause is "our dear mother," understood to be what we would consider an image of the Virgin, though the Nahuas rarely and reluctantly spoke of the religious paintings and statues they had in their house-holds for veneration as images, talking for all the world as though they were the saints themselves. Bárbara's Mary may be the Virgin of Guadalupe, though that is by no means a fore-gone conclusion even here in Guadalupe's local orbit when her cult is beginning to pick up some momentum, for other forms of the Virgin—Assumption, Immaculate Conception, Rosary, and others—had their devotees.

Note that here Mary is called "our dear mother," whereas in the preamble she was called "eternal virgin." It was varia-tions of this type that led me to conclude that the preamble of testaments was a frozen zone of orthodox expression estab-lished in the mid-sixteenth century and the body a changing arena where more colloquial and current speech might be displayed. When Nahuatl was first being written down under ecclesiastical auspices, the Spanish clerics, or aides acting thoroughly in their spirit, devised expressions which were mainly translations of Christian doctrine as literal as the language would allow. Specific objections were made at that time to calling the Virgin "our mother." Yet that is what the Nahuas ended up doing, and the usage of Spanish clerics in

Nahuatl eventually often followed them.

In the translation I have spoken of Bárbara's "having" the Virgin. The Nahuatl uses the verb *pia*, which was traditionally "to keep, guard, have custody of, have charge of," but by this time often was used as the equivalent of the Spanish verb *tener*, "to have." We really cannot decide unambiguously just where along the semantic continuum the meaning falls in this case.

The Virgin and the mule are not in the same clause by accident. It was common among the Nahuas to devote specific pieces of land to household saints and bequeath both saint and land to a relative, expecting the latter to use the land partly to maintain the saint's worship in the expected way. What was expected is well expressed here, to keep candles, flowers, and incense at the altar. Similar practices no doubt go back to preconquest times; by now they are merged with Christian beliefs and rites. No awareness of the double origin probably remains, but we can see something of it in the words used. "Candle" is a Spanish loanword. "Flower" is traditional Nahuatl, and the elaborate use of flowers in cult activities was a conspicuous Mesoamerican culture trait. "Incense" is the traditional Nahuatl word for copal, the resinous material used as incense before contact; by now it probably means incense of any origin. Since Bárbara has no land, her most precious possession, the mule, replaces it.

The person who should get the mule, one would think, would be Bárbara's daughter Juana Ursula. That that does not happen makes us imagine that Juana is an adolescent not yet capable of managing complex affairs as Bárbara herself does. So she has recourse to her nephew Juan Pedro, who presumably has the requisite experience. In effect she gives him the mule, but with the obligation of keeping up her household altar of the Virgin. Her speaking of the Virgin being maintained by the earnings of the mule implies that Juan Pedro will be renting it out; he may not, therefore, be in regional trade himself. The verb where the translation says that Juan Pedro is to "keep" the mule is again *pia*; it might mean "to have" in the fullest sense, or it might mean "look after," or "have custody of."

- yhuan vme metlatl macoz nochpontzin Juanna Orsola

- no ce metlatl monamacaz mocuiz — 6 tomi

- And two metates [grinding stones] are to be given to my daughter Juana Ursula.
- Another metate is to be sold; 6 tomines are to be taken for it.

That some metates should go to the daughter and that those in excess should be sold is natural. Knowing of the mule, we now look at every item with an eye to its salability. Three metates, though, is not yet enough for us to be able to deduce that Bárbara has been selling them.

- Jusana Dominican quipien ce peso — i peso
- Francisca quipie macuilpohualli cacahuatl no macuilpohualli xo-
coc ça hualmocuepaz
- Alonso Martin quipien yei tomi — 3 tomi
- Baolan quitlaniz yei tomi yehuatl quimati — 3 tomi
- Anna quipie macuiltomi — 5 tomi
- Esthevan quipie ome tomi — 2 tomi
- Juachin quipie medion — medio
- Domigo Pantlan quipie medio — medio
- Fabia quipien ome tomi — 2 tomi

- Susana Dominica has 1 peso [of mine].
- Francisca has 100 cacao beans and another 100 bitter ones; they are to be returned.
- Alonso Martín has 3 tomines.
- Pabla will demand 3 tomines; she knows about it.
- Ana has 5 tomines.
- Esteban has 2 tomines.
- Joaquín has half a tomín.
- Domingo Patlan has half a tomín.
- Fabián has 2 tomines.

This list of people who have Bárbara's money is the salient feature of the document and immediately engages our attention. Their "having" the money is once again *pia*. In this case one is much tempted to think it means the same thing as its special postconquest applicative form *pialia*, "to owe," which we have already seen above in the will of Juan de San Pedro of Culhuacan. In a very few clear cases, *pia* is indeed used that way. That the money is not actually theirs permanently is obvious from the very fact of its being mentioned here.

What has Bárbara been doing? Our first thought must be lending money; after much experience one finds that all the Nahua equivalents for "to owe" were long used primarily when money had changed hands, when the debtor was in a sense actually keeping and taking care of the money for the lender. Since we know or very strongly suspect, however, that Bárbara with her mule is involved in some sort of steady trading of goods requiring transport, more than we see any evidence of being produced in her establishment, she must have some way of acquiring the goods in the first place. Perhaps she has been advancing money to people who later deliver the product or products to her. Words of owing were not normally used for paying debts incurred through the sale of merchandise on credit, but we are after all dealing with a situation on the edge of current knowledge, and I would not absolutely affirm that some of the people on the list are not buyers of her merchandise who have not yet paid.

All the amounts are petty by Spanish standards and not large by any standard, the largest being of a single peso, and the total only a little over three pesos (of which three tomines is a debt of Bárbara's). But they are significant, and surely for an indigenous person. The cacao beans may seem out of place. In fact, they do belong under the heading of currency. The peso was rarely seen as a single coin in the local economy; the main coin was the *real* of silver, which the Nahuas persisted in calling a tomín from the Spanish usage of the conquest period; the smallest in normal circulation was the half real or half tomín. For amounts smaller than that, and purchases in the marketplace would often be, cacao beans were used as change, having served in that way ever since preconquest times. At any given time and place, the cacao bean was pegged to the coins, a tomín being worth so and so many beans. Despite having the status of a currency, cacao was still a consumable, perishable commodity, and quality had to be considered in assessing its value; hence the mention of the bitterness of one batch. Bárbara surely does not expect literally the same cacao beans to come back, but is merely describing the value to be rendered. In this case we can be sure that Bárbara lent or advanced the amount, because no one would have agreed in the abstract to pay such an odd assortment at a later time.

As we noticed, Bárbara herself has contracted a debt in some way, of the same order of size as the others, probably in the course of carrying on business. The Nahuatl phrase "to know it" (*quimati*) implies responsibility for something and discretion; Bárbara is essentially saying that whatever Pabla, the creditor, says will be right.

What of the people themselves? Most of them given only one name, they must be members of the local community and acquaintances of Bárbara's. They could never be identified legally by neutral authorities from the outside, even from other parts of the altepetl. They are identified only within Bárbara's circle. It could be that many of the people mentioned use only one name in everyday life. If they had a second name with any particular profile or prestige, it would doubtless be given. They are, then, humble folk. Of the three second names given, two are Christian names, forming the most common type of appellation for indigenous people, and the third is a Nahuatl name, with implications of yet lower rank. Four of the people in the list are women, five are men. A similar kind of dealing with both genders is implied. Although the principle is violated a bit, we see here a trace of the Nahuatl tendency to divide lists of people into two sets according to gender. Most often the men come first, but here it is the women.

- *Loreço den Sandon Domigo ocatcaya vmen huexolotl ocona ammo quixtlahua quitlaliz ce peso — i peso*

- The late Lorenzo de Santo Domingo took two turkey cocks and has not paid for them; he is to produce one peso.

Lorenzo de Santo Domingo (whose name is given the full treatment and who may have been a person of considerable substance) is still held responsible after his death for what he owed. More importantly, this clause gives our first definite evidence on what it is that Bárbara sells: in this case, turkeys.

- *Juanna ocatca nomonatzin nicpiellia — 9 tomi*
- *Maria tepitzin quipie ome peso çano ytomitzin nomonatzinn ocatcaya — 2 peso*
- *omen metlatl quipie Maria tepitzin çano nomonatzinn ocatcaya ytlatqui quitlalliz — 2 peso 4 tomi*

- I owe Juana, my late mother-in-law, 9 tomines.
- Little María has 2 pesos, likewise my late mother-in-law's money.
- Little María has two metates, likewise the property of my late mother-in-law; she is to come up with 2 pesos, 4 tomines.

At this point the picture begins to assume some generational depth. We can take it that Bárbara was married to the man who was the father of Juana Ursula, probably coming to live at his house, where his mother, Juana, was also still present. The husband, not being mentioned here, must have died some time ago. Bárbara's mother-in-law Juana seems to have died much more recently, for debts owed her are still outstanding and of concern. From the fairly considerable amounts, in the same range as Bárbara's own debts and credits, we can suspect that they were of a business nature. It looks very much like Juana was a trader before Bárbara, that Bárbara may have learned from her and later taken over for her, the daughter-in-law succeeding the mother-in-law.

With Little María we finally have some concession to the fact that nearly everyone has the same name: an attempt to distinguish one María from another of a type that is quite rarely seen. Possibly she is physically small, or young. She could be a relative, a business connection, or both.

The form "ocatcaya" used in the Nahuatl, meaning "who was, late," is a sort of double past not at all in favor with those who prided themselves on elegance in Nahuatl. The language and spelling of this particular notary, though competent, are very much on the lower end of the scale and would not do, for example, to record the proceedings of the municipal council of the great altepetl of Coyoacan, of which we are here in a minor constituent part.

- *yhua ce pitzotl monamacaz mocuiz ome peso ytech pohui totlaço-natzin nicnopiellia*
- *ynhua macuilteme huexolome monamacazque matlatlactomi mo-cuiz* — 6 *peso*
- *Francisca teoyotica noconeuh macoz çe cihuatotolli*

- And a pig is to be sold; 2 pesos are to be taken for it, to belong to [the image of] our dear mother that I have.
- And five turkey cocks are to be sold; 10 tomines each are to be taken for them — 6 pesos.
- A turkey hen is to be given to Francisca my godchild.

Now we are making progress on the nature of Bárbara's business. She has at least five turkey cocks and a turkey hen on hand, as well as a pig. She may buy and sell other items as well, but it looks very much as if turkeys and pigs, one an indigenous species and the other introduced but both prime sources of meat, are her main stock in trade.

The Nahuatl phrase "teoyotica noconeuh," since it means "my child through sacrament, or holy things," can refer to one's child in marriage, but it can also have the meaning "godchild," as here. The godchild is possibly the same Francisca who owes Bárbara the cacao beans and the same as the Francisca among the witnesses. Indeed, it is likely; but we must not take it as established.

- ymmixpam omochiuh yehuatini Grabiel Quauhtli Francisca Anna Ynsabel Beronica Luysan
- yhuan niquinotlatlauhtillia y noalbaçiashuan yehuantini Beronica Luisan Joa Baphtistan Juan Baphtista Tlacatecpam Miguel Sanchez tenanitlan yncatzinco Dios quimocuitlahuizque yn [. . .]

    Luis Margos fiscal   *Juan Pedro [. . .] escribano*

It was done before the following: Gabriel Quauhtli, Francisca, Ana, Isabel, Verónica Luisa.

And I implore my executors, who are as follows—Verónica Luisa, Juan Bautista, Juan Bautista of Tlacatecpan, Miguel Sánchez of Tenanitlan—in God's name to look after [my soul? my daughter?].

    Luis Marcos, fiscal.   Juan Pedro [. . .], notary.

The witnesses to the testament include a man with a humble name, listed first, and a certain number of women. I would not pretend to say just exactly how many. The punctuation in the translation represents a guess. Ana Isabel could be one person, Verónica Luisa conceivably two, though the immediate repetition in the same order made me think one more probable. The executors include both women and men, the woman first this time. Two of them are from other communities within Coyoacan, probably places where Bárbara does business, traveling there with her mule, turkeys, and pigs.

The fiscal was the highest Nahuatl official of the local church, and he often ended up intervening substantially in the carrying out of wills. Juan Pedro the notary ended his signature with a flourish that might be just a fancy rubric but might include an abbreviated version of an additional surname that I could not decipher. He is possibly the same person as the nephew of Bárbara's who is to get the mule, but as so often we cannot be sure. The limited repertoire of names the Nahuas used distinctly makes things more difficult.

Just what is to happen to money collected, once the church

staff and Pabla are paid what is owed them, is not specified, nor what is to happen to money owed Bárbara's mother-in-law that might come in. It would all appear to fall to Juana Ursula.

Again and again Bárbara Agustina's will seems to conjure up a woman's world, the business going from woman to woman, all the main characters women, many of the customers and witnesses women and sometimes listed first. Perhaps the impression is correct. But if so, men were not really excluded. Bárbara left her prize possession to Juan Pedro because Juana Ursula for whatever reason wasn't capable; more than half of her customers were male, and the same is true of the people she chose as executors of her will.

The three documents we have studied are much richer than average, indeed quite spectacular. The will of Juan de San Pedro, though, hardly seems exceptional at first sight among many other superficially similar texts in the Culhuacan collection, and the only thing that distinguishes Bárbara Agustina's testament to a quick glance is the list of apparent debts. One should always have one's faculties of observation and deduction tuned to a high pitch when reading documents, for the conjunction of routine elements can be extraordinarily revealing, and a short passage or a single word can be crucial.

In reading a sixteenth-century Nahuatl text I once came upon the word *camixatli*, which is the Spanish loanword *camisa*, "shirt," with the indigenous nominal absolutive ending *-tli*. The absolutive singular on loan nouns is extremely rare, and at that point I had never seen such a thing before. I was sure it was an error, but at least I copied it along with its date, place, and reference. Later I found a couple of loan nouns with absolutive in Molina's sixteenth-century dictionary and began to wonder; still, dictionaries are often artificial in giving citation forms. Later yet I found comparable forms in modern dictionaries of local varieties of Nahuatl and realized that the absolutive must have existed on certain loan nouns for hundreds of years. It took a long search, but I finally found the original instance in my notes, eventually came upon a couple more examples, and was able to conclude that from the earliest time the absolutive was used in a few cases where a word that was normally possessed occurred unpossessed. What had seemed an error or aberration found a reasonable explanation within the larger pattern of evolution.[9]

Any document whatever will substantiate a large number of meaningful inferences. Many texts, however, are so like one another that they become routine. I admit that when working with Spanish notarial documents, after a time I hardly glanced at the long internal formulas in powers of attorney. Perhaps I missed something important, but after finding nothing in several attempts I was willing to take the risk in order to be able to read closely a larger number of the meatier sections at the beginning and end of the documents.

Even when there is literally nothing more than routine matter, from a certain perspective, in a certain text, it can become very revealing when combined with others. I once came upon a notarial document in which the encomendero Pedro de Mendoza, one of the men of Cajamarca whom I was following, made what was called a *traspaso*, a transferral of debt. Merchants frequently engaged in these dealings, but anyone who was owed a debt and had occasion to buy something might do the same, so I thought nothing of it, though I noted it down on the principle of following Mendoza exhaustively. Later I found Mendoza involved in another traspaso, then another and another, and finally a whole sheaf of them all at once. I could no longer cherish any doubt that the man was a merchant by origin and was one of the few first conquerors who continued to function as such even after receiving an encomienda and taking permanent citizenship in a Peruvian city.[10]

I hope I have convinced you that almost any document will reveal patterned, interlocking information and concepts—a world—if you will read very, very closely, expecting anything and nothing, and make copious but reasonable deductions from what you see. Some people seem to be a great deal better at reading between the lines than others, and perhaps it is an

---

[9]The episode of *camixatli* made such an impression on me that this is the second time I have mentioned it publicly, the other time in a somewhat different context (Lockhart 1991, pp. 131–32).

[10]See Mendoza's biography in Lockhart 1972, pp. 305–7.

art, but I really fail to see why almost anyone couldn't do this sort of thing. And it is accompanied by one of the more rewarding feelings accorded to humans, an emotional identification across the distance with the people and the scene, a shock of recognition of its reality and inherent familiarity.

10. Some Unfashionable Ideas on the History of the Nahuatl Language

S TUDYING a remote language like Nahuatl tends to make one analytical and observant about it, much more than with more familiar tongues. If one works with the language as much as I have with Nahuatl, is of a grammatical bent from the beginning, spends a great deal of time and effort not only with texts but studying and even translating grammars,[1] and is at the same time a historian, one is likely to develop certain ideas about the evolution of the language even if one is not a professional linguist. Certainly I have done so. Many of my favorite notions first came to me some twenty years ago, at which time I shared them with some people in linguistics departments who were also working with Indian languages; I quickly discovered, to my great surprise, that my ideas were not received favorably. More angry than deflated, and having many other things to do, I stopped trying to communicate more broadly on these matters and indeed did no further active work in historical linguistics, but memory of the things I had noticed did not fade, and as I learned more about Nahuatl I felt that my earlier analysis stood up well, by my own criteria of course, and innerly it continued to evolve.

In this piece I want to elucidate the main points I have hit upon, in words as comprehensible to laypeople as possible. I have found similar material to be useful in helping those who have studied with me to master older Nahuatl vocabulary and morphology more quickly. For all my efforts, I imagine the matter here will be too technical for most readers into whose hands the present book might chance to fall. Yet I would like to have these things on record, even if in a very sketchy form. I am also hopeful that as time goes on history will come to consider linguistic analysis to be within its ordinary scope, as anthropology does, and that organized linguistics will

---

[1] I confess (see Chapter 12, p. 364) that I have long been working intermittently on a bilingual edition of Carochi's *Arte* (1645). At this writing the task is approaching completion.

broaden out again to share the interests and outlooks of other disciplines as it once did.

When I was first learning some Nahuatl I was impressed with how a string of letters that tends to look to us like a word sometimes had as much in it as one of our sentences and indeed functioned as a sentence. Every tiniest element had its own significance, and this proved to be true not only of the multitudinous affixes surrounding the root, but within the root itself, for many roots were obviously complex, and even those that at first seemed not to be later proved to divide into two or more parts with separate functions. In due course I came to the conclusion that in Nahuatl every single letter (that is, the sound segment it represents) had some separate recoverable semantic meaning or morphological-syntactic function.

After operating on this principle for a while, however, I retreated from it a bit. The smallest meaningful entity, if we think back to a remote and somewhat idealized time, would have been a consonant plus a vowel, a CV unit; where today we see V alone in a syllable in Nahuatl, it has been worn down from CV; where we see a consonant ending a CVC syllable, a final vowel has been lost, so that earlier it was CV-CV, with two units. The word *ā-tl*, "water," once began with a *p*; *tah-tli*, "father," once had the root *tata*.[2]

At the same time, things became more complex. A long vowel turned out sometimes to correspond to a short vowel plus glottal stop, implying that wherever there was a long vowel a whole potentially recoverable syllable had been lost. Thus the combining form of the root for "hand or arm" is usually *mā-*, but sometimes *mah-*, indicating that the root was once *maCV*. The original consonant must be considered un-identified at this point, for the syllable-final glottal stop is only a weak, rather unstable residue of some other obstruent.

---

[2]In this piece I use an orthography based on Carochi's, following him in indicating a long vowel with a macron above the letter but deviating in using *h* rather than a diacritic for the glottal stop and considering any unmarked vowel to be short rather than using a special diacritic for that purpose. All cases of *h* to mean glottal stop are syllable final; this *h* is not to be confused with the letter in *hu* (prevocalic [w]) or *uh* (syllable-final unvoiced [w]).

We do not have to look far for the identity of the final vowel, for it is still *i* in the citation form of the noun, *māi-tl*. (The principle that a long vowel compensates for the loss of a following segment or syllable is, of course, well established in the history of many languages.)[3]

Equipped with these tools, one can sometimes find remarkable correspondences in common Nahuatl vocabulary.

Nouns and verbs

The roots of nouns at times bear a suggestive resemblance to the roots (present-tense stems) of cognate verbs. Continuing with the example we were just discussing, let us consider the following:

māi-tl	hand or arm
mati	to know, think, feel, taste
maca	to give

The meaning of the two verbs here manifests a close and transparent relation to the notion "hand." The verb "to know, to feel," must have arrived at its present sense by the extension of an original meaning "to grasp, to hold in the hand." The verb "to give" must originally have been "to hand to someone." In these verbs it is hard to avoid the conclusion that the *ma* originally conveyed hand, while the two final syllables were verbalizing suffixes with meanings and func-

---

[3]I take it that in the normal Nahuatl processes of reduction, the loss of a consonant after a vowel always results in the lengthening of that vowel.

A quite distinct, much more limited process is the omission of one vowel and one consonant at morpheme boundary in the name of shortening Nahuatl's maze of affixes. At times this looks as if it occurs within morphemes. Thus *miqui-liz-tli* (to die-nominalizing ending-absolutive singular), "death," often appears as *miquiztli*. But *no-c-on-itta* (I-him-directional-see), "I go to see him," becomes *nocotta*; *itta-lō-ni* (see-nonactive-agentive), "something visible," becomes *ittōni*. Thus *miquiztli* must originate through omission of the final *i* of the verb stem *miqui-* and the *l* of the derivational suffix *-liz*. Either the vowel or the consonant omitted can come first, but the two segments must belong to two separate morphemes.

With reduction of this type, no compensatory lengthening takes place, as can be seen in both *miquiztli* and *nocotta*.

tions that are not easy to reconstruct at this remove in time. The element *ti* is ubiquitous in Nahuatl; it seems once to have been a verb "to be or become," and it appears as the final syllable of many intransitive verbs (*mati* has an intransitive variant). The element *ca* forms the second syllable of many four-segment verbs, mainly transitive.

It is sometimes said that the canonical form for Proto-Aztecan or Proto-Uto-Aztecan verbs was CVCV. I believe that to be true, but it is not as though the verbs were opaque four-segment entities, internally undifferentiated and impossible to analyze. The first syllable was more specific, lexical, often nominal, while the second, more general element verbalized the construction, at the same time giving it attributes such as transitivity or intransitivity. An examination of CVCV verbs in Nahuatl shows that the combinations of segments in the first syllable are much more numerous than those in the second syllable.

Can we then conclude that *mati*, "to know," and *maca*, "to give," are based on the noun *māitl*? I believe not. *Māi-tl* must once have been *maCi-tla* (we can deduce the *a* of the suffix because Nahuatl *tl* is the form that, in a great early shift, *t* took before *a*). The apparently cognate *mati* gives us a good idea of what the consonant might have been; we thus arrive at *mati-tla* as an earlier form of the noun "hand." I take it, then, that *māitl* is ultimately derived from *mati*, with the addition of the nominal singular absolutive (nonpossessed) ending which now takes the shape *-tli/-li/-tl*. This ending, which today seems to have no other function than to indicate that a word is a singular unpossessed noun, was perhaps once a substantive base, "thing" (*tla*, with the same shape the absolutive once had, is a verbal prefix indicating a nonhuman object, and the possibly closely related word *itlah* means "thing, something," while *tleh*, earlier *tlah*, means "what" and its negative "nothing"). Or possibly *-tla* formed an agentive noun, "that which." *Māitl* would then be "grasp-thing" or "that which grasps." The exact origin of *-tla* hardly matters.

Somewhere in the background is a nominal root *ma* with a short *a* that must have meant "hand," but it is of vast antiquity, several steps removed from the noun of that meaning that has been in Nahuatl for many centuries now. The morphology and syntax of the language at the time when many nouns were bare CV roots must have been very different than in any form of Nahuatl that we can readily reconstruct. But it seems to me that the language was once characterized by short, naked, opaque roots functioning as independent words. Over the centuries these words became enmeshed in an ever increasing number of affixes (themselves former words), so that the original nominal roots were no longer available in their simple form, and awareness of their separate meaning may have faded. Consequently a wave of renaming took place. One way to form a new noun would have been to add a verb descriptive of the action of the thing denominated to a substantive base or nominalizing suffix. As we will see, it is also possible that the verbs themselves were pressed into use as names or nouns. At that point, nouns would have been quite transparent; the years have obscured most of the meanings, but some can still be detected.

Indeed, if we look at the totality of nominal roots in current Nahuatl, they look a great deal like verb roots. To this day verbs and nouns share far more in Nahuatl than they do in European languages. Both have obligatory subject prefixes and can in themselves constitute complete statements. Nouns derived from verbs are not merely part of the standard vocabulary, but are readily formed ad hoc. Whether they belong to the standard lexicon or not, they bring with them verbal object prefixes, signs of transitivity and reflexivity, and markers of human or non-human objects. *Nitētlaçohtla* is "I love someone or people, I am loving," where *ni* is "I," *tē* is the indefinite personal object, and the rest is the verb "to love." "Love or loving (of people)" is *tētlaçohtlaliztli*, in which the object prefix is still included (-*liz*- makes a noun of action from a verb and itself consists of two verbal elements; -*tli* is the nominal absolutive singular). Deverbal nouns are often used where English or a similar language would use a verb: *Ca notlachīhual*, "For it is my made thing, my deed," meaning "I made or did it," instead of resorting directly to the verb *chīhua*, "to make or do."

But it is not only at the level of easily recognizable derivations that nouns resemble verbs. The simplest noun roots, at this point in time mainly resisting analysis into smaller units, are for the most part CVCV like the verb roots. That is, they can be reconstructed as such. All that is required with a CVC root such as *cac-tli*, "item of footwear," or *cal-li*, "house, structure to contain something," is that the lost vowel to the right be supplied. Even a noun with a root consisting of nothing more than a long vowel is of the right shape. The word "water" is *ā-tl*. We have already seen that the root earlier began with *p*; the long vowel implies a lost CV syllable to the right. It could very well have been the same ubiquitous *ti* as with *māitl*. An ancient root *pa*, "water," would have given rise to a verb *pati*, "to flow," which in turn would have formed the basis for *pati-tla*, "thing which flows, liquid, water." One's suspicion that such could have been the case is heightened by the Nahuatl word *pah-tli*, "medicine, poison," which is exactly the same root. The basic meaning "liquid" took a different semantic turn here. The old *p* was protected from loss in some fashion no longer clear, and the original consonant has been weakened only as far as glottal stop, not lost entirely with the result of lengthening the *a*, as with *pātl/ātl*.[4]

---

[4]A noun root consisting only of V*h* also poses no problem. The root of *oh-tli*, "road," was earlier *poh-*, and the *h* has the same impli-cations as with *pahtli*. To my knowledge the only nominal roots in the language whose shape does not seem to be compatible, historically, with that of a verb are a group of monosyllabic roots in short *e* such as *e-tl*, "bean"; *me-tl*, "maguey"; *te-tl*, "stone"; *tle-tl*, "fire." The last has a verbal cognate, *tlatla*, "to burn." (For reasons we have seen, the vowel in the noun must once have been *a*.) In the verb, the second syllable is a form of one of the more common verbalizing elements in ancient CVCV constructs. Does the verb derive directly from the noun root? Are these roots in *e* relics of the primordial bare CV nouns of the time before the whole Proto-Aztecan system took shape? I would main-tain that they are not.

The roots in question are no doubt worn down to ultimate sim-plicity from earlier longer forms. Long vowels are generally tenacious through the ages in Nahuatl, but they are reduced to short at the end of a word and sometimes even internally; thus *qualli*, "a good thing (originally something which is eaten)," is recorded as having a short *a*, not the long *ā* that we see in the verb from which it is derived. More immediately to the point, the Nahuatl glottal stop in classical times was a somewhat unstable element. In some common words (as in *tleh*, "what") it was omitted when a vowel followed; in others (as in *ilama*, "old woman," earlier *ilamah* and before that *ilamatqui*) it was lost

That *ātl* and *pahtli* have some sort of common origin is beyond doubt. But I would not wish to try to hide the complexities and uncertainties involved. *Pahtli* has the short *a* that we would expect if the roots of both words go back to an earlier *pati*. In classical Nahuatl, however, a vowel cannot be pronounced long if it is followed by a glottal stop. Even if the *a* of *pahtli* was historically long, that could not be detected from its current pronunciation; its present form is compatible with an earlier root *pāti*. A verb of that shape does indeed still exist, meaning for something to melt, i.e., become liquid or water. This verb I would, however, take to be a formation from the root of the second-generation noun for water before it lost the initial *p*. (There is also a verb *āti(ya)* with the same meaning, which must have been formed after the *p* was lost.) The verbal derivational suffix *ti* would have been involved in the evolution of the modern verb *pāti* two separate times; waves of loss and reestablishment of this element have been noticed in the Uto-Aztecan languages generally.[5]

Consider also the verb *pāca*, "to wash," which looks like one of the ancient Proto-Aztecan verbs. It has the same final syllable as the verb *maca*, and there is a similarity of meaning. With the latter, one uses the hand to give something to someone; with the former, one uses water to wash something. But whereas *ma* has a short vowel, *pā* has a long one. Is *pāca* already based on a second-generation noun? Was it once *patica*? Perhaps so.

Let us look at one of the most common and basic words in the language, *huēi*, "something big, large, great," which often translates as an adjective, although adjectives can hardly be said to exist in Nahuatl distinct from nouns, and this is definitely a noun word. Yet it never appears with the absolutive ending. It looks a great deal like an ancient CVCV verb, and one is immediately tempted to think that it was earlier *hueti*, in which *hue* had something to do with largeness and *ti* was "to

---

altogether. I have seen the written forms *teh-tzin-tli*, "stone, reverential or diminutive," and *tleh-co*, "in the fire." Hence I assume that all of these roots have lost a syllable-final glottal stop and ultimately the earlier following syllable that it implies.

[5]Langacker 1976.

be, become." And more than prima facie appearances speak in favor of such an interpretation. "Old man, elder" is *huēhueh* in Nahuatl; the first syllable is a reduplication of the second, original one. The word is a preterit agentive, belonging to a class derived from verbs, so that an old man is one who has grown big ("big" is a synonym for "old" in many languages). The original verb, now disappeared, can be reconstructed as *hueti*. It is true that the glottal stop at the end of *huēhueh* leaves the same ambiguities as with *pahtli* above (that the vowel might have been historically long), but here we are saved by the fact that the plural, *huēhuetqueh*, preserves both an unambiguous short vowel and the suspected *t*. With that much evidence, we can be positive both that there was a construct *hueti* and that it acted as a verb. To judge by its present-day descendant *huēi*, however, it may have acted as a noun as well.

Perhaps, then, the ancient CVCV constructs functioned as both verb and noun. I assume that they were primarily verbal, but could also refer to the thing or being carrying out the action; any Nahuatl verb can still function in that way if the particle *in* is preposed, and sometimes even if it is not. The very common preterit agentive noun in Nahuatl is essentially just a finite verb form interpreted nominally. This stage of virtual verb-noun merging may have been at the root of the now long tradition that Nahuatl nouns and verbs both have obligatory subjects—the same set of subjects, once independent pronouns and now reduced to attached prefixes. Subtle differences of stress or tone probably accompanied and defined the differing functions and account for the different shapes the corresponding descendant forms have today.[6]

At some point clarifying bases, later to become suffixes

---

[6] *Hueli* may be another of these ancient verb-nouns surviving into classical times. It presently means "ability, capability, power," and like *huēi* it does not demonstrably act as a verb (a few frozen phrases are ambiguous in this respect). It has given rise to the much more common particle *huel*, which acts as both an intensifier and an auxiliary element in phrases meaning "to be able to." It has the appropriate shape, and it never appears with an absolutive ending, but because of the ambiguities involved in its analysis, one cannot positively assert that it would not have an absolutive ending if it ever appeared in independent unpossessed nominal form.

(or perhaps they were derivational suffixes from the beginning), would have been added to the forms functioning
nominally. The *-tla* (now *-tli/-li/-tl*) ending was probably
primarily for inanimates. At one time there seems to have
been another ending for animates, something on the order of
*m*V or *n*V. Its remains are vestigial, a fairly short list of nouns
mainly for birds, small animals, insects and the like, with a
singular absolute in the shape of *-in*. We can confidently
deduce that the *i* was once part of the root; the remaining
syllable-final *n* could have been either *m* or *n* earlier and must
have been followed by some vowel which cannot be specified
further, for whereas *tl* identifies the following vowel as originally *a, m* and *n* are compatible with any earlier following
vowel.[7] These words, even more clearly than the inanimates,
must have been descriptive agentives, meaning one who car-
ries out such and such a characteristic action. The class is so
small and regressive, however, that I have not been able to
identify any cognate ancient verb roots, as with *-tl* words.

Paths of reduction
and the evolution of the verb classes

One sometimes sees statements in works of historical linguistics that a certain vowel or other segment in a proto-
language has become a certain other segment in the descendant language, presumably across the board and without
exception. Or it may be said that a given vowel has changed
into another in a certain environment, after or before a
certain consonant, or word-finally, or the like. Such dicta are
often entirely valid. They do not, however, speak to a process
which engages my interest much more directly, a process one
could call stable, ongoing, or cyclical, which affects individual words and roots without necessarily changing the
phonology of the language in general, at least in the short and
medium run.

In Nahuatl, for ages, when an *a*, usually at the beginning or

---

[7]In Nahuatl a syllable-final *m* regularly appears as *n*, so that a
final *n* could originally have been either. Such a form as *chiamātl* (lit.
chia-water), "chia oil," from *chian*, "chia," implies that the consonant
was *m*, but one would need more examples for certainty.

end of a root or word, begins to receive less stress and weaken, it becomes first *e*, then *i*, and then sometimes *y*, before disappearing entirely if the word can be pronounced and understood without it. Sometimes the changes are referred to as vowel raising, for in the series *a, e, i* each vowel is progressively higher, but from the point of view of Nahuatl this raising constitutes weakening, and the end result is disappearance. A regular avenue of weakening like this I call a path of reduction.

An example is the singular absolutive ending of nouns that I have referred to as *-tli/-li/-tl*. The alternative forms are by no means chaotic or arbitrary, but entirely expectable. As we saw, the ending was once *-tla*. Being at the end of the word, it was under attack, subject to weakening, for Nahuatl over time generated a forest of affixes around nuclear words, creating unwieldy constructs that were always being worn down and simplified as far as intelligibility and pronounceability would allow, at all the morpheme boundaries but above all word-finally. The form *-tla* must have weakened to *-tle*, although we have so few attestations of that shape that we must resort to deduction, and then it became *-tli*.

So far what has happened could be seen as mere vowel raising, but the next step makes clear what was going on. When the root to which *-tli* attached ended in a vowel, the final *i*, not being needed for pronunciation, was dropped. At a distant time, all noun roots would have ended in a vowel, but since the weakening process had also eliminated the final vowels of a great number of noun roots, many now ended in a consonant, in which case the full *-tli* had to be retained, for in Nahuatl a word cannot end in a consonant cluster. When the root ended in *l*, the same thing happened as always in Nahuatl, a simplification through assimilation of *ltl* [ltˡ] to *ll* [ll]. By the sixteenth to eighteenth centuries the result was *cen-tli*, "maize"; *cal-li*, "house"; and *ā-tl*, "water."[8]

---

[8]The path of reduction does not stop here. The next step is to lose the weakening ending entirely where that can be done without loss of essential morphological and semantic distinctions. In some modern varieties of Nahuatl, the *-li* form of the absolutive after *l* stems has been lost, leaving the bare root at the end of the word. The loss of *-tli* should come next. The form *-tl* might remain, taken by that time as

We have already seen aspects of another important path of reduction, in which a VCV string is reduced to a long vowel or to a short vowel plus glottal stop. Above we had the example of the root for hand going from *mati* to *māi*. The *i* is weak and on its way out; if another vowel follows, it is reduced to *y*, as in *māyeh*, "one who has hands, fieldhand." In time we would expect it to be lost altogether, as it is in the possessed form and in the related word *mātl*, in which "hand or arm" has the special meaning of a measure of length. The sequence of first loss of the medial consonant with compensatory lengthening of the preceding vowel and finally loss of the second vowel is, however, not the only possible path. This same root is preserved in some words as *mah*, as in *mahpilli*, "finger," or in etymological terms "hand-dependency." I believe that what has happened here is that the final vowel was lost first, leaving *matpilli*, and the final *t* was reduced to a glottal stop (Nahuatl shows a very low tolerance of syllable-final *t* and *p*). In cases like this, if and when the glottal stop is eventually lost itself, it no longer affects the vowel to the left (remember the roots in *e* mentioned earlier, in n. 4).

A case which exemplifies much of the story of reduction in Nahuatl is the development of the complex and opaque morphology of the preterits of verbs. It seems that at one time the preterit was formed by adding *cā* to the full CVCV form of a typical verb; thus *maca+cā* would be the past tense of the verb "to give."[9] At this stage, final long vowels may not yet have

---

part of the root.

The story of the nominal possessive ending, earlier *-huā*, is closely analogous. Always final in the singular, it came to be interpreted as short (it remained long in the plural, where it was protected by an additional suffix). As with the absolutive suffix, no distinct record of the *e* stage is preserved. In due course it became *-hui/-uh* under exactly the same conditions as *-tli/-tl*. By the sixteenth century, the *-hui* had largely disappeared, remaining only in a few archaic words or short words where the extra syllable was needed for bulk. The *-uh* was retained much more widely, though not universally, with vowel stems.

[9]Things did not begin at this point, of course. The form *cā* was already reduced, I would imagine from a *cati* that was the old present tense of Nahuatl's most general stative verb, *cah*. Earlier it must have

been pronounced short. The verbal plural was probably still -*t*, so that the preterit plural would have been *macacāt*.[10]

Important in the picture of what followed were three factors: the convention of pronouncing word-final long vowels short, so that if they never appeared elsewhere all sense of their being long could be lost; the evolution of the plural suffix from *t* to glottal stop; and the convention that any long vowel before a glottal stop would be pronounced short. Once these factors were in operation, the form of the preterit of *maca* would be *macaca* singular, *macacah* plural.

Now the sequence *a* > *e* > *i* > zero could enter into operation. The next stage would be *macaque*, *macaqueh*.[11] After this would come *macaqui*, but the vowel of the plural, protected by the following glottal stop, did not change, and has changed no further to this day. The glottal stop has continued to protect the vowel, and the entire indivisible suffix is needed to distinguish the plural from the singular. The singular continued to evolve, losing the final *i* in the normal way and becoming *macac*. If, however, the *c* suffix has occasion to occur in any protected, word-internal situation, it reveals itself as still the same *cā* as many centuries ago. The only place where that can happen is in the preterit agentive, which with a verb like this one is identical to the preterit of the finite verb. "He served people at table" is *tētlamacac*; the same form as an agentive means "one who serves at table"; the agentive's reverential is *tētlamacacātzīntli*.

Would that things had remained so straightforward! In fact, the eroding processes of reduction had meanwhile been

---

been an independent auxiliary verb postposed to the main verb, becoming an attached suffix by the time we are talking about here.

[10]We would suspect that the plural ending was once *t* merely from its shape and position, but the fact that it is still *t* in the related Pochutec establishes its origin beyond reasonable doubt.

Una Canger (1981) worked out a history of the development of the preterit with which I agree in most respects, and which anticipates much of what is said here. When her interpretation was published I had already hit on something similar independently and felt greatly heartened. I still interpret some things a bit differently, as will become clearer.

[11]In Nahuatl orthography, following Spanish models, [k] is written *c* before back vowels and *qu* before front vowels.

acting in different ways on differently constituted stems with results that can seem haphazard until we review the specific histories of how they evolved.

The verb we have been discussing, *maca*, belongs to what I call Class 1, of four classes of verbs according to how they form the preterit.[12] It is distinguished by not reducing its preterit stem, for at some time during the evolution sketched above, a great many verbs began to lose their final vowel in the preterit, retaining it in the present tense. Class 1, with unreduced preterit stems, consists mainly of verbs which cannot lose the vowel for phonological reasons, having been meanwhile transformed in other ways from a CVCV original shape. They had already lost their original first vowel, creating a consonant cluster which could not be pronounced without the final vowel, or they had been reduced to mono-syllables and had nothing more to lose, or two previous syllables had been reduced to a final long vowel, and a long vowel cannot be omitted. With a certain number of verbs in this class—*maca* as a verb ending in *ca* is one of them—the reasons for the failure to reduce are not understood and at any rate are not phonological.

Class 2 includes all those verbs which lose the final vowel in the preterit without any change beyond the normal adjustment the final consonant may have to make now that it is no longer medial. It appears that at one time the entire language was moving in the direction of final vowel loss in the verbal preterit, and that any verb not in Class 2 is in some sense an exception, prevented by special conditions from participating in the general wave of preterit reduction. It is hard to surmise just when in the sequence root-final vowel loss took place. With the verb *yōli*, "to live," the old *yōlicā*, plural *yōlicāt*, presumably became *yōlica*, *yōlicah*. But there is no way of knowing when the loss of the root-final *i* occurred

---

[12]J. Richard Andrews (1975) has the honor of having first pub-lished a satisfactory rationalization of the verb classes, which he called A, B, C, and D. They had escaped Carochi and even Launey. I had arrived at these classes, but had published nothing on the topic. Canger uses the same set but orders them differently. Andrews's order is preferable because, whether he so intended it or not, it puts the oldest class first and the variations on the second class last.

relative to the changes in the vowel of the suffix. The present situation is preterit singular *yōl*, preterit agentive singular *yōlqui*, plural of both the finite verb and the agentive *yōlqueh*. The agentive singular is an archaic form so preserved to distinguish it from the finite verb. It appears that whatever the exact relative sequence of reduction of the root-final vowel and the suffix, at some point the preterit singular finite verb was *yōlqui*, corresponding to the next to last stage of reduction with Class 1. It could not lose the final *i* as happened there because that would have resulted in an unpronounceable final consonant cluster (*yōlc*). It could, however, lose the entire suffix, because the loss of the final vowel alone distinguished it from the unreduced present tense. This the verbs of Class 1 could not do, for there was no difference between the present and preterit stems. The plural *-queh* was still needed in all classes to distinguish the singular from the plural.

It is with Class 3 that the difficulties really begin. These verbs end or appear to end in two vowels in the present tense—there are two types, *-ia* and *-oa*—and though they lose the final *a* in the preterit as with Class 2 verbs, they add a glottal stop after the *i* or *o*. I have long felt that these very numerous verbs are posterior to the ancient CVCV constructs and indeed are elaborations on them; they always have at least three syllables. Even so, they fit into approximately the same time frame as to the evolution of the preterit, for there is reason to think that they existed before the *t* to *tl* shift. In view of the paths of reduction we have already seen, the most likely explanation for the anomaly would seem to be that there was once a consonant between the two vowels, which was reduced differently in the present tense and in the preterit.[13] I think

---

[13]Canger 1981 actually makes such a suggestion with *ia* verbs, but she proposes a glottal stop from the beginning. This I would not consider probable, first because the preservation of a glottal stop over the millenia is not likely, and second because the glottal stop is virtually always syllable-final, except when the same vowel is being rearticulated.

The whole question of the status of the glottal stop has never been settled definitively. Today, in the great majority of dialects, the old glottal stop appears as aspirated [h]; for this reason some scholars

that the consonant was *t* (this by itself means that we are speaking of Proto-Aztecan times). The old verbal final syllable *ta* was once, I think, pervasive, creating a multitude of mainly transitive verbs from other kinds of elements, but it has largely been absorbed and is hard to recognize. Some direct evidence for it exists in the extant final syllable *tla*, the post-shift form of *ta*, as in *tlaçohtla*, "to love, esteem" (*tlaçoh-tli* is a noun word meaning "that which is dear, precious").

Let us take the verb *tlālia*, "to set down, place, issue, etc." Before the *tl* shift it would have been *tālita* in the present, *tālita-cā* in the preterit. The second *t* of the present was to be lost, not the final vowel (for most present-tense verbs have not lost the

---

have imagined that what was thought to have been glottal stop in classical times was [h] all along. Others have projected [h] separate from glottal stop far back into the proto-language.

I for one am convinced that what the Spaniards called a *saltillo* in the sixteenth to eighteenth centuries was a glottal stop, one reason being comments made at the time. The name itself, "little leap," tells us much, and Carochi (1645, f. 2) says it was like a hiccup, which is as good a description of the glottal stop as anyone will ever achieve. The other reason is that in the Nahuatl of classical times, as far as I have been able to discover, it is the reflex of stops exclusively, mainly *t* (exactly like the glottal stop replacing syllable-final [t] in the speech of many British people today), and does not replace continuants.

As for [h], I think it is a very recent phenomenon precisely replacing weakened continuants, above all syllable-final devoiced *uh* [w]. No change is seen in the writing of *uh* until the second half of the seventeenth century, after which it sometimes reduces to orthographic *h*. I presume the same thing was occurring in pronunciation, that is, that the rounding was being lost.

I believe that what happened was that in the late seventeenth and eighteenth centuries, as syllable-final [w] and possibly some other syllable-final continuants were being reduced to [h], the glottal stop too was being further weakened as part of a general strong erosion of syllable-final segments, and the glottal stop and [h] merged as [h]. Since the virtual disappearance of the glottal stop, weakened stops now become [h], as has happened with the [k] of the object prefix in many cases.

Thus neither glottal stop nor [h] should be posited as relatively stable consonants reaching back into Proto-Aztecan or Proto-Uto-Aztecan times. If a cognate glottal stop or [h] is found in another Uto-Aztecan language, that is because some consonant has undergone parallel weakening there.

final vowel to this day), but in line with what was happening with other verbs, the final *a* of the root would be lost in the preterit, giving something like *tālitca*, then *tālitque* and *tālitqui*; after the shift and further weakening, *tlālihqui* and then *tlālih*.

The problematic aspect of these plausible developments is that although the end result in the present, after the loss of *t*, should have been *tlālīa*, in fact the long vowel is nowhere reliably attested in the present tense. Because of the work of Canger, however, an explanation is at hand. She has shown that any given speaker or variety of Nahuatl makes no distinction between *ia*, *iya*, *īa*, and *īya* (or *oa*, *ohua*, *ōa*, and *ōhua*). Thus it would be impossible to detect the historically long vowel. But our troubles do not end here. When the present stem of the verb occurs word-internally, as it does in the imperfect, it is actually the root-final *a* that is long! Must we imagine this vowel as long historically? To do so would go against overwhelming evidence that the compensation for a lost segment occurs in the preceding, not the following vowel. Moreover, in parts of the paradigm, not only in the preterit, but also in other tenses, the *a* is dropped, something that does not happen to a long stem vowel in Nahuatl. Let us look at one of these tenses: the future of *tlālia* is *tlālīz*. Here the *i* is at last long as we would expect. Although some might say that it is long because of the loss of the *a*, I think it a very dubious proposition that a vowel should become long in compensation for the loss of another vowel. I believe this is the original long *ī* created in compensation for the loss of ancient *t*, able to show its length here because it is not followed by a neutralizing *a*. How and why there came to be a long *ā* in the word-internal present stem I do not know; after much thought the only thing that has occurred to me is the metathesis of vowel quantity, something known to have happened for example in Greek. Possibly there was also an influence from Class 4 verbs, where the apparently corresponding vowel is legitimately long. The situation is indeed anomalous and puzzling. It is normal and expectable, however, *except* for the long *ā* of the word-internal present stem.

Verbs in *-ia* are only half of the Class 3 story; verbs in *-oa* are at least as important. Nearly everything said above applies to the *-oa* verbs as well, including the effect of this combination in masking a long vowel. Some differences can be observed, however. Verbs in *-ia* are mainly transitive and only a certain number have intransitive cognates in *-i*. Those in *-oa* are also transitive more often than not, but they virtually always have an intransitive cognate in *-ihui* or *-ahui*. Thus *poloa*, "to lose or destroy something, etc.," has the cognate *polihui*, "to get lost, disappear." I propose that the *-oa* verbs arose by the addition of old transitivizing *ta* to a verb in V*hui*.[14] *Poloa* would originate as *polihuita*. In the history of Nahuatl the combination V*hu*V has often evolved into *ō*; *polihuita* would become *polōta*; when the medial *t* was lost as it was in all these verbs, the *ō* could change no more, already being long, but then its length was masked anyway, just as with *-ia* verbs. The rest of the picture is the same.

Class 3 is large and productive, constantly making new verbs, for the causative and applicative suffixes belong to this class, and *-oa* can form new verbs from nouns (as in *tamaloa*, "to make tamales"). Class 4 is very small and also is less problematic than Class 3. It consists of some verbs ending in a long *ā*, the length of which, of course, cannot be detected in the present tense. The preterit ends in an apparently short *a* plus glottal stop, so that this class shares a great deal with Class 3. It has indeed been suggested more than once that the Class 4 *ā* is in essence *aa*, parallel to Class 3's *ia* and *oa*. I believe that to be true, as far as it goes.

With the verb *qua* (*quā*), "to eat something," I would imagine the earliest reconstructable form to have been *quata*, with the same *ta* as the Class 3 verbs, reducing to *quāa* and then *quā* (pronounced *qua* in final position) in the present, *quat* and then *quah* in the preterit. Here the long vowel in the present is masked only by position, not by a related following glide. The imperfect *quāya* and the future *quāz* are just what

---

[14]Canger (1981) has suggested that the medial consonant in *-oa* verbs was *hu* [w] from the beginning. I resist this ingenious notion for several reasons, the most salient being that [w] is not a satisfactory origin for the glottal stop of the preterit (for as far as can be discovered, glottal stops in classical times always descended from some obstruent, most often *t*) and that the *-ia* and *-oa* verbs share too much not to share the main activating morpheme.

should be expected, and no anomaly is involved as with the long *a* in the word-internal present stem of Class 3 verbs.

Thus despite the apparent chaos of the formation of the preterit in Nahuatl verbs, they all began in the same way, with the full present stem plus *cā*, and they all moved in the direction of a shortened preterit stem, but the relationship was obscured with Classes 3 and 4 by the simultaneous loss of the consonant preceding the final vowel of the present, and reduction was prevented in Class 1, mainly by phonological barriers created by previous reductions, so that that class retained the old system of an unreduced stem. The suffixes *-c*, *-qui*, and *-queh* are all descendants of the old *cā*, which still exists as the form taken by *-c* and *-qui* in protected environments.[15]

Word order

Sometimes scholars attempt to deal with Nahuatl word order in terms of subject, object, and verb, by that meaning free-standing nouns and verbs as they can be found in the dictionary. Some languages are said to be SVO, some SOV, and so on, with large implications for the overall operation of the language concerned. My belief is that such analysis is not very applicable to Nahuatl in any form of the language that we know. What appears to be word order in Nahuatl is actually phrase order. It may be that in languages like English, words such as "child" or "leave" are in some sense descended from noun and verb phrases, but they normally cannot stand alone, being used rather as blocks in a larger utterance. In a language of the type of English, analysis of order in terms of S, O, and V is indicated.

In Nahuatl, only particles (uninflected words attached to

---

[15]Nahuatl has a tense which functions at times as a remote past, at times as a pluperfect. The stem is identical to that of the preterit in all classes; it differs in replacing *-c* or zero in the singular with *-ca*, the *-queh* of the plural with *-cah*. Canger suggests that this tense results from an amalgamation of the preterit when it was still *-cā* with the particle *ya*. I suggest that the pluperfect is neither more nor less than the old form of the preterit, kept that way to make a distinction just as the old *-qui* suffix was retained on preterit agentives but not on finite preterits.

nuclear words) could be said to need a larger construction to be meaningful. Every verb complex includes its subject, and if it is transitive its object as well; every noun has its subject prefix and is an equative statement in itself. "Child" is *piltzīntli* in the dictionary, but that is a third person singular form which by itself means "it is a child." To be incorporated in a larger utterance it needs subordination. "To leave" is in the dictionary as *cāhua*, but in actual use the verb must have its subject and object prefixes: *quicāhua* is "he, she, or it leaves him, her, or it." The subject and object can be further specified by external noun phrases, but they are already there in the verb complex.

Let us take a complete and fully specified sentence: *quicāhua in piltzīntli in calli*, "The child leaves the house." This should not be analyzed simply as VSO. All three of the primary elements are in the verb complex: "subject-object-leaves." The rest is in a kind of apposition to the subject and object prefixes. If you are curious as to what the subject is, "it is a child" (the subordination is shown overtly by the particle *in*); if you want to know what the object is, "it is a house."

The phrase order (and I will speak of Nahuatl as it is seen in texts of the central region in the sixteenth through eighteenth centuries) is far from fixed. When there is no special emphasis, the verb complex generally comes first, as in our example, followed by the noun phrases specifying subject and object, when present.[16] I have never been able to detect any marked tendency in the relative order of the phrase specifying the subject and the one specifying the object. The phrases seem to orient in relation to the verb complex according to emphasis, degree of focus, and weight. Our example could just as well be *quicāhua in calli in piltzīntli*, and indeed that sounds rather more natural to me, because the longer of the two noun complexes comes last. If one of the two phrases is notably longer than the other, it will almost always come at the end. If, however, one of the two phrases is topicalized or emphasized, it will come first, in front of the verb complex: *in piltzīntli quicāhua in calli*, "As to the child, it leaves the house,"

---

[16]Some short verb complexes, mainly modal or stative, and outstandingly *cah*, tend to come after the noun phrases.

or "The *child* leaves the house."[17] The object specification can also be preposed for purposes of emphasis or focus: *in calli quicāhua in piltzīntli*. With the addition of particles, possessed nouns, adverbial phrases, whole subordinated complex clauses, and a thick network of crossreference to tie the elements together, things become very complex, but our example suffices to show the most crucial points. The order of phrases is extremely flexible (and also apparently likely to change greatly with time and region). Which phrase refers to the subject, which to the object, seems not to be the crucial matter in phrase order. The one thing that stands out is a verb complex relative to which the rest is ordered.[18]

Finding little hold for subject-object-verb analysis in Nahuatl syntax, I looked at its morphology. After all, in many or most Nahuatl utterances the verb complex really *is* the sentence. Within that complex we find an inviolable order in precisely the right terms: subject (prefix), object (prefix), verb (root). I have no doubt that the prefixes were earlier independent words in themselves. The question is whether or not their order, which has not changed since the early sixteenth century, reaches far back into Proto-Aztecan times. It may, but I have no confidence that such is the case. Consider Spanish, where the order is subject (pronoun), object (pronoun, virtually prefix), verb; in Latin and even in older Spanish the object pronoun, then weightier and more independent, could come after the verb.

I think that a true analysis according to the order of "words" in the European sense would have to go back to the ancient times when *ma* was a noun, "hand," and *ti* was a verb,

---

[17]Preposing, especially of subject and object phrases referring to persons, was so common that it cannot have been very forceful, and I interpret it mainly as focus. The effect could be increased by putting the clause-introductory particle *ca* after the preposed element.

[18]For brevity's sake I do not discuss the fact that in many utterances a noun phrase, minimal or maximal, acts as the verb complex does here; such a statement lacks an object in the verbal sense, but can acquire the equivalent of one through noun possession: *nimotlamictīl in titlahuēlīlōc* (I-your-beaten-thing subordinator you-scoundrel), "I am your beaten thing, you who are a scoundrel," i.e, "you beat me, you scoundrel."

"to be or become," that is, to an age for which we have almost no information about syntax. A time will also come when the Nahuatl noun and verb complexes are so worn down semantically and morphologically that they can be counted as irreducible units in a larger scheme, but that time has not yet arrived, and is not likely to as long as every Nahuatl noun complex has an internal subject.

Appendix to Chapter 10: Equation in Nahuatl

A MATTER close to my heart has long been what I perceive as the absence of the equative verb "to be" (the copula) in Nahuatl. Though Nahuatl's manner of equation doubtless has a history, I know it not historically but simply as a striking feature of the language of the texts I have studied. Even so, I want to devote a word or two to the topic here; if my ideas on equation are not exactly historical, at least they bear somewhat on the historical matters discussed earlier, and they are unfashionable. The standard analysis of the situation by linguists in linguistics departments is that the verb *cah* is the copula, but that it is optional or missing in the present tense.

I maintain that *cah* is a stative verb, not the copula. The easiest way to understand it is to look at Spanish. Where English has only the all-purpose "to be," Spanish has two verbs: the stative *estar*, to be in a certain place at a certain time, to be momentarily sick or well, etc., and the equative *ser*, to be something (a woman, a man, a saint, a villain).[19] Nahuatl has only *estar*, which is *cah*, and lacks *ser*, using instead the obligatory subject prefixes of nouns and when necessary their crossreference.[20]

---

[19]Simple existence can be indicated by *ser*, but that sense is mainly covered by *hay*, "there is." Nahuatl has the equivalent expression, and indeed it uses *cah*, but only in combination with a directional prefix: *oncah*. Whereas in Spanish the existing thing is the object of the verb, in Nahuatl it is the subject.

[20]*Cah* was earlier *cati*, virtually identical to verbs in other Uto-Aztecan languages meaning "to sit." It is most suggestive that in the series of irregular stative verbs to which *cah* belongs there are words

When I was first studying Nahuatl texts and came upon such things as *nicocoxcātzīntli*, "I-poor-sick-person," where the only possible meaning was "I am a poor sick person," I began to get a glimmering of how the system worked, for all nouns referring to the first person had this prefix *ni*. Gradually I came to see that the absence of any prefix on third-person nouns was simply the way of indicating a third-person subject, and that the sense could be the same: *ahmō tīcitl*, "not healer (3rd person)," "he or she is not a healer." It was around this time that I read with the greatest imaginable pleasure the parts of J. Richard Andrews's grammar of Nahuatl (1975) laying out in no uncertain terms that every noun was an equative statement and bore an obligatory subject prefix, no less meaningful in the third person for being detectable only by reference to the form of the other persons. (The same is true with Nahuatl verbs, and no one ever doubted that they had obligatory subjects.) Later Michel Launey (1979) made the same point.

When one noun is to be equated with another, which generally happens in the third person, unless a proper name is involved, each starts as though it were a fully independent clause, but their conjunction and the identity of person and number creates a crossreference between them: *nacatl ītlaqual* (it-flesh it-its-food), "meat is its food," "it eats meat."

There is no denying that in tenses other than the present, the verb *cah* is used together with the equative noun clause.[21] But a remarkable fact gives us a clue about how to interpret the presence of the verb. "I was a child" is *nipiltzīntli nicatca* (or *ōnicatca*, with the specific preterit indicator). Note that *ni*, "I," appears in both the noun phrase and the verb phrase. In other words, the noun phrase still indicates the equation, and the verb merely puts it in a temporal context, one of the usual functions of *cah*.

In the following sentence one can feel the purely temporal

for lying and standing but not for sitting. Spanish *estar* was originally a verb meaning "to stand." Like *estar*, *cah* serves as an auxiliary in forming progressive verbs.

[21] It is never used with an equative noun phrase referring to the present, so one cannot properly speak of its being optional in the present tense.

thrust of *cah*: *in īpatiuh yez notech pōhuiz*, (subord. that-which-is-its-price it-will-be to-me it-will-belong), "Its future price (what is paid for it) will belong to me."

It is not quite right to say that equative noun phrases are unaccompanied by *cah* only in the present tense. The nominal equative statement is essentially timeless. When it lacks the accompanying stative verb we usually apply it to the present, but that is not necessarily the case. If someone has lost children and wants to have a mass said for them, he or she can say, *niquinchīhuilia mīxah[22] ca nopilhuān*, "I am having a mass said for them, for they (are, were) my children." In English we would have to take a position on the tense one way or the other, either of which would be somewhat awkward, but Nahuatl can easily solve the problem with its timeless, verbless way of equating one thing with another.

---

[22]In a text of classical times this word would actually be written "missa" or "misa."

11. Receptivity and Resistance

W HEN I was originally asked to give the presentation which became this chapter, the topic proposed was limited to resistance (resistance, that is, by indigenous American peoples to things European). It was at my own request that the notion of receptivity was added, in the name of discussing the entire spectrum of acceptance and nonacceptance of a European presence and European cultural elements by native peoples. For nowhere was there total acceptance or total nonacceptance, total penetrability or total imperviousness, and the balance between the two changed and evolved; what had previously failed to find acceptance often later found it, in a way potentially susceptible of systematic explanation.

For some reason, wherever one would expect to find discussion of the indigenous reaction to the presence from the outside, one more often than not finds this word resistance, in effect taking for granted that resistance is the normal reaction. Not long ago I was invited to chair a conference session on "Control and Resistance," the papers of which by their titles seemed to me simply to deal with various aspects of indigenous–European contact. Resistance is talked of so much more than the opposite that one even wonders just what to call it: receptivity, acceptance, adjustment, or something else. But that may have its good side, for the excessive standardization of the concept resistance has brought distortion and confusion.

Both resistance and receptivity used in this context are Eurocentric notions. They look at a process of interaction between those arriving and those already there and ask only what the indigenous group is willing or equipped to accept from the new group. It is as if one were working with a mortise and tenon and looked only at how the mortise takes the tenon rather than at the crux of the matter, how the two fit together; to the fit each member is equally important, and to achieve it either member can be adjusted.

As with a mortise and tenon joint, interaction between Europeans and indigenous peoples in the Western Hemisphere was not fully symmetrical. One group was deeply rooted in the local scene, the other not yet. One was initially much more numerous than the other. One, the European, possessed an array of techniques, attributes, and objects—steel weapons, firearms, horses, writing, ocean-going ships, greater linguistic and ethnic solidarity—the efficiency of which gave it the upper hand in any kind of direct conflict and thus an at least ostensible dominance, so that on the face of it influence appears to flow far more strongly from the European to the indigenous side than vice versa. But the processes in which we are interested definitely do go in both directions. "Receptivity" and "resistance" are found on the European side as well, and they follow some of the same principles.

Let us take a quick look at some of the things Europeans resisted and accepted. (Here as throughout, though I think the issues, dynamics, and trends are general in the hemisphere and probably beyond, I will be speaking primarily about Latin America, within that mainly Spanish America, within that Mexico much more than other areas.) The Spaniards (and in their way the Portuguese) long resisted even going in force to regions which did not have either dense sedentary populations or obvious wealth in precious metals, and hopefully both. The other side of the matter was that they eagerly accepted those precious metals, which were the economic basis of their whole enterprise, along with such technological aspects of indigenous mining as proved useful. They accepted the sedentary peoples to the extent of leaving them where they were and using the vast majority of their political, social, cultural, and economic mechanisms to underpin their own presence and extract benefits.

They accepted indigenous food and housing for themselves, grudgingly, faute de mieux, until they could grow and build European-style equivalents, which was usually very soon. But if wheat would not grow in an area, they would eat maize, and if not even maize, then cassava. Even in areas of denser European occupation, greater wealth, and greater suitability for European crops, the Spaniards gradually acquired a taste for indigenous foods, not as the staple—for the Spanish diet continued to be based on the European meats beef and mutton, on wheat bread not maize, and wine not pulque or chicha—but as accessories, so that in the end it was the indigenous items that gave the local flavor to Spanish American cuisine.

Indigenous mechanisms of permanent and temporary labor were not just for delivery of goods and services from the indigenous to the Hispanic world, they became built deeply into that world. Every Spanish household contained more or less permanent servants and employees coming out of native society, and it is no accident that they were long called by indigenous terms. Indigenous words designated labor practices of at least partly indigenous origin in both the Mexican and the Peruvian silver mining industries.

Just as indigenous foods gave a special flavor to the cuisine, indigenous words gave a special flavor to the language. The process went quite far even in the early occupation of the Antilles in the last years of the fifteenth and first couple decades of the sixteenth centuries.[1] The words virtually all referred to salient aspects of indigenous culture that were important in crosscultural contacts and possessed close equivalents in European culture but had a strong profile of their own: *cacique* for an indigenous ruler, "chief"; *canoa*, indigenous boat, and so on. All first-generation loans from indigenous languages that I know of were nouns, but with time some verbs appeared too. Even so, though the skeleton of the process of indigenous influence on Spanish can be detected, its yield is enormously less than the same types of influence in the other direction. Spanish was left hardly changed; Spanish American Spanish differs from the Spanish of Spain primarily as American English differs from the English of England, through leveling of dialects, archaisms, and other internal factors. One would need a far longer discussion to begin to deal with the nature of the mix of "resistance" and "receptivity" in the European reaction to indigenous culture and society, and the—apparent—overall strength of the former aspect compared with the latter. My main concern is merely to point out that both were in fact there, operating in ways in principle little different from their action among indigenous peoples.

Returning then from this disgression in which I have indulged in the name of perspective, I enter once again on the

---

[1] See Tuttle 1976.

topic proper. The reaction of indigenous peoples to European things, I repeat, depended on the fit of the two groups at various points and in various places as a result of previous centuries of experience. The notion of fit or match in most cases comes down to the degree of convergence, but it is not quite the same thing. Draft rotary labor, for example, was much more highly organized and used much more lavishly in the indigenous sedentary societies than in early modern Europe, but it was an excellent match with the needs of the Spaniards. In some respects the fit or lack of it was universal. No indigenous peoples had immunities to a set of Old World diseases headed by smallpox and measles but extending indefinitely, beyond our present certain knowledge. To use our key word in a very different sense, they had no resistance. The only variables here are the degree of dampness, the temperature (often a function of altitude), the relative proximity and numbers of Old Worlders and New Worlders, the duration of contact (for eventually immunities were acquired).

In a great number of more cultural matters, we can observe a radical difference in resistance/acceptance across the hemisphere, depending as I say on the relative fit of the two parties, in a kaleidoscopic, apparently chaotic fashion. And indeed, the result was not *exactly* the same in any two places, because each local society had a history and constitution to some extent unique. But for many years, since I first began giving undergraduate survey courses, I have used a rough, broad scheme of fully sedentary, semisedentary, and non-sedentary peoples.[2] Resistance of all kinds is the least in the first group, which shared an amazing number of characteristics with early modern European society, greater in the second, which shared much less, and maximal in the third, which shared a minimum of European traits.

It is in fact, as I view it, primarily the nature of indigenous society that accounts for the so varying reactions, not something on the European side, for all the Europeans were constituted much the same; surely that is true for the Spaniards, who alone met virtually every possible type of indig-

---

[2]This scheme is extensively illustrated in Lockhart and Schwartz, *Early Latin America* (1983).

enous society, with a very wide range of results. The history of nonsedentary peoples is much the same whether they faced Spaniards, Portuguese, or the English: prolonged all-out conflict to the point of dispersal or extinction if the Europeans persisted. Nor were European policy decisions the crux of the matter. Consider Powell's history of Spanish activity in the Mexican near north in the sixteenth and seventeenth centuries, in which every conceivable strategy and policy was successively applied, with more or less equal lack of success, until the mobile, fragmented peoples whom the Spaniards (following the Nahuas) called the Chichimecs were finally destroyed, absorbed, or confined to mountain fastnesses as the cumulative result of the Spanish occupation.[3] The first strategies used in the near north were the same ones used with such different results—quick acceptance—in central Mexico.

It is true that European numbers make a large difference in indigenous reactions. When Europeans come in numbers too small to represent any apparent threat, they and even bits and pieces of their culture may find quite ready and peaceful if sometimes fleeting acceptance, even among less sedentary peoples, as with Cabeza de Vaca's sixteenth-century wanderings in what is now the southern United States and northern Mexico. Larger numbers and the attempt to occupy the area invariably bring stiff military opposition at some early point, if not from the very first. Even larger numbers not only make the question of military resistance as good as irrelevant but through massive daily contact bring about the acceptance in some form of whole complexes of cultural patterns. In this way the Europeans (and the Africans accompanying them) surely make a crucial difference in the indigenous reaction from one place to another, but we must consider that the numerical aspect of their presence is itself often mainly a function of the nature of the indigenous people.[4] Europeans avoided nonsedentary peoples wherever and for as long as they could and, during the first couple of centuries, flocked

---

[3] Philip Wayne Powell, *Soldiers, Indians, and Silver: The Northward Advance of New Spain, 1550–1600* (1952).

[4] The point is made in a somewhat different context in "Three Experiences of Culture Contact," Chapter 8 in this volume, p. 204.

to areas with a dense sedentary population.

Conscious or patriotic resistance plays a much smaller role than it is imagined to, at least in many types of situations, and it is vastly fragmented. Lack of acceptance does not usually mean conscious opposition, which is what resistance is most often taken to mean, as in the French Resistance or in the widely discussed resistance of slave populations.[5] The topic needs division into, first, out-and-out general military action, which was ephemeral in many situations, and second, the developments when groups are reconciled to the European presence, totally or virtually abandoning military measures.

Combat

Let us first consider overt military combat (and thereby also the lack of it). Even this I would be reluctant to term resistance in a blanket fashion. With the less sedentary peoples especially, fighting against Europeans can take on the aspect of attack rather than resistance, in much the same sense as the Europeans were attacking them, not perhaps often with actual conquest or reconquest in mind, but at least in the spirit of the raiding that had gone back and forth between mobile groups, and sometimes by mobile groups against sedentary neighbors, far back in time.

Even where we see full-scale military campaigns with the avowed purpose of keeping the Europeans out, resistance per se is not usually exactly what happens, that is, in the highly fragmented sociopolitical and ethnic concatenations that are found almost everywhere, most groups and most members of those groups were simply thinking of the greatest good and largest quotient of independence they could attain within the situation as they had always known it, not of resistance to an outsider. Indigenous solidarity against the Europeans is pretty much unheard of. Initially and in most cases for a very long time, the indigenous people saw the Europeans as one

---

[5]Slave populations are always transported far from their homeland, living in a new situation largely determined by the owning group, so that their reactions are in much more direct relation to the owners and may have a much larger flavor of conscious resistance than among an indigenous population living where it always has, within a framework originally developed by itself.

more player on the local scene who by entering in a certain way into the local power balance might improve the position of one's own group in it.

Let us look at the well known conquest of central Mexico with these things in mind. The Spaniards, when they arrived in force in 1519, first came among the Totonacs of the Gulf coast. These peoples, who had only recently been made tributary to the Mexica ("Aztecs"), offered no overt resistance at all to the Spaniards, but gave them food and gifts and started talking about how they could be freed from Mexica tribute. All over the Indies, the most common reaction of indigenous groups which were in any way subjugated or dominated by another group was to begin to negotiate, if warily, with the new arrivals in order to lessen their dependence on that other local group.

As the Spaniards headed inland they met first sharp military attacks from the Tlaxcalans and then, for a couple of weeks, a series of pitched battles. After losing overwhelmingly in these tests, the Tlaxcalans came over to the Spaniards with offers of logistic and military help. They became the largest, most meaningful, most faithful collaborators with the Spaniards in the entire conquest of greater New Spain. The general lesson here is that the second power of a given region will likely become the Europeans' strongest support in the military phase of the conquest, looking to bring down the first power and take its place, not seeing the long-term consequences precisely because the Europeans were viewed only as one more comparable element rather than as something entirely new that would revolutionize the situation.[6]

Once the Spaniards and Tlaxcalans combined were on the

---

[6]As an aside, let me consider why the Tlaxcalans did first put up a stiff though brief fight. The reason can be seen as the fact that although on the macroregional scene they were a poor second to the Mexica, in the east central Mexican highlands they were the dominant power and had much to lose. They were themselves a confederation of groups, some of starkly different ethnicity; in fact, when they decided to work with the Spaniards, they blamed the fighting on the subordinate Otomi, from whom they had once taken the land and some of whom now served as border guards against the outside.

march toward Tenochtitlan, the other local ethnic states on the way, all paying tribute to the Mexica, generally received the Spaniards with what could be taken as either peace or submission; at least one can say that they fed and housed them and never thereafter caused the Spaniards any major concern.

Now it so happens that in an episode that everyone knows at least something about, the Mexica themselves, after having in a variety of ways tried to discourage the Spaniards from coming, received them peacefully when they got to Tenochtitlan. Let us pass over this ephemeral phenomenon for the moment, reserving it for discussion a bit later, and talk about the subsequent expulsion of the Spaniards, followed in turn by a Spanish siege and military resistance to the far edge of defeat, decimation, and starvation—the most serious and prolonged Spanish–indigenous warfare seen anywhere among sedentary peoples. It was the local physical setting that made such a stand possible, but the lesson is general. The leading power of a region will in short order offer all the military resistance it can to the arriving Europeans, not as a threat to indigenous civilization, but as a threat to its own dominance.

Both those who cooperated and those who actively resisted assumed that the Spaniards when victorious would demand tribute in approximately the same fashion as the Mexica had from the other local ethnic states, the *altepetl*. When finally ready to surrender, the Mexica, we are told, fell to conferring over what sort of tribute they would be willing to give to the Spaniards.[7] The other groups also seem to have thought the Spaniards would act in about the same fashion as previous, indigenous, conquerors. One may ask, if they thought that, why were they so willing to go over to the Spanish side? I suppose partly on the principle of playing one dominant power against another, and on the belief that a new boss can't be as bad as the old one. I have wondered if the Nahuas of greater central Mexico didn't prefer the Spaniards because they were so ignorant of the local scene and the language, unable to inspect in detail as the Mexica did, unlikely to understand the inner workings of the altepetl or to try to

---

[7]Lockhart, ed., *We People Here* (1993), p. 244.

subvert it through dynastic marriages. Their assessment was resoundingly wrong in the long run, but in the short run it was true enough, and many local states seemed unrepentent of the bargain even some time after the fact. The annals of the eastern Nahua state Quauhtinchan, written in the form we know around 1560, devote much space and emotion to the preconquest penetration of the Mexica but report the Spanish occupation laconically (after all, there was little or no military action involved), concentrating on new tribute arrangements and concerned above all to restore jurisdictions to where they had stood before the Mexica.[8]

The picture in central Mexico is the one we find everywhere in that any indigenous confederation or empire was an agglomeration of groups which were ethnically separate, structurally to a large extent self-governing, aware of earlier independence, and ready to consider regaining it. The self-contained nature of the local ethnic groups, from states to bands, is the primary reason for the character of their reaction to new arrivals. It would be wrong, though, to imagine that they themselves were monolithic. Various kinds of internal factionalism played an important role in the early stages of the European occupation of a given area.

Tenochtitlan had not transcended the system of being a single altepetl receiving tribute from a host of others built exactly like itself, each with its own ruler and set of constituent parts. But it had frequently married members of its own dynasty to members of the local dynasties in the expectation that some of the children, with close Mexica affiliations, would succeed to the local thrones. As a result, there tended to be a Mexica and an anti-Mexica party in the leading circles of the various central Mexican altepetl, especially those in or near the Valley of Mexico. As the Spaniards approached, the anti-Mexica parties proved uniformly stronger, the presence of the Spaniards and Tlaxcalans perhaps tipping the balance. But the Mexica elements continued to conspire; as resistance in Tenochtitlan took shape, many pretenders to the rulership in outlying altepetl, and even some actual rulers, went to

---

[8]For early postconquest historical writing by the Nahuas and some comment on it, see Lockhart, ed., 1993.

join it, taking many dissidents along with them.

This part of the process we can see, if dimly, through fragments in the Spanish chronicles and Nahua annals. Something similar must have happened in the commercial network which was as important to the creation of Tenochtitlan dominance and an "Aztec Empire" as actual conquest and dynastic intermarriage. The only way Tenochtitlan can have attained its apparent huge size is through spontaneous emigration of traders and producers from other parts of the area. The livelihood of many throughout the region must have depended on the markets of Tenochtitlan and its Mexica satellite Tlatelolco. My assumption is that many of the inhabitants of the Valley of Mexico who were more active in interregional trade also went to Tenochtitlan and joined the opposition, and many others must have sympathized, for to the extent that the capital was not actually blockaded it continued to be able to get supplies from the outside, even though all the altepetl in the valley had already made terms with the Spaniards.

In other words, the internal fights in local states (and they occurred among the Tlaxcalans too) were not so much between parties with differing attitudes about how to receive the Spaniards as between stronger and weaker parties, the weaker being forced into a position of active opposition to the Spaniards as a banner for dissidents. Had they been in power they would doubtless have acted the same as the rest. The core attitude of all the indigenous people of central Mexico in the conquest period was that the Spaniards were like a new if powerful altepetl on the local scene and would not otherwise transform it, so that one could oppose them or support them mainly on the criterion of which course seemed to favor the short-term interest of one's own party or state. It is often said that Cortés, or some other Spanish leader, or (by the more knowledgeable) the Spaniards in general skillfully manipulated indigenous authority figures. When we get deeper within the situation, it becomes hard to say who was manipulating whom. Moreover, the transaction was at bottom not usually between the Spaniards and some corrupt ruler looking to his own benefits, but between the Spaniards and a whole local ethnic state seeking as much autonomy as possible.

Let us now backtrack a bit to the moment of first contact. It is a notable fact that often if not usually even the dominant local powers whose interests impelled them toward outright opposition to the Spaniards, and who in fact soon went in that direction, hesitated initially. They so often vacillated to the point of allowing the newcomers into the physical presence of the ruler that to seize the cacique in a peaceful parley became part of the Spaniards' modus operandi, giving them an entree and the opportunity to use the ruler's powers on their own behalf during a transitional period.

In indigenous accounts, the events in central Mexico prior to the siege of Tenochtitlan are obscured by a mythological haze, but in this case they largely confirm contemporary Spanish accounts. The latter assert that Moteucçoma (Moctezuma, Montezuma), the Mexica ruler, made a number of futile efforts to discourage the Spaniards from coming to Tenochtitlan without ever taking decisive action, and in the end met them peacefully and ceremoniously at his city's gates, which led shortly to his capture and detention by the Spaniards. Virtually the same thing happened with the Incas. We have no truly reliable information on what the imperial rulers and others like them (along with their courts and hierarchies) were thinking. Perhaps they were as much as anything curious, or at any rate not wanting to make final decisions about something unknown until they had seen it. Perhaps, from their position of power, they could not believe that such a small number of newcomers as were reliably reported could possibly constitute a serious threat. Some sources, mainly late, report that the Mexica thought the Spaniards were gods (there are hints of the same in Peru), but the central Mexicans overall absolutely did not act as though they believed the Spaniards to be gods.

Whatever the explanation, major indigenous groups did not show uniform hostility at very first contact, a fact that must be added to indigenous factionalism and European technical superiority in explaining the ease of occupation. This early hesitance, however, was not in itself decisive. The demands made through the captured ruler quickly aroused resentment and some form of large-scale armed opposition, somewhat slower coming in Peru than in Mexico.

A striking feature of the New World scene is that the sedentary peoples, numerous, with great resources including large and elaborately organized armies, put up much less successful and prolonged military resistance to the Europeans than did poorer, less numerous, more mobile peoples. Let us run over the reasons, which quickly make it apparent that we are not dealing with any mystery or paradox. European technical superiority showed itself above all precisely in large pitched battles on level ground, a kind of fighting predominant among the sedentary peoples alone. Tied to the territory of a small local ethnic state, the sedentary peoples were not mobile. Their previous millenia of wars and conquests led them to think that a conqueror would demand tribute, fiddle a bit with the local dynasty and the pantheon of gods, and little more. Spanish procedures with the encomienda in fact allowed a local group to continue in its territory and live in a fashion that was recognizably the same at least during the first generation or so. There were so many common points between European and sedentary indigenous organization and procedures that no single generation of indigenous people in the sedentary areas ever saw its way of life or its immediate sociopolitical entities transformed beyond recognition.

The more mobile peoples did not have to stand and fight. Already moving periodically over larger territories, often on terrain very difficult in one respect or another, they could melt away almost at will without losing too much and also easily mount surprise counterattacks of various kinds. Because hunting played more of a role in their lives, agriculture less, and skirmishing was endemic, they were more skilled in war and had better weapons, especially really efficient bows and arrows, as well as in some cases poisoned missiles. Their sociopolitical units were more fluid; they could merge and converge much more easily than the sedentary peoples, irrevocably committed to a territorial state of very limited scope.

When conquered, there was no hope that the mobile peoples could continue to live in anything like the same fashion as before. Whenever they came under European dominance they soon found that out through experience, bringing on new military episodes, often for as long as the group continued to exist as such. In these postcontact outbreaks among less sedentary peoples we find something closely approaching the usual picture of resistance: raised to a conscious level, full of patriotic and religious sentiment, conceiving the outsiders as radically different and wholly evil, determined to cast them from the land and all their poisonous culture with them. These movements, often millenarian (the seventeenth-century rebellion of the Pueblos of New Mexico is an example), nevertheless were not devoid of European elements. The leaders had often been among the Europeans and were meaningfully acculturated, and European devices, including the horse, might play a role.[9]

The difference between the sedentary peoples and the others in positive and negative potential from the point of view of the Europeans brought on reactions on the part of the latter that strengthened the distinction, creating a self-reinforcing cycle. The light resistance of the sedentaries, their usable resources and similar mechanisms attracted floods of immigrants who made it yet easier to overcome further resistance of any kind. The high resistance potential among the less sedentary peoples, combined with their small numbers and few usable resources, meant that few Europeans were attracted to them, making the already effective opposition there even harder to overcome.

These characteristics that we have been discussing apply to people as groups. The moment an individual was detached from his or her cultural, social, and geographical setting, that person usually swung quickly to the acceptance end of the spectrum, regardless of the nature of the society of origin. In the conquest period, indigenous slaves taken in Nicaragua and brought to Peru quickly learned the Spanish language and way of life, including a large number of craft skills; except for their greater mortality from disease, they were occupying the same niche for skilled auxiliaries and intermediaries as the Africans slave and free who also accompanied the Spaniards.[10] They showed no inclination to join the great Andean rebellion a few years after the first conquest and never caused

---

[9]See Powell 1952 and Spicer 1962.
[10]See Lockhart 1994.

the Spaniards trouble in any other way. The nonsedentaries who were so intractable en masse were often taken as slaves, because there was no other way to make use of their labor, and the locale often had no other resource; once removed from their native ambience to a central area, they acted the same way as the transported Nicaraguans. Chichimecs from the north were a standard, though not a dominant feature of the Hispanic society of central Mexico in the sixteenth and seventeenth centuries.

Rebellion

If we look at a book on indigenous rebellions, we will usually find that it concerns the more mobile peoples on the Spanish periphery. Actually, it is too much to call most of these phenomena rebellions, carried on as they were by people who had never truly been brought under Spanish rule in the first place.[11] Large-scale rebellions were indeed rare in the central areas of Spanish America more than a few years past the conquest. More common was a spontaneous outbreak by the people of one local ethnic state, or as some say, village, in defense of their rights within the existing system. Movements of this type have been studied by William Taylor for Mexico.[12] To me they seem more self-assertion than resistance. The Spaniards called them *tumultos*, riots, apparently spontaneous action by the local populace or a part of it against local Spanish officials, the priest or district judge and tax collector for some new imposition or changed practice, or against a Spanish property owner or a neighboring ethnic group for encroachment, or the like. They were not in any detectable way against Spanish sovereignty or Christian religion; they asserted the group's autonomy within that context. They rarely indeed spread beyond the confines of a single local group (municipality, pueblo, minimal local ethnic state).

---

[11] Their experience dominated by the true conquests of the Caribbean, Mexico, Peru, and contiguous areas, the Spaniards were not prepared to think of indigenous groups as sovereign. In North American indigenous history, the first word one learns is "treaty," but both the word and the phenomenon are virtually absent from the Spanish American scene except on the farthest fringes.

[12] Taylor, *Drinking, Homicide & Rebellion* (1979), chapter 4.

These manifestations involved violent action but only occasionally deaths, and most were quickly past, sometimes gaining their point, sometimes being put down without many repercussions. I discuss them here as using force in opposition to actions of the established authorities, but in truth they are only part of a larger context involving peaceful cooperation. Within the normal framework of Spanish jurisprudence, indigenous groups were free to litigate in their own interest like any other individuals or groups, and from an early time they did so in Mexico, Peru, and elsewhere, using Spanish lawyers and developing much relevant expertise of their own.[13] Just as with the Spaniards themselves, grievances usually first took the form of petitions and lawsuits, by no means always unsuccessful. Usually a tumulto followed upon a long period of unsuccessful petitioning; it was really just a way of bringing one more degree of pressure, and seems to have been understood as such, in view of the frequent lightness of punishment of the perpetrators. In cases of protracted unsatisfactory litigating and repeated protests, tumultos could become fierce, desperate attacks leading to the death of one or several local Spanish and indigenous officers and other people, and were afterward punished accordingly. Actions of this type surely represent resistance, but also the highest level of attention-getting for a particular cause, a predictable phenomenon in a sense within the system.

The indigenous factionalism seen in the conquest period was still strong in the tumultos of later years. Very often those involved were dissidents acting primarily against the constituted authorities within the community itself, claiming that the latter were improperly elected or had behaved illegally. The uprisings in general were as much internal disputes as resistance against Spanish authority.[14]

As one gets farther from the center of the Spanish presence in Mexico, even short of the ever turbulent Chichimecs of the northern plains, one finds larger-scale movements. In 1712,

---

[13]Shown for Peru as well in Steve J. Stern, *Peru's Indian Peoples and the Challenge of the Spanish Conquest: Huamanga to 1640* (1982).

[14]See Robert Haskett, *Indigenous Rulers: An Ethnohistory of Town Government in Colonial Cuernavaca* (1991).

in the highlands of Chiapas in southern Mexico, a movement spread across a series of independent communities, settlements, or towns (in my terms historically local ethnic states), from a dozen to nearly thirty of them depending on the account and the criterion, based mainly among speakers of Tzeltal Maya but including also some Tzotzil Maya and Chol peoples. It started with an indigenous girl who had a vision of the Virgin Mary requesting a shrine in a fashion commonplace in both the Spanish and postconquest Mexican traditions. When she and her supporters were not given credence by Spanish officials, they created their own priests and special doctrine, making some use of preconquest-style shamanism and associated phenomena, within an otherwise orthodox Christianity; they killed priests, then Spaniards and Hispanic people in their area, and set up a loosely organized independent state with its own military hierarchy. They held on for several months before the movement collapsed, after Spanish mobilization and large-scale pitched battles.[15]

Many of the peoples of southern Mesoamerica (not all, and the topic has not been to my knowledge exhaustively studied), despite belonging to the same culture area as the Nahuas of central Mexico, having much the same calendar and counting system, writing, art, rulers and nobility, even basic crops, were not as fully sedentary. The famous Maya of Yucatan, builders of world-famous temples, practiced shifting agriculture at the time of the Spanish arrival. They shared many of the characteristics of semisedentary peoples and were correspondingly hard to conquer; the process took many more years than in central Mexico and stopped short of including the whole Yucatecan peninsula.

Thus the peoples to the north and south of central Mexico were in different ways structurally less similar to Europe and by that fact more prone to prolonged military opposition and later large-scale rebellion or protracted fighting. The situation in the south was compounded by the fact of its relatively small economic interest to the Spaniards and its location off the trunk line, with the result that the Spanish presence was

---

[15]Kevin Gosner, *Soldiers of the Virgin: The Moral Economy of a Colonial Maya Rebellion* (1992). See also Gosner 1998.

much thinner and the indigenous people less built into the Spanish society and economy.

The effect can be seen not only in macroregional terms but also locally. Chiapas had a trade route going through valley country toward Oaxaca to the north and Guatemala to the south. Along this route the economy was, though not thriving, at least more active, and many of the region's Spaniards and Hispanics were found here, as well as indigenous people trading with them and working for them. The rebellion, though extensive, was confined largely to the eastern highlands, off the trade route, with even fewer resident Spaniards than the rest of the region.

Normal interaction

I now enter on the topic that has interested me most in recent years, the question of what kind of European culture elements indigenous people were prepared to accept and under what conditions. I speak of people organized in their own sociopolitical entities on or near their traditional home ground; we have seen that when individuals are taken from this context and put among Spaniards, they quickly and successfully accept virtually everything. I will speak primarily of the situation I know best, that of the Nahuas of central Mexico, which I think can also be said to be the least badly understood situation in this hemisphere in general, with a few comparative remarks devoted to other Mesoamerican peoples and the Andeans.

My contention is that in the larger view of this matter conscious resistance plays a very small role, and to illustrate I mean to speak first of a sector where that is fairly clear from the beginning, namely language change, which since the great historical linguists of the nineteenth century has been understood to be a process as impersonal as plate tectonics, largely beneath the threshold of consciousness of the people who undergo it. Even so, it is perhaps necessary to emphasize how little any patriotic resentment of or resistance to foreign words and manners of speech came into play. Nowhere in all the Nahuatl texts I have ever seen, some of them very preachy, have I ever found any statement that one should retain pure native modes of speech and avoid Spanish expressions. From the time such expressions began to enter the language, they are found everywhere, even in formal texts such as histories and songs and in elevated conversation and speeches. The only people who took exception to these neologisms were Spanish ecclesiastics, who complained that the language was being corrupted and tried to keep phenomena of Spanish origin to a minimum in texts generated under their auspices.[16] A Spanish item, once in the Nahuatl vocabulary, was pronounced by Nahuatl rules and took on new if related meanings: *tomin*, from a Spanish word of the same spelling but not quite the same pronunciation, meant money in general, not just a specific coin; *camixatli* was the Nahuatl guise of *camisa*, shirt. It is clear that the Nahuas did not think of these as foreign terms; they did not think about them at all. The difference between them and the Spanish originals results from normal linguistic evolution, not resistance.

For the first postconquest generation, during what I call Stage 1, Nahuatl took only proper names from Spanish, otherwise using indigenous vocabulary to name the new things; the language as such could hardly be said to have changed. During about the next hundred years, in crudest terms 1550–1650, my Stage 2, Nahuatl took a myriad of words from Spanish. Indeed, there was almost no limit as to content; the limits were mainly linguistic. All words borrowed were nouns; pronunciation and grammar were virtually unaffected, and idiom just barely. Then from 1650 forward, in Stage 3, Nahuatl opened up to take words other than nouns, to translate idioms and create equivalences between Nahuatl and Spanish words, to add Spanish sounds to its phonology. It became able to take anything Spanish had, as needed, creating an open channel between the two language groups.

The question then arises, if Nahuatl was eventually going

---

[16]The writings of the seventeenth-century Tlaxcalan annalist Zapata are the only case known to me of an apparently conscious, culturally motivated if highly inconsistent avoidance of certain Spanish loanwords (today, however, attempts at linguistic purism in Nahuatl speaking communities are a standard part of the mix). See my *The Nahuas After the Conquest* (1992), p. 392. Further detail on most of what I say about the Nahuas on the following pages can be found scattered throughout that book.

to accept all these things, what kept that from happening immediately? One part of the answer is that we have here a progression with an inner logic and sequence; it much resembles a child's acquisition of language, in any language, and all over the world it has been noticed that nouns are borrowed from one language into another earlier and in greater numbers than verbs. A language-contact sequence something like the one among the Nahuas appears to approach universal validity, here cleanly worked out because it started from absolute scratch; but there is no apparent inherent reason why the whole process could not occur much more quickly, even in a single generation.

For that to happen, though, it would seem that there would have to be massive contact between the two populations, indeed a situation where the newcomers were not only dominant in various ways but more numerous than the indigenous people, and that was very far from being the case. A good deal of the relatively slow tempo of the process, then, can be ascribed not to any kind of resistance, however the term is defined, but to simple lack of opportunity for enough indigenous people to hear the Spanish words often enough: lack of contact, lack of exposure. Such, to me, is overwhelmingly the explanation for the generation-long Stage 1 of essentially no borrowing. There were few Spaniards in few places and vast numbers of Nahuas; even the Nahuas who got to hear some Spaniards speaking heard primarily a meaningless babble. The moment there were enough Spaniards present, in everyday situations, so that larger numbers of Nahuas could hear their words repeatedly, large-scale adoption of Spanish vocabulary began immediately. Thus there never had been a reluctance on the part of the Nahuas to borrow nouns, nor a structural inability of the language to borrow them.

On the positive side, everything borrowed denoted some new object, practice, or concept which the Spaniards brought with them and which impinged on the Nahuas meaningfully. The line between what was felt as new and what was not (and so could be called by existing words) is far from clear, and I still search for a systematic explanation of "newness." Taking in a new word was not the same thing as taking the thing itself (thus the word *caballo* was a part of Nahuatl long before many Nahuas had horses), but it was acceptance in the sense of something becoming a normal part of the Nahua mental horizon.

As we approach Stage 3 and the inundation of Nahuatl with a variety of Spanish linguistic phenomena, we reach the point where we can speak of some kind of (unconscious) resistance, reluctance, or inability. From not long after the onset of Stage 2 in the mid-sixteenth century, Nahuas had been not only hearing but understanding Spanish verbs, as we can tell by their influence on native vocabulary. No American indigenous language had a word "to have" as used in European languages; already in the sixteenth century the Nahuas began to change their verb *pia*, "to hold, keep, guard," to correspond to Spanish *tener* in meaning; but they did not borrow *tener* or any other Spanish verb. Not until the mid-seventeenth century— that is, not until Stage 3—do loan verbs appear regularly in Nahuatl texts (there were some isolated forerunners, one as far back as the last decade of the sixteenth century). Part of the problem was structural. It was by no means obvious how to borrow a Spanish verb into Nahuatl; the morphologies were very different. Finally Nahuatl fastened on the most noun-like part of the verb, the infinitive (all the more difficult to do because Nahuatl verbs lack an infinitive) and added native verb endings to it—a set of endings somewhat like our -*ize*, which makes verbs out of adjectives, as in "normalize." Taking prepositions was even more difficult. Nahuatl had no prepositions as they are known in European languages; all their comparable words acted like possessed nouns. When they finally started using Spanish prepositions just as in Spanish, with an "object" or complement, a grammatical revolution was required.

Over and above the structural obstacles, and far more important in the timing, was the necessity for a substantial sector of Nahuas to know Spanish really well. Stage 3 and all the phenomena that characterize it seem to coincide with the rise of a critical mass of bilingual Nahuas, so that the movement is again driven by increased contact, increased in intensity and intimacy between a larger group of Spanish speakers and a smaller group of Nahuatl speakers. The underlying facts in this respect cannot be demonstrated absolutely.

We know that the indigenous population of central Mexico in general was reaching its nadir in these years, and we know that the Spanish, mestizo and mulatto population was the largest yet and more dispersed into the countryside. We know that an increasing number of Nahuas were able to give legal testimony in Spanish, and more of them are referred to in various kinds of Spanish texts as *ladino*, fluent in Spanish. But the strongest evidence is circular; the kind of phenomena that appear in Nahuatl in Stage 3, the sorts of innovations we have been discussing and the acquisition of a large proportion of the other language's phonetic repertoire, are associated with bilingual settings all over the world in our own times.

Further corroboration comes from the nature of the things taken into Nahuatl at this time (continuing in the same vein until today wherever Nahuatl survives). Loans during Stage 2 usually involved items in categories familiar to the Nahuas, but so new and different from their own equivalents that they would have been hard put to describe them succinctly. That process continued into Stage 3 as the Nahuas got deeper and deeper into technical specialties such as the equipment and maintenance of horses, or the higher levels of legal chicanery. But a great many of the new words in Stage 3 involved meanings that could already be expressed, had been being expressed for centuries. The rationale of many Stage 3 phenomena cannot be understood until one compares the two languages and finds that there is a large disparity in the way they say something. Wherever that occurs, a Nahuatl innovation is likely. The reason can only be that it facilitated going back and forth between one language and the other. Here any notion of resistance is irrelevant to what the Nahuas were adopting or not adopting.

How did other indigenous languages behave in postconquest times? As we saw in Chapter 8, Yucatecan Maya, spoken in an area with a less active economy and far fewer resident Spaniards, especially outside the few cities, moved into something very closely approaching Nahuatl's Stage 2 at almost the same rate, but it stayed there indefinitely, retaining all the Stage 2 characteristics until at least the late eighteenth century. Mixtec, spoken by the immediate southern neighbors of the Nahuas, more isolated from the main Spanish presence than they but less so than the Maya of Yucatan, went farther through the process and closer in time to the Nahuas, perhaps twenty to fifty years behind in different respects, but their documents never show some of the characteristics of fully blown Stage 3 among the Nahuas. In these cases we seem to see the outlines of a process generally valid regardless of the structure of the particular language or even the special profile of the local culture, varying mainly with the density at different times of the local Spanish population.

The Andean case, however, fails to confirm such an analysis, although we cannot yet be sure of its import. All the Mesoamerican peoples took to European alphabetic writing quickly. The Andeans did not. One could say they mutely "resisted," i.e., they did not grasp the significance and method of the system very quickly because they had no analogue. Recently a few alphabetic texts have turned up in Quechua after all. Contrary to my expectation that Peru, in so many things like southern Mexico, would go through the language contact process very slowly, the texts show a language with nearly all the diagnostic criteria of Stage 3 as early as the first two decades of the seventeenth century. That evidence would indicate that Peru entered Stage 3, i.e., had a critical mass of bilingual indigenous people, even earlier than central Mexico. I tend to believe that the precocious development happened on the coast, where the Spanish speakers concentrated, and that it spread from there into areas of the highlands which had a meaningful Spanish presence. I provisionally envision a split development, with much of the country lagging far behind the leaders (unlike central Mexico, where the chronology was simultaneous across the entire Nahua culture area).[17]

To return to the Nahuas, change over the postconquest centuries across the board, in legal-political, religious, literary, and economic aspects of life, in the form of what at least superficially looks like acceptance of European culture elements, overall corresponds closely to the three stages of linguistic development. In broadest terms, for a generation

---

[17]For more detail on the content of the previous two paragraphs, especially the Andean case, see Chapter 8 in the present volume.

there was minimal change (change virtually equates with acceptance). In Stage 2, change and acceptance were often corporate in nature, mediated between the Spaniards and the indigenous mass by a small corps of translators and indigenous authorities who were sufficiently exposed to Spaniards to get a grasp of certain culture elements. At this point more than at any other, little tension existed between change and continuity, acceptance and "resistance." The best and often the only practical way to retain the core of one's own institutions and practices was to accept closely analagous Spanish institutions and practices, imbuing them of course with the spirit and substance of one's own tradition. In Stage 3, massive Spanish-indigenous contact began to cut into the integrity of the larger indigenous corporate phenomena, so that the new change was more at the level of the individual, an individual now sufficiently prepared for dealing with Spaniards directly, bypassing the corporation. Now change and acceptance were often not predicated upon already existing close analogies as in Stage 2 but aimed precisely at remaining differences between the two cultures, with the effect if not the intention of reducing them to a minimum for easy communication and interaction. I think the reader will see how difficult it is to bring the concept of resistance to bear on this evolution, which is best analyzed in other terms.

From here forward I will proceed in a very skeletal way; the topic becomes vast, representing the entire postconquest history, in the widest possible sense, of the peoples involved. Changes in the household regime, kinship, and landholding at the household level among the Nahuas were smaller and slower than in the more corporate aspects of life, as follows naturally from the nature of Stage 2 as explained above. But even in Stage 3 many things remained the same, including a single-entry walled compound for the household, with separate structures inside for nuclear families, and many separate small landholdings worked by the various family members. The entity remained the household and whoever lived there, not a "family" in the modern European sense. Stage 3 did see some adaptations in the conceptualization of kinship, but as I say, changes in this sphere were small. The reason for the relative inertness seems to be not "resistance" but the lack of Spanish-indigenous contact at this level.[18]

As we saw in Chapter 4, at the beginning of Stage 2 the Spaniards reorganized the local Nahua political regime, creating a Spanish-style city council for each local ethnic state. The Nahuas offered no open resistance to this innovation, and the institution quickly took root. As time went on, offices and practices came to be somewhat closer to the Spanish, but in the end it was quite clear even to the Spaniards that the councils were as much like preconquest governments as like their Spanish counterpart. It was not resistance but continuation, the result of a striking but only partial convergence between Spanish and Nahua traditions. In Stage 3 much friction came to surround this system, leading to endless litigation and sometimes to the tumultos mentioned above, with appeals and complaints to Spanish authorities, but the phenomenon was not resistance to the Spaniards; rather it was fragmentation of the local indigenous states, the altepetl, into their constituent parts. Each part would now prefer to deal with the Spaniards directly, bypassing the larger altepetl, something which could be done much more easily under Stage 3 conditions of widespread bilingualism and the constant presence of Spaniards and Hispanics everywhere.

In religion, in view of the Mesoamerican tradition of acceptance of the gods of a conquering group, resistance was

---

[18]A separate problem is why women seemed to "resist" certain kinds of change more than men, especially in matters of dress and certain technology (a phenomenon seen in many areas worldwide). Men wore shirts and pants, women the preconquest *huipilli* (a long one-piece, unfitted blouse) and *cueitl* (wraparound skirt). Men worked European looms, women the preconquest backstrap loom. One might say this is the natural consequence of men going out into the world more and being employed by Spaniards. It is true that the household and its tasks were the special domain of women, but they were not restricted to it. They were prominent if not dominant in the markets that supplied Spaniards with much of their daily fare and household objects. They were ubiquitous as servants and often mistresses in Spanish households. Indeed, in the conquest period it was women who, because of this type of contact, were often the first in a family to learn Spanish. We are far from having established the facts on this matter.

not the normal reaction to Christianity, nor was conversion necessary. What was needed, as the Spanish clerics saw, was instruction; they spoke constantly of indoctrination and rarely of conversion (far less did they call themselves "missionaries"). The Nahuas thought that they could continue their old practices and beliefs along with the new. During Stage 1 the results of this attitude were partially, provisionally tolerated (though occasionally fiercely punished). With the Stage 2 reorganization, creating a parish and an indigenous church organization in each local unit, parallel to and intermeshed with the political organization much as it had been in preconquest times, the continuation of blatantly preconquest practices was pushed to the margins, virtually to the level of European witchcraft and sectarianism,[19] because the needs of the mainstream of Nahua nobles and commoners were met by the local forms of Christianity, which soon gained their allegiance.[20]

Where Christianity provided no equivalent, however, the old tended to continue in some form. Christianity was inadequate at the level of shamanism—curing, conjuring, hallucinogenic substances, etc.—and practices of this type long persisted among the populace in general, not so much in a spirit of resistance to Christianity as of supplementing it within a larger system. Sometimes members of the indigenous Christian church organization themselves attended to the shamanistic aspect, but with time it fell to more and more marginal figures, as in some parts of central Mexico to this day. Even preconquest incantations, mentioning pagan gods, might be performed in a Christian framework, with Christian formulas added to the beginning and end, and indigenous holy substances might be devoted to a saint's image. At a certain

---

[19]See Serge Gruzinski, *Man-Gods in the Mexican Highlands* (1989). The book treats several dissident indigenous religious prophets and movements in central Mexico from Stage 1 into Stage 3. Either the locale is the far edge (Sierra de Puebla), the scene is an entity of secondary or tertiary importance, the personnel are of the lowest rank, or the personnel are marginalized to the extent of transience, without a base in any one altepetl and wandering from one to another. In many cases, all of these conditions obtain.

[20]For more detail on these matters see Chapter 4 in this volume.

point, usually after they had long existed, Spanish clerics began to take notice of such things and Nahuas became aware of the disapproval; after that the practices can be put under the heading of resistance to the extent that they were hidden as well as possible.[21]

In central Mexican economic affairs the indigenous people, unlike the inhabitants of some parts of the hemisphere, had no problems operating with money; as we have seen, one of the first words they borrowed meant money or cash, broadened from a particular coin, the *tomín*, as has often happened in history. They used money among themselves as well as in dealings with Spaniards. The reason, as usual, was that they already had an analogue; their currencies included the cacao bean and the tribute blanket, the former for small change, the latter for larger amounts. Likewise, having virtual equivalents, they immediately understood private landowning and the sale of land. They also possessed professional traders or merchants, and had no problems with investment and commercialization. They had their own terminology for all these things. Their performance in these matters long retained a particular flavor, which as in religion or politics was the residue of a less than total convergence. It did take them some time to adjust to the concept of lending and borrowing money; their first stabs were in the direction of taking care of the money for someone else. They also tended to merge borrowing with pawning and leasing and to confuse them with sale by installment, largely I think because of their own lack of cash. But there was none of the kind of thing often reported for North America, where it seems that buying and selling was confused with gift giving and fictive kinship obligations.

Religion and politics were grafted onto basic institutions of the indigenous ethnic state. The economic equivalent was the market. The marketplace did survive, but it never received a tenth of the attention, generated few records, and above all was not just an indigenous venue but a place of interaction of Spaniards and Nahuas. Household aspects of Spanish life depended on it for centuries, and it became correspondingly

---

[21]See Ruiz de Alarcón, *Treatise on the Heathen Superstitions* . . . (1984).

inundated with Hispanic personnel and practices, at the same time retaining much that was indigenous down to the present day. Here is an area where our present knowledge is radically insufficient.

The overall picture in central Mexico is that of an indigenous system readily accepting, though also transforming, anything from the outside that was closely parallel in structure and function but wanting to continue with those aspects of the system not compensated for. Nothing was resisted simply because it was foreign; foreignness of culture items was not a category of importance to the Nahuas (as opposed to degree of inherent familiarity and utility).

Let it be understood that the Nahua experience is not universal in its content; it stands at one end of a wide spectrum. Spanish-style municipal government took root among most sedentary peoples, wherever there was a strong local ruler and a well defined nobility. In more isolated situations, as in southern Mexico and the Peruvian highlands, the ruler continued in a recognizably preconquest form for longer. Among semi- and nonsedentary peoples without tight territoriality, powerful rulers, and a nobility, the system was hard to establish, because it failed to correspond with anything in the local tradition.

Among sedentary peoples who were on the periphery of the Spanish presence, again as in southern Mexico and much of the Peruvian highland, preconquest religion and Christianity were often slow in merging, with each maintained separately and, from the point of view of the indigenous unit, publicly, though hidden as far as possible from the Spaniards. In time, with greater Spanish penetration, greater integration took place, but recognizably preconquest cults and religious experts survived to some extent in many places of this type. Practitioners of traditional religion sometimes showed overt hostility to Christianity, but the population in general seems to have given its allegiance to both. Whereas actual opposition to Christianity was only a very small countercurrent among sedentary peoples, it often gained the upper hand among the more mobile peoples, where it was part of the reaction of groups who correctly felt that their whole way of life and group existence was threatened.

*   *   *

In all of these matters the basic determinants are the fit of European and indigenous culture and the contact between two populations, which involves both relative numbers and type of contact—peaceful and day-to-day, or intermittent, or through trade and hostilities. Within the framework of convergence as the principal determinant, I do not mean to neglect the fact that what indigenous people saw as being to their advantage, as working better, was crucial. Some methods, tools, and materials have an actual efficiency that may not be quite a universal objective fact, but nearly enough so that all peoples see it. No people to my knowledge has ever failed to see the utility of steel knives. Such things will be accepted under the most adverse conditions. As I say, all this still occurs within the framework of convergence; efficiency is most appreciated when it concerns something the group already has or does. Prestige accruing from the position of the conqueror is another large factor, but it too operates within convergence.

In general, then, I see acceptance and resistance as being primarily a function of degree of convergence, especially in the longer run.[22] Among the sedentary peoples, "resistance," that is, difference between indigenous and European beliefs, structures, and practices at a given time and place, was the residue left after the operation of the primary convergences that made the European occupation possible. Gradually, in the layered, sequential process we have seen, daily contact between the two populations worked to reduce that difference, not only by bringing the indigenous closer to the European, but acting in some important respects also in the other direction. Things always stopped short of the achievement of identity or complete acceptance. Much of this rapprochement occurred within the context of a situation where each side

---

[22]Studying "resistance" head-on is like studying *mestizaje* (race mixture), which we have almost stopped doing, because it is the byproduct of widespread factors that in themselves are not related to race mixture, such as Iberian family organization, the type of employment dictated by the economy, and many other kinds of intermediate causative elements.

tended to presume that the approximately equivalent phenomenon on the other side was actually identical to its own, something I have called Double Mistaken Identity.[23]

It is quite possible to view the burden of what is said here as a matter of semantics or use of terminology. The concept of resistance can be a valid tool if it is understood as one pole of a bipolar reaction by indigenous people, seen from only one direction of a two-direction transaction between native inhabitants and new arrivals, and occurring beneath the level of consciousness more often than not. Even so, I believe that many of the most basic instances of crosscultural change and continuity in the Western Hemisphere bear little relation to resistance no matter how much the notion is refined.

---

[23]See Chapter 4 in this volume. For North America, Richard White hit on a quite similar notion ("what amounts to a process of creative, often expedient misunderstandings"), although it is more in a context of creating something quite new to both sides than of already well established partially convergent phenomena. See White's *The Middle Ground* (1991), p. x.

12. A Historian and the Disciplines

I LACK ANY very firm disciplinary foundation. Before and during elementary school, through junior high school, and into the first years of high school I was a quite eager reader of whatever came to hand, whether my father's books in the high old cases my grandfather had made, the *Wonder Books of World Knowledge* acquired specifically with me in mind (the ones on archaeology and ancient history, music, and animals were my favorites; I still have the one on animals), my father's prize World War I vintage Encyclopædia Britannica (above all the parts on ships and cannon), the small libraries of grade school classrooms, or the larger holdings of the junior high and high school libraries, and also newspapers, the funnies, comic books, dime westerns and mysteries from the drugstore, the *Saturday Evening Post*, the *Readers' Digest*, even *Life* and *Look*, anything so long as it was in English and wasn't impossible to hold while you lay in bed falling asleep.

It's true that a life of Alexander the Great made a great impression on me, but so did a collection of dog stories and the Tarzan books. Sometime in the middle of high school I lost that omnivorous reading pattern and for many years thereafter did reading focused on the project or passion of the moment,[1] until rediscovering reading for amusement and breadth in retirement. I think I may still have somewhere some lists I have made at different times of things I absolutely must read soon in the name of being able to call myself an educated person; eventually I read a good many of them for various reasons, but never because they were on the lists.

In high school my favorite subject was Latin.[2] In college I

---

[1]Indeed, during this long time I frequently expatiated on the evils of too much broad reading, which had robbed many people of originality and momentum, and even served as a pretext for getting nothing done. I now see the other side of the matter, and yet I am far from convinced that I was wrong.

[2]My second favorite was Spanish. To this day I am not quite sure of the reason for preferring one over the other. Maybe it was just two years of Latin versus one term of Spanish, or the greater intelligence

tried journalism, education, English, and a bit of Spanish. I had little idea what I should go into; my parents having been high school teachers and teaching having been in the family for two or three generations, it looked like I might become a college professor of some kind.

Before finishing my BA I went into the Army Signal Corps, as much because I was doing badly in school as because I might be drafted. They tested me, sent me to the Monterey language school to learn German, and then off to Germany. The German experience was somehow decisive for me. I read with some enthusiasm, half for language improvement, in history, philosophy, and some novels, especially Thomas Mann (as a possible example of how you could be analytical and balanced and still write novels), and developed an interest in German medieval architecture. And I got to know many Germans, mainly professional people, plus, as they called them, *leichtsinnige Mädchen* ("frivolous girls"). It was my first immersion in another culture, becoming totally absorbed and obsessed with it, loving it, even going German to a point, and yet being outside it.

I also discovered the way that as you get deeper and deeper inside a different culture, not only the more familiar does it become as itself, but the more like your own it seems, and you are driven to put your finger on and rationalize the relatively few though crucial things that make it different. You discover the analysis of culture. I could very well have ended up in German studies for good, but I became disillusioned with some German phenomena. After dipping into a few philosophers,

---

and dedication of the Latin instructor. Or was it that Latin came wrapped in history and cultural analysis? At any rate, I was soon convinced that any utterance whatever sounded best in Latin. Yet I made no move to study the language in college, something I have repeatedly regretted. (From time to time I have studied Latin a bit on my own, not without profit, but I still can't read most texts without running to dictionaries and experts.) Latin and geometry had been sold to me as good for mental development, not as something to make a career of. Today, although I do feel the thrust of Jorge Luis Borges's bon mot "El español es el latín venido a menos" (Spanish is Latin come down in the world, or fallen on hard times), I admire both languages equally, Latin for its majesty and Spanish for its dry vigor (twenty-five years ago I suppose I would have said its manliness).

each as dogmatic as the last, I decided that there was no point to this massive system-building, with the problems covered by the German language, in the obscurities and ambiguities of which the philosophers gloried. It seemed about as promising as medieval theology. I eventually saw that Thomas Mann was trying to be philosophically "deep" in the German sense and laugh at it at the same time, that in the last analysis he probably thought German culture was simply superior. It got through to me that a great many ordinary and not so ordinary Germans were quite unrepentant about the Nazis and the war, or oblivious that anything unusual had happened, concerned only as far as it had affected their eating, sleeping, and housing. And though I wrote a few commentaries, in German, actually, as a language exercise, in the end I wanted to go elsewhere. (As a side enterprise, when I got to that point, I learned enough French from an expatriate Frenchwoman to find my way through scholarly books in that language to this day.)

What I was supposed to be doing in Germany was working with a low-level intelligence agency, part of the Signal Corps, as a translator. Letters crossing the Iron Curtain in both directions were routinely opened and photocopied (by both sides, I think). Copies of the ones coming west in German, from East Germany and from ethnic Germans in various countries, ended up in our office, for us to see what there might be of value for American intelligence in them. Precious little, actually—sometimes some hint of morale, or of something people were excited about. For me, it was mainly language instruction and human interest. Someone hit on the idea of making a journal to be sent back periodically to Washington, with selections from what seemed the most significant or typical letters, and a few comments giving context where necessary. (The journal was a distant forerunner, perhaps, of the volume I did with Enrique Otte called *Letters and People of the Spanish Indies, Sixteenth Century* [1976]). I became principal editor, making the choices of what went in and doing the final versions of the translations. Other people around were more highly trained in various kinds of German and had degrees, some of them advanced degrees. The main difference I felt between myself and them was that they put both the documents and the experience in certain already existing categories and didn't see and adjust to what was actually before them as much as I did, not that I did totally myself, but the fact that I did as much as I did was the reason I gravitated to the center of the operation.

In the process I began to become radically dissatisfied with the modern categorization of human activity. I had by the time I was a freshman in college conceived a vague notion—too vague to act upon—that perhaps I ought to be a novelist, because I seemed to be inclined to books and writing and was told that novels were the locus of originality, creativity, even beauty and deeper truth. I was simply not finding it to be the case. I was finding both English and German novels that I read in my spare time to be often derivative, exaggerated and stereotypical, even unintelligent, surely not repositories of truth and beauty; more like a pastime. I found I didn't even particularly like to read novels; I bought a lot that I never read more than a couple of pages of. The histories of Jacob Burckhardt seemed to have as much or more of all those desirable qualities, but equally the mundane letters from individuals to individuals that we were reading in the office. Understanding them, translating them, commenting on them, seemed to have as much art and search of truth about it as writing novels or the normal kind of histories, sometimes more.

Even before this time I had been struck by finding in eighteenth and nineteenth century texts the term literary referring not only to novels and poetry but to history writing and even to studies in geology, astronomy, or medicine. It was the same with philosophy and philosopher, which could refer to wisdom and sages in many branches of human activity. That was what I wanted, a framework within which terms like art, literature, and creativity applied to the whole range of what people do.

I was already beginning to feel that I would not be entirely at home in any of the slots set up in the twentieth century for those who observe, study, and write. I had a strong feeling for the flavor of individual human lives, particularly as expressed on paper in very concrete circumstances. But I had an equally strong feeling about what I thought of as truth, which as I examine it many years later didn't mean some allegedly

transcendent or religious truth, nor—although it included it—
the truth about what actually happens, surface event by
surface event. My concern with truth went beyond the concrete, although never dismissing it, to try to make sense of
what happens, to see patterns in it. Although you never saw
them all, the patterns you saw were really there, as true as the
individual happenings.[3] And I wanted to express all that, to
get it on paper in a straightforward form that would please
me, in that sense to be a writer.

Back in the States, I finished college with an English major
and a German minor giving (too much) credit for my army
schooling and experiences. Where to go from there seemed to
come down to finding something I was somewhat qualified
for, hopefully involving the study of texts in various languages. A buddy of mine in the army (Richard Hampsten, his

---

[3]My belief in and interest in truth never went away. The dossiers
that the University of Wisconsin sent out to employers in the 60's
included a half sheet for the job candidate to make a statement. Mine
centered on getting closer to the truth and destroying false clichés
and stereotypes; it wouldn't go over at all today, and perhaps it didn't
then either. From the beginning I have been very skeptical about the
objective truth of any particular statement, more so I think than the
postmodernists who pride themselves on their skepticism and
purport to believe in no objective truth at all (despite which they try
to convince us of things and act as though they believe in the objective existence of texts and their writers, and even—too much—in
the efficacy of those writers' conscious plans and intentions). When I
was around eight or ten it occurred to me that perhaps everyone and
everything else was an illusion, but some rudimentary testing and
thinking convinced me that such was not the case. I used to hide in
the corner behind the kitchen stove shutting my eyes, and when I
would open them with lightning speed to catch the nothingness,
everything was always there as before, everyone going about their
business as normal. In the long run it was impossible not to believe
in the objective existence, truth, of human beings with certain genes
and fingerprints conceived and born at a certain time and place,
dying at another, and certifiably doing and saying a long series of
things in between. Even the most biased text ever written, seen in the
context of a larger corpus, contains any number of true, objective, not
trivial facts unrelated to the main ostensible message. It also
contains the vocabulary, grammar, syntax and rhetoric of its time
and place, which is another kind of truth. Truth is not exhaustible,
but it is there and available to us.

name was) was entering a field called comparative literature, which sounded to me like precisely the opportunity to study texts in various languages. There were few programs in operation at that time; he knew of one at the University of Washington and another at Wisconsin, which was where my new wife Mary Ann was from, so there I went.

I became dissatisfied with comparative literature almost immediately. As part of the program I was allowed to take courses in the German department and even ended up teaching German to undergraduates, all of which in a way I greatly enjoyed, but it didn't get me past the problematics of German studies in general. And I did all right in some courses in English and American literature because at that time the reigning school was something called the New Criticism, which involved looking very closely at the texts themselves and ignoring everything else. Comparative literature proper, as it was there and then, wasn't at all what I expected. I thought it would be the study of a vast corpus of texts without the barriers and parochialisms of the individual language departments. I found it was being used as a way of reducing the already small text corpus preferred by the departments to almost nothing, abstracting from them, replacing them with an empty jargon. It was my first real experience of gobbledy-gook; the language of the German philosophers was nothing to it.[4] I was later to experience the jargons of the political scientists, the sociologists, the anthropologists, the linguists, and though I didn't like any of them, they were based on something, which with comparative literature talk I couldn't see. At that time I formed a theory that I still think valid, that the more you restrict the corpus studied, the more baroque the language of the studies will become, in an effort to find something new to say about the same old stuff, or at least to hide the fact that you have nothing new to say. In the second year I gave up on comparative literature and by extension any kind of literary study in the narrower sense.

---

[4]Looking back I am surprised at my prescience. Comparative literature in those days (the late 50's and early 60's) had hardly begun to be the refuge of meaningless terminology that it has since become. Indeed, my reaction then seems unjustified except in the light of what came later. Perhaps I intuited where it was all leading.

After a while working in a paper box factory and indulging my passion for the music of the Renaissance, I decided on history as being, as far as I could see, the most straightforward and least specialized of the disciplines studying humans, and also as being based on a much greater volume and variety of texts than literary study as I knew it, or any other discipline. I went into Latin American history partly because of the Alliance for Progress, then big, partly because I knew some Spanish, and partly because people I talked to in United States and European history seemed to be crowding all over themselves, taking ever more miniscule dissertation topics. I wanted scope and no one looking over my shoulder.[5]

But since I had very few history courses in my transcript, and my protest against comparative literature had taken the form of getting a large number of incompletes and leaving the program without a degree, I wasn't qualified to enter the Wisconsin graduate program in history directly. I got in through the avenue of an MA in Hispanic Studies, which was nearly the same thing as what in most places today is called Latin American Studies. One took two disciplinary concentrations, I believe, and dabbled in some others at the rate of a course or two each. In addition to history I did Spanish, which was more or less where I was coming from, and a few courses in anthropology, geography, and political science.

The history was fine; actually, what I did was mainly European medieval, and I could have fun basing my papers on

---

[5]In the course of the years I have come to realize that no field is ever truly exhausted, and surely not North American and European history, vast as they are in range. One does not have to follow the momentary flow of research at any given time, and indeed it may be best not to if one wants to achieve originality and a profile. But not knowing such things, I was unduly impressed by the graduate student who told me how he and his peers were doing dissertations on ever smaller temporal and regional samples of the Wisconsin dairy industry, or by the number of books I was told were in existence on a single Italian city of the early modern period. I was perhaps, in view of my experiences with the literary disciplines, still too sensitive to the restriction of the field of study. But I was not wholly wrong, either. In North American or European history I could not have taken the social history of an entire important country in the generation of its refounding as a doctoral dissertation.

older German scholarship, such as that on Visigothic law. To
my horror, I liked Spanish best. It was somewhat accidental,
the result of two professors to whom I responded. One, a
Catalan, spoke in a dry and sardonic manner of Spanish
Golden Age literature, with no bombast, no undue hero
worship. I will never forget his remark on the pastoral
romance: that whereas at times the hero of the romance of
chivalry does nothing, relaxing from battle with a tepid bath,
the hero of the pastoral romance never does anything ever—
no hace nada nunca. And the other professor, though
supposed to be teaching literature, actually did little but
grammar; I am a grammatical animal, and I loved it. In both
cases the cast of mind of the professor and the way he
conceived his subject struck a chord in me. It began to be
clearer that you have to look at least as much at the
individual as at the discipline, that the discipline subsumes
only the shallowest of individuals.

Geography (of which only historical geography impinged
on me) had no impact. At that time and place it gave a good
impression of a dying discipline. Anthropology and political
science did have an impact, by no means a fully positive one,
but valuable in helping orient my future work. The subject
matter of anthropology, insofar as it was the indigenous
population of this hemisphere, was fascinating to me. To the
subject matter of political science I was profoundly in-
different. Anthropology seemed to be interested in everything
about a given people, to take the position that everything
affected everything else, not giving any one branch of life
primacy, whereas political science appeared to think that
something called policy was crucial, and that the policy was
the result of the conscious decisions of the policy makers and
how they and their constituents were organized. I never
believed that for a second; I thought also that to the extent
there was something to it it was very superficial, the product
of more subterranean processes I was more interested in.

What hit me about anthropology as an approximate equivalent to history (in those days, the early 60's, one didn't use
the word ethnohistory) was its apparent unevenness across
time. For the earliest periods there was archaeology, with a
set of refined techniques one could only admire, a kind of

detective work I felt great sympathy with and could wish to be involved in. And then skipping centuries there was ethnography, studies based on the closest kind of long-term observation of, experience and interaction with, a local group of people. Also admirable in its way. But what about the centuries in between? They seemed largely ignored; the ethnographers picked up with the archaeology as though there were no other context, and they were distinctly not interested in context anyway. The archaeologists did a bit of what I think is called upstreaming, using the ethnography as an interpretive context despite the temporal interval, which sometimes works but is often wrong. Anthropology in the New World seemed to have dedicated itself entirely to indigenous peoples, determined to ignore Europeans even when they were a huge influence on those very indigenous populations. And it seemed wedded to two techniques, the use of the spade and the field notebook or tape recorder, leaving the study of written texts to historians.

Even at that time, however, anthropology did not totally ignore the written word. Archaeology delivers some stunning information, but not always very much about human organization, concepts, and behavior. So the anthropologists working on Latin America became readers and students of the postconquest Spanish chronicles telling about the indigenous people in the sixteenth century and at second hand about earlier times as well. With my apparently inborn feeling for the subtlety and often factual unreliability of texts, and my experience with the New Criticism (even though I hated the very name of literary studies at that moment), I was shocked to see that the anthropologists were taking the Spanish chroniclers very straight, in the most naive and unacceptable fashion. I could see immediately that based on unanalytical, ethnocentric Spanish interpretations based in turn on partisan indigenous reports, they were projecting a far too strong, monolithic, almost modern European-style Inca empire.

The only sign of any sophistication among them was the work of John Rowe, who went through the whole corpus of Spanish chronicles asking which had the best version of a particular topic, but presuming that some version or other must be right. He also cared nothing for the time of writing in

relation to the time of the event, which as any textually-
oriented person knows is at least as crucial to text interpretation as layering is to archaeological digs; in fact, his great
favorite was the latest of the lot, Bernabé Cobo—a fine
historical mind but not a source for the Incas in the first half
of the sixteenth century. Passing right by the fact that the
Incas had no regular calendrical scheme going beyond one
year, Rowe established a sequence of Inca rulers and their
dates of rule, and decided what areas were conquered by
which, all illustrated in a map which seemed to appear in any
book on Peru that you might pick up. I didn't believe in a one
of the dates and was most skeptical even about the identity of
the rulers and their number and sequence.[6]

------

[6]Some years later I read with malicious enjoyment and a sense of
vindication a work of Åke Wedin (1966) using a detailed study of the
chronicle corpus to show with devastating force that it was impossible to determine the date of the death of the last undisputed
Inca ruler within five years, and that dating and naming the Inca
rulers before that was an idle enterprise.

During these years most of my anthropological reading had to do
with the Andes, but I also became aware of George Foster's *Culture
and Conquest* (1960). It struck me as the product of a first-rate mind.
At the same time it had, in a marked degree, the characteristics of
anthropological studies of a historical nature, especially the unintegrated handling of present-day ethnography and the study of
older documents, along with a lack of skepticism about the contents
of historical texts and the works of historians. Like the art historian
George Kubler (see pp. 361–62), Foster took Robert Ricard at face
value and allowed his work to replace independent investigation,
with serious consequences. Foster and Kubler are somehow much
alike in many ways.

At the time of writing *The Men of Cajamarca* (1972) I went back to
Foster's book as one of the few things deeply concerned and analytical about the early stages of the formation of specifically Spanish
American society and culture. I was encouraged and inspired to find
some of my own evolving ideas confirmed by a very different approach. I felt very much at home in that Foster, like me, entirely
ignored the superficial effect that any one particular policy maker
may have had. In some sense we were operating at the same level. It
has happened to me repeatedly that I am most deeply impressed and
affected by work reaching conclusions or using methods which I
myself have already at least partially anticipated.

I did and still do differ with some of Foster's conclusions, which I
think arose largely because he like others of that time, and especially

It seemed that historians should be the ones dealing with this aspect of the topic—the social, political, cultural world of the Incas and similar peoples in the late preconquest centuries and the long stretch from then on until the tape recorder picks up (for the anthropologists of that time used the texts *only* to make deductions about the preconquest period). Historians were in the right time slot and working with somewhat the right kind of sources, but they had conceived their topic as Europeans only, or at most European attitudes toward and treatment of indigenous inhabitants. From this concatenation of things a long-term plan was born, to see if something could be done about a more adequate textually based exploration of the indigenous world shortly before contact as well as in the centuries thereafter. I did not in fact first go in that direction; for good reason, I think.[7] That came many years later and in a different part of the hemisphere, and I carried out only a part of the program, but the basic notion had been fairly well formed in my mind since being exposed to those anthropology courses on the Incas.

With political science, which seemed to come in a package with economics and sociology, I quickly learned that my Alliance for Progress motivation had been all wet. I didn't really want to help some benighted people by analyzing their ills and making policy recommendations; the more I learned about these people the more I was simply interested in them. Both the indigenous sedentary peoples and the Spaniards in America seemed to have been highly developed long ago; maybe they had it behind them. It didn't seem to be up to us to

outside the circle of historians, had little awareness of the nature and importance of Spanish civil society in the Indies. (A brief pronouncement on these matters may be found in Lockhart 1972, pp. 116–17.)

[7]The decisive reason was that I would not have known where to begin, i.e., what documents to use for such a purpose. But even had I known, I would probably not have studied indigenous society immediately. What I was doing in those years was going one step beyond current Latin American historiography in subject matter and sources, and that led first to Spanish society. It was just as well, for postconquest indigenous society is nearly incomprehensible without an understanding of the Hispanic civil society that was in the final analysis the main cause, or at least catalyst, of change.

put them through our notion of development. I resisted the
pervasive concept of modernization, I shuddered at the distinction between traditional and modern. As far as I could see,
the Spaniards and other Europeans from their first arrival
had been acting much as we today would under the circumstances. And there were vast differences between the various
indigenous peoples and their reactions. Even a more apt dichotomy wouldn't have been right.[8]

But the social scientists were looking for more or less
objectively detectable and valid patterns not immediately
obvious to either observers or participants, the same thing
essentially that I wanted to do. So I accorded them respect
even though I didn't really like their enterprise, and most
especially the jargons in which they were beginning to clothe
it (it was in a political science class that I first heard the word
"coopt," which I intensely disliked immediately and still do,
although on occasion I find myself using it). Before long I
could and often did rattle off a series of objections to the
typical social science procedures. The latter were often very
closely tied to policy recommendations, particularly in relation to the United States; it was no way to get at the truth.
They were the products of a system with a strong government,
well developed bureaucracies and other hierarchies, formidable statistics, a large "middle class," and other attributes
all of which were projected in some fashion onto Latin
America, bad enough for the present but disastrous for the
past. The social scientists' methods implied sources that
didn't exist, but they didn't seem very worried about sources
anyway. They read newspapers, governmental reports, governmental macrostatistics, maybe carried out some inter-
views and questionnaire campaigns, and voilà.

I would have been happy enough simply to part company
with political-science-style social science at that point, and I
never later worked with anyone in those disciplines as I did
with some anthropologists and linguists, nor did works in

---

[8]Affected by the world history of William McNeill (1963), I began
to see that the dichotomy even where there was one was not (despite
McNeill's title, emphasizing the West) between western Europe and
the rest of the world but between Indians and non-Indians, to express it in the terms in which I thought in those days.

that style have any particular influence on me. They did on quite a few other Latin American historians, though, including some working in the early period, to which I was immediately drawn.[9] And so I felt I had to fend off social science encroachment. At the beginning of the conclusion to my first book *Spanish Peru* (1968), on Hispanic society in Peru in the conquest period, I put a rather impassioned statement saying that the process of reconstructing a whole complex social world was very different from proving a narrow preconceived hypothesis, and that the concluding chapters of studies of the two types look very different and have a different function.[10] In a historiographical article a few years later I wrote the following:

> The social sciences as we know them arose in industrialized countries in the late nineteenth and twentieth centuries; they often presuppose an easily available, trustworthy informational base, and strong, uniform institutions. Nothing could be further from the early Latin American situation. Ideas from the social sciences can serve to inspire interpreters as well as any others—but no better. Each new external element must be tested critically for applicability; otherwise we are in danger of repeating the mistake made with the anachronistic concepts the field has now overcome. Unsophisticated work on insufficient sources with the newest European methods and concepts is, as Rolando Mellafe has said, nothing but an amusing intellectual game.[11]

This had a certain impact on the field, and the passage was quoted ten years later by a social scientist (a cultural anthropologist specializing in the modern period, at least) as an

---

[9]John Johnson was the great channel of social science influence on Latin American history in the first phase. Johnson and a bevy of somewhat more theoretical writers had a profound impact on John Phelan, my mentor at Wisconsin, and though I respected his work and was not altogether untouched by it, I heartily resented that aspect as a simple imposition from the outside and distanced myself from it in all ways possible.

[10]This outcry, which may have seemed gratuitous and/or naive to those who were not cognizant of the background, was omitted from the second edition of 1994, but a note at that point goes far toward explaining my position both early and late.

[11]Lockhart 1972a (also Chapter 2 in this book, p. 77).

example of a reaction going on in the 70's not only in early Latin American history but among the anthropologists who by that time could be called ethnohistorians, notably John Murra, to reject premature application of models and methods based mainly on recent Europe and the US, not to orient their research within that framework, but develop interpretations closer to the situation as the local sources show it to have been.[12]

Meanwhile, working toward *Spanish Peru*, I wasn't motivated mainly by an antagonism to the social sciences or even thinking of them, just fascinated with the new things I was finding left and right. It was true I had more than half expected to find such things. The narrative-institutionalist version of the occupation of Spanish America by so-called "soldiers," officials, and priests, as set forth by the historians of the field up to that time, simply didn't make sense, nor did the stereotyped statements that passed for analysis of Spanish American society. Even in the chronicles and governmental reports that were at the root of that way of looking at things, at moments numbers of Spanish women, African slaves, and working artisans would pop out as elements in the mix.[13] So I was operating inside the early Latin American historiographical tradition, extending the subject matter and the sources by one step. When *Spanish Peru* came out, I was quite irritated that a couple of institutional-narrative historians saw the book as an unwelcome intrusion of the social sciences into the field.

The most obvious, weighty and bulky source was the notarial records. Their main characteristic was that they contained a huge amount of fresh, authentic information about individual people and transactions, ultralocal, ultracontemporaneous, in a highly fragmented form. I put the bits together by two main techniques, first following the lives of people who occurred several times, and second following key words— social and economic categories like *tratante*, which turned

---

[12]George A. Collier, in his introduction to Collier, Rosaldo, and Wirth 1982, pp. 1–2.

[13]See my 1972 remarks to this effect in Ch. 2 in this volume, p. 39. The methods of *Spanish Peru* are also discussed there (pp. 68–70).

out to be a usually illiterate, always badly connected petty trader in local goods, as opposed to the *mercader*, who dealt in imported goods and was part of a network. Adding up the numbers of people in categories sometimes led to tables, but they were arrived at in a very different way than those in works of sociology, were in a different context, and had a somewhat different kind of significance. Although I did sometimes use them in a rough way as random samples, their original meaning was simply to prove that a group existed. You say that Spaniards in America in the conquest period wouldn't work with their hands or attend to the economy? Here is a table of 824 working artisans, divided according to their trades, whom I found named in the records. I think anyone, either historian or social scientist, who was confronted with the kind of records and trying to find out the things that I was would have been likely to hit on much the same methods. Enrique Otte was doing something quite similar at the same time with the merchants of Seville, within a tradition of Spanish economic history which had had a much more institutional, statistical, macro approach until then.[14]

But I did do some things others didn't, even a good many of those who came after me, and it had to do mainly with this textual sensitivity that I seem to have had from an early age, honed in the army in Germany, and developed further in my exposure to the literary studies that I now detested. The Spaniards of the sixteenth century were extraordinarily aware of the nuances of names and titles. They used them with the greatest subtlety and expressive significance, and they hit the roof when anyone used them wrong or in an unexpected way.

When I came along, an operating generalization was that Spanish peninsular social distinctions quickly disappeared among Spaniards in America, that everyone was called *don*. Historians (and literary scholars) had been through reams of texts and documentary material without ever challenging that dictum. But when I started reading the documents,

---

[14]Aside from a myriad of articles from the early 60's forward, see Otte's *Las perlas del Caribe: Nueva Cádiz de Cubagua.* (1977), and *Sevilla y sus mercaderes a fines de la Edad Media* (1996).

whether they be notarial, trial records, reports, or even chronicles, I found that hardly anyone was called "don." The tiny minority who were so denominated *always* bore the title; don Alvaro de Toledo was not by any means to be confused with Alvaro de Toledo. My first intimation of the true nature of the situation was the discovery that don Martín Pizarro, the indigenous interpreter as it later turned out, was not the same person as Martín Pizarro the plebeian first conqueror and often regidor of the cabildo of Lima. (The decisive clue was that don Martín could sign part of his name, while plain Martín produced only empty rubrics.) The title was used only by those with close connections to the highest nobility of Spain or by people who had it by virtue of holding very high office. Women used the *doña* rather more liberally, as they did in Spain itself, but usage was still invariable with a particular person. I found only half a dozen irregularities in the use of don and doña in all of Peru in the conquest generation. Don and doña were such a crucial part of a name that indexes of notarial volumes, which were organized by first name, put all the dons and doñas under *D*. The breakdown of social distinctions had been vastly exaggerated.

It can be harder to recognize that something is missing altogether, but a textually oriented researcher is attuned to such things. I was taught that the Indies were occupied by soldiers and missionaries. But I soon noticed that my notarial records, even those made in the very course of the conquest campaigns, never mentioned the word *soldado*. It turned out to be lacking in the entire archival record. What's more, when I turned to reading chronicles seriously, I found that those written contemporaneously with the events also lacked it entirely. The hundreds of scholars who must have read those texts had never noticed, but went right ahead mentally translating Spaniard, Christian, footman, horseman, and the like into their stereotyped notion of soldier.[15] This terminological disparity led me to further research showing that these people had little or no formal military training or experience and few of the other attributes

---

[15]The use of *soldado* picked up in later years. See Lockhart 1994, p. 155.

associated with the term soldier, but were more like a type of immigrant we are very familiar with from United States history.[16] Nor did *misionero* ever surface, in any kind of source. The consequences here are more subtle, and I won't go into them. I only repeat that important aspects of my books *Spanish Peru* and *The Men of Cajamarca* were made possible by a kind of philology not unrelated to what has sometimes been seen in literary studies and allied sorts of cultural history.

While I was in Peru doing research, anthropology and anthropologists didn't affect my work very much. I still didn't know much about what John Murra was doing, but I heard of him. I met Tom Zuidema, who was reading a lot of the same chronicles I was for a very different purpose. Once to make conversation and to show how little I believed in the Rowe view of the Inca empire, I told him that to the Spaniards the Inca emperor was just one more cacique. He replied that they were right—that is (though he did not explain then and there), that the Inca was not a European monarch but a figure thrown up by the workings of a numerical rotational system in a multiethnic setting. He also didn't believe in Rowe's chronology, which warmed my heart. Of course, it soon turned out that he cared quite little for chronology of any kind.

The next phase of my career brought me into closer contact with, actual active cooperation with some scholars in other disciplines. After my Peruvian work I directed my attention to Mexico, looking for balance and a broader overall base, also meaning to come forward in time chronologically. To me the entity was always the early Latin American field (I suppose in effect Spanish American mainly), not some particular country; I viewed and view the countries within the field much as a United States historian might view the states. At the same time I wanted to broaden my work in another way, ethnically, and with each year that aspect of it became more important to me, perhaps in line with the general climate of the time. When I was on my *Spanish Peru/Men of Cajamarca* research trip in 1964/65, the most meaningful members of my

---

[16]As shown in some detail in the first part of my *The Men of Cajamarca* (1972).

cohort were Fred Bowser, working on Africans in Peru, and Karen Spalding, working on indigenous Andeans. From the first moment I was interested in everybody, in the whole conglomeration of human beings in the country, but with my methods I was committed to those who appeared directly in the documentation, not to those who were merely talked about at a distance. My documentation—that is, nearly everything written down in Peru to 1560—provided direct views of non-Spanish European foreigners, Spanish women, some early mestizos, Africans, slaves and servants from Nicaragua, and a stratum of Andeans who got caught up in Spanish society as servants, employees, and intermediaries, but it distinctly did not extend to the larger indigenous population living away from Spanish centers, seen only in stereotyped remarks, synthesizing reports, and histories.

As I became more focused on somehow studying the indigenous population in a style comparable to that of my studies of Hispanic society, I realized that it could be done only with access to sources created by the people themselves, in their own language, revealing their outlook, their rhetoric, their genres of expression, the intimacies of their lives, above all their categories. Looking back to Peru, I saw nothing like that on the horizon, no known documentation in Quechua by Andeans (since then some has appeared). John Murra had opened up the visitas, Spanish inspections of Andean localities in the sixteenth century, containing information that made the Inca area look much more variegated, with more local autonomy, tradition, and fragmentation than in the Rowe picture, just as I had always imagined. But the materials were census-like, done by Spaniards in Spanish (though some key terms were sometimes left in indigenous languages).

In Mexico, however, Nahuatl had been written from an early time, and there was a tradition of studying it. The best-known texts were done under Spanish auspices and mainly looked back to preconquest times, but they had implications of a broader and more contemporaneous document production. I asked a student of mine, David Szewczyk, who was doing research in Mexico, to see if there was such a thing as Nahuatl notarial records and the like and send me copies of a few examples if possible. He did a tremendous job. Mundane Nahuatl records were reported to exist in the Archivo General de la Nación in large quantities, though scattered and hard to put your finger on. David sent me an important cache concerning Coyoacan and a testament from Tlaxcala, a corpus which later became the core of the collection *Beyond the Codices*. So I was in business.

The next thing was to learn Nahuatl; I didn't know a word of any indigenous language. Though some of the documents were accompanied by Spanish translations done at the time or not long after, at first I couldn't figure out any correspondence at all between the text and the translation. I got the great sixteenth-century dictionary of fray Alonso de Molina, but in Nahuatl the roots of the words are wrapped in multitudinous prefixes and suffixes, and I was unable to recognize them. A grammar and anthology by Angel María Garibay,[17] a Mexican literary-historical scholar specializing in classical Nahuatl, did help me a good deal, but I still couldn't handle the texts. Garibay, his famous student Miguel León-Portilla, and some associated scholars in Mexico formed an interesting group with much potential, operating in an almost nondisciplinary fashion somewhere in the area of literature, history, and anthropology. The problems from my point of view were that they were working with only the earliest and most formal texts, with an eye to the precontact period; that they were acting in a spirit of generous patriotism and nationalism, and also Europeanizing their subjects; and that they weren't really interested in close textual analysis, though León-Portilla did go into certain Nahua concepts embodied in special words.[18]

I clearly needed help and company. Who knew Indian languages in this country? Anthropologists and linguists. Who knew them in any time depth, from written texts? Almost no one. The main method of both groups, which sometimes partially merge, is to work with informants, present-

---

[17]*Llave del náhuatl* (1970).

[18]*La filosofía náhuatl* (1956) and many later writings in a similar vein. But see also León-Portilla 1983, a substantial analysis of genres of written expression.

day native speakers. I did take an informal beginning class in classical Nahuatl from a UCLA linguist, William Bright. The course was inherited from a Chicago linguist who had it from the historian/anthropologist/poet/grammarian Charles Barlow, who had developed it in Mexico. It helped a great deal in getting a grasp of some basic vocabulary and morphology. When I tried taking one of my texts to Bright, though, it proved somewhat beyond his ken; no doubt he could have made large progress if he had studied it full time, but after all he had things of his own to do.

It turned out to my good fortune that some anthropologists, Arthur Anderson and Charles Dibble, had done massive translation of an important early formal Nahuatl text, Sahagún's Florentine Codex, and one of them, Anderson, lived within reach of Los Angeles. William Bright himself recommended that I seek him out. I contacted him, he was interested in opening up postconquest mundane texts, and we started working on the ones my student David Szewczyk had sent, plus some others that turned out to be in the UCLA special collections. Frances Berdan, an anthropologist interested especially in the economy of early Mesoamerica, had already been working with me, trying to crack the Tlaxcalan will that Szewczyk had sent. She was, like me, a neophyte in Nahuatl, so we were in the same boat, but in something apparently so forbidding and unexplored, companionship was important. The three of us, Anderson, Berdan, and myself, went gradually from a study group to a translation team.

Now what I was after was not anthropological or linguistic concepts and methods; for better or worse, I had a conceptual framework and I had methods. I wanted help in understanding the documents. I was a bit surprised at first to find that our texts were causing my distinguished collaborator Arthur a certain amount of difficulty. Of course he got most of the meaning and was a tremendous, indispensable help; but there was a large difference of genre, vocabulary, and idiom between the classical texts and these working documents. Again to my surprise, I was able to be of some help myself from the beginning. The dominant genre was the testament, changed in some respects from the Spanish form, but still closely modeled on it, and I knew the testament form backwards. I was also attuned to a type of special Spanish vocabulary that appeared in strange forms in the texts. And then there were the parts that none of us could understand, belonging to a living, changing practice that we had to grasp from the context or sometimes from Spanish translations of the time (though before long we learned we couldn't trust the translations implicitly, nor did they always render everything, by a long shot). After a year or two we had served our apprenticeship, and though still nearly beginners in this kind of thing, published a collection of samples from the documentation which had a certain impact and were to serve me as important source material in future work.[19]

There was nothing particularly disciplinary about what we had done. Arthur and Charles had distanced themselves from the archaeologists and the ethnographers and had, in the classic manner of philology in any of the humanities, set about filling that temporal gap that I too had noticed by concentrating on texts in indigenous languages. I think it may be true, and surely it is true in my vicinity, that those prepared to get into interdisciplinary work are often quite marginal in their own disciplines, or to put another light on it, are mavericks or different, perhaps pioneers; it's not just a matter of trading around the orthodoxies of two or more disciplines.

I continued to do translation projects with Anderson and Berdan for a while, but my large long-term enterprise, which became *The Nahuas After the Conquest* (1992), was separate. It essentially involved an adaptation of *Spanish Peru* methodology to a new topic. Here, although there ended up being plenty of documents, you didn't find many dense concentrations for particular localities or particular times, so I was more or less forced to do what I wanted to do anyway, cover the whole area where Nahuatl was spoken during the whole time that it was written. *Spanish Peru* methodology, as we saw, involved two main ingredients, career pattern work, i.e., sets of parallel lives known in considerable detail as the basis of structural analysis and generalization, and philology centering on key words and categories in the texts. In Nahuatl texts, you only rarely caught the same individual a second

---

[19]Anderson, Berdan, and Lockhart, *Beyond the Codices* (1976).

time and even if you did, you weren't sure, because everyone was named Juan Francisco or María Juana. Following words, concepts, practices, genres directly rather than people as the bearers of them was pretty much dictated. And also the language varied greatly from place to place and over time. You couldn't possibly ignore it, because you had to struggle simply to understand. But it was immediately obvious that this was the stuff of cultural analysis, a precipitation of cultural evolution. I was pushed straight into a classic kind of philology, very close analysis of a single document, even publication of a document with comment, something I would hardly have thought of when I was working with Spanish, which I did by the ream, because it was so uniform in vocabulary and conventions.[20]

And also I was getting fairly close to linguistics, at least the way linguistics used to be. Spanish words were showing up in my sources in the strangest forms; usually I would eventually figure them out, but felt ill equipped to understand the patterns in the distortions. I began studying and later collaborating in publications with a linguist, Frances Karttunen. She didn't know any Nahuatl to begin with, though she had worked with rare languages and learned fast. She taught me some very basic phonology and something of what to expect in language contact situations, which is that the recipient language borrows words equating any sound it lacks with the closest sound it does have. When you learn about voiced and unvoiced obstruents, point of articulation, and the like, and know that Nahuatl had no voiced obstruents, it is obvious, expectable, inevitable that for the Spanish voiced dental obstruent *d* it will substitute the unvoiced dental obstruent *t*, that for "don Pedro" you will get "ton Petlo" or "Petolo." And on and on; all the substitution was boringly normal. That in itself was not trivial; interactions between Spaniards and Nahuas were not sui generis, but fit right into the spectrum of interaction between peoples worldwide and over the millenia.

---

[20]Lockhart 1991a contains a somewhat fuller discussion. On reflection, I realize that Lockhart and Otte, *Letters and People* (1976) consists mainly of translated Spanish documents with commentary, but the analysis is far less technical and textual than with the things of my Nahuatl phase, and the work is not meant as primary research.

Working together we developed a description of the phenomena we were finding in phonology, lexicon, and to a certain extent syntax that I probably could not have managed, and certainly not expressed as clearly, without some exposure to professional linguistics. Much of the working out of the picture over the centuries, however, got its impetus from me as the historian, the person concerned with chronology or at least the pattern in change over time. Linguistics, having been eminently historical in the nineteenth century, had become the opposite, making much of the primacy of synchronic over diachronic analysis. So it was at my initiative, I believe, that we began putting the date of attestation on the entries in our word lists and keeping track of when certain sorts of phenomena first appeared. In this way a three-stage evolution emerged: first a generation of virtually no change in the language, second a hundred years of massive noun borrowing, and third the acceptance of verbs and particles, phonological and syntactic change, the translation of idioms, the whole range of phenomena often associated with massive bilingualism.[21] The entire movement seemed to be driven by increasing contact between the two populations, though that was simply a deduction; no one at the time had talked about it. No one had talked about or apparently even been aware of the whole huge and hugely significant evolution. We published a volume in a linguistic monograph series with our findings.[22] On my own I kept going with the three-stage process, finding it again in every branch of human interest: to simplify, a generation of little structural change, a hundred years of corporate change, and then change at the level of the individual, all driven by

---

[21]See the fuller discussion in Chapter 8 of this volume.

[22]Frances Karttunen and James Lockhart, *Nahuatl in the Middle Years* (1976). In retrospect I have sometimes been amazed at how quickly the introduction to older mundane Nahuatl went and some of the basic methods and findings took shape. I began to look about for a way to attack Nahuatl seriously in 1972. It was in 1973, I believe, that I began to work with Anderson and Berdan, and at the same time with Karttunen. In 1976 both *Beyond the Codices* and *Nahuatl in the Middle Years* appeared. *Beyond the Codices* was actually completed first and was originally expected out in late 1975. I blush at some of the translations in it, but it mainly did the job, and in *Nahuatl in the Middle Years* few signs of the novitiate remained.

the progressively closer contact and interpenetration of Nahuas and Spaniards. This process is at the core of my book *The Nahuas*.

Something on the order of linguistic work, then, was essential to the kind of philological ethnohistory that I have developed. Some technical linguistic terms and some lore common among professional linguists were important. But you mustn't imagine that there was any substantial contact between me and linguistics as done by the central figures in the most prestigious linguistics departments in this country. Those people are devoted to a kind of abstract analysis, mainly syntactic, that aims at language universals and tends to look down on the study of any individual language, especially the Indian languages that used to be in linguistics departments because there was no other place for them. A famous MIT linguist from time to time descends on the UCLA department and excoriates those few who still have anything to do with cataloguing and analyzing rare indigenous languages.

I couldn't help finding out a little bit about this stuff, and my reaction was in the general area of repugnance and soon avoidance. I'm not alone; when I was at the Institute for Advanced Study one year, discussing parallel change in culture and language with the anthropologist Clifford Geertz, I mentioned professional linguistics, and he said "Oh, the linguists. They're useless." Many of the mainline linguists believe that rules actually cause mental and behavioral phenomena. The only way I can understand a rule is as an attempted explanation or generalization, often very very good but never perfect, concerning a certain phenomenon that exists independently of it. And though claims of universality are made, as long as I stuck with it it seemed to me that generalizations were being made overwhelmingly on the basis of English. *The* example is the copula, i.e., the verb "to be" in an equative sense, which seems to be taken to be part of the universal human mental and linguistic equipment. Yet I was from an early time convinced that it didn't exist in Nahuatl.[23]

---

[23]See the discussion of this matter in the appendix to Chapter 10, pp. 301–3, in this volume.

I gradually came to believe it didn't in Maya or Quechua either (Quechua may come a little closer than the others). The modern European languages have it, but if you go back only as far as Latin and Greek it begins to become problematic. I could never convince my linguist collaborator, who stayed true to her origins, but over time my position on the copula (hardly mentioned in public) got a lot of support from people studying the language, entirely independently of me and at first mainly of one another.

J. Richard Andrews wrote a large grammar in which it is seen that the obligatory connection of a subject prefix with a noun is the way Nahuatl does equation.[24] Andrews has lived his life in Spanish departments. He got interested in the languages of the people the Spaniards encountered, like the Arabs or the Nahuas; he started with Nahuatl with William Bright, the same UCLA linguist whose course helped me. He became one could say a linguist, at least a grammarian, but fully outside linguistics departments and the discipline proper. The Frenchman Michel Launey also wrote a grammar taking the same position.[25] He has become a theoretical linguist specializing in Nahuatl, and I don't know his origins quite as well, but he apparently came out of literary study and anthropology. The Dane Una Canger also takes the same position; she would always have called herself a linguist, but she works in a sociology department and is somewhat estranged from American professional linguistics.[26] All of these people know one another and read one another's work, and I guess I should be included.

My belief is that a group like this, miscellaneous in terms of disciplinary origin, can be the germ of real innovation in linguistics, or possibly of the creation or recreation of a different kind of linguistics, either as a discipline in itself or as a well defined subfield in anthropology, history, and language departments. It can do so because it is over the disciplinary border, safe from being forced back into orthodoxy

---

[24]Andrews 1975.

[25]Launey 1979.

[26]See Canger 1980 for a major example of her work, though it does not treat this particular question.

by the linguistics-department linguists, much as those of us who are in this country can say what we really think about the legend of the Virgin of Guadalupe, without fear of the repercussions that often strike those who speak out in Mexico.

Going back to *The Nahuas*, although I did not collaborate actively with any anthropologists at this time, the work of some of them came in by way of source or precedent, much as previous historical work might have been expected to. Pedro Carrasco, based in both Mexico and the United States, had hit upon a set of detailed local censuses from the Cuernavaca region, from the late 1530's into the early 1540's apparently, written in Nahuatl by native speakers, the earliest large-scale Nahuatl texts known.[27] Carrasco was not a deep student of the language, but he used a helper, Luis Reyes, who knew it as well as anyone. He was primarily analyzing the size and organization of households and communities, and the operation of tribute, with quantitative methods. His work gave me an overview quickly and was most helpful, although I soon went over to a more detailed philological analysis of the texts.[28]

The Mexican scholar Fernando Horcasitas collected all the Nahuatl plays he could find, pretty much exclusively Christian religious in type, transcribed and translated them, and published a volume that aided me immensely, *El teatro ná-huatl*.[29] It was wonderful material for cultural and intellectual history.

In neither case was it of any particular importance to me that the scholars concerned were in anthropology, nor did they really function as anthropologists per se in the work I was interested in. Carrasco, it is true, had a Marxist orientation common in the main Mexican school of anthropology, but that didn't affect me, and even more importantly, it hardly affected the work except in certain interpretive paragraphs,

---

[27]For the most essential publications see the items listed under Carrasco's name in the bibliography of Lockhart 1992.

[28]I also made use of the philological publication of Eike Hinz referred to in n. 30. S. L. Cline has since published a volume of the census with the full treatment: transcription, translation, and extensive commentary on substance and language (Cline 1993).

[29]Horcasitas 1974.

the rest being straightforward statistical aggregation and
disaggregation that could be done in the name of any of
various social sciences or history. Horcasitas was mainly the
collector and translator, a person interested in resuscitating
any form of Nahua culture that came into his view; analysis
of the plays was minimal, and what there was was of a more
or less literary historical type. I suppose I should include Luis
Reyes here; he has been associated with some anthropologists
but is hardly an anthropologist. He is a native Nahuatl
speaker who became a document cataloguer and then did some
of the best translations of older Nahuatl texts that exist, and I
have duly used them.

I shouldn't forget the Germans. Günter Zimmermann and
his successor Eike Hinz, at Hamburg, working within the
broad older school of German anthropology, are important as
philologists, publishing texts that were very valuable to me.
Zimmermann put out a transcription, untranslated and with
no apparatus beyond some notes, of the work of the early
seventeenth-century annalist Chimalpahin; I used it for a
hundred purposes and refer to it constantly in *The Nahuas*.[30]

So though I was not being conceptually and methodolog-
ically nourished by the anthropologists, their work, not that
of historians, provided me with precedents and sources, some
kind of context, even though I was an early Latin American
historian operating quite fully within the traditions of that
field. I felt that these anthropologists—not necessarily anthropologists in general—were at least interested in many of
the same things I was. The big exception in history was the
work of Charles Gibson, which led straight into mine, insti-
tutionally oriented work preceding more social and cultural
work as it so often has in our field.[31]

To get back to the anthropologists, and going beyond the
type I have just been talking about, who in different ways were
working with postconquest written texts in the name of
ethnohistory, the writings of Mesoamerican anthropologists
dealing with the preconquest period come to my attention to

---

[30]Chimalpahin 1963–65. From Hinz the main item is Hinz et al.
1983.
[31]See Lockhart 1991a.

some extent. Wonderful progress has been made in deciphering Mayan hieroglyphics, which are often historical/genealogical, as I had imagined they would be, and show normal warfare and dynastic politics, rather than the idealized peaceful and intellectual Maya. What rather disturbs me is the interpretation of the new information. Those most involved do have the sophistication not to take the statements about people and battles as objective fact. But elite planning and manipulation, which was definitely a factor, is taken for the whole explanation. The strong ethnic feelings and local ethnic states of which the elites were only a manifestation are virtually ignored; there is little awareness of a local ethnic group or state as the determining entity. The visual artifacts are dealt with as a complete communication system, when in fact they were only one part of a unified two-track system in which oral presentation was at least equally essential. I like to think that the work I and my students and former students have been doing can have some impact here, but after all, there's not only the disciplinary boundary, but the fact that any alphabetic document that is ever going to be found will be written after the conquest. The precontact implications are clear enough to us, but the work is bound to be in the first instance about the postcontact state of things.

And yet maybe there will be some impact. Not long ago I got a letter from two anthropologists who basically do Meso-american archaeology, accompanied by an article they have written. They have absorbed my notion of cellular or modular organization as laid out in *The Nahuas* and are trying to use it instead of what has been the dominant interpretation among anthropologists, which sees the regional entities in terms of urbanization and "central place." I am delighted; I have innerly opposed those notions for a long time. A Nahua sociopolitical entity is a set of rotating independent constituent ethnic parts. There isn't even a word for city as opposed to the whole entity, and Nahuatl hardly could be said to have a word meaning center. If this kind of thing can cross the barrier, perhaps there's hope that I can get through to the field of anthropology about something equally important. When anthropologists dealing with the preconquest speak of the state, they mean the empire; smaller entities they see as chiefdoms, something very different. But to me the local entities were states; they had all the structures and mechanisms of the empires and were much less ephemeral; an empire was just a situation in which one of them became dominant for a while.

The linguists are generally more impervious than the anthropologists. Even so, cooperation and influence back and forth are not out of the question.[32]

Art history has not been as central and close to me as anthropology and linguistics, but connections exist. I was introduced to the work of George Kubler while I was a graduate student, then studied it seriously when I began to teach, in the late 60's. Kubler aroused a sense of recognition in me, the spectacle of a person doing something truly first-rate, large-scale, and original in a way I could wish for myself, that was all too rare in the early stages of my study of the Latin American field, though I did feel it sooner or later with Woodrow Borah, Charles Gibson, Mario Góngora, and in some ways with C.H. Haring, Lewis Hanke, Raúl Porras Barrenechea, Robert Ricard, and François Chevalier.[33] I detected something

---

[32]Pamela Munro, in linguistics at UCLA, Kevin Terraciano, in history there, and myself are contemplating a small project comparing the manner of borrowing Spanish verbs in Zapotec, Mixtec, and Nahuatl against the background of hundreds of years of language contact and the grammars of the three languages concerned.

[33]Another of these figures was Philip Curtin, at the University of Wisconsin when I was a graduate student there, because of his way of taking an entire field, reevaluating and reorganizing it from scratch, which was just what I wanted to do. Although his area was Africa, which I increasingly saw as not a model for Latin America, and his interest was less in internal social and cultural analysis than mine was (and is), so that there was little substantive influence, he was my main inspiration at Wisconsin. He reinforced my belief that one can be very sure of one's direction and conclusions, applying the best of one's intelligence in a unified fashion to every aspect of the history business, from pencils and tape recorders to the trajectories of universal human evolution, without resorting to obscurities and pretentious words. He also happened to be from northern West Virginia, as my family is, and made me aware that that sort of origin, which amounts to being a sort of Mark Twain nineteenth-century American, like being Canadian, or Jewish American, can let one understand scholarly and other developments in this country from the inside and at the same time retain a perspective on them that most people seem to lack, as though one were also an outsider.

familiar in Kubler that I didn't recognize at first, then later decided it was some affinity with or influence on Gibson, who proved to have been his student across the disciplines. Here was someone who could be meticulous, methodical, indefatigable, and at the same time sharp and imaginative.[34] He was a model for interdisciplinary work, braving his way into general Latin American history, Spanish urbanization, and even demography. But as I got to know both Kubler and our own field better, I realized that whereas in his direct line of research he examined everything with an entirely open and critical mind, challenging any received tradition before confirming or demolishing it and building past it, in fields other than art history he tended to abandon his sophistication, or rather he applied it to the findings of others as a given without ever questioning them. In particular, and quite centrally, he swallowed the work of Robert Ricard whole, including Ricard's conception of the mendicant friars as the only agent for the introduction of anything remotely cultural to New Spain; this view extended even to his treatment of Spanish civil urbanization, rendering it unacceptable as a whole no matter how many interesting details it might contain. Yet if one just excised the Ricard and concentrated on what Kubler had done for himself from direct evidence, much was left that was congruent on the one hand with the social history movement in early Latin American history starting in the late 60's and on the other with the philological ethnohistory coming even later, adding a valuable dimension.

The same was true of Kubler's successor John McAndrew and his work on open chapels in the Mexican monastery complexes (though he retained or even heightened the Ricardian emphasis).[35] McAndrew was somehow lesser, but his focus

---

[34]Gibson was just the same, at least as original if not more so, but he didn't *seem* superficially to have the sparkle often found in Kubler. The Kubler who affected me was the one who worked on postconquest Mexican architecture and related topics (above all in Kubler 1948), not the one who went on to extensive investigation of preconquest art which is possibly better known to the world at large, but which I am not entirely convinced had all the qualities of his earlier work.

[35]McAndrew 1964.

on a more specific topic brought out new things, and after all he had some of the same qualities as Kubler. Long before I developed my notion of the pervasiveness of cellular organization in the Nahua world, McAndrew in a notable paragraph had pinpointed and described it in indigenous architectural ornamentation.[36] Donald Robertson had done something similar with indigenous manuscript painting techniques.[37] These examples could then be added without further ado to my display of variants of cellular organization in *The Nahuas*.

In a third generation, Jeanette Peterson, who had begun studying with McAndrew, did a detailed study of the frescoes in the cloister of the Augustinian establishment of Malinalco. It served me, although not so conceived by her, as a perfect example for *The Nahuas* of Stage 2 in the arts.[38] By the time she did it, there had been considerable contact between us, for she took a field in early Latin American history with me and studied Nahuatl quite seriously for a while before the logistics of long-distance commuting made it impossible. Not only did I have a certain influence (not basic, I believe) on her work, but as it developed it opened my eyes to things I had not seen before. I remember that during one of her presentations to an informal group of anthropological enthusiasts she commented on the fact that in the frescoes when the general Mesoamerican speech scroll referred specifically to song, a series of lines across it divided it into compartments. Thinking immediately of my discovery, part of my exploration of cellular organization, that the archetypal song was in eight verses, I hazarded the prediction that there would be eight of the compartments. Later counting proved the prediction true— in the main, just as with the songs.

Since Peterson, a steady stream of graduate students in art history[39] has joined the ongoing informal UCLA Nahuatl seminar,[40] often to the point of outnumbering the history

---

[36]The passage is in McAndrew 1964, p. 199. It was first brought to my attention by Frances Karttunen.

[37]Robertson 1959.

[38]The version that I used was Peterson's doctoral dissertation (1985). A book based on it has since been published (1993).

[39]Sent by their sympathetic mentor Cecelia Klein.

[40]Now led by Kevin Terraciano, Lisa Sousa, and Stafford Poole.

students. One outstanding performer among them was Dana Leibsohn, who did a dissertation on the Historia Tolteca-Chichimeca beginning what must surely become a tradition of giving the alphabetic text (in Nahuatl) and the pictorial component equal weight in the study of such documents.[41] Others are coming in her wake, still operating within the tradition of art history but noticeablely affected by philological ethnohistory. I have wondered why they seem to do so well with Nahuatl and with the approach. Part of it, at least, is that unlike many students in history and the social sciences, they are open to subject matter that is exotic, removed from them in time and place. They are also sensitive or observant and meticulous. I have seen in them relatively little of what one might expect in view of the fact that art history overall has become a haven for elaborate vacuous terminology second only to comparative literature.

I shouldn't forget to mention the person who I have often felt was the closest collaborator I ever had—Horacio Carochi, the Italian-born Jesuit who worked in Mexico City in the first half of the seventeenth century and in 1645 published the best grammar of Nahuatl there has ever been or perhaps ever will be.[42] All the other instruction in Nahuatl I had was just on the way to him, and from then on it was a matter of working with texts and looking about in Carochi for help in understanding anything I found puzzling. The answer was often there, though sometimes located after I had figured it out for myself. The whole school of grammarians mentioned earlier is based on him, the result of the rediscovery and close examination of his work. It is true we have added some things, but it is as though he were our strict contemporary, much more so than say Angel María Garibay, who flourished from the 1940's into the 1960's. Carochi was very much a Jesuit and trained in a Latinate school of grammar, but neither of those things seem to define him; he was simply a lucid intelligence opening up the patterns of the Nahuatl language, fascinated with it, not approving or disapproving. One of my current projects is an edition of Carochi with voluminous commentary. I guess I wouldn't call it history exactly, but it's by no means extra-

---

[41]Leibsohn 1993.   [42]Carochi 1983.

neous to my more specifically historical work.

Recently, with two collaborators—Stafford Poole, a historian who has written a well known book on the Guadalupe legend, and Lisa Sousa, a former doctoral student of mine—I have been doing an edition, including transcription, translation, and extended commentary, of the version of the Guadalupe story published in Nahuatl in 1649 by bachiller Luis Laso de la Vega, the priest in charge of the Guadalupe chapel.[43] By very close analysis of the language, its morphology, grammar, idiom, affinity with Spanish, and its relation to other published texts, involving the discovery of several subtle but distinct language errors, we were able to come close to establishing that this text, often thought to have been written by a Nahua far back in the sixteenth century or at least the product of Nahua oral tradition, was mainly composed by Laso de la Vega himself, taking most of his material from a book published the previous year in Spanish by his friend the priest Miguel Sánchez. As far as I am concerned this work of ours is simply history, maybe cultural history, and all the people doing it are history-department historians. But when it came to an outside reader, they sent it to an anthropologist; she said the translation was fine, the analysis telling, but it was mainly linguistics. Linguistics-department linguists would find that notion a source of considerable mirth.

So by now I've worked myself into a position where anthropologists tend to think what I do is linguistics and linguists tend to think what I do is anthropology; historians wonder. Actually, I mustn't exaggerate about historians. As I think is quite clear by now, the work of myself and my circle comes out of the specifically early Spanish American historical tradition and remains part of it. One of our main present concerns is to tie studies of indigenous people and Europeans in Latin America more closely together, as they were in real life—that is, to reunite the early Latin American historical field.[44]

---

[43]Sousa, Poole, and Lockhart 1998.

[44]Rebecca Horn's *Postconquest Coyoacan: Nahua-Spanish Relations in Central Mexico, 1519–1650* (1997) is a large step in this

With any luck, I think I might have been considered part of the fraternity even if there weren't such good reason. One of the most real meanings of the discipline groups is that they form reading circles. If you have a PhD in Latin American history and are hired in a history department, other people of that description will take at least a look at what you write no matter what it is. The same happens with anthropologists and linguists. Few people indeed ever really cross the border; I think in our field the anthropologist John Chance may have.

Aside from being boxes for jobs, salaries, and readerships, I consider the disciplines to be quite superficial phenomena. I don't know when the word discipline even first became part of my vocabulary, that is, other than as in parental discipline, or a sense of discipline. I think not until graduate school. Before that I believe I just said field, which may put it in a better light. Of course we usually speak of fields within a discipline, and indeed, I begin to pick up a sense of reality more at the level of the discipline-internal field. The evolutions of the early field and the modern field (nineteenth and twentieth centuries) in Latin American history are quite separate, and their crossdisciplinary affinities are very distinct. I see much of the significance in what you could call schools or movements inside the fields, with their own coherence and profile, their own affinities.

What I have been doing with the second half of my career, a kind of activity in which several people have joined me, I call a New Philology. It centers on indigenous-language texts, though including any other likely source of information as well, and combines career pattern research where possible with a philology not unlike that of the classicists (though equipped with some new techniques such as an awareness of things like the three stages and blessed with more direct sources), seeking patterns in the language and in behavior across a very broad spectrum. The scope coincides in ways with those of anthropology and linguistics but in a somewhat different context. I am happy to call it history, because

direction. Matthew Restall has been at work on projects on early Yucatan which would bring Spaniards, people of African descent, and the Maya into a single framework of research and interpretation.

history is the broadest and most flexible of the "disciplines," and I hardly know where else it could be. I tend to view history, like philosophy, as the mother of other disciplines; it is more likely to engender new ones than merely to need to run to others for enlightenment. Scholars whose interests and expertise touch without being identical can definitely help each other; the cooperation between them I tend to call nondisciplinary rather than crossdisciplinary, for disciplinary rigidities, orthodoxies, and preconceptions are often the greatest hurdle.

Appendix: Details
on the Chapters

THE FIRST chapter, "Encomienda and Hacienda,"[1] is well enough known not to need another reprinting. Yet I wished to accompany it with an epilogue I drafted a few years ago, sketching out the development of my thinking on the topic in the time since the article was first written.

A form of Chapter 2, "The Social History of Early Latin America," is also not unknown.[2] No sooner was it published in 1972, however, than I began using it as the point of departure for graduate historiography courses, adding notes and removing some of the more ephemeral material as the years went by. Finally in 1989 I reworked the piece quite thoroughly and added an epilogue as of that date, already thinking of some sort of publication, which has not eventuated until now.

Chapter 3 is to a large extent the introduction that *Letters and People of the Spanish Indies* (Lockhart and Otte 1976) never had.[3] It also points to aspects of transatlantic unity at

---

[1] Originally published with its present title in *Hispanic American Historical Review*, 49 (1969): 411–29.

[2] Originally published as "The Social History of Colonial Spanish America: Evolution and Potential," *Latin American Research Review*, 7 (1972): 6–45. "Spanish" rather than "Latin" was a last-minute editorial error, and I have always used "Latin" in my own references to the piece. I did at that time voluntarily use the term "colonial." As the years went by, I noticed that many people were giving the word a connotation foreign to me, and as I began to consider that the trees, the rivers, and even the language and customs of the people of that time were not particularly colonial, but simply what they were—indigenous or Iberian or some convergence or mixture, staying the same, adapting, evolving, in a highly autonomous way, leading gradually to what they are today—I began to rebel against the term itself, and I use it as little as possible. "Early," as employed by the more responsible among United States historians, is a far better category, implying the importance that attaches to a beginning and a series of unbroken continuities looking forward. It also has affinities with the very meaningful historical category "early modern."

[3] Originally published with its present title, "Letters and People to Spain," in *First Images of America: The Impact of the New World on the Old* (1976), ed. by Fredi Chiappelli, pp. 783–96.

the level of individual, family, and organization. I would have been tempted to add an epilogue here too, but Ida Altman took up the challenge of transatlantic social history and has made further remarks superfluous.[4]

During the time when my book *The Nahuas After the Conquest* (1992) was in gestation, I would occasionally receive requests to speak to people curious about what it could be I was taking so long to do. I had two standard talks for the purpose. One was an overall summary of the ongoing work (which appeared in 1991 as the first chapter of my *Nahuas and Spaniards*); the other, published in 1985, was called "Some Nahua Concepts in Postconquest Guise," showing the continuity of indigenous ideas and procedures inside ostensibly Hispanic forms.[5] As *The Nahuas* took shape, nearly all of the 1985 article's subtopics came to be treated more thoroughly there, and its substantial historiographical introduction was actually incorporated into the book. Still, I had a fondness for the notion of Double Mistaken Identity which I had hit on in the original article, and the talks I gave gradually centered more on that point. In 1993 I rewrote the piece, not meaning to go beyond *The Nahuas* in substance, but organizing the material in such a way as to highlight the key concept, which I also put in the main title. It is that version that is published here.

The fifth chapter[6] responds more to its subtitle, "The Spanish Reaction to American Resources," that having been the assignment given me for a Columbian quincentenary conference at Ohio State University, than to its main title, "Trunk Lines and Feeder Lines." I had meant to do only the quickest analysis of the Spaniards as being economically rational, even sophisticated, and concentrate more on the large-scale network of routes they devised to organize the Indies, but the opposite happened. That was doubtless no ac-

---

[4]See Altman, *Emigrants and Society* (1989) and, when it appears with Stanford University Press, her study on Puebla and Brihuega.

[5]*History of European Ideas*, 6 (1985): 465–82. From this version only the title concept and a good number of sentences and paragraphs, often put in a new light, remain in the present Chapter 4.

[6]Originally published with its present title in *Transatlantic Encounters: Europeans and Andeans in the Sixteenth Century* (1991), ed. by Kenneth J. Andrien and Rolena Adorno, pp. 90–120.

cident. Perhaps it is not possible to do much more than lay out the structure and function of the trunk lines without more research of a quite daunting type, which would need to embrace a large number of areas separated by great distances and still be primary enough to catch family, business, and institutional networks at the level of the individual.

For many years I wanted to do something with the theme of mercantile organization in early Spanish America over the long haul, but the gap between the sixteenth century and the eighteenth was too wide. When Luisa Hoberman filled in the seventeenth, my aim became somewhat feasible, and the piece which is now Chapter 6 was written and published in a Festschrift in honor of Enrique Otte, who has contributed so much to this kind of history.[7]

Chapter 7 is a byproduct of a volume I edited called *We People Here* (1993), containing several Nahuatl accounts of the Spanish conquest of Mexico, of which Book Twelve of Sahagún's Florentine Codex is the largest by far. Using Book Twelve as an example, I explain the procedures I deem necessary in such enterprises to capture and reflect, as well as one can, the characteristics of indigenous texts and writers, especially with texts done under ecclesiastical auspices, where two sets of authors and intentions are involved.[8]

The main item on my research agenda is now and for some time has been to broaden out from the Nahuas of central Mexico to any other indigenous peoples of the hemisphere who have left us written evidence in their own languages of their experiences in the postcontact centuries. Chapter 8, published in virtually the form it has here as recently as 1998,[9] was actually done in 1992, yet it remains up to date about my current opinions on these matters, for the truth is

---

[7] Originally published with its present title in *Ibero-Amerikanisches Archiv: Zeitschrift für Sozialwissenschaften und Geschichte*, 20 (1994): 223–46 (pp. 219–451 constitute the Festschrift).

[8] The original was published with its present title in *Critical Issues in Editing Exploration Texts* (1995), ed. by Germaine Warkentin, pp. 125–47.

[9] Originally published with its present title in *Native Traditions in the Postconquest World* (1998), ed. by Elizabeth Hill Boone and Tom Cummins, pp. 31–53.

that despite my intentions I have spent most of my scholarly time since then completing already existing projects in Nahuatl philology. Indeed, I have since lost ground in the study of Yucatecan Maya and Quechua. The main thrust of the article is already anticipated somewhat in the conclusion of my book *The Nahuas*, but the linguistic analysis of Quechua is new, one of the few examples of primary research in the volume, and although provisional I believe quite significant.

The remaining chapters have not been published in any form. Chapter 9, "Between the Lines," largely explains its own origins. The piece is a slight gesture toward replacing a book on Spanish American paleography and the method of social and cultural research that I have often dreamed of but may never get around to in view of other enterprises. Perhaps it is not for everyone to look as closely at texts as is done here, but I am optimistic, and those who carry out and above all manage to enjoy such exercises can gain vastly from them.

Chapter 10 is an excursion into a field, Nahuatl historical linguistics, that has been of perennial interest to me, in which despite my amateur status I want to say some things that I consider important, even ultimately to cultural history. I hope that despite the technical language in which topics like this must be discussed, scholars other than professional linguists will eventually take such matters to heart.

The last two chapters are the result of presentations I gave early in 1998 at Johns Hopkins and Emory Universities respectively. After a time of enjoying not going anywhere to give talks, I responded to an invitation from Hopkins specifying the theme of resistance, because over the years that concept had become quite problematic to me. My interest in the topic began to surface at the time of the composition of Lockhart and Schwartz, *Early Latin America* (1983), and it became more acute during the work leading to *The Nahuas* (1992), in which the matter receives a good deal of scattered mention. The piece that came out of my visit to Hopkins (Chapter 11) goes over ground I have covered previously but focuses on the question of how the distance between indigenous and European beliefs, practices, and structures in the Americas should be conceived. The question I take to be a very important one.

My assignment at Emory, which resulted in Chapter 12,

was originally to speak on some aspect of interdisciplinary research; I suggested that I talk about my own experiences of that kind. As I began putting something together, it seemed that the actual research projects needed to be seen in the light of my overall exposure to the disciplines, which led back to graduate school and even earlier, so that something like a particular kind of abbreviated memoir resulted. The piece is wide ranging, but it does not pretend to do justice to all my personal and intellectual connections *within* the early Latin American field (though some of them inevitably crop up).

First appearing across a stretch of nearly thirty years in a variety of organs, the previously published pieces had widely varying conventions for citing references. I have gone a long way toward unifying them, but although I mainly cite an item by author and date alone, I still feel free to mention a title when that seems indicated. In a couple of cases, some citations in the body of the text were built into the original by editorial policy, and it would now be artificial to remove them.

Bibliography

Aiton, Arthur Scott. 1927. *Antonio de Mendoza, First Viceroy of New Spain*. Durham, N. C.

Alden, Dauril. 1968. *Royal Government in Colonial Brazil, with Special Reference to the Administration of the Marquis of Lavradio, Viceroy, 1769–1779*. Berkeley and Los Angeles.

Altman, Ida. 1988. "Emigrants and Society: An Approach to the Background of Colonial Spanish America," *Comparative Studies in Society and History*, 30: 170–90.

———. 1989. *Emigrants and Society: Extremadura and Spanish America in the Sixteenth Century*. Berkeley and Los Angeles.

———. 1991. "Spanish Society in Mexico City After the Conquest," *Hispanic American Historical Review*, 71: 413–45.

———. Forthcoming. *Transatlantic Ties in the Spanish Empire: Brihuega, Spain and Puebla, Mexico, 1560–1620* (provisional title). Stanford, Calif.

Altman, Ida, and James Horn, eds. 1991. *"To Make America": European Emigration in the Early Modern Period*. Berkeley and Los Angeles.

Altman, Ida, and James Lockhart, eds. 1976. *Provinces of Early Mexico: Variants of Spanish American Regional Evolution*. Los Angeles.

Anderson, Arthur J. O., Frances Berdan, and James Lockhart. 1976. *Beyond the Codices*. Berkeley and Los Angeles.

Andrews, J. Richard. 1975. *Introduction to Classical Nahuatl*. Austin, Texas.

Bakewell, P. J. 1971. *Silver Mining and Society in Colonial Mexico: Zacatecas, 1546–1700*. Cambridge, Eng.

———. 1984. *Miners of the Red Mountain: Indian Labor in Potosí, 1545–1650*. Albuquerque, N. M.

———. 1984a. "Mining in Colonial Spanish America." In Leslie Bethell, ed., *The Cambridge History of Latin America*, 2 (Cambridge, Eng.): 105–51.

———. 1988. *Silver and Entrepreneurship in Seventeenth-Century Potosí: The Life and Times of Antonio López de Quiroga*. Albuquerque, N. M.

Barbier, Jacques. 1970. "The Restoration of the Chilean Elite and the Bourbon Reforms." (Paper read at the American Historical Association conference.)

———. 1980. *Reform and Politics in Bourbon Chile, 1755–1796*. Ottawa.

Barrett, Ward. 1970. *The Sugar Hacienda of the Marqueses del Valle*. Minneapolis.

Bataillon, Marcel. 1995. *La colonia: ensayos peruanistas*. Compiled by Alberto Tauro. Lima.

Bermúdez Plata, Cristóbal, ed. 1940–46. *Catálogo de pasajeros a Indias*. 3 vols. Seville.

Bills, Garland D., Bernardo Vallejo C., and Rudolph C. Troike. 1969. *An Introduction to Spoken Bolivian Quechua*. Austin, Texas.

Borah, Woodrow (*see also* Cook). 1951. *New Spain's Century of Depression*. Ibero-Americana, 35. Berkeley and Los Angeles.

⸺. 1954. "Race and Class in Mexico," *Pacific Historical Review*, 23: 331–42.

Borah, Woodrow, and Sherburne F. Cook. 1958. *Price Trends of Some Basic Commodities in Central Mexico, 1531–1570*. Ibero-Americana, 40. Berkeley and Los Angeles.

Borchart de Moreno, Christiana. 1976. "Kaufmannschaft und Handelskapitalismus in der Stadt Mexico (1759–1778)," Doctoral dissertation, Rheinische Friedrich-Wilhelms-Universität, Bonn.

Borde, Jean and Mario Góngora. 1956. *La evolución de la propiedad rural en el Valle del Puangue*. Santiago, Chile.

Bourne, Edward Gaylord. 1904. *Spain in America, 1400–1580*. New York.

Bowser, Frederick P. 1974. *The African Slave in Colonial Peru, 1524–1650*. Stanford, Calif.

Boxer, C. R. 1952. *Salvador de Sá and the Struggle for Brazil and Angola, 1602–1686*. London.

⸺. 1957. *The Dutch in Brazil, 1624–1654*. Oxford.

⸺. 1962. *The Golden Age of Brazil, 1695–1750: Growing Pains of a Society*. Berkeley and Los Angeles.

⸺. 1965. *Portuguese Society in the Tropics: The Municipal Councils of Goa, Macao, Bahia, and Luanda, 1510–1800*. Madison, Wis.

Boyd-Bowman, Peter. 1964–68. *Indice geobiográfico de cuarenta mil pobladores españoles de América en el siglo XVI*. 2 vols. 1: 1493–1519. Bogotá (1964). 2: 1520–1539. México (1968).

⸺. 1969. "Negro Slaves in Early Colonial Mexico," *The Americas*, 26: 134–51.

⸺. 1976. "Patterns of Spanish Emigration to the Indies until 1600," *Hispanic American Historical Review*, 56: 580–604

Brading, D. A. 1971. *Miners and Merchants in Bourbon Mexico, 1763–1810*. Cambridge, Eng.

⸺. 1978. *Haciendas and Ranchos in the Mexican Bajío: León 1700–1860*. Cambridge, Eng..

Bricker, Victoria R. 1981. *The Indian Christ, the Indian King: The Substrate of Maya Myth and Ritual*. Austin, Texas.

Bronner, Fred. 1977. "Peruvian Encomenderos in 1630: Elite Circulation and Consolidation." *Hispanic American Historical Review*, 57: 633–59.

Campbell, Leon G. 1972. "A Creole Establishment: The Audiencia of Lima in the Later Eighteenth Century." *Hispanic American Historical Review*, 52: 1–25.

Canger, Una. 1980. *Five Studies Inspired by Nahuatl Verbs in -oa*.

Copenhagen.

Capoche, Luis. 1959. *Relación general de la Villa Imperial de Potosí.* Ed. by Lewis Hanke. In *Relaciones histórico-literarias de la América meridional.* Madrid.

Carochi, Horacio. 1983. *Arte de la lengua mexicana con la declaración de los adverbios della.* Facsimile of 1645 edition, with introduction by Miguel León-Portilla. México.

Cartas de Indias. 1877. Madrid.

Castillero Calvo, Alfredo. 1967. *Estructuras sociales y económicas de Veragua desde sus orígenes históricos, siglos XVI y XVII.* Panamá.

———. 1970. *La sociedad panameña: historia de su formación e integración.* Panamá.

Celestino Solís, Eustaquio, Armando Valencia R., and Constantino Medina Lima, eds. 1985. *Actas del cabildo de Tlaxcala, 1547–1567.* México.

Céspedes del Castillo, Guillermo. 1957. "La sociedad colonial americana en los siglos XVI y XVII." In *Historia social y económica de España y América,* 3: 387–578. 5 vols. Barcelona.

Chance, John K. 1978. *Race and Class in Colonial Oaxaca.* Stanford, Calif.

———. 1989. *Conquest of the Sierra: Spaniards and Indians in Colonial Oaxaca.* Norman, Okla.

Chaunu, Pierre and Huguette. 1955–60. *Seville et l'Atlantique, 1504–1650.* 13 vols. in 8. Paris.

Chevalier, François. 1952. *La formation des grands domaines au Mexique: terre et société aux XVIe–XVIIe siècles.* Paris.

———. 1963. *Land and Society in Colonial Mexico: The Great Hacienda.* Berkeley and Los Angeles.

Chimalpahin Quauhtlehuanitzin, don Domingo Francisco de San Antón Muñón. 1963–65. *Die Relationes Chimalpahin's zur Geschichte Mexico's.* Ed. by Günter Zimmermann. 2 vols. Hamburg.

Cline, S. L. 1986. *Colonial Culhuacan, 1580–1600.* Albuquerque, N. M.

———, ed. and trans. 1993. *The Book of Tributes: Early Sixteenth-Century Nahuatl Censuses from Morelos.* UCLA Latin American Center Nahuatl Studies Series, 4. Los Angeles.

Cline, S. L., and Miguel León-Portilla, eds. 1984. *The Testaments of Culhuacan.* UCLA Latin American Center Nahuatl Studies Series, 1. Los Angeles.

Cole, Jeffrey A. 1985. *The Potosí Mita, 1573–1700: Compulsory Indian Labor in the Andes.* Stanford, Calif.

Collier, George A., Renato I. Rosaldo, and John D. Wirth, eds. 1982. *The Inca and Aztec States, 1400–1800: Anthropology and History.* New York.

Cook, Noble David. 1981. *Demographic Collapse: Indian Peru, 1520–1620.* Cambridge, Eng.

Cook, Sherburne F., and Woodrow Borah. 1971–79. *Essays in Population History.* 3 vols. Berkeley and Los Angeles.

Davidson, David M. 1966. "Negro Slave Control and Resistance in Colonial Mexico, 1519–1650," *Hispanic American Historical Review*, 46: 235–53.

Davies, Keith A. 1984. *Landowners in Colonial Peru*. Austin, Texas.

Díaz del Castillo, Bernal. 1947. *Verdadera historia de la conquista de la Nueva España*. Biblioteca de Autores Españoles, 26. Madrid.

Diffie, Bailie W. 1945. *Latin American Civilization, Colonial Period*. Harrisburg, Pa. Reprint 1967, New York.

Elliott, J. H. 1970. *The Old World and the New, 1492–1650*. Cambridge, Eng.

Espinoza Soriano, Waldemar, ed. 1964. *Visita hecha a la provincia de Chucuito por Garci Díez de San Miguel en al año 1567*. With an ethnohistorical analysis by John V. Murra. Lima.

Fair, Theopolis. 1972. "The *indiano* during the Spanish Golden Age from 1550–1650." Doctoral dissertation, Temple University.

Fals Borda, Orlando. 1961. *Campesinos de los Andes: estudio sociológico de Saucío*. Bogotá.

Farriss, Nancy M. 1984. *Maya Society Under Colonial Rule: The Collective Enterprise of Survival*. Princeton, N. J.

Florescano, Enrique. 1969. *Precios del maíz y crisis agrícolas en México (1708–1810)*. México.

Flory, Rae. 1978. "Bahian Society in the Mid-Colonial Period: The Sugar Planters, Tobacco Growers, Merchants, and Artisans of Salvador and the Recôncavo, 1680–1725." Doctoral dissertation, University of Texas, Austin.

Flory, Rae, and David Grant Smith. 1978. "Bahian Merchants and Planters in the Seventeenth and Early Eighteenth Centuries," *Hispanic American Historical Review*, 58: 571–94.

Foster, George M. 1960. *Culture and Conquest: America's Spanish Heritage*. Chicago.

Fraser, Valerie. 1989. *The Architecture of Conquest: Building in the Viceroyalty of Peru, 1535–1635*. Cambridge, Eng.

Freyre, Gilberto. 1933. *Casa grande e senzala*. Rio de Janeiro.

Friede, Juan. 1965. "Proceso de formación de la propiedad territorial en la América intertropical," *Jahrbuch für Geschichte von Staat, Wirtschaft und Gesellschaft Lateinamerikas*, 2: 75–87.

Gakenheimer, Ralph A. 1967. "The Peruvian City of the Sixteenth Century." In Glenn H. Beyer, ed., *The Urban Explosion in Latin America: A Continent in the Process of Modernization*, pp. 33–56. Ithaca.

Ganster, Paul B. 1974. "A Social History of the Secular Clergy of Lima during the Middle Decades of the Eighteenth Century." UCLA doctoral dissertation.

Garibay K., Angel María. 1964–68. *Poesía náhuatl*. 3 vols. México.

———. 1970. *Llave del náhuatl: Colección de trozos clásicos, con gramática y vocabulario, para utilidad de los principiantes*. 3rd ed. México.

_____, ed. 1943. "Huehuetlatolli, Documento A." *Tlalocan*, 1: 31–53, 81–107.

Gauderman, Kimberly. 1998. "Women Playing the System: Social, Economic, and Legal Aspects of Women's Lives in Seventeenth-Century Quito." UCLA doctoral dissertation.

Gibson, Charles. 1952. *Tlaxcala in the Sixteenth Century*. New Haven, Conn.

_____. 1964. *The Aztecs Under Spanish Rule: A History of the Indians of the Valley of Mexico, 1519–1810*. Stanford, Calif.

_____. 1966. *Spain in America*. New York.

Glave, Luis Miguel. 1989. *Trajinantes: caminos indígenas en la sociedad colonial siglos XVI–XVII*. Lima.

Gonçalez Holguin [González Holguín], Diego. 1952. *Vocabulario de la lengua general de todo el Peru llamada lengua Qquichua o del Inca*. Lima.

Góngora, Mario (*see also* Borde). 1960. *Origen de los "inquilinos" de Chile central*. Santiago, Chile.

_____. 1962. *Grupos de conquistadores en Tierra Firme (1509–1530)*. Santiago, Chile.

_____. 1971. *Encomenderos y estancieros: estudios acerca de la constitución social aristocrática de Chile después de la conquista, 1580–1660*. Santiago, Chile.

Gosner, Kevin. 1992. *Soldiers of the Virgin: The Moral Economy of a Colonial Maya Rebellion*. Tucson, Ariz.

_____. 1998. "Religion and Rebellion in Colonial Chiapas." In Susan Schroeder, ed., *Native Resistance and the Pax Colonial in New Spain*, pp. 47–66.

Greenleaf, Richard E. 1969. *The Mexican Inquisition of the Sixteenth Century*. Albuquerque, N. M.

Grondín N., Marcelo. 1971. *Runa simi: Método de quechua*. Oruro, Bolivia.

Gruzinski, Serge. 1989. *Man-Gods in the Mexican Highlands*. Stanford, Calif.

Guaman [Huaman] Poma de Ayala, don Felipe. 1980. *El primer nueva coronica y buen gobierno* [1615]. Ed. by John V. Murra and Rolena Adorno. Translation and analysis of the Quechua by George L. Urioste. 3 vols. México.

Hamnett, Brian R. 1971. *Politics and Trade in Southern Mexico, 1750–1821*. Cambridge, Eng.

Hanke, Lewis. 1949. *The Spanish Struggle for Justice in the Conquest of America*. Philadelphia.

_____. 1956. *The Imperial City of Potosí*. The Hague.

_____. 1965. *Bartolomé Arzáns de Orsúa y Vela's History of Potosí*. Providence, R.I.

_____. 1971. "A Modest Proposal for a Moratorium on Grand Generalizations: Some Thoughts on the Black Legend," *Hispanic American Historical Review*, 51: 112–27.

Haring, Clarence R. 1947. *The Spanish Empire in America*. New York.

The Harkness Collection in the Library of Congress. Documents from Early Peru, the Pizarros and the Almagros, 1531–1578. 1936. Washington, D. C.

Haskett, Robert. 1991. *Indigenous Rulers: An Ethnohistory of Town Government in Colonial Cuernavaca*. Albuquerque, N. M.

Hassig, Ross. 1985. *Trade, Tribute and Transportation: The Sixteenth-Century Political Economy of the Valley of Mexico*. Norman, Okla.

Herrera, Robinson Antonio. 1997. "The People of Santiago: Early Colonial Guatemala, 1538–1587." UCLA doctoral dissertation.

Himmerich y Valencia, Robert T. 1983. "The Encomenderos of New Spain." UCLA doctoral dissertation.

_____. 1991. *The Encomenderos of New Spain, 1521–1555*. Austin, Texas.

Hinz, Eike, Claudine Hartau, and Marie-Luise Heimann-Koenen, eds. 1983. *Aztekischer Zensus. Zur indianischen Wirtschaft und Gesellschaft im Marquesado um 1540: Aus dem "Libro de Tributos" (Col. Ant. Ms. 551) im Archivo Histórico, México*. 2 vols. Hanover.

Hoberman, Louisa Schell. 1991. *Mexico's Merchant Elite, 1590–1660*. Durham, N. C.

Horcasitas, Fernando. 1974. *El teatro náhuatl*. México.

Horn, Rebecca. 1997. *Postconquest Coyoacan: Nahua-Spanish Relations in Central Mexico, 1519–1650*. Stanford, Calif.

Hunt, Marta Espejo-Ponce. 1974. "Colonial Yucatan: Town and Region in the Seventeenth Century." UCLA doctoral dissertation.

_____. 1976. "The Processes of the Development of Yucatan, 1600–1700." In Altman and Lockhart, eds., *Provinces of Early Mexico*.

Iglesia, Ramón. 1969. *Columbus, Cortés, and Other Essays*. Berkeley and Los Angeles.

Jara, Alvaro. 1966. *Tres ensayos sobre economía minera hispanoamericana*. Santiago, Chile.

Karttunen, Frances. 1985. *Nahuatl and Maya in Contact with Spanish*. Texas Linguistic Forum, 26 (Department of Linguistics, University of Texas). Austin, Texas.

Karttunen, Frances, and James Lockhart. 1976. *Nahuatl in the Middle Years: Language Contact Phenomena in Texts of the Colonial Period*. University of California Publications in Linguistics, 85. Berkeley and Los Angeles.

Karttunen, Frances, and James Lockhart, eds. 1987. *The Art of Nahuatl Speech: The Bancroft Dialogues*. UCLA Latin American Center Nahuatl Studies Series, 2. Los Angeles.

Keith, Robert G. 1976. *Conquest and Agrarian Change: The Emergence of the Hacienda System on the Peruvian Coast*. Cambridge, Mass.

Kicza, John E. 1979. "Business and Society in Late Colonial Mexico City." UCLA doctoral dissertation.

_____. 1983. *Colonial Entrepreneurs: Families and Business in Bourbon Mexico City*. Albuquerque, N. M.

Kirchhoff, Paul, Lina Odena Güemes, and Luis Reyes García, eds. 1976. *Historia tolteca-chichimeca*. México.

Kirkpatrick, F. A. 1939. "Repartimiento-Encomienda," *Hispanic American Historical Review*, 19: 372–79.

Klein, Herbert S. 1967. *Slavery in the Americas: A Comparative Study of Virginia and Cuba*. Chicago.

Konetzke, Richard. 1945. "La emigración de las mujeres españolas a América durante la época colonial," *Revista Internacional de Sociología*, 3: 125–50.

_____. 1949. "La esclavitud de los indios como elemento en la estructuración social de Hispanoamérica," *Estudios de Historia Social*, 1: 443–79.

_____. 1951. "La formación de la nobleza en Indias," *Estudios Americanos*, 3: 339–357.

_____, ed. 1953–62. *Colección de documentos para la historia de la formación social de Hispano-América*. 3 vols. Madrid.

Kubler, George. 1948. *Mexican Architecture of the Sixteenth Century*. 2 vols. Yale Historical Publications, History of Art, 5. New Haven, Conn.

Langacker, Ronald W. 1976. *Non-Distinct Arguments in Uto-Aztecan*. University of California Publications in Linguistics, 82. Berkeley and Los Angeles.

Launey, Michel. 1979. *Introduction à la langue et à la littérature aztèques*. Vol. 1: *Grammaire*. Paris.

León-Portilla, Miguel. 1956. *La filosofía náhuatl estudiada en sus fuentes*. México.

_____. 1983. "Cuicatl y tlahtolli: Las formas de expresión en náhuatl," *Estudios de Cultura Náhuatl*, 16: 13–108.

Levillier, Roberto. 1935–42. *Don Francisco de Toledo, supremo organizador del Perú*. 3 vols. Madrid.

Leibsohn, Dana. 1993. "The Historia Tolteca-Chichimeca: Recollecting Identity in a Nahua Manuscript." UCLA doctoral dissertation.

Liebman, Seymour B. 1970. *The Jews in New Spain*. Miami, Fla.

Lobo, Eulalia Maria Lahmeyer. 1967. "Imigração e colonização no Chile colonial (1540–1565)," *Revista de História*, 35: 39–59.

Lockhart, James. 1968. *Spanish Peru, 1532–1560*. Madison, Wis.

_____. 1969. "Encomienda and Hacienda: The Evolution of the Great Estate in the Spanish Indies," *Hispanic American Historical Review*, 49: 411–29.

_____. 1972. *The Men of Cajamarca: A Social and Biographical Study of the First Conquerors of Peru*. Austin, Texas.

_____. 1972a. "The Social History of Colonial Latin America: Evolution and Potential," *Latin American Research Review*, 7: 6–45.

_____. 1975. "Españoles entre indios: Toluca a fines del siglo XVI." In Francisco de Solano, ed., *Estudios sobre la ciudad iberoame-*

ricana, pp. 435–91. Madrid.

_____. 1976. "Introduction." In Altman and Lockhart, eds., *Provinces of Early Mexico*, pp. 3–28.

_____. 1976a. "Capital and Province, Spaniard and Indian: The Example of Late Sixteenth-Century Toluca." In Altman and Lockhart, eds., *Provinces of Early Mexico*, pp. 99–123.

_____. 1976b. "Letters and People to Spain." In Fredi Chiappelli, ed., *First Images of America: The Impact of the New World on the Old*, pp. 783–96. Berkeley and Los Angeles.

_____. 1984. "Social Organization and Social Change in Colonial Spanish America." In Leslie Bethell, ed., *The Cambridge History of Latin America*, 2: 265–319. Cambridge, Eng., and New York.

_____. 1985. "Some Nahua Concepts in Postconquest Guise," *History of European Ideas*, 6: 465–82.

_____. 1987. Review of *Reliving the Past: The Worlds of Social History*, ed. by Olivier Zunz. *Hispanic American Historical Review*, 67: 499–501.

_____. 1991. *Nahuas and Spaniards: Postconquest Central Mexican History and Philology*. Stanford, Calif., and Los Angeles.

_____. 1991a. "Charles Gibson and the Ethnohistory of Postconquest Central Mexico." In James Lockhart, *Nahuas and Spaniards*.

_____. 1991b. "Trunk Lines and Feeder Lines: The Spanish Reaction to American Resources." In Kenneth J. Andrien and Rolena Adorno, eds., *Transatlantic Encounters: Europeans and Andeans in the Sixteenth Century*, pp. 90–120. Berkeley and Los Angeles.

_____. 1992. *The Nahuas After the Conquest: A Social and Cultural History of the Indians of Central Mexico, Sixteenth Through Eighteenth Centuries*. Stanford, Calif.

_____. 1994. *Spanish Peru, 1532–1560: A Social History*. 2nd ed. Madison, Wis.

_____. 1994a. "The Merchants of Early Spanish America: Continuity and Change." In Günter Vollmer, ed., *Comerciantes, indios tributarios, curas y otra gente sin o con importancia que hicieron o soportaron historia en la Nueva España. Ocho ensayos dedicados a Enrique Otte. Ibero-Amerikanisches Archiv: Zeitschrift für Sozialwissenschaften und Geschichte*, 20 (1994): 223–46 (pp. 219–451 constitute the Festschrift).

_____. 1995. "A Double Tradition: Editing Book Twelve of the Florentine Codex." In Germaine Warkentin, ed., *Critical Issues in Editing Exploration Texts*, pp. 125–47. Toronto.

_____. 1998. "Three Experiences of Culture Contact: Nahua, Maya, and Quechua." In Elizabeth Hill Boone and Tom Cummins, eds., *Native Traditions in the Postconquest World*, pp. 31–53. Washington, D. C.

_____, ed. 1993. *We People Here: Nahuatl Accounts of the Conquest of Mexico*. Berkeley and Los Angeles.

Lockhart, James, Frances Berdan, and Arthur J. O. Anderson. 1986.

The Tlaxcalan Actas: A Compendium of the Records of the Cabildo of Tlaxcala (1545–1627). Salt Lake City.

Lockhart, James, and Enrique Otte, eds. 1976. *Letters and People of the Spanish Indies, Sixteenth Century*. Cambridge, Eng., and New York.

Lockhart, James, and Stuart B. Schwartz. 1983. *Early Latin America: A History of Colonial Spanish America and Brazil*. Cambridge, Eng., and New York.

Love, Edgar F. 1971. "Marriage Patterns of Persons of African Descent in a Colonial Mexico City Parish," *Hispanic American Historical Review*, 51: 1.

McAlister, Lyle N. 1963. "Social Structure and Social Change in New Spain," *Hispanic American Historical Review*, 43: 349–70.

———. 1984. *Spain and Portugal in the New World, 1492–1700*. Minneapolis.

McAndrew, John. 1964. *The Open-Air Churches of Sixteenth-Century Mexico*. Cambridge, Mass.

McBride, George. 1923. *The Land Systems of Mexico*. New York.

MacLeod, Murdo J. 1973. *Spanish Central America: A Socioeconomic History, 1520–1720*. Berkeley and Los Angeles.

———. 1984. "Aspects of the Internal Economy of Colonial Spanish America: Labour; Taxation; Distribution and Exchange." In Leslie Bethell, ed., *Cambridge History of Latin America*, 2: 219–64. Cambridge, Eng.

McNeill, William H. 1963. *The Rise of the West*. Chicago.

Mannheim, Bruce. 1991. *The Language of the Inka Since the European Invasion*. Austin, Texas.

Matienzo, Juan de. 1967. *Gobierno del Perú*. Paris and Lima.

Mellafe, Rolando. 1970. "Commentary," *Latin American Research Review*, 5: 93–100.

Mendels, Franklin F. 1970. "Recent Research in European Historical Demography," *American Historical Review*, 75: 1065–73.

Miranda, José. 1965. *La función económica del encomendero en los orígenes del régimen colonial. Nueva España (1525–1531)*. 2nd ed. México.

Mörner, Magnus. 1967. *Race Mixture in the History of Latin America*. Boston.

Molina, fray Alonso de. 1970. *Vocabulario en lengua castellana y mexicana y mexicana y castellana* (1571). México.

Moore, John Preston. 1966. *The Cabildo in Peru under the Bourbons*. Durham, N. C.

Moreno geb. Borchart, Christiana Renate. *See* Borchart.

Moreno Toscano, Alejandra. 1968. *Geografía económica de México (siglo XVI)*. México.

Morse, Richard M. 1962. "Some Characteristics of Latin American Urban History," *American Historical Review*, 67: 317–38.

———. 1971. "Trends and Issues in Latin American Urban Research,

1965–1970," *Latin American Research Review*, 6: 3–52, 19–75.

Murphy, Michael E. 1986. *Irrigation in the Bajío Region of Colonial Mexico*. Boulder, Colorado.

Murra, John V. *See* Espinoza Soriano and Guaman Poma.

Offutt, Leslie Scott. 1993. *Una sociedad urbana y rural en el Norte de México: Saltillo a fines de la época colonial*. Saltillo, Mexico.

Otte, Enrique. 1965. "Das genuesische Unternehmertum und Amerika unter den katholischen Königen," *Jahrbuch für Geschichte von Staat, Wirtschaft und Gesellschaft Lateinamerikas (JGSWGL)*, 2: 30–74.

_____. 1966. "Cartas privadas de Puebla," *JGSWGL*, 3: 10–87.

_____. 1966a. "Los mercaderes vascos y los Pizarro," *TILAS* (Strasbourg), 6: 25–44.

_____. 1967. "Träger und Formen der wirtschaftlichen Erschließung Lateinamerikas im 16. Jahrhundert," *JGSWGL*, 4: 226–66.

_____. 1968. "Mercaderes burgaleses en los inicios del comercio con México," *Historia Mexicana*, 18: 108–44.

_____. 1969. "Die europäischen Siedler und die Probleme der Neuen Welt," *JGSWGL*, 6: 1–40.

_____. 1977. *Las perlas del Caribe: Nueva Cádiz de Cubagua*. Caracas.

_____. 1978. "Wirtschaftskräfte Andalusiens an der Schwelle der Neuzeit: die 'traperos'." In *Beiträge zur Wirtschaftsgeschichte*, 4: *Wirtschaftskräfte und Wirtschaftswege I: Mittelmeer und Kontinent: Festschrift für Hermann Kellenbenz*, 297–312. Nürnberg.

_____. 1990. "Los mercaderes transatlánticos bajo Carlos V," *Anuario de Estudios Americanos*, 47: 95–121.

_____. 1993. *Cartas privadas de emigrantes a Indias, 1540–1616*. Seville.

_____. 1996. *Sevilla y sus mercaderes a fines de la Edad Media*. Seville.

Pérez de Tudela, Juan, ed. 1963–65. *Crónicas del Perú*. 5 vols. Madrid.

_____. 1964. *Documentos relativos a don Pedro de la Gasca y a Gonzalo Pizarro*. 2 vols. Madrid.

Peterson, Jeanette Favrot. 1985. "The Garden Frescoes of Malinalco." UCLA doctoral dissertation.

_____. 1993. *The Paradise Garden Murals of Malinalco*. Austin, Texas.

Phelan, John Leddy. 1967. *The Kingdom of Quito in the Seventeenth Century: Bureaucratic Politics in the Spanish Empire*. Madison, Wis.

Pike, Ruth. 1966. *Enterprise and Adventure: The Genoese in Seville and the Opening of the New World*. Ithaca, N. Y.

_____. 1967. "Sevillian Society in the Sixteenth Century: Slaves and Freedmen," *Hispanic American Historical Review*, 47: 344–59.

Poole, Stafford, C. M. 1995. *Our Lady of Guadalupe: The Origins and Sources of a Mexican National Symbol, 1531–1797*. Tucson, Ariz.

Porras Barrenechea, Raúl, ed. 1959. *Cartas del Perú (1524–1543)*. Lima.

Prescott, William H. n.d. *History of the Conquest of Mexico* and *History of the Conquest of Peru*. New York (Modern Library).

Ramírez, Susan E. 1986. *Provincial Patriarchs: Land Tenure and the Economics of Power in Colonial Peru*. Albuquerque, N. M.

Restall, Matthew. 1992. "The World of the *Cah*: Postconquest Yucatec Maya Society." UCLA doctoral dissertation.

_____. 1997. *The Maya World: Yucatec Culture and Society, 1550–1850*. Stanford, Calif.

Ricard, Robert. 1933. *La "Conquête spirituelle" du Mexique*. Paris.

Riley, G. Michael. 1972. *The Estate of Fernando Cortés in the Cuernavaca Area of Mexico, 1522–1547*. Albuquerque, N. M.

Robertson, Donald. 1959. *Mexican Manuscript Painting of the Early Colonial Period: The Metropolitan Schools*. Yale Historical Publications, History of Art, 12. New Haven, Conn.

Rowe, John H. 1963 (orig. 1944). "Inca Culture at the Time of the Spanish Conquest." In Julian H. Steward, ed., *Handbook of South American Indians*, vol. 2, *The Andean Civilizations*, 183–330. New York.

Roys, Ralph L., ed. and trans. 1939. *The Titles of Ebtun*. Washington, D. C.

Rubio Mañé, J. Ignacio, ed. 1966. *Gente de España en la ciudad de México, año de 1689*. In *Boletín del Archivo General de la Nación* (México), 8: nos. 1, 2.

Ruiz de Alarcón, Hernando. 1984. *Treatise on the Heathen Superstitions and Customs that Today Live among the Indians Native to this New Spain, 1629*. Trans. and ed. by J. Richard Andrews and Ross Hassig. Norman, Okla.

Russell-Wood, A. J. R. 1968. *Fidalgos and Philanthropists: The Santa Casa da Misericórdia of Bahia, 1550–1755*. Berkeley and Los Angeles.

Sahagún, fray Bernardino de. 1975. *Historia general de las cosas de la Nueva España*. 3d ed. México.

_____. 1950–82. *Florentine Codex: General History of the Things of New Spain*. Trans. by Arthur J. O. Anderson and Charles E. Dibble. 13 parts. Salt Lake City and Santa Fe, N. M.

_____. 1978. *The War of Conquest: How It Was Waged Here in Mexico*. Trans. by Arthur J. O. Anderson and Charles E. Dibble. Salt Lake City.

_____. 1979. *Códice Florentino*. El Manuscrito 218–220 de la colección Palatina de la Biblioteca Medicea Laurenziana. Facsimile edition. Florence.

_____. 1986. *Coloquios y doctrina cristiana*. Ed. by Miguel León-Portilla. México.

_____. 1989. *Conquest of New Spain, 1585 Revision*. Trans. by Howard F. Cline and ed. by S. L. Cline. Salt Lake City.

Salomon, Frank, and George L. Urioste, trans. and eds. 1991. *The Huarochirí Manuscript: A Testament of Ancient and Colonial Andean Religion*. Austin.

Santo Tomás, fray Domingo. 1951. *Grammatica o Arte de la lengua general de los indios de los reynos de Peru*. Ed. by Raúl Porras Barrenechea. Lima.

_____. 1951a. *Lexicon o vocabulario de la lengua general del Peru llamada quichua*. Ed. by Raúl Porras Barrenechea. Lima.

Sauer, Carl Ortwin. 1966. *The Early Spanish Main*. Berkeley and Los Angeles.

Schroeder, Susan. 1991. *Chimalpahin and the Kingdoms of Chalco*. Tucson, Ariz.

_____, ed. 1998. *Native Resistance and the Pax Colonial in New Spain*. Lincoln, Nebr.

Schwartz, Stuart B. 1970. "Magistracy and Society in Colonial Brazil," *Hispanic American Historical Review*, 50: 715–30.

_____. 1973. *Sovereignty and Society in Colonial Brazil: The High Court of Bahia and its Judges, 1609–1751*. Berkeley and Los Angeles.

_____. 1985. *Sugar Plantations in the Formation of Brazilian Society: Bahia, 1550–1835*. Cambridge, Eng., and New York.

Seler, Eduard. 1927. *Einige Kapitel aus dem Geschichtswerk des Fray Bernardino de Sahagún aus dem Aztekischen übersetzt*. Ed. by Cäcilie Seler-Sachs, Walter Lehmann, and Walter Krickeberg. Stuttgart.

Sell, Barry David. 1993. "Friars, Nahuas, and Books: Language and Expression in Colonial Nahuatl Publications." UCLA doctoral dissertation.

Sigal, Peter H. 1995. "Maya Passions: Colonial Yucatecan Ideas of Sexuality, Gender and the Body." UCLA doctoral dissertation.

Simpson, Lesley B. 1965. *The Encomienda in New Spain: The Beginning of Spanish Mexico*. Berkeley and Los Angeles.

_____. 1934–40. *Studies in the Administration of the Indians of New Spain*. 4 vols. Berkeley and Los Angeles.

Smith, David G. 1974. "The Mercantile Class of Portugal and Brazil in the Seventeenth Century: A Socio-economic Study of the Merchants of Lisbon and Bahia, 1620–1690." Doctoral dissertation, University of Texas, Austin.

Socolow, Susan Migden. 1978. *The Merchants of Buenos Aires, 1778–1810: Family and Commerce*. Cambridge, Eng., and New York.

Sousa, Lisa. 1998. "Women in Native Societies and Cultures of Colonial Mexico." UCLA doctoral dissertation.

Sousa, Lisa, Stafford Poole, C. M., and James Lockhart, eds. and trans. 1998. *The Story of Guadalupe: Luis Laso de la Vega's Huei tlamahuiçoltica of 1649*. UCLA Latin American Center Nahuatl Studies Series, 5. Stanford, Calif., and Los Angeles.

Spalding, Karen. 1967. "Indian Rural Society in Colonial Peru: the

Example of Huarochirí." Doctoral dissertation, University of California, Berkeley.

_____. 1984. *Huarochirí: An Andean Society Under Inca and Spanish Rule*. Stanford, Calif.

Spicer, Edward H. 1962. *Cycles of Conquest: The Impact of Spain, Mexico, and the United States on the Indians of the Southwest, 1533–1960*. Tucson, Ariz.

Stern, Steve J. 1982. *Peru's Indian Peoples and the Challenge of Spanish Conquest: Huamanga to 1640*. Madison, Wis.

_____, ed. 1987. *Resistance, Rebellion, and Consciousness in the Andean Peasant World, Eighteenth to Twentieth Centuries*. Madison, Wis.

Stone, Lawrence. 1971. "Prosopography," *Daedalus*, 100: 46–79.

Strickon, Arnold. 1965. "Hacienda and Plantation in Yucatan. An Historical-Ecological Consideration of the Folk-Urban Continuum in Yucatan," *América Indígena*, 25: 35–63.

Super, John C. 1973. "Querétaro: Society and Economy in Early Provincial Mexico, 1590–1630." UCLA doctoral dissertation.

_____. 1976. "The Agricultural Near North: Querétaro in the Seventeenth Century. " In Altman and Lockhart, eds., *Provinces of Early Mexico*.

_____. 1983. *La vida en Querétaro durante la Colonia, 1531–1810*. México.

_____. 1988. *Food, Conquest and Colonization in Sixteenth-Century Spanish America*. Albuquerque, N. M.

Tannenbaum, Frank. 1946. *Slave and Citizen: The Negro in the Americas*. New York.

Taylor, William B. 1972. *Landlord and Peasant in Colonial Oaxaca*. Stanford, Calif.

_____. 1979. *Drinking, Homicide and Rebellion in Colonial Mexican Villages*. Stanford, Calif.

Terraciano, Kevin. 1994. "Ñudzahui History: Mixtec Writing and Culture in Colonial Oaxaca." UCLA doctoral dissertation.

_____. Forthcoming. *The Mixtecs of Colonial Oaxaca: A History of Ñudzahui Writing and Culture* (provisional title). Stanford, Calif.

Tezozomoc, don Hernando [Fernando] de Alvarado. 1949. *Crónica mexicayotl*. Trans. and ed. by Adrián León. Publicaciones del Instituto de Historia, series 1, no. 10. México.

Thayer Ojeda, Tomás. 1939–41. *Formación de la sociedad chilena*. 3 vols. Santiago, Chile.

_____. 1950. *Valdivia y sus compañeros*. Santiago, Chile.

Trelles Aréstegui, Efraín. 1982. *Lucas Martínez Vegazo: Funcionamiento de una encomienda peruana inicial*. Lima.

Tutino, John M. 1976. "Creole Mexico: Spanish Elites, Haciendas, and Indian Towns, 1750–1810." Doctoral dissertation, University of Texas, Austin.

Tuttle, Edward F. 1976. "Borrowing Versus Semantic Shift: New World

Nomenclature in Europe." In Fredi Chiappelli, ed., *First Images of America: The Impact of the New World on the Old*, pp. 596–611. Berkeley and Los Angeles.

Urioste, George, ed. 1983. *Hijos de Pariya Qaqa: La tradición oral de Waru Chiri (mitología, ritual, y costumbres)*. 2 vols. Foreign and Comparative Studies, Latin American Series, of Maxwell School of Citizenship and Public Affairs, Syracuse University, no. 6. Syracuse, N. Y.

Van Oss, A. C. 1978. "Comparing Colonial Bishoprics in Spanish South America," *Boletín de Estudios Latinamericanos y del Caribe* (Amsterdam), no. 24 (June 1978), 27–65.

Van Young, Eric. 1981. *Hacienda and Market in Eighteenth-Century Mexico: The Rural Economy of the Guadalajara Region, 1675–1820*. Berkeley and Los Angeles.

Vázquez, Mario C. 1961. *Hacienda, peonaje y servidumbre en los Andes peruanos*. Lima.

Verlinden, Charles. 1970. "Italian Influences in Iberian Colonization." In H. B. Johnson, Jr., ed., *From Reconquest to Empire: The Iberian Background to Latin American History*, pp. 55–67. New York.

Wedin, Åke. 1966. *El concepto de lo incaico y las fuentes*. Uppsala, Sweden.

West, Robert C. 1949. *The Mining Community of Northern New Spain: The Parral District*. Ibero-Americana, 30. Berkeley and Los Angeles.

_____. 1952. *Colonial Placer Mining in Colombia*. Baton Rouge, La.

Wethey, Harold E. 1949. *Colonial Architecture and Sculpture in Peru*. Cambridge, Mass.

White, Richard. 1991. *The Middle Ground: Indians, Empires and Republics in the Great Lakes Region, 1650–1815*. Cambridge, Eng., and New York.

Wightman, Ann M. 1990. *Indigenous Migration and Social Change: The Forasteros of Cuzco, 1520–1720*. Durham, N. C.

Wiznitzer, Arnold. 1960. *Jews in Colonial Brazil*. New York.

Wood, Stephanie G. 1984. "Corporate Adjustments in Colonial Mexican Indian Towns: Toluca Region." UCLA doctoral dissertation.

Zavala, Silvio. 1935. *La encomienda indiana*. Madrid.

_____. 1940. *De encomiendas y propiedad territorial en algunas regiones de la América española*. México.

_____. 1945. *Contribución a la historia de las instituciones coloniales en Guatemala*. México.

Zuidema, R. Tom. 1989. *Reyes y guerreros: ensayos de cultura andina*. Lima.

Index

Absolutive endings in Nahuatl: 284, 287, 288 n6, 289, 290; with Spanish nouns, 278–79

Acceptance of cultural elements from one group by another: 304–32 passim

Acculturation: 20, 43, 194, 316. See also Stages

Actual, current official: 106

Admonitions in Nahuatl documents: 110, 260, 270

Adventure, irrelevance of in comprehending Spanish actions: 122

Africa: 120, 132–33, 147 n34, 361 n33

Africans: general characteristics, x–xi n3; in middle positions and among Europeans, 13, 14, 128, 130, 308, 316; historiography of, 26, 63, 67, 346, 350, 366 n44; distribution, 43; marriage patterns, 45; in Brazil, 51, 66; in Peru, 147 n34, 218

Age structure of transatlantic migration cycle: 180

Aguirre, Lope de, demented conqueror: 125

Agustina, Bárbara, Nahua market woman: 267–78

Aides of ecclesiastics: Nahua, 183–202, (especially 184–85, 194–95, 202), 271; Andean, 224

Aiton, Arthur: 148

Alcaldes: Nahua, 104, 105, 106, 107; Spanish, 168, 177

Alcaldes mayores: 13

Alden, Dauril: 50

Alphabetic writing by indigenous people: in Mesoamerica, 106, 325; by Nahuas, 117, 183–85, 188–91, 194–96; by Mixtecs, 205; in Yucatan, 213–15; in Andes, 218–24, 325; postconquest phenomenon, 360; need for art history to consider, 364

Altepetl, Nahua ethnic state: form under Spaniards, 99–108; and "titles," 110; and religion, 114, 116; other mentions, 199, 210, 217, 256, 266, 311, 312, 327, 328 n19

Altman, Ida: 147, 151 n45, 156, 180 n78, 369

Almacenero, wholesaler: 165 n16

Amatlacuilo, writer: 106

Andalusians: 47, 178, 180, 190

Andeans: work of Spalding on, 62–63; postcontact linguistic and cultural evolution, 218–27; in the will of a Peruvian encomendero, 230–54 passim; other mentions, 19 n31, 99, 131, 139, 140, 146, 153, 154, 207, 226, 316, 325, 350

Anderson, Arthur: 187, 192, 196–99, 352, 353

Andrews, J. Richard: 293 n12, 302, 357

Anthropology: and ethnohistory general-

ly, 60, 61, 79, 80, 148, 152–53 n48; and J. Lockhart in particular, 340–43, 346, 351–52, 358–59; of preconquest Mesoamerica, 360–61; converging with history, 365, 366

Antilles: 4–5, 6, 12 n24, 132, 133, 306. See also Caribbean

Aragonese in early Peru: 231–33

Archaeology: 340–41, 360

Archive of the Indies: 83

Arequipa: 94, 129, 135, 146, 150–51, 152

Aristocracy, alleged: 9, 11, 21, 50, 51, 162

Art: 117. See also Art history

Art history: 201, 361–64

Asymmetry, partial, in acceptance and resistance between natives and intruders: 304–06

Attraction, general process: 143 n28

Audiencia, high court: historiography of, 26, 35, 48–50; mentioned, 96, 108, 143

Augustinians, 84, 117

Autonomy: of social-cultural evolution, 77, 207; of early Latin American historiography, 77–78; Nahua sociopolitical, 103; of Mexican mercantile community, 105; autonomy of Mexican mercantile community, 161, 165; of Nahuatl philology, 203; object of uprisings, 317; local in Andes, 350. See also Localization

Avío, supply: 169

Axtell, James: 211

Bakewell, Peter: work on Zacatecas and implications, 43–44, 50, 64; work on Peru, 56 n9, 60; other mentions, 78, 136–37, 148

Balboa, Vasco Núñez de, not an explorer: 123–24

Bandos, factions: 91

Barbier, Jacques: 45

Barlow, Charles: 352

Barrera, Juan de, merchant: 172, 173

Barrett, Ward: 66

Basques: 123, 175, 178

Batab, Mayan ruler and governor: 225

Bataillon, Marcel: 31

Benalcázar, Sebastián de: 122

Beneficencia, Spanish charitable organization: 52

Berdan, Frances: 352

Beyond the Codices, by Anderson, Berdan, and Lockhart: 351, 353, 355 n22

Bilbao: 175

Bifurcation of evolution in the central Andes: 224, 227

Bilingualism: 208, 211, 223, 323–24, 325, 327

Bloch, Marc: 64

Borah, Woodrow: 41, 42 n3, 43, 44, 361

Borchart, Christiana: section partially based on, 164–70

Library of Congress Cataloging-in-Publication Data

Lockhart, James.
    Of things of the Indies : essays old and new in early Latin
American history / James Lockhart.
       p.   cm.
    Includes bibliographical references (p.   ) and index.
    ISBN 0-8047-3809-2 (cloth : alk. paper). — ISBN 0-8047-3810-6
(pbk. : alk. paper)
    1. Latin America—History—To 1830. I. Title.
F1411.L793   1999
980'.01—dc21   99-16980

This book is printed on acid-free paper.

Original printing 1999
Last figure below indicates year of this printing:
08 07 06 05 04 03 02 01 00 99